FACT BOOK ON WOMEN IN HIGHER EDUCATION

compiled by

Judith G. Touchton and Lynne Davis

with the assistance of
Vivian Parker Makosky

American Council on Education   **M**   Macmillan Publishing Company
NEW YORK

Collier Macmillan Canada
TORONTO

Maxwell Macmillan International
NEW YORK   OXFORD   SINGAPORE   SYDNEY

Macmillan Publishing Company
866 Third Avenue, New York, N.Y. 10022

Collier Macmillan Canada, Inc.
1200 Eglinton Avenue East, Suite 200
Don Mills, Ontario M3C 3N1

Library of Congress Catalog Card Number: 90-20408

Printed in the United States of America

printing number
1 2 3 4 5 6 7 8 9 10

Library of Congress Cataloging-in-Publication Data
Touchton, Judith G.
    Fact book on women in higher education / compiled by Judith G. Touchton and Lynne Davis; with the sistance of Vivian Parker Makosky.
        p.   cm.—(American Council on Education/Macmillan series on higher education)
    Includes bibliographical references (p.) and index.
    ISBN 0-02-900951-0
    1. Women—Education (Higher)—United States—Statistics. 2. Women in education—United States—Statistics. 3.Minority women—Education (Higher)—United States—Statistics. 4. Education, Higher—Unite States—Statistics. I. Davis, Lynne. II. Makosky, Vivian Parker. III. Title. IV. Series.
    LC1756.T68   1991
    376′.65′0973021—dc20   90-2

AMERICAN COUNCIL ON EDUCATION

Board of Directors 1990

Alice Chandler, President
State University College at New
    Paltz
*American Association of State
    Colleges and Universities*

Gene A. Budig, Chancellor
University of Kansas
*Association of American
    Universities*

Joseph A. O'Hare, S.J., President
Fordham University
*Association of Catholic Colleges
    and Universities*

Thomas Savage, S.J., President
Rockhurst College
*Association of Jesuit Colleges
    and Universities*

Keith G. Briscoe, President
Buena Vista College
*Council of Independent
    Colleges*

Henry Ponder, President
Fisk University
*National Association for Equal
    Opportunity in Higher
    Education*

Dorothy Ann Kelly, OSU,
    President
College of New Rochelle
*National Association of
    Independent Colleges and
    Universities*

Chase N. Peterson, President
University of Utah
*National Association of State
    Universities and Land-Grant
    Colleges*

**Elected Officers of
Associations—Ex officio for
1-year term:**

James E. Shanley, President
Fort Peck Community College
*American Indian Higher
    Education Consortium*

A. Dallas Martin, Jr., President
*National Association of Student
    Financial Aid Administrators*

**Washington Higher Education
Secretariat Representative—
1-year term:**

Kay J. Kohl, Executive Director
*National University Continuing
    Education Association*

Executive Secretary

Irene L. Gomberg
*American Council
    on Education*

CONTENTS

FACULTY   **87**

ADMINISTRATORS, TRUSTEES, AND STAFF   **101**

STUDENT AID   **109**

FOREWORD

Equal treatment of women and men in society—in education, employment, politics, religion, and social situations—has been addressed in dramatic ways over the last two decades. This has resulted in important gains for women's status and influence in most fields, especially higher education. Understanding the gains, recognizing the problems that still exist, and charting an appropriate course for the future require a comprehensive and accurate presentation of data. This ACE *Fact Book on Women in Higher Education* offers the first presentation of data on women faculty, students, administrators, staff, and trustees available in a single volume, an approach designed to make existing data more accessible to a larger number of users.

The completion of this book is an important milestone for the Office of Women in Higher Education. The Office was begun in 1973 with a mandate to increase the number of women in higher education administration, especially at the presidential level. The need for data on the status of women in higher education was recognized early on as a critical part of the planning process, and the Office soon became regarded as the only reliable source of data on women administrators. Although the ACE *Fact Book on Higher Education* has extended its coverage of data on both majority and minority women and on minority men over the years, there remained a need to have in one volume as much of the data on women in higher education as possible. This need gave rise to the idea of having a separate fact book in the ACE *Fact Book* series focusing on women in higher education.

A day rarely goes by in the Office during which there are no calls requesting data on women for use in campus planning and research offices, for graduate students, for college presidents making speeches on the status of women, or even for newspaper or journal articles. This book is a rich resource and makes a major contribution toward providing these data. It will help the Office plan for the next decade of service to women in higher education and will be an important reference for colleges, universities, and other associations like ours as they address the challenges they face in the twenty-first century.

From the development of current scenarios, through a reconstruction of the past, to projections for the future, it is now possible to track and plan for women's progress in an easier and more systematic way. The following are only a few examples of what can be learned about the scope of the task ahead from the *Fact Book*:

- Although the number of women presidents of colleges and universities has doubled over the last decade, only 11% are headed by women.

- Despite efforts to equalize financial aid for women, women are still more likely than their male colleagues to pay for their own educations, and on average they receive fewer dollars in their award packages.

- Both in and out of higher education, the wage gap between men and women exists at every level of employment, making it abundantly clear that women get less monetarily from their investment in higher education than their male colleagues.

- Women now receive 56% of all associate's degrees, 51% of all bachelor's degrees, 50% of all master's degrees, and 35% of all doctoral degrees but are not yet fully represented throughout the range of possible fields.

These examples illustrate the need for continued attention to improving the education of women—to prepare them for their own futures and to help them assume their rightful places of leadership in our society.

Signs of progress are also evident in reading this *Fact Book*. The growing number of women faculty and the dramatic increases of women earning first-professional degrees are two excellent examples of the "good news." Certain areas of progress are not yet fully tracked for inclusion in this *Fact Book* but are important indicators of how women are advancing in higher education. For example, more women are assuming important leadership roles, and the number of women presidents is increasing. There are also more women serving as State Higher Education

Officers (women constituted 10% of the total in 1988), more heading higher education consortia (women constituted 20% of the total in 1988), and more in executive positions in higher education associations.

Data on curriculum are rarely included in statistical reports on higher education. However, the development of women's studies has formed the intellectual and conceptual basis for much of the change that has taken place in this area, and has made the current status of women's studies an important issue. An estimated 30,000 courses in women's studies are presently offered on our nation's campuses. Fifty-four institutions have free-standing women's studies programs that offer a bachelor's degree in women's studies; 6 offer a master's degree; and a few are investigating Ph.D. programs. Many other women's studies programs enable students to create interdisciplinary majors, offer a minor or a concentration in women's studies, or offer a certificate in women's studies. Over 100 campuses now have curriculum transformation projects that focus essentially on how we can reshape the way we think about knowledge. These are important indicators at this time in our history. (For more information on women's studies programs, see Table 112.)

The data presented in the *Fact Book*, coupled with the vision, philosophy, information, strategies, and practical advice provided in the Office's *Educating the Majority: Women Challenge Tradition in Higher Education* (ACE/Macmillan, 1989), should serve to guide institutions in preparing women for their own futures and to join fully with their male colleagues in assuming the leadership roles so important to the future of our nation.

DONNA SHAVLIK
Director, Office of Women
 in Higher Education
American Council on Education

ACKNOWLEDGMENTS

The Office of Women in Higher Education of the American Council on Education is pleased to be publishing the first *Fact Book on Women in Higher Education,* and we wish to acknowledge the contributions of a number of people to this project.

Judy Touchton had general responsibility for the project. She was joined by Lynne Davis, an Ed.D. candidate at Columbia University then serving as a doctoral intern in the Office, who was hired as a Research Associate specifically for this project. Judy and Lynne worked closely together throughout the project. Lynne had the principal role in seeking out desired data from many sources and in compiling the initial charts, graphs, and summaries for all sections. In the subsequent process of revision and refinement, Judy and Lynne were joined by Vivian Parker Makosky, who, as a consultant to ACE, added her insight and perspective to the writing of trends, observations, and highlights for each area. Each section was then reviewed by research staff employed in ACE's Division of Policy Analysis and Research.

We are grateful to Charles Anderson for his work on the Demographics and Transitions sections; to Cathy Henderson, former staff member and a frequent consultant to ACE, for her work on the Enrollments and Degrees sections; to Cecilia Ottinger and Jennifer Hess for their work on the Faculty and Administrators sections; and to Laurent Ross and Pat Smith in ACE's Division of Government Relations for their work on the Student Aid section. At various stages over the two years of production we also received wise counsel from Deborah Carter and Drew Malizio, whose experience in producing previous ACE fact books was invaluable. In every case these reviewers were exceedingly thoughtful and detailed in their review of the data, data sources, graphic illustrations, and observations, and we appreciate their comments and helpful suggestions.

Although nearly all of the data in this book were initially presented elsewhere, there are two areas in which special tabulations of data were requested and are presented for the first time. With the assistance of Martha Provenzano at the College and University Personnel Association, we were able to obtain special tabulations of data on administrators by sex and race from the "1988 Administrative Compensation Survey." Laurent Ross, our colleague at ACE, prepared and interpreted special tabulations of selected student aid data by sex from the National Postsecondary Student Aid Study files of the National Center for Education Statistics. We appreciate their contribution. Boichi San also helped ably with the analysis of women's colleges and with technical assistance.

In our own office, everyone who has been employed or served an internship with us within the last two years has been engaged in this project in some way. We are grateful to Deborah Ingram-Peek for her consistent help and support, as well as to Dulie Kahn, Jaymie Lewis, Darrell Williams, Alice Cornelison, Bari Anhalt, Sarah Sayeed, and Eileen O'Brien for their contributions at critical times.

We invited a number of our colleagues who share our interest in research and data on women to advise us when we conceived and launched this project. They constituted an Advisory Board that met once in March, 1988. We have also had informal conversations with some Board members as the project evolved. The Board was helpful in suggesting data resources and issues of particular concern, and in offering support to the project. We appreciate their ideas and encouragement. Members of the Advisory Board were Charles Anderson, Department of Policy Analysis and Research, ACE; Eleanor Babco, Commission on Professionals in Science and Technology; Deborah Carter, Department of Policy Analysis and Research, ACE; Betty Dooley, Women's Research and Education Institute, Congressional Caucus for Women's Issues; Myrna Goldenberg, Editor of *Women Today*; Anne Hafner, National Center for Education Statistics, U.S. Department of

Education; George Marx, University of Maryland (then Dean in Residence at the Council of Graduate Schools); Marsha Matyas, Project on Women in Science, American Association for the Advancement of Science; James Palmer, American Association of Community and Junior Colleges; Janice Petrovich, ASPIRA; Sam Ping, National Center for Education Statistics, U.S. Department of Education; Marie Racine, University of the District of Columbia; Martha Provenzano, College and University Personnel Association; Sara Rix, Women's Research and Education Institute, Congressional Caucus for Women's Issues; Bernice Sandler, Project on the Status and Education of Women, Association of American Colleges; Betty Vetter, Commission on Professionals in Science and Technology; and Jacqueline Woods, Association of Governing Boards.

Clearly, a project of this magnitude required financial support, and we wish to give special thanks to those who provided it. Alison Bernstein of the Ford Foundation, who has been a source of support and encouragement for our Office's data-gathering and dissemination activities for several years, provided seed money for the project and the challenge of matching funds. The Henry Luce Foundation provided the major funding for the project, enabling us to expand our book in both concept and size and to make it part of the established *ACE Fact Book on Higher Education* series. We thank Melissa Topping of the Foundation for her interest. James Murray, Director of Publications at ACE, was always helpful in our negotiations with Macmillan to publish the book. Elaine El-Khawas, Director of ACE's Division of Policy Analysis and Research, was supportive throughout this project, both personally and through her staff. And Lloyd Chilton, our editor at Macmillan, was magically effective in the congenial way in which he kept us on schedule.

Finally, we wish to recognize the contribution of Donna Shavlik, Director of the Office of Women, to the entire project. Donna was the first person to talk about the need for a resource like the *Fact Book* in the early 1970s, so it is not surprising that she has been part of the process all along. She played a crucial role in seeking and obtaining funding and was actively involved in the identification of topics and in reading and commenting on successive drafts. Her enthusiasm for the project was always evident, her managerial support was critical to completion of the project, and her personal support was always felt.

While we recognize the contributions of the many people who have been involved in the process of compiling, writing, reviewing, and editing so necessary to such a project, we reserve for ourselves the responsibility for any errors that may become evident. We hope they are few.

We hope this *Fact Book on Women in Higher Education* will address the need for better information on the education and status of women and help improve the condition of women in our society.

JUDITH G. TOUCHTON
Deputy Director, Office of
Women in Higher Education
American Council on Education

LYNNE DAVIS

I

Introduction

Just as economists in recent years have recognized the need for better statistics on the economic status of women, so have educators recognized the need for better data on the educational status of women. The American Council on Education's Office of Women in Higher Education has produced the *Fact Book on Women in Higher Education* to meet this need. The *Fact Book* is a compendium of information from the best data sources available, covering all women in higher education (minority and majority) in all of their academic roles—as students, faculty, administrators, and staff. This valuable resource takes existing data and presents it in some new formats, thus making the information available to a wider number of readers.

Rationale

The 1960s and 1970s were vitally important decades for women in higher education. Due largely to the impetus generated by federal, state, and local legislation and regulations, many aggressive policies were created to promote nondiscrimination, equity, and advancement for women. Major federal legislation includes:

- Executive Order 11246 (as amended by Executive Order 11375), mandating the use of affirmative action;

- Title VII of the Civil Rights Act of 1964, as amended, prohibiting discrimination in employment on the basis of race, color, religion, sex, or national origin;

- Title IX of the Elementary/Secondary Education Act of 1972, the first law prohibiting discrimination against students on the basis of sex, and also including some aspects of employment;

- Title VI of the Civil Rights Act of 1964 (minority women included in 1964), prohibiting discrimination on the basis of race, color, or national origin;

- Section 503 of the Rehabilitation Act of 1973, prohibiting discrimination on the basis of handicap;

- Age Discrimination in Employment Act of 1967, as amended, prohibiting discrimination on the basis of age;

- Equal Pay Act of 1963, as amended, prohibiting differential pay rates for women and men doing the same work; and

- Pregnancy Discrimination Act of 1978, amending Title VII and providing that pregnant women will be treated the same for all employment-related purposes as other persons not so affected but similar in their ability or inability to work.

In 1979 women constituted a majority of students for the first time in our nation's history, a trend that continued through the 1980s. As we begin the 1990s, a number of people—administrators, faculty, policymakers, advocates, and researchers in public and private sectors—are asking vital questions relative to the status of women of all races and ethnic groups. Some of these questions are:

- What gains have women in higher education made in recent years? Where have the gains occurred? What has yet to be done?

- What changes have taken place in women's rate of participation in higher education, in their access to the professions, in their upward mobility in diverse fields, and in their share of leadership positions?

- How do women faculty compare with men with respect to access, advancement, salary level, promotion, and tenure?

- What are the differences between men and women students with respect to earned degrees, part-time enrollment status, and financial aid?

- How do gains for minority women compare with those for majority women in all areas?

The purpose of the *Fact Book on Women* is to provide an accessible, easy-to-use source of information, data, and statistics to answer these and other such questions. The content and format of the book have been guided by the experience of ACE's Office of Women in Higher Education and by our Division of Policy Analysis and Research in answering questions about the status of women over the years. The book is designed to provide information on all women, including minority women to the fullest extent possible, in the areas of greatest inquiry in higher education. These areas include enrollment patterns, earned degrees, employment status, salary, promotion and tenure of faculty, administrative ranks and other leadership positions, and emerging areas of interest such as freshman aspirations, financial aid, majors, and career choices, among others. It is also designed to be used by a wide variety of people, including researchers, generalists, policymakers, administrators, faculty, students, reporters, advocates, and others who are interested in the status of women.

The *Fact Book on Women* is also "user friendly" in its adaptation to different learning styles and information needs. Accordingly, data are presented in three ways: (1) in narrative form in the "Highlights and Trends" section, which lists the important areas within each of the major topics and gives summary findings as to these areas; (2) in chart and graph form, accompanied by brief comments augmenting the data shown; and (3) in source tables from which the charts, graphs, and narrative comments are drawn.

For many people, data on women in higher education are not easily obtained. This is a common experience, for many reasons. At best, the information exists in a variety of sources, many of which are not easily accessible. At worst, information on women is not collected, or if collected, not reported. Too often, the collection, analysis, and reporting processes do not address minority women. For the *Fact Book on Women*, we sought the best data on women from the sources available, provided trend data as well as current data wherever possible, and included data by race or ethnicity as well as sex wherever we found them.

Our purpose in producing this resource was to make it easier for readers and users both to obtain answers to their questions and encourage them to ask more questions. We know that much has happened for women in the past two decades—we can see and feel the progress. But there remains a great need for better assessment of what gains actually have been made and what has yet to be accomplished. In our data-oriented society,

there is no substitute for quantitative measures. We have attempted to provide a resource by which others can assess change in areas of greatest interest to them. We hope this book will serve as a prototype for subsequent data-gathering and data-reporting activities at the state and regional levels, at individual campuses, and within systems. Those who are not satisfied with the current status of women in higher education may be guided by the comments of Juanita Kreps, former Secretary of Commerce:

> A vague sense of injustice is not adequate to attract attention and action. It takes statistics to influence Government's decisions. It takes statistics to determine the flow of dollars. Individual cases of discrimination can be ignored, rationalized, hushed up, or settled with little fanfare. It is much more difficult to ignore persistent and shocking statistics.*

Similarly, it takes statistics to influence our campuses—national statistics to set a context, and campus-based statistics to focus the inquiry. If we were to take Kreps' comments about women, statistics, and national priorities and apply them to the campus, we could add that our campuses, like our political system, "respond to problems but they respond more quickly to problems that are documented clearly and thus elevated in the hierarchies of priorities" (Kreps, 1979). For this reason it is essential that each campus begin, if it has not already done so, to collect data on its own women students, faculty, administrators, and staff.

How to Use This Book

The *Fact Book on Women* is divided into three main parts. Part One is an introduction that sets the context for the book and offers useful recommendations and guidance for readers. Part Two contains highlights and trends in narrative and visual form. It features major findings from each of the seven topical sections: demographic and economic trends significant

---

* Juanita Kreps, former Secretary of Commerce, in a conference on "Issues in Federal Statistical Needs Relating to Women," Bureau of the Census, Current Population Reports, Special Studies, Series P-23, No. 83, 1979.

to higher education; the transition from high school to college; enrollments; earned degrees; faculty; administrators, trustees, and staff; and student financial aid. Then, for each of these seven sections, Part Two presents data in chart or graph form, combined with observations in narrative form. Within sections, page headings indicate the topics covered both in the charts or graphs and in the accompanying narrative comments. The narrative comments generally contain information that expands on or gives the context for data shown in the charts or graphs. In some cases, however, the same information is presented in both formats for emphasis.

Part Three of the book contains a section on Data Issues and Sources, including a Guide to Sources, a complete bibliography, and the source tables on which information in Part Two is based. The inclusion of the source tables is designed to enable readers to do their own research, answering questions of interest that may not be specifically addressed elsewhere in this volume.

The *Fact Book on Women* may be used in a number of ways, depending on the reader's familiarity with the data, depth of interest, and available time. Some readers may choose to begin by scanning the Highlights and Trends. Others may use the Contents to identify topics of interest, then turn to the pages containing charts or graphs with narrative comments. Still others may use this *Fact Book* as a research sourcebook, making extensive use of the tables. We hope our readers will use this book in all of these ways, depending on their particular interests and needs at various times.

Recommendations

The underlying assumption of the *Fact Book on Women* is that "statistics do more than tell us what is happening—they also cause things to happen" (Kreps, 1979). Accordingly, we have several recommendations to offer campuses:

1. Make this book a resource readily available on campus to those who are responsible in any way for women students, faculty, administrators, and staff.
2. Note the national trends within the various areas covered in the *Fact Book on Women* and compare

the experience of your campus with national trends.

3. Determine whether your campus is involved in institutional research to illuminate the status of women students, faculty, administrators, staff, and trustees. Note what the research consists of, who is collecting the information, and how it is being disseminated.

Some examples of questions which should be asked are:

What are the number and percentage of women and men students in each major and at each degree level?

What are the number and percentage of women and men faculty by rank in each department, division, and college? What are the promotion rates for women and men in each category?

What are the number and percentage of women and men at the various administrative levels?

What are the number and percentage of women trustees on your campus? *

4. If you have an institutional research program, either centralized or decentralized, find out whether it routinely disaggregates and reports its data by sex and race/ethnicity. If it does not, recommend that this be done and follow through with your recommendation.
5. Support the collection and reporting of data on women on your campus. Study the results for any action or change that would enable your campus better to serve the needs of women students, faculty, staff, and administrators.

Overview of Data Sources

Information contained in the *Fact Book on Women* is based on the latest available data from many sources. While we gathered no new data, the *Fact Book on Women* presents certain data for the first time, in an original format, based on special tabulations of existing data tapes that we requested for this purpose. Government sources for national data include the Equal Employment Opportunity Commission, the National Academy of Sciences' Na-

* A detailed checklist with 5 separate categories (including social-educational climate) is available in the *Institutional Self-Study Guide on Sex Equity for Postsecondary Institutions*, 1981, by Karen Bogart, available from the Association of American Colleges' Project on the Status and Education of Women, 1818 R Street, N.W., Washington, DC 20036.

tional Research Council, the U.S. Department of Commerce's Bureau of the Census, the U.S. Department of Education's National Center for Education Statistics, the U.S. Department of Labor's Bureau of Labor Statistics, and various postsecondary education associations. The *1989–90 Fact Book on Higher Education* was also used extensively, as many of its tables are based on unpublished tabulations of government statistics available only on tape. For more information on data sources, see the listings in the Guide to Sources and the Bibliography.

Care should be taken in looking at data on racial and ethnic minorities because these data are collected and reported in different ways by various organizations. Data on minorities have increased substantially since the mid-1970s, when Hispanic, Asian/Pacific Islander, and American Indian data were first reported, but regrettably these data have not always been collected or reported. Even when such data are available, the editors of this book often found that the number of Asian/Pacific Islanders and American Indians was so small in comparison to other groups that they could not be meaningfully included in some graphical presentations.

The editors also wish to alert readers to the fact that, in some cases, categories are not mutually exclusive. For example, Hispanics may be white or black in terms of race, and in addition have many national origins (for example, Cuban, Puerto Rican, Mexican, and so forth). If both race and ethnicity are reported in the same table, caution should be used in adding racial/ethnic numbers, or numbers higher than the actual totals may result. Users of this book are urged to read tables and footnotes carefully. In general, they will find that the National Center for Education Statistics reports data on Hispanics separately, as a mutually exclusive category, and that the U.S. Census Bureau reports Hispanics both as "Hispanics" and as "black" or "white," as appropriate. The editors of the *Fact Book on Women* have attempted to add a note indicating that "Hispanics may be of any race" on all tables and charts where this statement seems to apply.

Caveats

Though this first *Fact Book on Women in Higher Education* presents data and trends on women in many areas of higher education, it will not satisfy all the needs of those who use it. However, used in conjunction with ACE's other fact books, the *1989-90 Fact Book on Higher Education* and the *Community College Fact Book*, this book will allow readers to understand many of the general trends in higher education. For further statistical information the reader may use several resources, including the *American Statistics Index*, the *Statistical Reference Index*, and ERIC's *Resources in Education*.

II

Highlights and Trends

Demographic and Economic Data

Population

- In 1990, the total U.S. population is estimated to be 250 million. Women will constitute 51% of the population (128 million), and men 49% (122 million). (See Table 2.)

- Women have constituted 51% of the total population since 1960. Their share of the total population is projected to increase slightly to 52% by 2040. (See Table 2.)

- Minority populations in the United States are growing at much faster rates than the majority population. Between 1985 and 2000, the Hispanic population is projected to increase by 46%, and blacks and other minorities by 23%. The white population is projected to increase by only 10% during this period. (See Figure 1.)

- In 1990, blacks are estimated to constitute 13% of the U.S. population, and Hispanics 8%. Black women are expected to outnumber black men (16.5 million vs. 14.9 million), but the number of Hispanic women and men is expected to be the same (9.9 million of each). (See Table 1.)

- In 1990, the total traditional college-age population (18–24 year olds) is projected to be 26 million, of which 49% will be women and 51% men. Population experts predict a sustained slight decline in the total 18–24 year old population over the next several decades. (See Table 3.)

- By 2000, 1 in 5 persons age 18–24 (20% of the women and 19% of the men) will be in minority groups. (See Figure 2.)

Educational Attainment

- There has been a substantial increase over the last 40 years in the number of people completing 4 years of college. In 1950, 5% of the women and 7% of the men age 25–34 had completed 4 or more years of college. By 1987, the comparable figures were 23% for women and 25% for men. (See Figure 5.)

- In 1986, the number of white women and men age 25 and older completing 1–3 years of college was the same (17% of each), but considerably fewer white women than men had completed 4 or more

years of college (16% of the women compared to 24% of the men). (See Table 5.)

- In 1986, the proportion of persons age 25 and older who had completed 4 or more years of college was:

16% of white women	24% of white men
11% of black women	11% of black men
7% of Hispanic women	9% of Hispanic men

(See Figure 4.)

Labor Force

- In 1986, the civilian U.S. labor force was 118 million, up from 105 million in 1979. The 1986 total consisted of:

44.6 million white women	57.2 million white men
6.3 million black women	6.4 million black men
3.1 million Hispanic women	4.9 million Hispanic men
1.5 million Asian women	1.8 million Asian men

(See Table 8.)

- In 1986, 55% of the women and 76% of the men age 16 and older were participating in the labor force. By 2000, the proportion of men is expected to remain stable at 75%, but the proportion of women is expected to increase to 62%. (See Figure 6.)

- The participation of women in the labor force has increased substantially in the last 20 years, and this trend is expected to continue. White women accounted for 50% of the growth in the labor force between 1972 and 1986 and are projected to account for 47% of the increase between 1986 and 2000. (See Figure 6.)

- By 2000, the total work force is projected to be composed of:

39% white women	45% white men
6% black women	6% black men
4% Hispanic women	6% Hispanic men
2% Asian women	2% Asian men

(See Figure 6.)

- In 1987, most women with children were participants in the labor force, but participation rates were higher for mothers of school age children than for those with children under 6.

- For women with children age 6–17, 71% of married women with husbands present, 73% of separated women, and 85% of divorced women were in the labor force.

- For women with children under age 6, 57% of married women with husbands present, 55% of separated women, and 71% of divorced women were in the labor force. (See Table 12.)

Income

- Women in every ethnic and racial group earn lower median salaries than men in any ethnic or racial group. (See Figure 15.)

- The return on a college education differs greatly for women and for men. In 1987, the median salary for men with 4 years of high school ($25,394) was higher than the median salary earned by women with 4 years of college ($23,406). (See Table 18.)

- In 1987, women with 4 or more years of college had a median income of $25,645; for men the comparable figure was $37,854. (See Table 18.)

High School and the Transition to Higher Education

- In every racial and ethnic group, a slightly larger percentage of women complete high school than do men in the same group. The high school completion rate for women and men by race/ethnic group in 1986 was:

87% of white women	85% of white men
80% of black women	77% of black men
62% of Hispanic women	59% of Hispanic men

  (See Figure 19.)

- Women make higher grades than men as shown in estimated high school grade point averages, but score lower than men on Scholastic Aptitude Tests. (See Figure 20.)

- The percentage of women high school graduates enrolled in or completing one or more years of college increased from 35% to 55% between 1960 and 1986, surpassing by a small margin the percentage of men doing so. (See Figure 22.)

Freshman Characteristics

- Women's aspirations for advanced degrees are increasing, and the long-term objectives of freshman women and men are becoming more similar. In 1987, over one-half of both women and men (56% of each) aspired to some kind of advanced degree, and more than one-third (35% women and 36% men) aspired to a bachelor's degree. (See Figure 23.)

- The percentage of first-time freshman women aspiring to doctoral or professional degrees nearly doubled from 1970 to 1985, from 10% to 20%. At the same time, the percentage of men aspiring to doctoral or professional degrees declined from 25% to 20%. (See Figure 23.)

- There is still a wide gap between women's and men's interest in technological fields such as engineering. In 1987, 3% of freshman women anticipated majoring in engineering compared to 17% of the men. (See Figure 24.)

Enrollment

- Since 1979, women have constituted a majority of students enrolled in higher education. In 1987, women were 53% of the 12.5 million students enrolled in higher education (6.7 million women, 5.9 million men). (See Figure 28.)

- In 1987, women constituted 51% of all students enrolled in 4-year institutions and 56% of all students enrolled in 2-year institutions. (See Figure 29.)

- In 1985, women constituted 52% of undergraduate students, 49% of graduate students, 34% of those in first-professional programs, and 59% of unclassified students. (See Figure 34.)

- In 1984, among women enrolled as undergraduates, 80% were white, 11% were black, and 9% were either Hispanic, Asian, or American Indian. Among graduate and first-professional students, a slightly higher percentage of women were white (84–85%), and a lower percentage were black (6–7%) or Hispanic, Asian, or American Indian (4–7%). (See Table 45.)

- In fall 1986, 4 in 5 women (81%) and men (80%) in higher education were enrolled in public institutions. (See Figure 30.)

Attendance Status

- Part-time enrollments have increased substantially for all students in the past two decades, but the trend is especially evident for women. In 1986, almost one-half (47%) of the women were enrolled as part-time students, compared to 39% of the men. (See Figure 32.)

- In 4-year institutions more than 2 in 3 students attend full-time. In 2-year institutions the majority of all students attend part-time. But in both 4-year and 2-year institutions, women are more likely than men to be enrolled part-time. (See Figure 33.)

Age

- Enrollment of women age 25 and older has increased steadily in the past 15 years. Today more than 40% of women college students are age 25 or more. (See Figure 35.)

- Women age 35 and older represent the fastest growing group of college students; their numbers tripled between 1972 and 1985. (See Figure 35.)

Racial/Ethnic Groups

- In 1986, minority enrollment in higher education was 18% of the total, up slightly from 16% 10 years previously. In almost every case, the increase in minority women's enrollment was greater than the increase in minority men's enrollment. Black men constituted the only group experiencing a decline in enrollment between 1976 and 1986; their enrollment declined by 7%. (See Figure 36.)

- In 1986, minority women outnumbered minority men in higher education in every racial/ethnic group, with the exception of Asians. In that year women comprised:

  60% of black students;

  56% of American Indian students;

  53% of Hispanic students; and

  47% of Asian students.

(See Figure 36.)

Freshman Characteristics

- Between 1976 and 1986, business and management was the most popular major field for both women and men students, but the gains for women in this field were especially dramatic. In 1986, women accounted for 46% of the majors in the field (undergraduate and graduate students combined). (See Figure 39.)

- At both the undergraduate and graduate levels, women continue to be seriously underrepresented in engineering and the physical sciences. (See Figure 39.)

Women's Colleges

- Enrollment in women's colleges has remained relatively stable during the last decade (about 100,000 students), despite some reduction in the number of women's colleges. (See Figure 37.)

Earned Degrees

- In 1986, women received 49% of the total degrees awarded (bachelor's and higher). Beginning in 1987–88, women were projected to receive a larger proportion of the total degrees earned than men. (See Figure 42.)

- Women's share of degrees at all levels has risen over the past decade. In 1986, women received:

  56% of associate's degrees, up from 46% in 1976;

  51% of bachelor's degrees, up from 46% in 1976;

  50% of master's degrees, up from 46% in 1976;

  35% of doctorates, up from 23% in 1976; and

  33% of first-professional degrees, up from 16% in 1976.

- (See Tables 56 and 61.)

Associate's Degrees

- Women received about 55% of the associate degrees awarded each year since 1983. The number of associate degrees awarded to women annually has remained stable, around 250,000. (See Figure 48.)

- In 1985, minorities received 16% of all associate degrees awarded. Within this group, minority women received a higher proportion of associate degrees (9%) than minority men (7%). (See Table 111.)

- Of the 237,000 women receiving associate degrees in 1985, 84% were white, 9% were black, 4% were Hispanic, 2% were Asian or Pacific Islander, and 1% were American Indian/Alaskan Native. (See Table 111.)

Bachelor's Degrees

- In 1986, women received 501,900 bachelor's degrees, 51% of the total awarded that year. (See Figure 49.)

- In 1985, 12% of all bachelor's degrees were awarded to members of minority groups. Minority women earned slightly more of these degrees than did minority men. (See Table 65.)

- Between 1976 and 1985, the number of bachelor's degrees awarded to black women increased 3%, and the number awarded to white women increased 15%. During that same period, bachelor's degrees awarded to black men decreased 10%, and similar degrees awarded to white men decreased 9%. (See Figure 51.)

- Between 1976 and 1985, the number of bachelor's degrees awarded to Hispanic women increased 73%, although they still received only 3% of all bachelor's degrees awarded to women in 1985. (See Figure 51.)

- In 1985, Asian women received 2% of the bachelor's degrees awarded to women. (See Figure 51.)

- The largest number of bachelor's degrees awarded to both women and men was in the field of business and management. The number of degrees awarded to women in this field almost quadrupled between 1976 and 1986, from 28,000 to 109,000. (See Figure 49.)

- Between 1976 and 1986, the number of women receiving bachelor's degrees in education dropped 41%. For men, the percentage drop was 50%. (See Figure 49.)

- In 1985, minority women received 10% of the bachelor's degrees in education awarded to women, which is slightly lower than the 12% they received in 1976. Minorities as a group received 10.5% of the education degrees in 1985. (See Figure 50.)

- Between 1976 and 1986, the number of women receiving bachelor's degrees in engineering increased notably; however, in 1986 women received only 14% of the bachelor's degrees in engineering awarded that year. (See Figure 49.)

Master's Degrees

- In 1986, women received 145,000 master's degrees, 50% of the total master's degrees awarded in that year. (See Figure 53 and Table 67.)

- The proportion of master's degrees awarded to women increased substantially between 1960 and 1980, then leveled off, and is now rising slightly.

In the 1990s, women are projected to receive 51% to 52% of all master's degrees awarded annually. (See Figure 53 and Table 67.)

In 1984–85, minority women received 11% of the 141,000 master's degrees awarded to women that year, about the same proportion that they received in 1976. Black women received 6%, Hispanic women 3%, Asian women 2%, and American Indian women less than 1% of these degrees. (See Table 68.)

Among the 30,000 minorities who earned master's degrees in 1985, minority women constituted slightly more than one-half (54%) of the recipients. (See Table 68.)

First-Professional Degrees

- In 1986, women received 24,600 first-professional degrees, 33% of the total of such degrees awarded in that year, up from 16% of the total in 1976. By 1995, women are projected to receive 40% of all first-professional degrees awarded annually. (See Tables 71 and 74.)

- Women are receiving an increasing proportion of degrees in professional fields. In 1986, women received:

  52% of degrees in pharmacy;
  48% of degrees in veterinary medicine;
  39% of degrees in law;
  31% of degrees in medicine;

22% of degrees in dentistry; and
19% of degrees in theology.

(See Table 74.)

Doctorates

- In 1986, women received 12,000 doctoral degrees, 35% of all the doctorates awarded in that year, up from 23% of the total in 1976. Women are projected to receive 46% of all doctorates awarded in 1998. (See Figure 58 and Table 75.)

- In 1986, women received more than one-half of the doctorates awarded in seven fields: English, French, German, Spanish, education, anthropology, and psychology. (See Figure 59.)

- Although many more women are choosing to study mathematical and scientific fields, they are still greatly outnumbered by men in these fields, especially at the doctoral level. In 1986, women earned 21% of the doctorates in chemistry, 17% of the doctorates in mathematics, and 9% of the doctorates in physics. (See Tables 76, 77, and 78.)

- In 1985, minority women received 11% of all doctorates awarded to women. Black women received 5%, Hispanic women 2%, Asian women 3%, and American Indian women less than 1%. (See Table 80.)

- Of the 3,050 minority students who earned doctorates in 1985, minority women constituted less than 2 in 5 of the recipients (39%). (See Table 80.)

Faculty

- For over a century, the proportion of women faculty has fluctuated widely. The highest proportion of women faculty actually occurred in 1880, when women constituted 36% of faculty. Since 1900 the number of women faculty has grown substantially, but the proportion of women compared to men has been slow to change. Women constituted 20% of the faculty in 1910, 28% in 1940, 23% in 1970, and 29% in 1984. (See Figure 63.)

- Although the numbers are increasing, between 1975 and 1985 the proportion of women faculty remained steady at just over one-fourth of the total, and the percentage of these women faculty who are minorities has remained at 12%. (See Tables 81 and 89.)

- The greatest increases in the number and proportion of women faculty have come at the rank of assistant professor, where the proportion of women increased from 24% of all assistant professors in 1972 to 38% in 1985. (See Figure 64.)

- At the rank of assistant professor in 1985, women as a proportion of total full-time faculty were as follows: white women, 31%; black women, 3%; Asian women, 1%; and Hispanic and American Indian, less than 1% combined. (See Figure 64.)

- In all types of institutions, women are tenured at much lower rates than men. In 1985, 46% of the full-time women faculty were tenured compared to 66% of the full-time men faculty. (See Figure 65.)

- Women in all types of private institutions are less likely to be tenured than in all types of public institutions. (See Figure 65.)

- In nearly every major discipline in 1985, women faculty were much less likely to be tenured than men faculty. A notable exception was computer science/information systems, where women and men were equally likely to be tenured. (See Figure 66.)

- The probability of a woman faculty member being tenured varies tremendously by state, with only 9 states having a majority of women faculty tenured in 1985. In every state, women faculty were considerably less likely to be tenured than men. (See Figure 67.)

- The proportion of women faculty who are minorities remained stable between 1975 and 1985 at 12%. (See Table 89.)

- Of the 53,608 tenured women faculty in 1985, 3,790 were black (7%), 1,078 were Hispanic (2%), 1,344 were Asian/Pacific (3%), and 138 (less than 1%) were American Indians. (See Figure 69.)

- In 1985, minority women constituted 12% of newly hired women faculty. Minority men constituted 14% of all newly hired male faculty. (See Figure 69.)

- Women faculty at all ranks and in all types of institutions have lower average salaries than men. (See Figure 73.)

- The gap between women's salaries and men's salaries is widening. In 1985–86, with all ranks combined, women faculty salaries averaged 80% of those of men faculty. Almost a decade earlier, in 1976–77, women's salaries averaged 82% of men's salaries. (See Figure 72.)

- Faculty salaries are increasing, but at higher rates for men than for women. Between 1976 and 1986, the average salary of women faculty rose from $15,000 to $27,576, an increase of 83%. For men, the average salary rose from $18,378 to $34,294, an increase of 87%. (See Figure 73 and Table 93.)

- Both men and women earn highest average salaries in private universities, but in these institutions in 1985–1986, the average salary for women ($31,174) was 74% of the average salary for men ($41,929). (See Figure 73.)

- The percentage of women at the rank of full professor has changed very little over the last 13 years. In 1986, 12% of all full professors were women, a figure only slightly higher than the 1973 figure of 10%. (See Table 82.)

- In both public and private institutions, the proportion of women faculty (all ranks combined) is lowest in universities and highest in 2-year institutions. (See Table 82.)

Administrators, Trustees, and Staff

Presidents

- In 1989, there were 328 women chief executive officers of colleges and universities, constituting 11% of all CEOs of institutions accredited by the six major regional accrediting associations. (See Figure 75.)

- Between 1975 and 1989, the number of women college and university presidents more than doubled, from 148 to 328. (See Figure 75.)

- In 1989, 55% of the women presidents headed private institutions and 45% headed public institutions. Their institutions included major research universities, comprehensive colleges and universities, liberal arts colleges, community and junior colleges, and system offices. (See Figure 75.)

- In 1989, minority women represented 13% of all women presidents. They were located mostly in public institutions. (See Figure 75.)

Administrators

- Women are more likely to hold high-level administrative positions in private institutions than in public institutions. (See Figure 77.)

- Women administrators are more likely to be found in student affairs and external affairs than in academic and administrative affairs. At the highest positions in all these areas, however, women are greatly outnumbered by men. (See Figure 76.)

- In 1987, 27% of the deans in academic areas were women. This percentage ranged from a high of 97% women for Deans of Nursing to a low of 8% for Deans of Law. Women held more than one-half of the senior positions only in the areas of nursing (97%) and home economics (77%). (See Figure 76.)

- The proportion of women administrators increases at lower levels of the organization. For example, in Admissions offices in 1987, women held 28% of the Director of Admissions positions, 50% of the Associate Director positions, and 66% of the Assistant Director positions. (See Figure 76.)

- In 1987, minority women and men combined held only 8% of all positions in administration.

Of all minority administrators in 1987, 44% were women. (See Figure 78.)

- In 1987, minority women held only 2% of all Dean positions. (See Figure 78.)

- Minority women were most likely to be found as Director of Affirmative Action/Equal Opportunity (holding 24% of such positions in 1987), and next most likely to be found as Director of Financial Aid or Director of Student Counseling; they held 7% each of these positions. (See Figure 78.)

- In 1987, minority women represented 10% of all women administrators, whereas minority men represented 7% of all men administrators. (See Figure 78.)

- Overall, in most major positions in administration, women have lower median salaries than men in the same positions, but the differences vary by sector. (See Figure 79.)

- In 1987, the median salaries of women and men in chief academic officer positions were almost the same in 4- and 2-year public institutions. In private institutions, both 4- and 2-year, men's salaries were notably higher than women's in these positions. (See Figure 79.)

Staff

- In 1985, 44,000 women (35% of a total of 124,000) were full-time executives, managers, or administrators in higher education institutions. Of these women administrators, 86% were white non-Hispanic, 10% were black non-Hispanic, 2% were Hispanic, 2% were Asian/Pacific Islander, and less than 1% were American Indian. (See Figure 80.)

- In 1985, there were 2.1 million full- and part-time employees in institutions of higher education. Of these, 23% were part-time employees. More of the part-time faculty were men and more of the part-time secretarial, clerical, and technical paraprofessionals were women. (See Figure 80.)

Trustees

- In 1985, women made up 23% of the voting members of higher education governing boards in public institutions and 20% of the members in independent institutions. (See Figure 81.)

- Of the women and men serving as voting members of governing boards in higher education in 1985, 90% were white, 6% were black, 1% were Hispanic, and 3% were in other categories. Public institutions had slightly higher percentages of black and Hispanic members than private institutions. (Data by race/ethnicity and sex were not available.) (See Figure 81.)

Student Aid

- In all types of institutions, women are more likely than men to be financing their own educations. Of all undergraduate students, 1 in 4 women (25%) and 1 in 5 men (18%) indicated they were solely responsible for financing their higher educations. (See Figure 82.)

- Three out of 5 undergraduates reported using no outside source of financial aid. These women (60%) and men (61%) reported using their own and their families' money to finance their education. (See Figure 82.)

- Students in private institutions are more likely to receive some form of financial aid than students in public institutions. (See Figure 83.)

- Black students, both women and men, are more likely than other students to receive some form of financial aid. In fall 1986, of the total enrollment, 57% of black women received financial aid, compared to 36% of white women and 36% of all other women; and 50% of black men received financial aid, compared to 36% of white men and 37% of all other men. (See Figure 83.)

- Almost one-third (31%) of all undergraduates enrolled in 1986 received some form of federal financial aid. (See Figure 84.)

- In fall 1986, in all categories in which federal aid was awarded, women received on average fewer dollars than men. The greatest discrepancy was in federal work-study awards, where men received 34% more than what women received (an average of $1,621 for men compared to $1,211 for women). (See Figure 85.)

- In fall 1986, an undergraduate man received an average of 7% more in total financial aid than an undergraduate woman ($3,996 compared to $3,740). (See Figure 85.)

- In fall 1986, women and men undergraduates received about the same average amount in federal grants (just over $1,500), but the average nonfederal grant for a man was 11% higher than that for a woman ($2,046 compared to $1,848). (See Figure 85.)

- With respect to support for doctoral studies, between 1974 and 1987 the greatest overall discrepancy between women and men occurred in the awarding of research assistantships. In 1974, women received 12% fewer of these awards than men; in 1985 and 1987, women received 15% and 10% fewer awards, respectively. (See Figure 86.)

- Although men and women in 1983–84 borrowed about the same amount of money while in college, the ability of women to repay their debts differed from that of their male colleagues because of the differences in average starting salaries. For example, 13% of women college graduates with debts faced a loan burden of 10% or more of their first year's earnings, compared to 6% for men. (See Table 113.)

Demographic and Economic Data

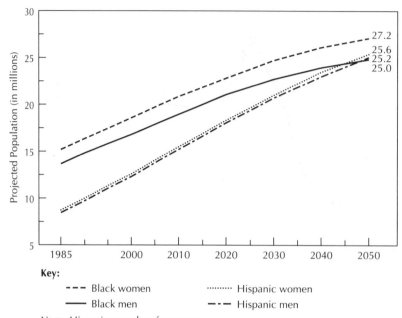

Key:

‑ ‑ ‑ Black women   ·········· Hispanic women
——— Black men   ‑·‑ Hispanic men

NOTE: Hispanics may be of any race.

- 1950 was the first year in which women outnumbered men in the total U.S. population (76.4 to 75.8 million). By the year 2050, women are projected to constitute 52% of the total population of 309.5 million.
- The segment of the population 65 and over is rapidly growing. In 1900, it constituted 4% of the total population; by 2000, it is projected to be 13%. Between 1986 and 2000, this age group will increase by 20%.
- Between 1985 and 2000, the Hispanic population is projected to increase by 46% (from 17.3 to 25.2 million), while the population of blacks and other minorities is projected to increase 23% (from 29.1 to 35.8 million). The white population is projected to increase by 10% (from 203.1 to 222.6 million).
- Between 2000 and 2050, the Hispanic population is projected to more than double (to 50.8 million), while the population of blacks and other minorities is projected to increase by 46% (to 52.3 million), and the white population by only 7% (to 238.3 million).

NOTE: Population includes armed forces overseas.

SOURCES: U.S. Bureau of the Census, *Current Population Reports*, Ser. P-25, No. 995, "Projections of the Hispanic Population: 1983–2080," Table 2; No. 952, "Projections of the Population of the U.S. by Age, Sex, and Race: 1983–2080," Table 6. ACE/Macmillan, *1989–90 Fact Book on Higher Education*, Table 1.

See Tables 1 and 2.

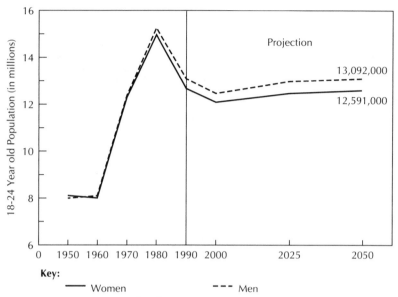

Key:
⎯⎯ Women   - - - Men

NOTE: Hispanics may be of any race.

- Between 1960 and 1970, the number of 18–24 year old men and women (the traditional college-age population) increased by 53%, from 16.1 to 24.7 million, with equal proportions of women and men represented. This age group peaked in 1981 at 30.4 million (15.0 million women and 15.4 million men).
- In 1960, 13% of the women and 12% of the men age 18–24 were minorities. By 2000, 20% of the women and 19% of the men age 18–24 will be minorities.
- In 1960, blacks constituted more than 90% of the 18–24 year old minority population (1.8 to 2.0 million minorities). By 2000, blacks will be less than 80% of the 18–24 year old minority population (3.8 of 4.8 million), due to the increase in other minority groups.

SOURCE: ACE/Macmillan, *1989–90 Fact Book on Higher Education*, Table 3.

See Table 3.

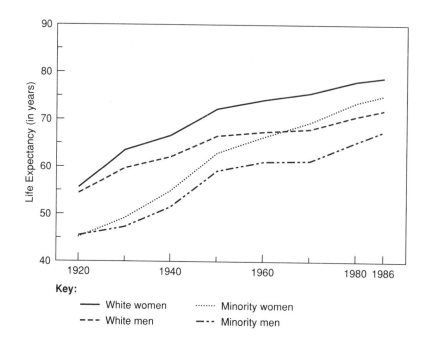

Key:

— White women ⋯⋯ Minority women
--- White men —·— Minority men

- Since 1920, the average life expectancy for women has increased from 55 to 78 years. For men, the average life expectancy has increased from 54 to 71 years.
- In 1986, the life expectancy of black women was 74 years, as opposed to 79 years for white women. For black men, life expectancy in 1986 was 66 years, as compared to 72 years for white men.
- For minorities in general (including blacks), the average life expectancy has increased from 45 years in 1920 to 71 in 1986.

SOURCE: U.S. Bureau of the Census, *Statistical Abstract of the United States, 1988*, Table 106.

See Table 4.

4

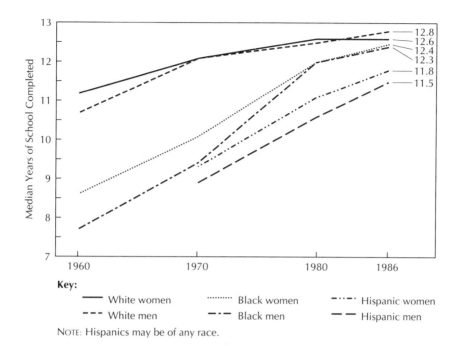

Key:

—— White women .... Black women – · · –· Hispanic women
– – – White men –·– Black men – – Hispanic men

NOTE: Hispanics may be of any race.

- Since 1960, the educational attainment of the U.S. population has consistently increased. Educational attainment of blacks and Hispanics continues to lag behind that of whites, though the gap has narrowed in the past 20 years.
- In 1986, about the same proportion of white men and women had completed 1–3 years of college (17% of each); however, considerably fewer women than men had completed 4 or more years of college (16% of women and 24% of men).
- Among the black population in 1986, 11% of both women and men had completed 4 or more years of college. In 1970, 5% of black women and 4% of black men had completed the same amount of education.
- Among the Hispanic population in 1986, 7% of the women and 9% of the men had completed 4 or more years of college. In 1970, 3% of Hispanic women and 6% of Hispanic men had completed the same amount of education.
- In 1986, Hispanic women had completed fewer years of school (median of 11.5 years) than had any other racial or ethnic group.

SOURCE: U.S. Bureau of the Census, *Statistical Abstract of the United States, 1988*, Table 202.

See Table 5.

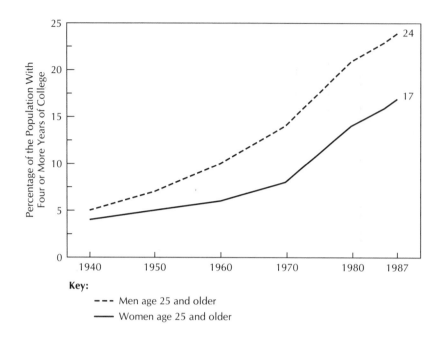

Key:

--- Men age 25 and older

—— Women age 25 and older

- Between 1940 and 1987, the proportion of all women age 25 and over completing 4 or more years of college increased from 4% to 17%. For men, the comparable figures were from 5% to 24%.
- In 1940 only 5% of the women and 7% of the men age 25–34 had 4 or more years of college. By 1987, 23% of the women and 25% of the men in this age group had 4 or more years of college.
- In 1986, 20% of whites age 25 and older had completed 4 or more years of college. The rate for blacks was 11%, and for Hispanics, 8%.

SOURCES: U.S. Bureau of the Census, *Current Population Reports*, Ser. P-20, No. 428, "Educational Attainment in the United States, March 1987 and 1986," Table 11; *Statistical Abstract of the United States, 1988*, Table 203.

See Tables 6 and 7.

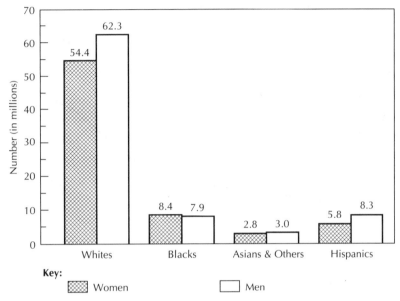

Key:

▨ Women ☐ Men

NOTE: Hispanics may be of any race.

- White women accounted for 50% of the growth in the labor force between 1972 and 1986 (15.4 of a total of 30.8 million people added to the labor force). In the period 1986–2000, they will account for 47% of the increase in the labor force (9.8 of a projected 20.9 million).
- In 1986, 55% of the women and 76% of the men age 16 and over were participating in the labor force. By 2000, 62% of the women and 75% of the men 16 and over are expected to participate in the labor force.
- By the year 2000, the total work force is projected to be composed of: 39% white women; 6% black women; 4% Hispanic women; 2% Asian women; 45% white men; 6% black men; 6% Hispanic men; and 2% Asian men.

NOTE: In 1979, a white woman age 25 had a worklife expectancy of 24 years; black and other women this age had a worklife expectancy of 23 years. For infants born in that year, the worklife expectancy for white females increases to 30 years, and for black and other females to 27 years. "Others" include Asians, American Indians, Alaskan Natives, and Pacific Islanders. Persons of Hispanic origin may be of any race.

SOURCES: U.S. Bureau of Labor Statistics, *Monthly Labor Review*, Sept. 1987, Table 5. U.S. Bureau of the Census, *Statistical Abstract of the United States, 1988*, Table 606.

See Tables 8 and 9.

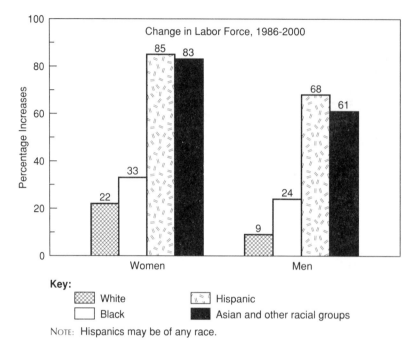

Change in Labor Force, 1986-2000

Key:

White   Hispanic
Black   Asian and other racial groups

NOTE: Hispanics may be of any race.

- The proportion of all women entering the labor force is increasing, a trend that holds true regardless of race or ethnicity.
- In 1986, 55% of white women and 77% of white men participated in the labor force. By 2000, participation rates are expected to increase to 62% for white women, but to decrease slightly to 75% for white men.
- In 1986, 57% of black women and 71% of black men participated in the labor force. By 2000, participation rates are expected to increase to 62% for black women, but to remain constant at 71% for black men.
- In 1986, 56% of the women and 75% of the men who were classified as "Asian and other" racial groups participated in the labor force. By 2000, participation rates for these groups is expected to increase to 60% for women, but to decrease slightly to 72% for men.
- In 1986, 50% of Hispanic women and 81% of Hispanic men participated in the labor force. By 2000, participation rates are expected to increase to 57% for Hispanic women, but to decrease slightly to 80% for the men.

NOTE: "Asian and other" racial groups include American Indians, Alaskan Natives, Asians, and Pacific Islanders.

SOURCE: U.S. Bureau of Labor Statistics, *Monthly Labor Review*, Sept. 1987, Table 5.

See Table 10.

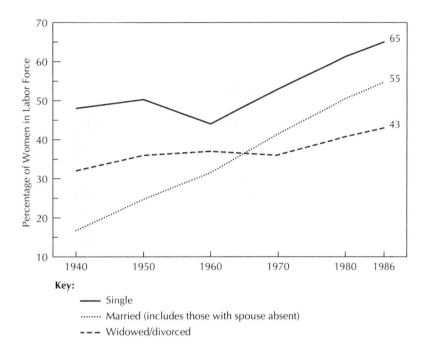

Key:
——— Single
········ Married (includes those with spouse absent)
--- Widowed/divorced

- In 1986, among all women in the population who were age 16 and older, 65% of single women (never married) were in the labor force, as were 55% of married women, and 43% of widowed or divorced women.
- Between 1940 and 1986, the proportion of all women in the labor force married with husband present increased from 30% to 55%.
- In 1940, single women (never married) constituted 49% (6.7 million) of the women in the work force. By 1986, single women (never married) constituted 25% (13.1 million) of the female work force.
- In 1986, married women (including those with absent spouses) accounted for 59% of the female work force; and single, widowed, or divorced women accounted for 41%.

NOTE: Single, as noted above, means never married. Divorced and widowed women are grouped in a separate category in this case.

SOURCE: U.S. Bureau of the Census, *Statistical Abstract of the United States, 1987*, Table 653.

See Table 11.

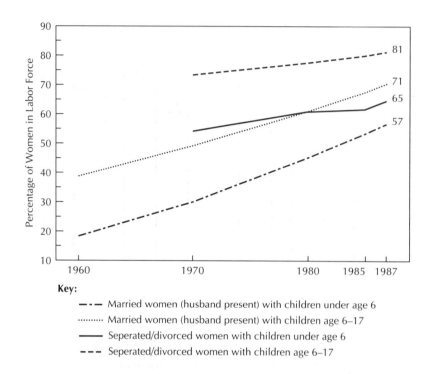

Key:

—·— Married women (husband present) with children under age 6

·········· Married women (husband present) with children age 6–17

——— Seperated/divorced women with children under age 6

— — — Seperated/divorced women with children age 6–17

- Between 1960 and 1987, the percentage of women in the labor force who were married but had no children under age 18 increased from 35% (5.7 million) to 48% (13.2 million).
- Between 1960 and 1987, the percentage of women in the labor force who were married with children age 6–17 increased from 39% (4.1 million) to 71% (9.0 million).
- Between 1960 and 1987, the percentage of women in the labor force married with children under age 6 increased from 19% (2.5 million) to 57% (7 million).

SOURCE: U.S. Bureau of the Census, *Statistical Abstract of the United States, 1988*, Table 624.

See Table 12.

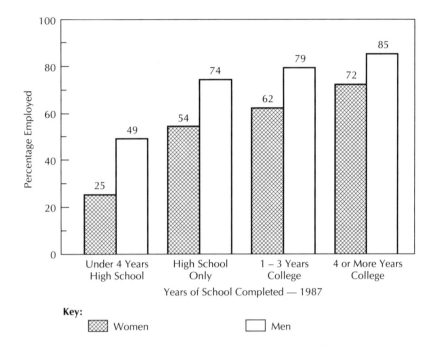

Years of School Completed — 1987

Key:
Women   Men

- As with men, the more education a woman has, the more likely she is to be employed. In 1987, 54% of women with only a 4-year high school education were employed, whereas 62% of women with 1–3 years of college and 72% of women with 4 or more years of college were employed.
- The disparity between the proportion of men and women who are employed decreases with higher levels of education.

NOTE: Employment data are for the civilian noninstitutional population.

SOURCES: U.S. Bureau of the Census, *Current Population Reports*, Ser. P-20, No. 428, "Educational Attainment in the United States, March 1987 and March 1986," Table 11; *Statistical Abstract of the United States, 1988*, Table 628.

See Tables 6 and 13.

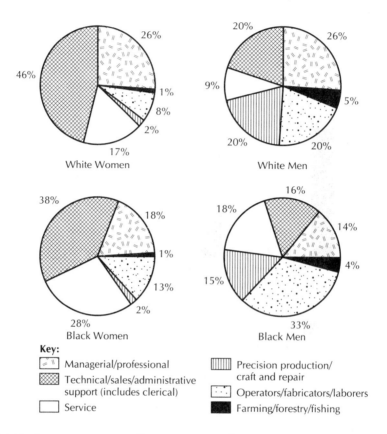

Key:

Managerial/professional	Precision production/ craft and repair
Technical/sales/administrative support (includes clerical)	Operators/fabricators/laborers
Service	Farming/forestry/fishing

- In July 1988, there were 47.8 million women and 60.6 million men age 20 and older employed in the United States.
- The same proportion of white women as white men are employed in occupations classified as managerial/professional (26%), but for blacks, a higher proportion of women are in these occupations than men (18% compared to 14%).
- Of the 44 major occupational groups identified by the Bureau of Labor Statistics, women were most likely to be found in the "other administrative support, including clerical" group (5.7 million) and the "secretaries, stenographers, typists" group (4.5 million); 22% of all women in the labor force were in these two categories.
- The proportion of black women employed in service occupations is higher than for white women, or for white or black men.

NOTE: The managerial/professional category includes all management and administrative positions (such as financial, personnel, purchasing, advertising, education, and health managers), as well as professions such as teaching, engineering, and law. The technical/sales/administrative support category includes secretaries and clerical assistants; and the service category includes household, protective service, food preparation, and personal service occupations.

SOURCE: Bureau of Labor Statistics, *Employment and Earnings*, Aug. 1988, Tables A-22, A-23. See Tables 14 and 15.

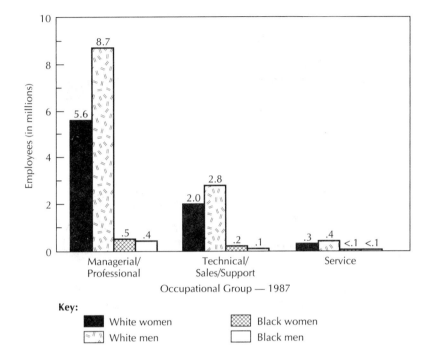

Occupational Group — 1987

Key:

White women   Black women
White men   Black men

- In 1987, white women with 4 or more years of college accounted for 24% of all employed white women. White men with the same level of education accounted for 29% of all employed white men. Comparable figures for black women and men were 16% and 14%, respectively.

- In 1987, 70% of the employed white women and 68% of the employed white men with 4 or more years of college were in managerial/professional positions. 68% of employed black women with 4 or more years of college were in managerial/professional positions, but only 57% of black men with similar education were in such positions.

- In 1987, for both black and white women with a high school diploma or 1–3 years of college, the most likely occupation was in the technical/sales/administrative support area.

- In 1987, 60% of black women and 35% of white women with less than 4 years of high school were employed in service occupations (including private household work).

NOTE: The managerial/professional category includes more than 40 occupations, including finance, purchasing, accounting, engineering, medicine, nursing, teaching, library science, and counseling. The technical/sales/support category includes technicians, cashiers, secretaries, receptionists, and clerks; and the service category includes household, protective service, food preparation, and personal service occupations.

SOURCE: U.S. Bureau of the Census, *Statistical Abstract of the United States, 1988*, Table 628.

See Table 13.

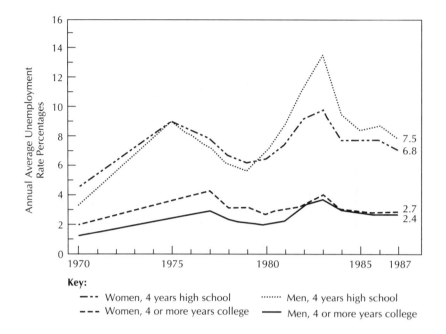

Key:
- — ·· — Women, 4 years high school
- — — — Women, 4 or more years college
- ········ Men, 4 years high school
- ——— Men, 4 or more years college

- Between 1960 and 1987, average annual unemployment rates were higher for women age 20 and older than for men of the same age, except in 1982 and 1983. In 1987, the annual average unemployment rate for both women and men age 20 and older was 5.4%.

- Since 1969, the average unemployment rates for both women and men age 16–19 has been greater than 15%, except for men in 1973, where the rate dipped to 13.9%.

- Between 1977 and 1987, unemployment rates for whites with 4 or more years of college were consistently lower than the rates for blacks or Hispanics with the same educational attainment. Of these three groups, black college graduates most frequently had the highest unemployment rates.

- In 1987, the unemployment rate for white college graduates was 2.3%; for Hispanics, 2.6%; for blacks, 5.3%. In the same year, the average unemployment rate for white high school graduates was 6.2%; for Hispanics, 9.4%; and for blacks, 14.3%.

SOURCES: U.S. Bureau of the Census, *Statistical Abstract of the United States, 1988*, Table 634. ACE/Macmillan, *1989–90 Fact Book on Higher Education*, Table 41.

See Tables 16 and 17.

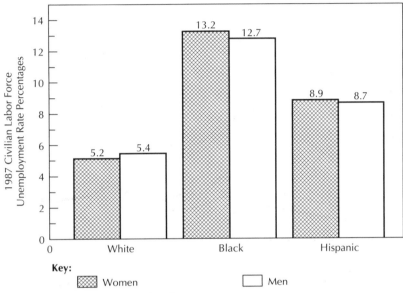

Key:
▨ Women   ☐ Men

NOTE: Hispanics may be of any race

- In 1987, the overall unemployment rate was lowest for whites and highest for blacks, with Hispanics between these groups. Although white women fared better than white men, unemployment rates for black and Hispanic women were higher than those for black and Hispanic men.
- In 1987, when comparing unemployment in various regions, black and white women and men, and Hispanic women, all had their lowest unemployment rates in New England. For both white women and white men in this region, the average unemployment rate was 3.2%. For black women, the rate was 7.0%; for black men, 6.4%; for Hispanic women, 4.2%; and for Hispanic men, 7.5%.
- In 1987, the highest unemployment rate for white women (7.3%) was in the West South Central area. For black women, the highest unemployment (18.1%) was in the East North Central area. For Hispanic women, the highest unemployment rate (15.6%) was in the West North Central area.

NOTE: New England includes Connecticut, Maine, Massachusetts, New Hampshire, Rhode Island, and Vermont. West North Central includes Iowa, Kansas, Minnesota, Missouri, Nebraska, North Dakota, and South Dakota. East North Central includes Illinois, Indiana, Ohio, Michigan, and Wisconsin. West South Central includes Arkansas, Louisiana, Oklahoma, and Texas.

SOURCE: U.S. Bureau of Labor Statistics, *Geographic Profile of Employment and Unemployment: 1987*, Table 1.

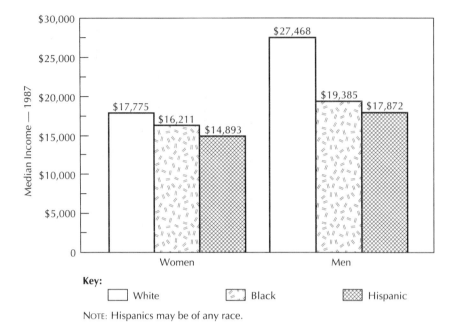

NOTE: Hispanics may be of any race.

- Women in every racial and ethnic group earned lower median salaries than men in any racial or ethnic group.
- The median incomes of year-round, full-time women workers are substantially lower than those of their male counterparts. In 1987, black women earned 84% as much as black men; Hispanic women earned 83% as much as Hispanic men; and white women earned 65% as much as white men.
- In 1987, white women age 15 and older who were year-round, full-time workers earned an average of $17,775 per year. Black women who were year-round, full-time workers earned $16,211, or 91% of the average white woman's salary.

SOURCE: U.S. Bureau of the Census, *Current Population Reports*, Ser. P-60, No. 161, "Money Income and Poverty Status in the United States: 1987," Table 7.

See Table 18.

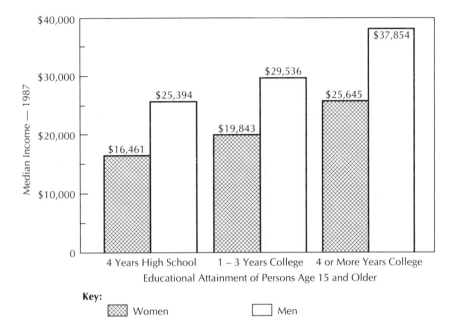

Key:

▨ Women   ☐ Men

- The return on a college education differs greatly for women and men. In 1970, women age 25 and older with 4 years of college earned an average of $8,156 per year, or 61% of the average salary of men with the same level of education ($13,264). By 1985, this gap had narrowed only slightly. Women with 4 years of college earned an average of $21,389, or 65% of the average salary of men with 4 years of college ($32,822).
- For persons age 15 and older, in 1987 the median salary for men with 4 years of high school ($25,394) was higher than the median salary earned by women with 4 years of college ($23,406).

SOURCES: U.S. Bureau of the Census, *Current Population Reports*, Ser. P-60, No. 161, "Money Income and Poverty Status in the United States: 1987," Table 7. National Center for Education Statistics, *Digest of Education Statistics*, 1988, Table 237.

See Tables 18 and 19.

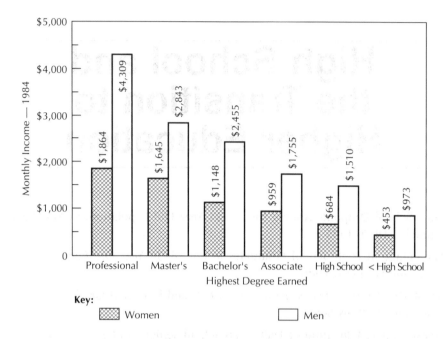

Key:

Women   Men

- In 1984, the average monthly income of all women was $734; the average for all men was $1,620.
- In 1984, the average monthly income for all people with bachelor's degrees was $1,841; the average for those with advanced degrees was $2,711.
- In 1984, a woman with a high school diploma could expect to earn 60% as much as a woman with a bachelor's degree; and a woman with a bachelor's degree could expect to earn 62% as much as a woman with a professional degree. A man with a high school diploma could expect to earn 62% as much as a man with a bachelor's degree; and a man with a bachelor's degree could expect to earn 57% as much as a man with a professional degree. But at both ends of the continuum, a woman could expect to earn less than one-half of what a man with comparable education could expect to earn.

NOTE: Income figures are for all employed persons, including full-time, part-time, and seasonal employees.

SOURCE: *Chronicle of Higher Education* 34, No. 7 (Oct. 14, 1987): A 36.

See Table 20.

High School and the Transition to Higher Education

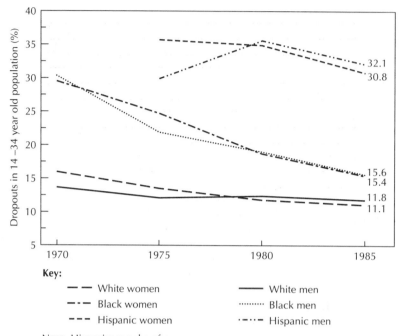

Key:

— — White women   ———— White men

—·— Black women   ·········· Black men

— — Hispanic women   ·—··— Hispanic men

NOTE: Hispanics may be of any race.

- Between 1975 and 1985, among 14–34 year olds, the percentage of white women and men not completing high school was consistently below 15%.
- Between 1975 and 1985, among 14–34 year olds, the percentage of Hispanic women and men not completing high school was consistently above 30%.
- Between 1975 and 1985, the percentage of black women and men not completing high school dropped steadily. In 1985, the percentage of blacks who dropped out was about the same (15%) as for whites in 1970.
- For all sex, racial, and ethnic groups except Hispanic males, the percentages of people age 14–34 who are high school dropouts has decreased since 1975.
- Since 1980, in all racial and ethnic groups, women have been slightly less likely to drop out than men.

NOTE: Dropouts are those people not enrolled in school who are not high school graduates. People with General Educational Development credentials are counted as graduates.

SOURCE: National Center for Education Statistics, *Digest of Education Statistics*, 1987, Table 72.

See Table 21.

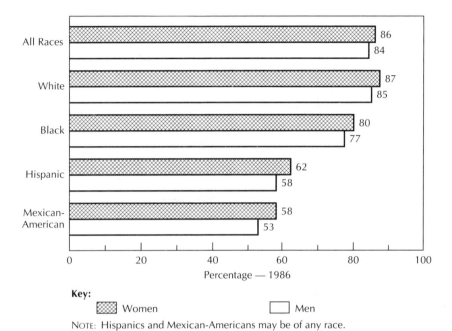

Percentage — 1986

Key:

▨ Women   ▢ Men

NOTE: Hispanics and Mexican-Americans may be of any race.

- Overall, only 14% of women age 18–34 did not have a high school diploma in 1986.
- Between 1976 and 1986, for all racial and ethnic groups, the percentage of people age 18–34 who graduated from high school increased.
- In 1986, in all racial and ethnic groups, a higher percentage of women than men age 18–34 were likely to be high school graduates. White women were most likely to be high school graduates (87%); Mexican-American women least likely (58%). Of black women in this age group, 80% were high school graduates.
- Between 1976 and 1986, Mexican-American women made the most progress in educational attainment; the proportion having a high school diploma increased from 48% to 58%.

SOURCES: U.S. Bureau of the Census, *Current Population Reports*, Ser. P-20, No. 319, "School Enrollment—Social and Economic Characteristics of Students," Table 1; No. 429, Table 1.

See Table 22.

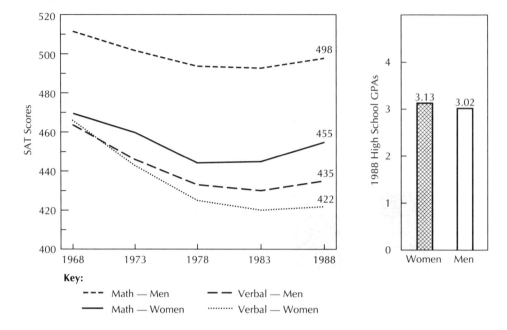

Key:

- - - Math — Men   — — Verbal — Men
——— Math — Women   ········ Verbal — Women

- Women make higher grades than men as shown in estimated high school GPAs, but score lower than men on SATs.
- In 1985, for students who took the SAT exam, the mean GPA for women was 3.07, and for men 2.98 (on a 4.0 scale); the combined verbal and math SAT score was 877 for women and 926 for men. In 1988, women who took the SAT exam had an average high school GPA of 3.13, while men had an average GPA of 3.02; the combined verbal and math SAT score was 877 for women and 933 for men.
- In each year since 1974, more women than men have taken the SAT exam. In 1988, 1.1 million people took the exam, 52% of them women.

NOTE: Data refer to "college-bound" high school seniors, not to all high school students.

SOURCES: The College Board, *Profiles, College-Bound Seniors, 1985*, pp. 10, 20; and *College-Bound Seniors: 1988 Profile of SAT and Achievement Test Takers*, Table A, and unpublished data.

See Tables 23 and 24.

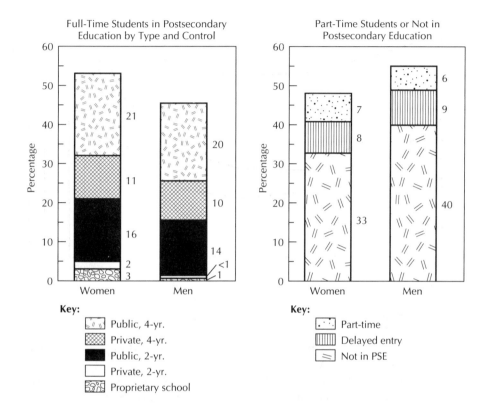

Full-Time Students in Postsecondary Education by Type and Control

Part-Time Students or Not in Postsecondary Education

Key:
- Public, 4-yr.
- Private, 4-yr.
- Public, 2-yr.
- Private, 2-yr.
- Proprietary school

Key:
- Part-time
- Delayed entry
- Not in PSE

- Three-fifths (59%) of the women and over one-half (52%) of the men who were high school seniors in spring 1980 entered some kind of postsecondary educational institution in fall 1980.

- Among those 1980 high school seniors who entered postsecondary education in fall 1980, the largest percentage attended either a public 4-year institution (21% of the women and 20% of the men) or a public 2-year community college (14% of the women and 13% of the men).

- The proportion of women vs. men who attended private 4-year institutions was slightly higher (11% women, 10% men).

- Among black high school seniors in 1980, 32% entered public institutions and 10% entered private institutions in fall 1980.

- Cubans were more likely than other Hispanic groups to enter higher education; 32% entered 2-year community colleges and 31% entered 4-year institutions. For Mexicans, 17% entered community colleges and 13% entered 4-year institutions. For Puerto Ricans, 6% entered community colleges and 30% entered 4-year institutions.

- Those who were seniors in Catholic or other private schools in 1980 were almost twice as likely to enroll in 4-year institutions as those graduating from public high schools.

SOURCE: National Center for Education Statistics, "The Timing of Abnormal Progression Among 1980 High School Seniors Entering Postsecondary Education in October 1980," from unpublished tabulations from the "High School and Beyond" survey.

See Table 25.

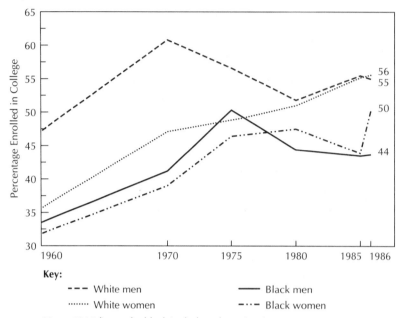

Key:

- - - White men   ——— Black men

········ White women   -··- Black women

NOTE: 1960 figures for black includes other minority races.

- The percentage of women high school graduates enrolled in or completing 1 or more years of college has increased from 35% to 55% in the past 25 years and now surpasses, by a small margin, the percentage of men enrolled in or completing 1 or more years of college.
- The percentage of black women high school graduates enrolled in or completing 1 or more years of college increased by 58% in the years 1960–1986. For white women, the increase was 56%.
- The percentage of black women high school graduates enrolled in or completing 1 year of college increased sharply in 1986, from 44% in 1985 to 50% in 1986.

NOTE: 1960 figures for blacks include blacks and other races.

SOURCE: U.S. Bureau of the Census, *Statistical Abstract of the United States, 1988*, Table 233.

See Table 26.

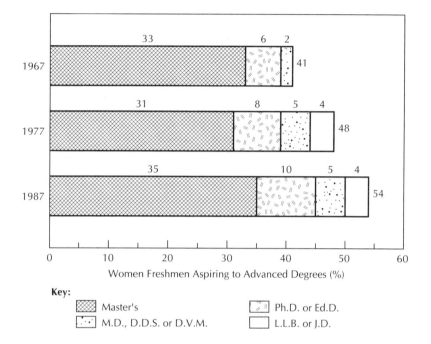

Women Freshmen Aspiring to Advanced Degrees (%)

Key:

Master's	Ph.D. or Ed.D.
M.D., D.D.S. or D.V.M.	L.L.B. or J.D.

- In 1987, the overall level of educational aspirations of women and men was nearly identical, with 56% of both women and men aspiring to some kind of advanced degree, and 35% of the women and 36% of the men aspiring to a bachelor's degree.
- The percentage of first-time freshman women aspiring to doctoral or professional degrees doubled from 1970 to 1985 (from 10% to 20%); at the same time, the percentage of men aspiring to doctoral or professional degrees declined (from 25% to 20%).
- Since 1970, the proportion of women aspiring to medical degrees has increased by two and one-half, and the proportion aspiring to law degrees has more than quadrupled. Men's interest in both of these degrees has declined somewhat, as proportionally more men aspire to the master's degree.

NOTE: These data were based on samples of first-time, full-time students enrolled in 2- and 4-year institutions, both public and private.

SOURCES: Astin, A. W., Green, K. C., & Korn, W. S., *The American Freshman: Twenty Year Trends*, 1987. Astin, A. W., Green, K. C., Korn, W. S., and Schalit, M., *The American Freshman: National Norms for Fall 1987*, 1987.

See Table 27.

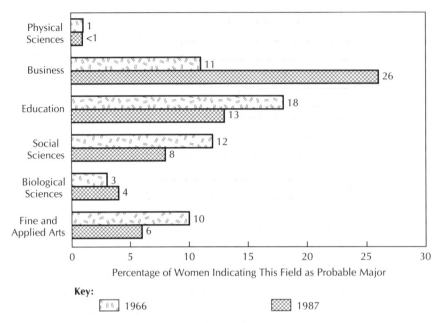

Percentage of Women Indicating This Field as Probable Major

Key:
1966   1987

- Between 1977 and 1987, the field of business showed the greatest increase in popularity for first-time, full-time freshmen. The percentage of women reporting business as their probable major increased during this period from 21% to 26%; for freshman men, the increase was from 24% to 29%.
- Humanities, fine and performing arts, and social sciences have all declined in popularity in the last 20 years. For example, the percentage of freshman women planning to major in English declined from 7% in 1966 to 2% in 1987; the percentage for men also declined, from 2% to 1%. The percentage of women planning to major in fine and applied arts decreased from 10% in 1966 to 6% in 1987; for men, the percentage declined from 7% to 5%.
- The percentage of freshman women planning to major in engineering has increased slightly, but there is still a wide gap between women's and men's interest in this field. Between 1977 and 1987, the proportion of freshman women anticipating majors in engineering increased from 2% to 3%. For men, the proportion anticipating this major was 17% in each of these years.

SOURCE: ACE/Macmillan, *1989–90 Fact Book on Higher Education*, Table 121.

See Table 28.

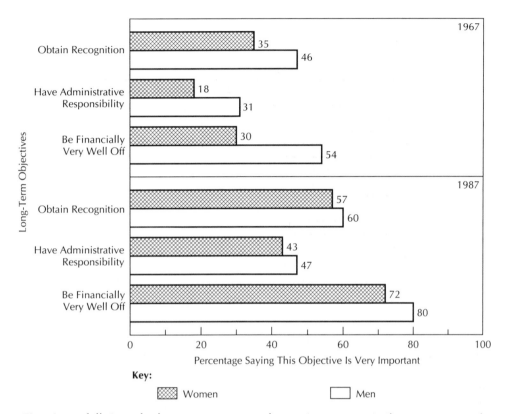

Percentage Saying This Objective Is Very Important

Key:

▨ Women   ☐ Men

- First-time, full-time freshman women are becoming more similar to men in their long-term achievement goals, such as the desire to obtain recognition, to have administrative responsibility, and to be financially very well off. More men still report these goals as very important, but the gap is narrowing.

- In 1987, 4 of the top 5 ranking objectives were the same for women and men: to be an authority in one's field, to be well off financially, to obtain recognition from colleagues, and to raise a family. For women, the fifth top objective was to help others who are in difficulty; for men, the fifth objective was to be successful in their own business.

- Developing a meaningful philosophy of life has decreased dramatically as a goal for college freshmen, both women and men, in the past 20 years. In 1967, 88% of the women and 79% of the men indicated it was an essential or very important goal. In 1987, only 39% of the women and 40% of the men considered it essential or very important.

- Raising a family was listed as an essential or very important goal by proportionately fewer women in 1987 than in 1967, but this goal is still very important to more women than men. In 1970, 72% of freshman women and 64% of freshman men indicated raising a family was an essential or very important life goal; in 1987, only 60% of the women and 56% of the men listed this as essential or very important.

SOURCE: Astin, A. W., Green, K. C., & Korn, W. S., *The American Freshman: Twenty Year Trends*, 1987, pp. 49, 73. Astin, A. W., Green, K. C., Korn, W. S. & Schalit, M., *The American Freshman: National Norms for Fall 1987*, 1987, pp. 28, 44.

See Table 29.

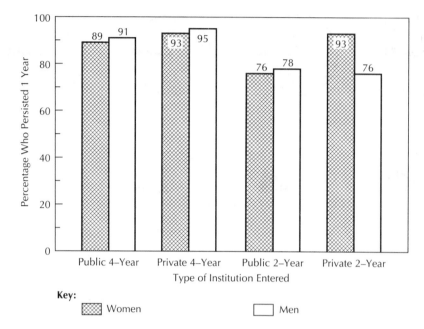

Key:
⬚ Women   ☐ Men

- Of the women who were high school seniors in 1980, 59% entered some form of postsecondary education during the 1980-81 academic year.

- Of the women who were high school seniors in 1980, 21% entered public 4-year institutions, 14% entered public 2-year institutions, and 11% entered private 4-year institutions in fall 1980.

- Of the 1980 high school seniors from families in the lowest socioeconomic status (SES) quartile, 47% attended some kind of postsecondary institution in the 6-year period 1980–1986. At the same time, those whose families were in the top SES quartile were nearly twice as likely (88%) to attend some form of postsecondary institution.

- In three sectors—4-year public, 4-year private and 2-year public institutions—about the same number of women and men who entered higher education in fall 1980 persisted through their first year of college, although the persistence level of men was slightly higher. In 2-year private institutions, the persistence level of women was higher than that of men, and the gap between them was much wider.

- Asian students had the highest persistence levels of any race or ethnic group. More than 99% of Asian 1980 high school seniors who entered higher education in the fall of 1980 completed their first year of college.

NOTE: Socioeconomic status was measured by a composite score of parental education, family income, father's occupation, and household characteristics in 1980.

SOURCE: National Center for Education Statistics, "The Timing of Abnormal Progression Among 1980 High School Seniors Entering Postsecondary Education in October 1980," Tables 1 and 2, unpublished tabulations from *High School and Beyond: Senior Second Follow-up,* July 1986.

See Tables 25 and 30.

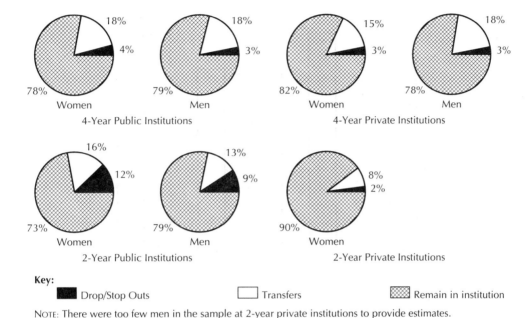

4-Year Public Institutions   4-Year Private Institutions

2-Year Public Institutions   2-Year Private Institutions

Key:

■ Drop/Stop Outs   □ Transfers   ▨ Remain in institution

NOTE: There were too few men in the sample at 2-year private institutions to provide estimates.

- At all types of institutions, at least 88% of both women and men 1980 high school seniors who completed 1 year of higher education in 1980–81 continued their college education, either in the same institution or by transferring to another institution. At 4-year institutions, both public and private, the level was higher, between 96% and 97%.
- In public 4-year institutions, women were about as likely as men to remain in the same institution (78% of women, 79% of men). In private 4-year institutions, women were a little more likely than men to remain in the same institution (82% of women, 78% of men).
- The highest dropout rate for both women and men was in 2-year public institutions (9% for women, 8% for men).

NOTE: Proprietary and public 2-year technical institutions were excluded from these analyses.

SOURCE: National Center for Education Statistics, "The Timing of Abnormal Progression Among 1980 High School Seniors Entering Postsecondary Education in October 1980," Tables 3A and 3 B, unpublished tabulations from *High School and Beyond: Senior Second Follow-up*, July 1986.

See Table 31.

Enrollment

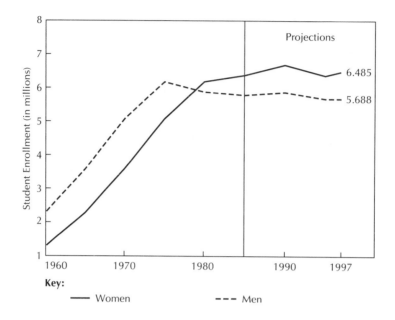

Key:
——— Women   --- Men

- Between 1950 and 1987, the opening fall enrollment of college students at all institutions increased more than fivefold, from 2.3 to 12.5 million. The number of women enrolled in 1987 (6.7 million) was more than nine times greater than in 1950 (.7 million); the number of men enrolled more than tripled (from 1.6 to 5.9 million) during this period.
- 1979 was the first year in which women outnumbered men in the opening fall enrollment figures (6.0 million women vs. 5.7 million men). Since 1979, women have consistently outnumbered men; in 1987, they constituted 53% of the total enrollment.
- Between 1977 and 1987, the enrollment of women increased by 20%, while the enrollment of men remained relatively constant.
- Enrollment of men in colleges and universities peaked in 1975 at 6.2 million, and by 1987 had dropped 5%, to 5.9 million. In 1987, enrollment of women was still continuing to increase.

SOURCES: *Chronicle of Higher Education* 35, no. 14 (Nov. 30, 1988): A 34. ACE/Macmillan, *1989-90 Fact Book on Higher Education*, Table 46.

See Tables 32 and 33.

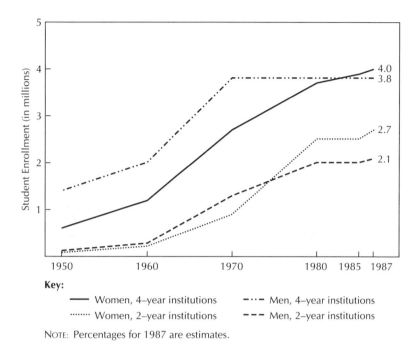

Key:
— Women, 4–year institutions   –·–· Men, 4–year institutions
······· Women, 2–year institutions   – – – Men, 2–year institutions

NOTE: Percentages for 1987 are estimates.

- Between 1965 and 1987, enrollment of women in 2-year institutions increased sixfold, while enrollment of men almost tripled.
- Between 1965 and 1987, enrollment of women in 4-year institutions more than doubled, while enrollment of men increased by about 30%.
- In 1987, women made up 51% of the student body in 4-year institutions and 56% of the student body in 2-year institutions.

SOURCE: ACE/Macmillan, *1989–90 Fact Book on Higher Education*, Tables 59 and 61.

See Tables 34 and 35.

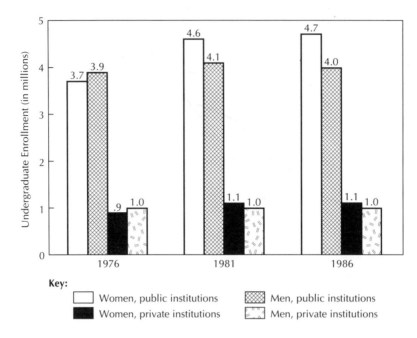

Key:

☐ Women, public institutions   ▨ Men, public institutions
■ Women, private institutions   ▨ Men, private institutions

- Between 1970 and 1986, women's undergraduate enrollment in public institutions almost doubled, from 2.4 to 4.7 million. During that same period, men's enrollment increased 24%, from 3.2 to 4.0 million.
- Between 1970 and 1986, enrollment of undergraduate women in private institutions increased 52%, from .7 million to 1.1 million. During that same period, men's enrollment remained essentially the same (1.0 million).
- In fall 1986, 4 in 5 of the women (81%) and the men (80%) in higher education were enrolled in public institutions of higher education.

NOTE: Enrollment figures include full- and part-time students.

SOURCE: National Center for Education Statistics, *Digest of Education Statistics 1988*, Table 125.

See Table 36.

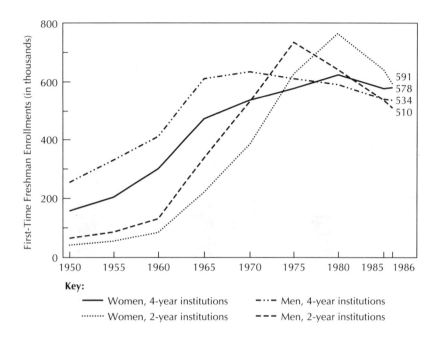

Key:
——— Women, 4-year institutions   — ·· — Men, 4-year institutions
············ Women, 2-year institutions   — — — Men, 2-year institutions

- Since 1977, women have constituted more than one-half of the first-time freshman enrollment.
- In 4-year institutions, enrollments of first-time freshman women peaked in 1980; by 1986, enrollment in this group had declined 7%. Enrollments of first-time freshman men peaked in 1970, and by 1986 had declined 15%.
- In 2-year institutions, enrollment of first-time freshman women peaked in 1981 and steadily declined through 1986. Enrollment of first-time freshman men peaked in 1975 and by 1986 had declined 30%.
- Between 1975 and 1976, in 2-year institutions, the proportion of men vs. women entering as first-time freshmen changed significantly. In 1975, women constituted 46% of those students; in 1976, they constituted 51%. By 1978, their proportion increased to 54%, where it remained in 1986.
- Between 1981 and 1986, the total number of students enrolling as first-time freshmen declined by 16%. The rate of decline was similar for women and men: 17% for the women, 15% for the men.

SOURCE: ACE/Macmillan, *1989–90 Fact Book on Higher Education*, Tables 75, 80, and 82.

See Tables 37, 38, and 39.

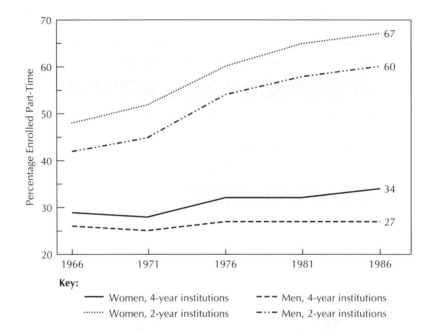

Key:

——— Women, 4-year institutions   – – – Men, 4-year institutions
·········· Women, 2-year institutions   – ·· – Men, 2-year institutions

- Between 1965 and 1982, there was an overall shift toward part-time enrollment, but the shift was more pronounced for women.
- Between 1965 and 1986, the percentage of women students in higher education who were enrolled part-time increased from 31% to 47%. For men, the comparable increase was from 28% to 39%.
- The number of women enrolled part-time in higher education more than quadrupled between 1965 and 1986, while the number of men enrolled part-time more than doubled.
- In 1986, nearly one-half of the women (47%) were enrolled as part-time students. In the same year, 39% of the men were enrolled part-time.

SOURCE: ACE/Macmillan, *1989–90 Fact Book on Higher Education*, Tables 69, 70, 73, and 74.

See Tables 40, 41, 42, and 43.

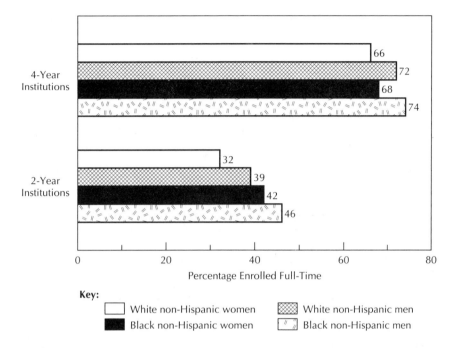

Key:

☐ White non-Hispanic women   ▨ White non-Hispanic men

■ Black non-Hispanic women   ▨ Black non-Hispanic men

- At 4-year institutions, most women and men were enrolled on a full-time basis. In 1986, 2 in 3 white, non-Hispanic women (66%) and almost 3 in 4 white, non-Hispanic men (72%) who were enrolled in all 4-year institutions attended full-time.
- Of the black, non-Hispanic women enrolled in 4-year institutions in 1986, 68% were enrolled full-time; the percentage for black, non-Hispanic men enrolled full-time was 74%.
- At 2-year institutions, most women and men enroll on a part-time basis. In 1986, 58% of the black, non-Hispanic women were enrolled part-time, while 68% of the white, non-Hispanic women were enrolled part-time.
- In both 2- and 4-year institutions, for both black and white students, women are less likely than men to be enrolled full-time.

SOURCE: National Center for Education Statistics, "Trends in Minority Enrollment in Higher Education, Fall 1976–Fall 1986," April 1988, Table 3.

See Table 44.

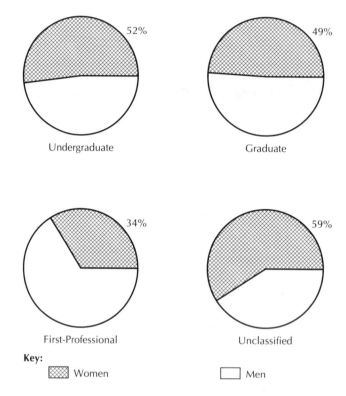

- Between 1976 and 1985, the proportion of women students in every level of higher education increased. First-professional programs had the biggest gains, but also the smallest percentages of students who were women.
- In 1976, women constituted 22% of those enrolled in first-professional programs; in 1985, their percentage had risen to 34%.
- Between 1976 and 1985, the percentage of women in graduate school increased from 45% to 49% of the total graduate enrollment.
- In 1976, women constituted 48% of the undergraduate enrollments in U.S. colleges and universities; by 1985, they constituted 52%.
- In both 1976 and 1985, women were a majority of those enrolled as unclassified students in institutions of higher education. In 1976, women enrollees constituted 52% of a total of 1.2 million in this category; in 1985, they constituted 59% of a total of 1.4 million.

NOTE: The "unclassified" category includes all undergraduate and graduate students not enrolled for a degree.

SOURCES: National Center for Education Statistics, *Digest of Education Statistics*, 1987, Table 131; *Digest of Education Statistics*, 1988, Table 120.

See Tables 45 and 46.

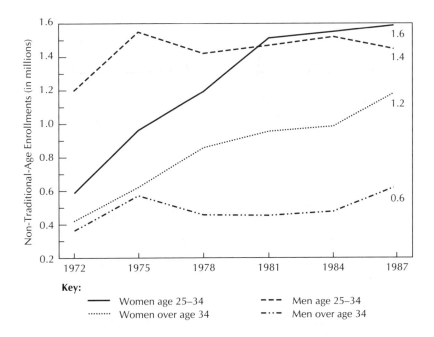

Key:
— Women age 25–34   – – – Men age 25–34
········ Women over age 34   –··– Men over age 34

- In 1987, women made up 53% of those enrolled in higher education (6.6 of a total of 12.5 million).
- Between 1972 and 1987, among traditional college-age students (age 18–24), men's enrollment increased from 3.5 to 3.9 million, while women's enrollment increased from 2.7 to 3.8 million.
- In 1987, women age 25 and older constituted 22% of all students enrolled in U.S. colleges and universities (2.7 of a total of 12.5 million); this group constituted 41% of the 6.6 million women enrolled in higher education.
- Since 1972, women age 35 and older have been the fastest growing group of college students; this group almost tripled in size between 1972 and 1987.

SOURCES: U.S. Bureau of the Census, *Statistical Abstract of the United States, 1988*, Table 234; and unpublished data, 1989.

See Tables 47 and 48.

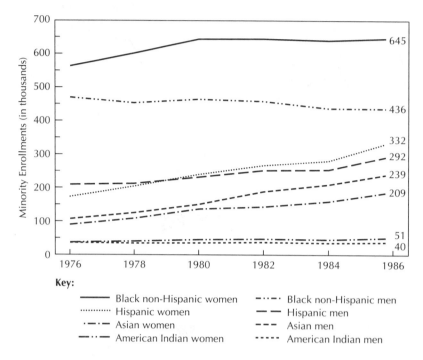

Key:

— Black non-Hispanic women   —··— Black non-Hispanic men
·········· Hispanic women   — — Hispanic men
·—·— Asian women   — — — Asian men
—··— American Indian women   ····· American Indian men

- In 1976, minorities made up almost 16% of all enrollments in higher education institutions; by 1986, their percentage increased to 18%.

- In almost every case, the increase in minority women's enrollment was greater than the increase in minority men's enrollment. The only minority group that experienced a decline in enrollment between 1976 and 1986 was black men, whose enrollment declined by 8%.

- Between 1976 and 1986, the enrollment of white, non-Hispanic women increased 23%. During this period, enrollment of Asian/Pacific Island women more than doubled; enrollment of Hispanic women increased 91%; enrollment of American Indian women increased 34%; and enrollment of black women increased 15%.

- In 1986, women constituted a majority of all minorities, with the exception of Asians. In that year, women made up 56% of American Indian enrollments, 60% of black enrollments, 53% of Hispanic enrollments, and 47% of Asian enrollments.

NOTES: Minorities include students who are classified as black, non-Hispanic; Hispanic; Asian or Pacific Islander; and American Indian/Alaskan Native. Nonresident aliens were excluded from the above analyses.

SOURCE: National Center for Education Statistics, "Trends in Minority Enrollment in Higher Education 1976–1986," Table 1.

See Table 49.

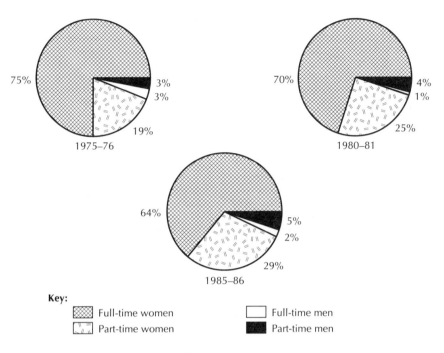

1975–76

1980–81

1985–86

Key:

Full-time women   Full-time men

Part-time women   Part-time men

- In 1985–86, a total of 104,454 students (97,142 women and 7,312 men) were enrolled in the 102 institutions that reported themselves as women's colleges.
- In 1985, the 97,142 women enrolled in women's colleges represented 1.5% of all the women enrolled in higher education in that year (over 6.4 million).
- Enrollment in women's colleges between 1975 and 1985 remained essentially stable (100,000 to 110,000), although the number of women's colleges continued to decrease during the 10-year period.
- Part-time enrollment in women's colleges has increased faster than part-time enrollment in private institutions as a whole. Between 1975 and 1985, the proportion of students enrolled part-time in private institutions increased from 27% to 30%; in women's colleges, part-time enrollment increased from 22% to 34% of the total.

NOTE: Women's colleges are those that reported their institutions as such on the Higher Education General Information System (HEGIS) forms. All but two women's colleges were private.

SOURCE: ACE, special 1988 tabulations from the Higher Education General Information System computer tapes.

See Table 50.

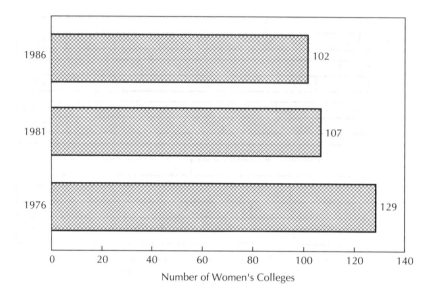

Number of Women's Colleges

- The number of women's colleges declined between 1976 and 1986, although the total enrollments remained at approximately 100,000.
- The decrease in the number of women's colleges has occurred because some institutions have declared themselves to be coed, some have merged with other institutions, and some have closed.

NOTE: Women's colleges are those that reported their institutions as such on the Higher Education General Information System (HEGIS) institutional characteristics form.

SOURCE: ACE, special 1988 tabulations from the Higher Education General Information System computer tapes.

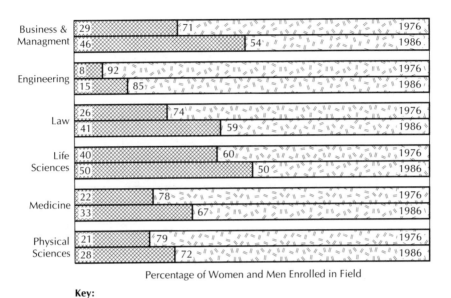

Percentage of Women and Men Enrolled in Field

Key:

Women   Men

- Between 1976 and 1986, more students, both women and men, were enrolled in business and management than in any other field. In 1976, women represented 29% of the enrollment in this field; in 1986, they accounted for 46% of the enrollment.
- Between 1976 and 1986, enrollment of women in veterinary medicine increased from 28% to 53% of the total in that field.
- Between 1976 and 1986, the number of women enrolled in dentistry more than doubled as a percentage of the total in that field (from 11% to 27%).
- Between 1976 and 1986, women's enrollment in engineering increased from 8% to 15% of the total enrollment in that field.

NOTE: Enrollment includes both undergraduate and graduate students.

SOURCE: National Center for Education Statistics, *Digest of Education Statistics,* 1988, Table 142.

See Table 51.

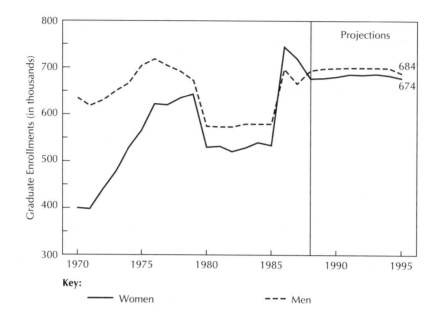

- In 1929, there was a total of 47,255 graduate students in U.S. institutions of higher education, of whom 38% were women. By 1949, the proportion of women graduate students had dropped to a low of 27%. The proportion of women has increased ever since, and in 1986, 52% of graduate students were women.
- By 1997, there are projected to be 1.3 million graduate students in the United States, about one-half of whom are expected to be women.
- Since 1970, about 30% of the women and 40% of the men enrolled in graduate programs have been full-time students. These percentages are projected to remain the same during the 1990s, although the numbers are projected to increase.
- In 1970, 25% of the women graduate students and 33% of the men graduate students were enrolled in private institutions. By 1985, 32% of the women and 39% of the men in graduate programs were enrolled in private institutions.

NOTES: Graduate enrollment includes unclassified postbaccalaureate students. The figure above is based on Table 53.

SOURCES: National Center for Education Statistics, *Digest of Education Statistics*, 1987, Table 111; and unpublished projections. ACE/Macmillan, *1989–90 Fact Book on Higher Education*, Table 84.

See Tables 52 and 53.

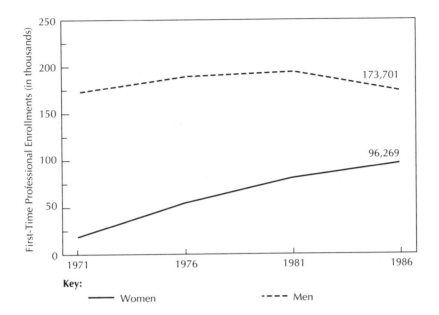

Key:

——— Women   - - - - Men

- In 1970, there were almost 15,000 women (about 9% of the total) enrolled in first-professional programs in U.S. colleges and universities. By 1986, there were about 96,000 women (36% of the total) enrolled in such programs.
- In 1986, about 9% of both women and men in first-professional programs were enrolled on a part-time basis. In 1970, slightly more of both men and women had been enrolled part-time in these programs (11%).
- Between 1980 and 1986, enrollment of women in first-professional programs increased 23%, while enrollment of men in similar programs declined 13%.
- In 1986, about 3 in 5 of the women (57%) and of the men (60%) in first-professional programs were attending private institutions.

NOTE: The National Center for Education Statistics defines first-professional programs as those in dentistry, medicine, optometry, osteopathic medicine, pharmacy, podiatric medicine, veterinary medicine, chiropractic medicine, law, and theology.

SOURCE: National Center for Education Statistics, *Digest of Education Statistics*, 1988, Table 128.

See Table 54.

Earned Degrees

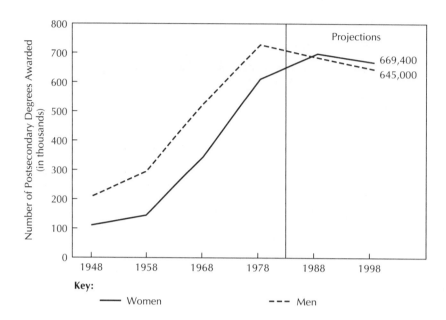

Key:
——— Women   - - - Men

- Between 1950 and 1986, the number of women receiving bachelor's and higher degrees increased more than fourfold, while the number of men receiving degrees increased 85%.

- Beginning in 1987–88, women were projected to receive a larger proportion of the total degrees earned in any given year than men.

- In 1948, degrees conferred by private institutions constituted about one-half (51%) of the total number awarded. In 1986, they constituted only 36% of the degrees awarded.

- Between 1986 and 1998, the total number of degrees conferred is projected to decline by 5%, but the number of degrees conferred to women is expected to decline by only 2%.

SOURCE: ACE/Macmillan, *1989–90 Fact Book on Higher Education*, Table 123.

See Table 55.

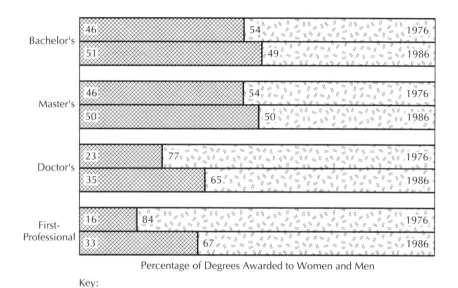

Percentage of Degrees Awarded to Women and Men

Key:
Women   Men

- In 1960, women received 34% of all degrees awarded. In 1986, they received 49% of all degrees. Projections call for their share to rise to 51% and remain there until the end of the century.
- Women's share of bachelor's degrees has risen from 43% in 1970 to 51% in 1986. Their share of master's degrees has risen from 40% in 1970 to 50% in 1986. Their share of doctoral degrees has risen from 13% in 1970 to 35% in 1986.
- In 1970, women received 5% of first-professional degrees awarded that year. In 1986, they received 33% of first-professional degrees. In 1998, they are projected to receive 43%.
- Between 1983 and 1987, women made their biggest gains in first-professional degrees, where their proportion increased from 30% to 35% of the degrees.
- In the half century 1948–1998 (with current projections holding), the proportion of women receiving doctoral degrees will increase from 12% to 46% of the yearly total.

SOURCE: ACE/Macmillan, *1989–90 Fact Book on Higher Education*, Table 128.

See Table 56.

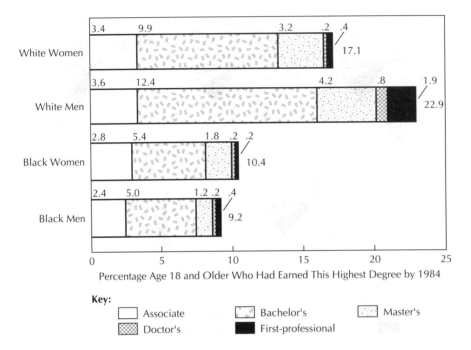

Percentage Age 18 and Older Who Had Earned This Highest Degree by 1984

Key:

☐ Associate   ▨ Bachelor's   ▦ Master's
▨ Doctor's   ■ First-professional

- In 1984, less than 1% of the U.S. population—black or white, female or male—had doctoral degrees. In that year 147,000 white women, 558,000 white men, 18,000 black women, and 14,000 black men in the United States had doctoral degrees.
- In 1984, 10% of white women age 18 and older had bachelor's degrees as their highest degree. In that same year, 12% of white men, 5% of black women, and 5% of black men had bachelor's degrees as their highest degree.
- About one-third of the black men (31%), black women (34%), and white men (33%) who were age 18 and older had attained only a high-school diploma; for white women, the comparable figure was 39%.
- In 1984, more than one-third of the black population of the U.S. who were age 18 and older, both women (38%) and men (39%), were not high-school graduates. About one-fourth of the white population (25% of women, 23% of men) also were not high-school graduates in that year.
- In 1984, a large proportion (62%) of the total population age 18 and older had a high-school diploma or less. This included 57% of white men, 64% of white women, 71% of black men, and 72% of black women.

NOTE: Degrees include vocational, associate's, bachelor's, master's, professional, and doctoral degrees.

SOURCE: U.S. Bureau of the Census, *Current Population Reports*, Ser. P-70, No. 11, "What It's Worth: Educational Background and Economic Status, Spring 1984," Table 11.

See Table 57.

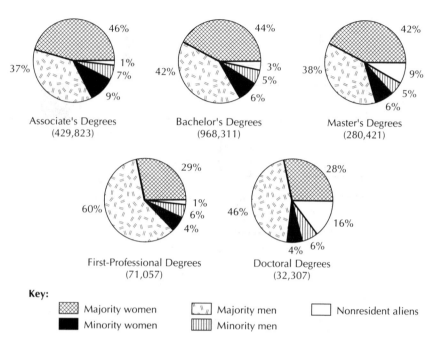

Associate's Degrees
(429,823)

Bachelor's Degrees
(968,311)

Master's Degrees
(280,421)

First-Professional Degrees
(71,057)

Doctoral Degrees
(32,307)

Key:

Majority women   Majority men   Nonresident aliens

Minority women   Minority men

- In 1985, white women received 46% of all associate's degrees, 43% of all bachelor's degrees, 42% of all master's degrees, 28% of all doctorates, and 29% of all first-professional degrees.

- As a group, minority women received 9% of all associate's degrees awarded in 1985, 6% each of all bachelor's and master's degrees, and 4% each of all doctorates and first-professional degrees.

- Black women received more than one-half of the degrees awarded to minority women in 1985. In that year they earned 5% of all associate's degrees, 4% of all bachelor's degrees, 3% of all master's degrees, and 2% of each of all doctorates and first-professional degrees.

- Hispanic women received 3% of all associate's degrees awarded in 1985, 1% of all bachelor's and master's degrees, and less than 1% of all doctorates and first-professional degrees.

- Asian/Pacific Island women received approximately 1% of all degrees awarded at each level in 1985, and American Indian/Alaskan Native women received .5% or less of all degrees awarded at each level.

SOURCE: National Center for Education Statistics, Ed Tabs, "Earned Degree Data," Jan. 1988, Table 7.

See Table 58.

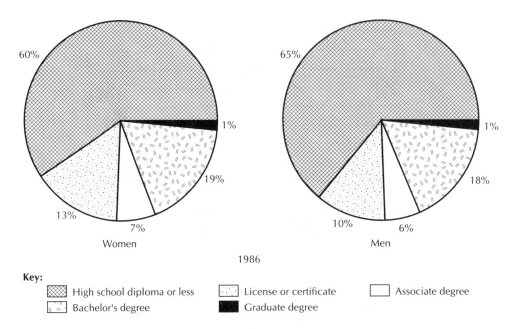

1986

Key:

High school diploma or less   License or certificate   Associate degree

Bachelor's degree   Graduate degree

- Fewer than 1 in 5 (20%) students who were high school seniors in spring 1980 had earned a bachelor's degree by spring 1986.
- A slightly higher proportion of women who were high school seniors in spring 1980 had earned bachelor's and associate's degrees by spring 1986 than men: 19% of the women vs. 18% of the men had attained bachelor's degrees; and 7% of the women vs. 6% of the men had attained associate's degrees.
- Slightly more men than women who were high school seniors in spring 1980 had earned graduate or professional degrees by spring 1986, but the percentage for both was less than 1%.
- Asians who were high school seniors in 1980 had the highest educational attainment by spring 1986: 27% had received a bachelor's degree, and 2% had completed graduate or professional degrees. 20% of whites, about 10% of blacks and American Indians, and 7% of Hispanics had completed a bachelor's degree within the 6 years following their senior year in high school.
- Those who graduated from a Catholic (33%) or other private school (37%) in 1980 were more than twice as likely to have completed a bachelor's degree by spring 1986 than were those who graduated from a public high school (16%).
- Of the 1980 seniors who were in the lowest socioeconomic status group, 12% had achieved an associate's or bachelor's degree by spring 1986. Of those from the highest socioeconomic group, 43% had completed a 2- or 4-year degree.

NOTE: Socioeconomic status in 1980 was measured by a composite score of parental education, family income, father's occupation, and household characteristics.

SOURCE: National Center for Education Statistics, *Digest of Education Statistics*, 1988, Table 214.

See Table 59.

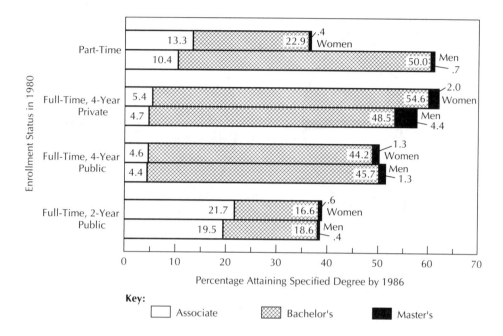

Percentage Attaining Specified Degree by 1986

Key: ☐ Associate ▨ Bachelor's ■ Master's

- Of those who were high school seniors in spring 1980, 1 in 4 (25%) had attained some postsecondary degree (associate's, bachelor's and/or master's) by spring 1986. For women, the percentage was 26%.
- Women who had entered 4-year private institutions as full-time students in fall 1980 were more likely to have attained a postsecondary degree by spring 1986 than were either women who entered other types of institutions or men who entered 4-year private institutions: 62% attained some degree, and 55% completed a bachelor's degree. Of the men who entered 4-year private institutions as full-time students, 58% attained some degree, and 49% completed a bachelor's degree.
- Of those who entered a college or university as part-time students directly after high school, men were more likely than women to have completed a bachelor's degree in 6 years (50% as opposed to 23%).
- Very few of those seniors who had not enrolled in college directly after high school had earned a postsecondary degree 6 years after leaving high school (8% of the men and 7% of the women).

NOTE: Data for private 2-year institutions were not reported separately in this study. In preparing the graph, part-time enrollments in 4-year private, 4-year public, and 2-year public institutions were summed.

SOURCE: National Center for Education Statistics, "Highest Degree Attained by 1980 High School Seniors by Sex, Race, Type of Community and Type of High School as of Spring, 1986," unpublished tabulations, Tables 2 & 3.

See Table 60.

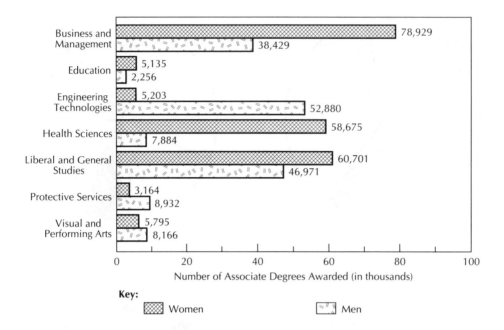

Number of Associate Degrees Awarded (in thousands)

Key: Women | Men

- Women received about 55% of the associate's degrees awarded each year since 1983. The total number of these degrees awarded to women has remained fairly stable, around 250,000.
- Women received two-thirds of the associate's degrees in the field of business management in 1986; of those, more than 25% were in secretarial and related programs.
- Women received 88% of the associate's degrees in the health sciences field in 1986; of those, nearly 3 in 5 degrees were in nursing fields.
- In 1986, women received one-fourth (25%) of the degrees in protective services, and less than 10% of the associate's degrees in engineering technologies.

SOURCES: National Center for Education Statistics, *Digest of Education Statistics*, 1988, Table 170; unpublished tabulations from "Associate Degrees and Other Awards Below the Baccalaureate, 1983–1985," Table 1.1.

See Table 61.

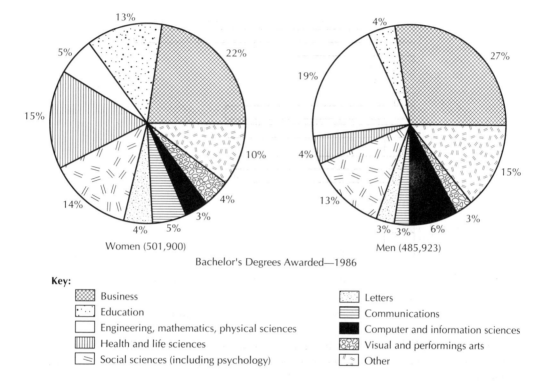

Women (501,900)   Men (485,923)

Bachelor's Degrees Awarded—1986

Key:

Business		Letters	
Education		Communications	
Engineering, mathematics, physical sciences		Computer and information sciences	
Health and life sciences		Visual and performing arts	
Social sciences (including psychology)		Other	

- In 1976, 420,821 bachelor's degrees were awarded to women. By 1986, 501,900 degrees were awarded to women, a 19% increase over 10 years. By contrast, bachelor's degrees awarded to men during this same period declined 4%, from 504,925 to 485,923.

- Between 1976 and 1986, the number of women receiving bachelor's degrees in education dropped 41%, from 112,737 to 66,235. For men, the percentage drop during the period was 50%, from 42,070 to 20,986.

- The largest number of bachelor's degrees awarded in 1986 to both women and men was in the field of business and management; the number of degrees awarded to women in this field almost quadrupled between 1976 and 1986.

- The number of women receiving bachelor's degrees in engineering increased dramatically between 1976 and 1986, from 822 to 11,195. However, even in 1986, women received only 14% of the 76,333 engineering degrees awarded that year.

NOTE: "Other" includes agriculture/natural resources, architecture/environmental design, area/ethnic studies, communications technologies, engineering technologies, foreign languages, home economics, law, liberal/general studies, military sciences, multi/interdisciplinary studies, parks/recreation, philosophy/religion, theology, protective services, and public affairs.

SOURCES: National Center for Education Statistics, "Trends in Bachelor's and Higher Degrees 1975–1985," Tables 2A and 2B; "Bachelor's and Higher Degrees Conferred in 1985–86," Table 2.

See Tables 62 and 63.

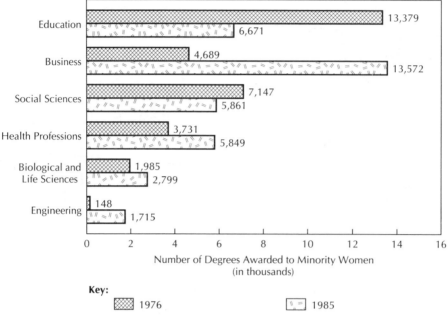

Number of Degrees Awarded to Minority Women
(in thousands)

Key:

☒ 1976   ▨ 1985

NOTE: Nonresident aliens were excluded from this analysis.

- Between 1976 and 1985, the largest gain in bachelor's degrees for all minority women was in the field of business; in 1976, one-third (32%) of all degrees awarded to minority women were in business, compared to one-half (51%) in 1985.
- Women, both minority and majority, greatly increased the number of engineering degrees they received from 1976 to 1985. However, women still represented only 15% of the total receiving engineering degrees in 1985.
- Between 1976 and 1985, the number of social-science degrees awarded to black women decreased 37%, but increased for all other groups of minority women, as follows: 19% for Hispanic women, 72% for Asian/Pacific Islander women, and 8% for American Indian women.
- Minorities as a group received only 10% of the bachelor's degrees in education conferred in 1985 and in 1976.
- Between 1976 and 1985, degrees awarded to women in education decreased 63% for black women, 40% for white women, and 37% for American Indian women. In the same time period,education degrees awarded to Hispanic women increased 3%, and those awarded to Asian/Pacific Islander women increased 9%.

SOURCE: ACE, "Minorities in Higher Education: Sixth Annual Status Report, 1987," Table 4A.

See Table 64.

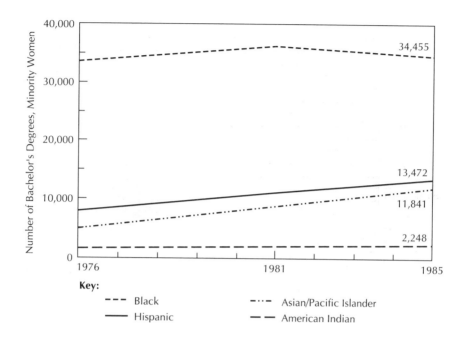

Key:
- – – – Black
- ——— Hispanic
- – · – Asian/Pacific Islander
- – – American Indian

- Overall, between 1976 and 1985, the number of bachelor's degrees awarded to women increased 18%, while those awarded to men decreased 5%.
- In 1985, 12% of all bachelor's degrees were awarded to members of minority groups. Minority women earned slightly more of the degrees (13%) than did minority men (11%).
- Between 1976 and 1985, bachelor's degrees awarded to black women increased 3%, and those awarded to white women increased 15%. During that same period, bachelor's degrees awarded to black men decreased 10%, and those awarded to white men decreased 9%.
- Between 1976 and 1985, the number of bachelor's degrees awarded to Hispanic women increased 73%, although they still received only 3% of the degrees awarded to women in 1985.
- Bachelor's degrees awarded to Asian-American women more than doubled between 1976 and 1985, though this group still received a very small proportion (2%) of the total bachelor's degrees awarded to women. Asian/Pacific Islanders are the only minority group in which men earned more bachelor's degrees than women.

SOURCE: ACE, "Minorities in Higher Education: Sixth Annual Status Report, 1987," Table 3A.

See Table 65.

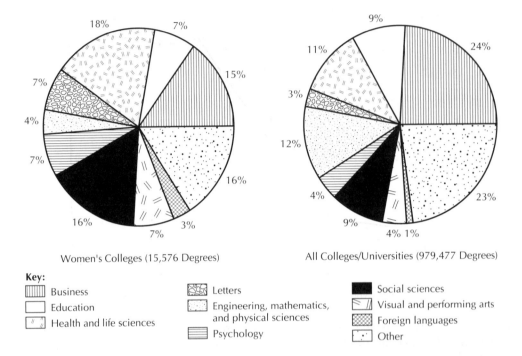

Women's Colleges (15,576 Degrees)   All Colleges/Universities (979,477 Degrees)

Key:

Business		Letters		Social sciences	
Education		Engineering, mathematics, and physical sciences		Visual and performing arts	
Health and life sciences				Foreign languages	
		Psychology		Other	

- In 1985, the 102 colleges that defined themselves as women's colleges awarded 15,576 bachelor's degrees. They awarded about 3% of all bachelor's degrees awarded to women that year.
- In 1985, women's colleges awarded the same proportion of their bachelor's degrees to minorities as did colleges and universities in general (12%).
- Among women, white women received 88% of the degrees; black women, 7%; Hispanic women, 3%; Asian women, 2%; and American Indian women, less than 1%. Men received 3% of the degrees granted at women's colleges.
- Women's colleges produce a higher proportion of graduates with degrees in health/life sciences, letters, social sciences/psychology, visual/performing arts, and foreign languages than do colleges and universities in general.
- Women's colleges award fewer degrees in business and education (22% combined) than do colleges and universities in general (33% combined).

NOTE: Women's colleges are those institutions that report themselves as such on the Higher Education General Information System's institutional characteristics form. "Other" includes agriculture, architecture/environmental design, area/ethnic studies, communications, computer/information science, home economics, law, liberal/general studies, library/archival sciences, multi/interdisciplinary studies, philosophy/religion, theology, public affairs, and other majors.

SOURCES: ACE, unpublished tabulations from the Higher Education General Information System computer tapes. National Center for Education Statistics, *Digest of Education Statistics*, 1987, Table 154.

See Table 66.

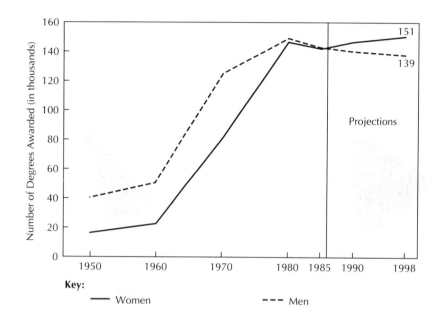

Key:

——— Women   - - - Men

- In 1977, for women and men combined, the number of master's degrees awarded peaked at 318,241. By 1984, the number had dropped 11% from the 1977 peak. Since 1984, the number has climbed again; projections to 1998 indicate a stabilization in the upcoming decade at about 290,000 degrees per year.
- In 1977, the number of master's degrees awarded by public institutions peaked at 209,689, and has declined every year since then. Master's degrees awarded at independent institutions have continued to increase each year, and in 1986 constituted 41% of all the master's degrees awarded.
- Since 1986, women have received slightly more master's degrees than men, a trend that is expected to continue. In the 1990s, women are projected to receive 51% to 52% of all master's degrees awarded annually.

SOURCE: ACE/Macmillan, *1989–90 Fact Book on Higher Education*, Table 126.

See Table 67.

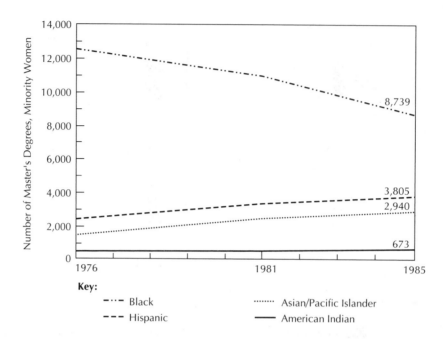

Key:

  – ··· – Black   ········ Asian/Pacific Islander
  – – – Hispanic   ———— American Indian

- In 1985, minority women received 11% of the 141,000 master's degrees awarded to women.
- In 1985, black and white women both had declines in the total number of master's degrees received compared to 1976. Master's degrees conferred to black women declined 30%; and to white women, 5%.
- Between 1976 and 1985, the number of Hispanic women who received master's degrees increased 57%, although in 1985 they still received less than 3% of the master's degrees awarded to women.
- Asians, both women and men, almost doubled the number of master's degrees they received between 1976 and 1985, although their combined number of degrees still represented only 3% of the total awarded in 1985.

SOURCE: ACE, "Minorities in Higher Education: Sixth Annual Status Report, 1987," Table 3B.

See Table 68.

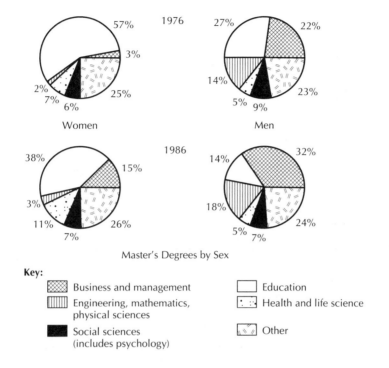

Master's Degrees by Sex

Key:

▦	Business and management	☐	Education
▥	Engineering, mathematics, physical sciences	⬚	Health and life science
■	Social sciences (includes psychology)	◿	Other

- In 1986, women received one-half of the master's degrees awarded.
- Although the total number of master's degrees awarded to women remained fairly stable between 1976 and 1986, women increased their proportion of degrees awarded in every major field, in part because of the large declines in the number of master's degrees awarded to men.
- In the period 1976–1986, the number of women receiving master's degrees in computer science increased more than sixfold; however, in 1986 women still received only 30% of the master's degrees awarded in that field.
- In 1986, women received 73% of the master's degrees awarded in education, 31% of the master's in business administration, 76% of the master's degrees in health sciences, and 62% of the master's degrees in public affairs.

SOURCES: National Center for Education Statistics, "Trends in Bachelors and Higher Degrees: 1975–1985," Tables 3A and 3B; and "Bachelors and Higher Degrees Conferred 1985–86" (bulletin), Table 3.

See Tables 69 and 70.

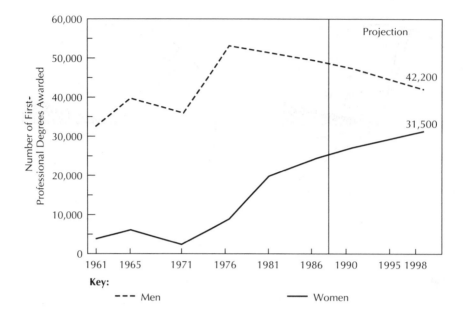

Key:

--- Men   —— Women

- Between 1970 and 1980, the number of women receiving first-professional degrees increased more than ninefold, from 1,908 to 17,415. The increase for men was less than 60%, from 33,344 to 52,716.
- In 1985, women received one-third of the professional degrees awarded that year; by 1998, they are projected to earn 43% of the first-professional degrees.
- For the period 1986–1998, the number of women receiving first-professional degrees is projected to increase by more than 20%, while the number of men receiving such degrees is projected to decrease by 10%.

NOTE: First-professional degrees, according to the National Center for Education Statistics, are those that are required for beginning practice in the fields of dentistry, medicine, optometry, osteopathic medicine, pharmacy, podiatric medicine, veterinary medicine, chiropractic, law, and theological professions.

SOURCES: Vetter, B. M. & Babco, E. L., *Professional Women and Minorities: A Manpower Data Resource Service*, 1987, Table 3-2. National Center for Education Statistics, *Digest of Education Statistics*, 1988, Table 180. ACE/Macmillan, *1989–90 Fact Book on Higher Education*, Table 125.

See Tables 71, 72, and 73.

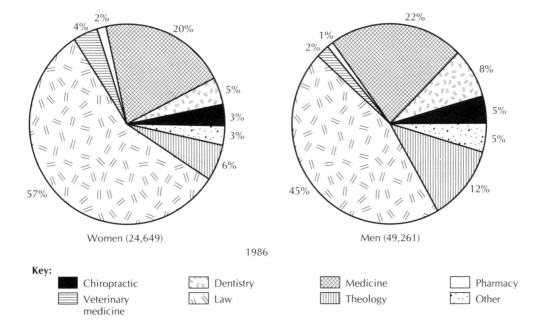

Women (24,649) Men (49,261)

1986

Key:

■ Chiropractic	⬚ Dentistry	▨ Medicine	☐ Pharmacy
▤ Veterinary medicine	◫ Law	▥ Theology	⬚ Other

- In 1986, women received one-third (33%) of the total first-professional degrees awarded that year.
- Between 1971 and 1986, the number of women receiving medical degrees annually increased from 809 to 4,916, which was 31% of the total medical degrees awarded in 1986.
- In 1986, women received about one-half (52%) of the pharmacy (471) and 48% of the veterinary medicine (1,079) degrees.
- The number of women receiving law degrees has increased dramatically since 1971, when only 1,240 women received that professional degree. In 1986, almost 14,000 women received law degrees, 39% of the total awarded in that field that year.
- The number of women receiving dentistry degrees each year increased almost fivefold in the years 1976–1986.
- The number of women receiving veterinary medicine degrees each year increased almost fourfold in the years 1976–1986.
- The number of women receiving degrees in the theological professions each year more than tripled in the years 1976–1986.

SOURCES: National Center for Education Statistics, "Trends in Bachelors and Higher Degrees 1975–1985," Table 5; "Bachelors and Higher Degrees Conferred in 1985–86," (bulletin), Table 5; *Digest of Education Statistics*, 1988, Table 180.

See Tables 73 and 74.

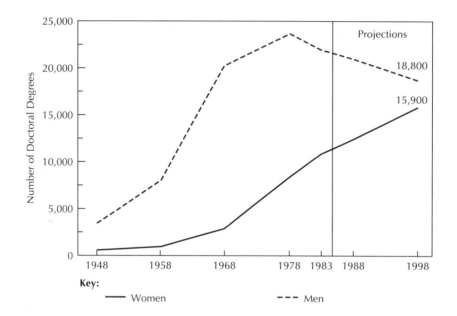

Key:

——— Women   - - - Men

- Between 1948 and 1986, the number of doctoral degrees received by women each year increased from approximately 500 to 12,000.
- Between 1950 and 1970, the proportion of all doctorates earned by women increased by a small margin, from 10% to 13% of the total. By 1986, however, the proportion of all doctorates awarded to women had risen to 35%.
- By 1998, women are projected to receive 46% of all doctorates awarded in that year.

SOURCE: ACE/Macmillan, *1989–90 Fact Book on Higher Education*, Table 127.

See Table 75.

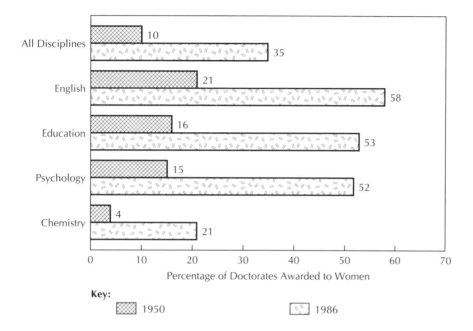

Percentage of Doctorates Awarded to Women

Key:

▨ 1950   ▨ 1986

- Historically, compared to men, women have received the largest percentage of doctoral degrees in the humanities, with French and Spanish consistently ranking the highest.
- In 1986, women received the majority of the doctorates awarded in 7 major fields: Anthropology (51%), Education (53%), English (52%), French (74%), German (52%), Psychology (52%), and Spanish (64%).
- Between 1950 and 1975, the percentage of doctorates awarded to women increased as follows: in economics, from 4% to 8%; in chemistry, from 4% to 11%; in mathematics, from 6% to 11%; and in physics, from 1% to 5% of the degrees awarded. The trends in these fields continued, and by 1986, the percentages were 20% of all doctorates in economics, 21% of all doctorates in chemistry, 17% of all doctorates in mathematics and 9% of all doctorates in physics.

SOURCE: ACE/Macmillan, *1989–90 Fact Book on Higher Education*, Table 130.

See Table 76.

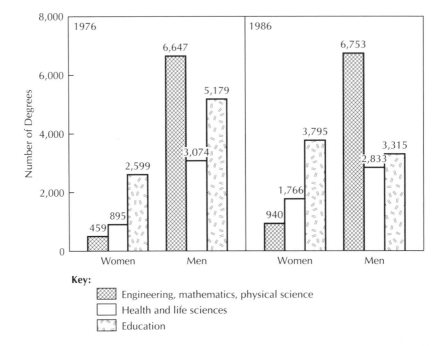

Key:
- Engineering, mathematics, physical science
- Health and life sciences
- Education

- Between 1976 and 1986, the number of women each year receiving doctorates increased in every major field except two: foreign languages, where they decreased by one-third, and letters, where they decreased by one-sixth. During the same period, the number of men receiving doctorates declined in more than one-half of the fields.
- Between 1976 and 1986, the number of women receiving doctorates in psychology increased 94%.
- The largest numbers of doctoral degrees awarded to women in 1986 were in education (3,795), psychology (1,591), and life sciences (1,129). In the same year, only 6 women received doctorates in law, 228 in engineering, 124 in math, and 588 in physical sciences.
- In 1986, 45 women and 299 men received doctorates in computer science; in the same year, 228 women and 3,172 men were awarded doctorates in engineering.

SOURCES: National Center for Education Statistics, "Trends in Bachelors and Higher Degrees 1975–85," Tables 4A and 4B; and "Bachelors and Higher Degrees Conferred in 1985–86," (bulletin), Table 4.

See Tables 77 and 78.

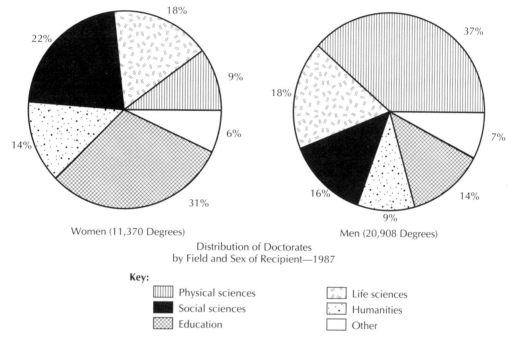

Women (11,370 Degrees)   Men (20,908 Degrees)

Distribution of Doctorates
by Field and Sex of Recipient—1987

Key:

▤ Physical sciences	▧ Life sciences
■ Social sciences	⊡ Humanities
▨ Education	☐ Other

- Women received 11,370 doctorates in 1987, 35% of the total number of 32,278 awarded that year.
- The median age of women receiving doctorates in 1987 was 35.4 years; the median age for men was 32.8 years.
- In 1987, 52% of the women receiving doctorates were married, as were 60% of the men.
- In 1987, 42% of the women and 34% of the men receiving doctorates anticipated teaching as their primary employment activity on completion of their degrees.
- In 1987, 16% of the women, and 35% of the men anticipated research and development as their primary employment activity.
- More than one-half (51%) of the women and men (57%) awarded doctorates had a bachelor's degree in the same field as their doctorate.

SOURCE: National Research Council, "Summary Report 1987: Doctorate Recipients from United States Universities," preliminary tabulations, Table 2.

See Table 79.

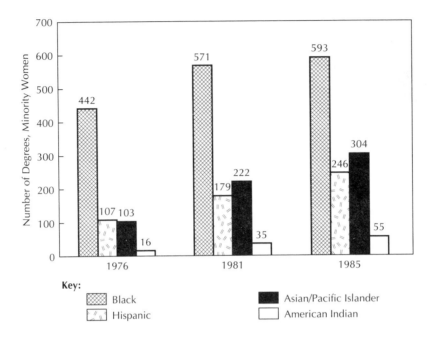

Key:

⬚ Black   ■ Asian/Pacific Islander

⬚ Hispanic   □ American Indian

- Of the 11,011 women who received doctorates in 1985, 81% were awarded to white women, 5% to black women, 2% to Hispanic women, 3% to Asian/Pacific Island women, less than 1% to American Indian women, and 8% to nonresident alien women.
- Between 1976 and 1985, the number of black women receiving doctoral degrees increased by about one-third, from 442 to 593.
- Between 1976 and 1985, the number of Hispanic women receiving doctoral degrees more than doubled, from 107 to 246.
- Between 1976 and 1985, the number of Asian/Pacific Islander women receiving doctorates increased about threefold, from 103 to 304.
- Between 1976 and 1985, the number of American Indian women receiving doctorates increased more than threefold, from 16 to 55.

SOURCE: ACE, "Minorities in Higher Education: Sixth Annual Status Report, 1987," Table 3C.

See Table 80.

Faculty

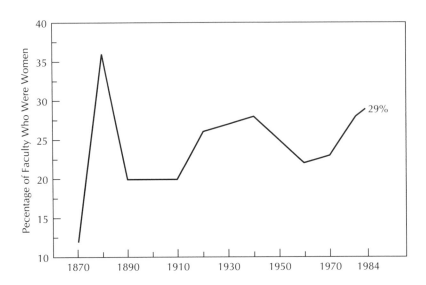

- Since 1900, there has been a continuing increase in the number of women faculty, but the proportion of faculty who were women has fluctuated widely. Only in 1980 did the proportion of women faculty exceed the pre–World War II high of 28%.
- Between 1900 and 1940, the number of women faculty increased from 20% to 28% of the total faculty.
- Between 1940 and 1960, women as a percentage of the total faculty dropped from 28% to 22%.
- Between 1960 and 1982, the proportion of women faculty increased from 22% to 29% of all faculty.

NOTE: "Faculty" is defined as the total number of persons not reduced to full-time equivalents. This includes both part-time and full-time faculty. Percentages before 1900 are estimates; from 1970 on the percentages are estimates of senior instructional staff, excluding graduate assistants.

SOURCE: Vetter, B. M. & Babco, E. L., *Professional Women and Minorities: A Manpower Data Resource*, 1987, Table 5–17.

See Table 81.

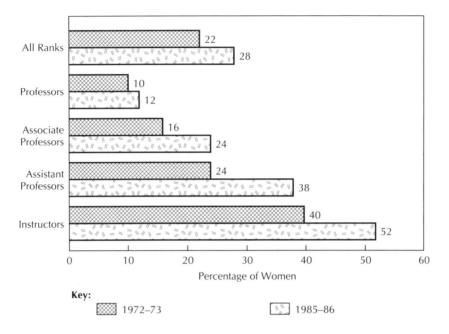

Key:

▨ 1972–73   ⬚ 1985–86

- Although the percentage of women faculty increased in each academic rank in the aggregate of higher education institutions between 1972 and 1985, women made up only 28% of the total full-time instructional faculty in 1985.

- The greatest gains for women faculty have come at the rank of assistant professor, where they moved from constituting 24% of full-time instructional faculty in 1972, to 38% in 1985.

- In 1985, women constituted the following proportions of total full-time assistant professors: white women, 31%; black women, 3%; Asian women, 1%; and Hispanic and American Indian women, less than 1% combined.

- Only at the ranks of instructor and lecturer were women and men represented in nearly equal numbers in 1985. Women constituted 52% and 49% of the faculty in these ranks, respectively.

- In 1985, over one-half (55%) of all women working in ranked faculty positions were either assistant professors or instructors. In contrast, 70% of all men in ranked positions were either professors or associate professors.

NOTE: Faculty are full-time instructional faculty on 9- to 12-month contracts.

SOURCES: Vetter, B. M. & Babco, E. L., *Professional Women and Minorities: A Manpower Data Resource Service*, 1987, Table 5–7. ACE, "Minorities in Higher Education," 1988. ACE/Macmillan, *1989–90 Fact Book on Higher Education*, Table 108.

See Tables 82, 83, and 84.

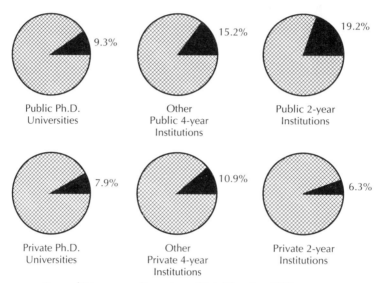

Tenured Women as a Percentage of Total Faculty—1985

NOTE: The National Center for Education Statistics makes the distinction between universities and other 4-year institutions when reporting these data.

- In all types of institutions, women continue to be tenured at much lower rates than men. In 1985, overall, 46% of the full-time women faculty were tenured, whereas 66% of the full-time men faculty were tenured.
- Of all tenured faculty in 1985, 21% were women and 79% were men.
- Women at all types of private institutions are less likely to be tenured than are women in all types of public institutions.
- In 1985, 25% of the women who were tenured were full professors, and 38% were associate professors. Of the tenured men, 52% were full professors and 32% were associate professors.

SOURCES: Vetter, B. M. & Babco, E. L., *Professional Women and Minorities: A Manpower Data Resource Service*, 1987, Table 5–7. Equal Employment Opportunity Commission, "1985 EEO-6 Summary Report," preliminary tables.

See Tables 83 and 85.

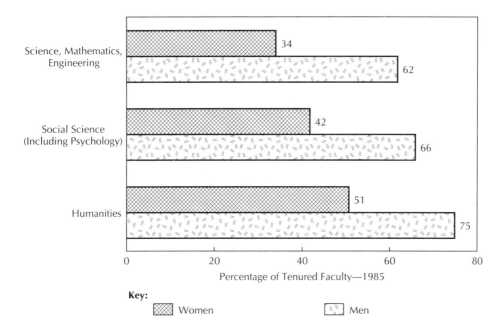

Percentage of Tenured Faculty—1985

Key:

Women   Men

- In nearly every major discipline in 1985, women faculty were much less likely to be tenured than men faculty. A notable exception is computer science/information systems, where women and men were equally likely to be tenured.
- Although over one-half of the women faculty in the humanities were tenured (51%), the proportion of men faculty who were tenured (75%) was much greater.
- In 1985, English and mathematics had the highest percentage of their women faculty tenured, with 54% of the women in both disciplines being tenured.

SOURCE: Vetter, B. M., & Babco, E. L., *Professional Women and Minorities: A Manpower Data Resource Service*, 1987, Tables 5–4 and 5–5.

See Tables 86 and 87.

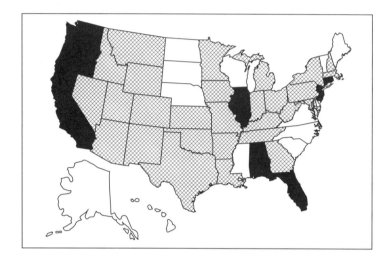

Key:

☐ Less than 35% (12 states)

▨ 35% – 49% (30 states)

■ 50% or more (9 states)

- In 1985, women constituted 28% of the total full-time faculty in the U.S. and outlying areas. Their percentages in that year ranged from a low of 21% in Montana to a high of 37% in Mississippi.
- In 1985, 46% of the full-time women faculty members in the U.S. and outlying territories were tenured. Their percentage in various states ranged from a low of 10% in Alaska to a high of 68% in California.
- In every state, women faculty were considerably less likely to be tenured than men. The greatest disparities in tenure status existed in Delaware, where 61% of the men but only 28% of the women were tenured, and in Montana, where 68% of the men but only 35% of the women were tenured.
- In only 9 states (Alabama, California, Connecticut, Florida, Illinois, New Jersey, Oregon, Rhode Island, and Washington) are the majority of women faculty members tenured. The majority of men are tenured in every state except Alaska, Mississippi, and North Carolina.

SOURCE: ACE/Macmillan, *1989–90 Fact Book on Higher Education*, Table 106.

See Table 88.

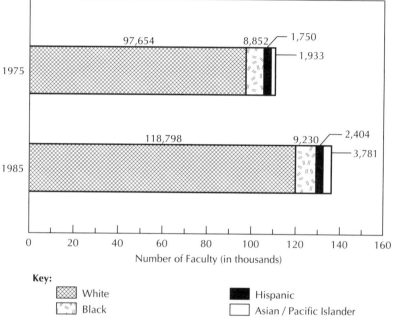

Number of Faculty (in thousands)

Key:

White

Black

Hispanic

Asian / Pacific Islander

NOTE: American Indian faculty were too few in number to be represented on the graph.

- The proportion of full-time faculty who are women increased slightly between 1975 and 1985, from 25% to 28%.
- The proportion of women faculty who are minorities remained steady between 1975 and 1985, at 12%.
- In both 1975 and 1985, minority women accounted for 3% of all full-time faculty members, although there was a 23% increase in the number of minority women faculty over that decade.
- Between 1975 and 1985, the number of black women faculty increased by 4%, from 8,852 to 9,230. In 1985, they represented 7% of the women faculty in colleges and universities.
- Between 1975 and 1985, the number of Hispanic women faculty increased by 37%, from 1,750 to 2,404. However, in 1985 Hispanic women represented less than 2% of the women faculty in colleges and universities.
- The number of Asian-American women faculty members almost doubled between 1975 and 1985, from 1,933 to 3,781, but they accounted for less than 3% of all women faculty in 1985.

SOURCE: ACE, "Minorities in Higher Education: Seventh Annual Status Report, 1988," Table 11.

See Table 89.

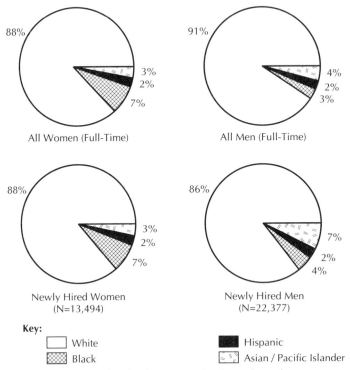

All Women (Full-Time)

88%
3%
2%
7%

All Men (Full-Time)

91%
4%
2%
3%

Newly Hired Women
(N=13,494)

88%
3%
2%
7%

Newly Hired Men
(N=22,377)

86%
7%
2%
4%

Key:

☐ White   ■ Hispanic

▨ Black   ▨ Asian / Pacific Islander

NOTE: American Indian faculty were too few in number to be
represented on these graphs.

- In 1985, minority women constituted 12% of newly hired women faculty and of all women faculty. Minority men constituted 14% of all newly hired men faculty and 10% of all men faculty.
- Of all women who were faculty members in 1985, white, non-Hispanics constituted 88% of the tenured, 87% of the nontenured, and 89% of the other faculty.
- Of the 53,608 tenured women faculty in 1985, 3,790 (7%) were black; 1,078 (2%) were Hispanic; 1,344 (3%) were Asian/Pacific Islanders; and 138 (less than 1%) were American Indians.
- Of all women faculty hired in 1985, 51% were tenured or in tenure track position. Of all men faculty hired that year, 55% were tenured or in tenure track positions.

SOURCE: Equal Employment Opportunity Commission, "1985 EEO-6 Summary Report," preliminary tables.

See Table 85.

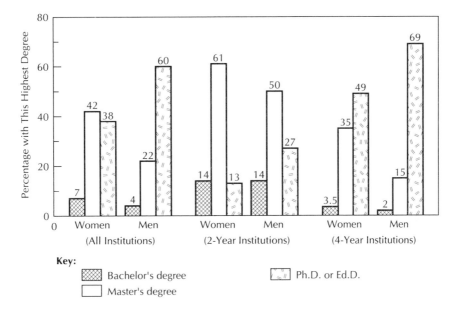

Key:

▨ Bachelor's degree   ⬚ Ph.D. or Ed.D.
☐ Master's degree

- In 1975, 34% of the women and 55% of the men faculty members in all institutions had either a Ph.D. or an Ed.D. degree. By 1984, 38% of the women and 60% of the men faculty held one of those two degrees.
- In 4-year institutions, one-half (50%) of the women faculty in 1984 had a doctoral degree, compared to over two-thirds (70%) of the men. In 2-year institutions, 13% of the women and 28% of the men had doctorates.
- In 1984, 38% of the women faculty in 4-year institutions had a master's degree or less; in 2-year institutions, the percentage was 74%.
- In 1984, women faculty in 4-year institutions most commonly held their highest degree in the humanities (16%), education (15%), social science (14%), or health science (13%). Popular fields for men faculty were physical sciences (16%), social science (15%), and humanities (13%).
- In 1984, about one-third (33% of the women, 36% of the men) of the faculty members in all institutions were between the ages of 41 and 50. However, 35% of the men were over age 51, compared to 26% of the women.

SOURCE: ACE/Macmillan, *1986–87 Fact Book on Higher Education*, Tables 120 and 121.

See Table 90.

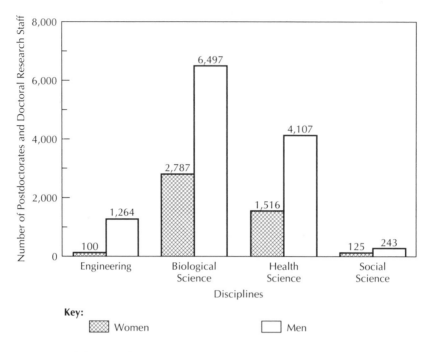

Key:

[Women] Women   [ ] Men

- In 1985, 24% of the postdoctorates were women.
- In 1985, women accounted for 13% of the postdoctorates in mathematics (29) and in the physical sciences (600), 34% of those in the social sciences (125), and 45% of those in psychology (225).
- Of all nonfaculty doctoral research staff members in 1985, 25% were women.

NOTE: Data on minorities in postdoctoral research staff positions were not available.

SOURCE: Vetter, B. M. & Babco, E. L., *Professional Women and Minorities: A Manpower Data Resource Service*, 1987, Table 5–14.

See Table 91.

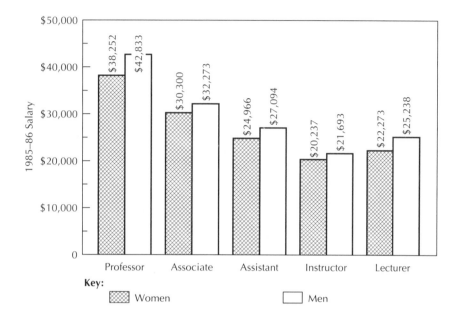

Key:

▨ Women   ☐ Men

- In current dollars, the average faculty salary has increased by 84% between 1976 and 1986. Women's salaries increased 83%, and men's, 87%.
- In 1985–86, in all ranks combined, women faculty salaries averaged 80% of those of men faculty. In 1976–77, the comparable percentage was 82%.
- At every rank, the average salary for women faculty in 1985–86 was less than that of their male counterparts. The difference was greatest at the rank of full professor, where the average salary for women was 89% of that of men. At the ranks of associate professor and assistant professor, the average salary for women was 94% and 92%, respectively, of that of men.

SOURCE: National Center for Education Statistics, "College Faculty salaries, 1976–1986," Aug. 1987, App. Table B.

See Table 92.

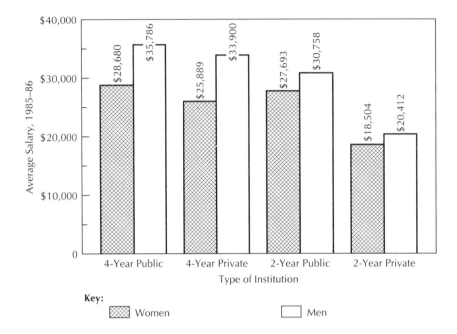

- Women faculty have lower average salaries than men faculty at every type of institution.
- Between 1976–77 and 1985–86, the average salary of women faculty increased by 83%, to $27,576. The average for men faculty increased 87%, to $34,294.
- Both women and men earned highest average salaries in private universities, but in these institutions in 1985–86, the average salary for women ($31,174) was only 74% of the average salary for men faculty ($41,929).

NOTE: Faculty are defined as full-time instructional faculty on 9- or 10-month contracts.

SOURCE: National Center for Education Statistics, "College Faculty Salaries, 1976–1986," Aug. 1987, Appendix Table C.

See Table 93.

Key:

——— Women   - - - Men

- Average faculty salaries in constant 1985–86 dollars declined for both women and men at all ranks between 1976 and 1986. During this period, at the rank of full professor, the average salary of women and men declined 4%. At the rank of associate professor, the comparable decline was 5% for women and 4% for men; and at the rank of assistant professor, it was 5% for women and 1% for men.
- Women faculty in all ranks have lower average salaries than men of the same rank. In 1985–86, the greatest disparity was at the rank of lecturer, where women earned 88% of the salary of men, and at the rank of full professor, where women earned 89% of the salary of men. At other ranks women earned at least 92% of men's salaries.
- Between 1976 and 1986, the gap between the salaries of women and of men (all ranks combined) increased slightly, with women receiving 82% as much as men in 1976–77, and 80% as much as men in 1985–86.

NOTE: Salaries are in constant 1985–86 dollars, using the Consumer Price Index to adjust figures in previous years to control for inflation.

SOURCE: National Center for Education Statistics, "College Faculty Salaries 1976–1986," Aug. 1987, p. 9.

See Table 94.

Administrators, Trustees, and Staff

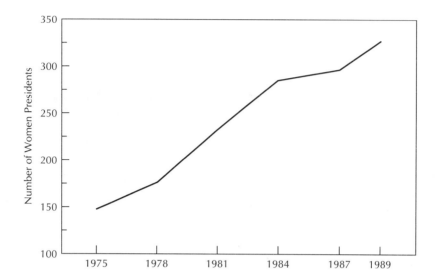

- Between 1975 and 1989, the number of women college and university presidents more than doubled (from 148 to 328). In 1989, women held 11% of all such positions, up from 5% in 1975.
- The proportion of all women presidents in public institutions increased substantially from 1975 to 1989. In 1989, there were nine times as many women presidents in public institutions as in 1975 (from 16 to 146), while in private institutions, the increase was only 38% (from 132 to 182).
- In 1989, 45% of women presidents were in the public sector, compared to 11% in 1975.
- In 1989, 55% of women presidents were in private institutions, compared to 89% in 1975.
- Of the women presidents in 1989, 23% were members of a religious order, compared to 55% in 1975.
- Minority women represented 13% of all women presidents in 1989. They were located mostly in public institutions.

NOTES: "President" refers to any person serving as chief executive officer of a regionally accredited system, institution, or campus. According to the Council on Postsecondary Accreditation, in 1989–1990 there were approximately 3,000 institutions accredited by the six regional accrediting associations.

SOURCE: ACE, Office of Women in Higher Education, "Women Chief Executive Officers in U.S. Colleges and Universities, Table XII, December 1989" (table prepared July 1990).

See Table 95.

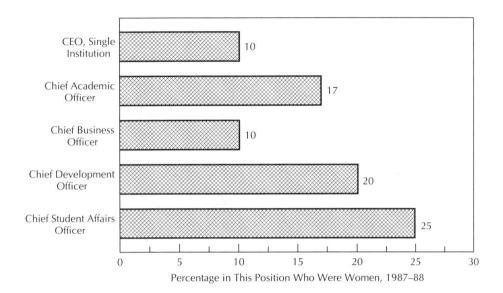

Percentage in This Position Who Were Women, 1987–88

- Women are more likely to be found in student affairs and external affairs than in academic and administrative affairs. In 1987, at the highest positions in all these areas, women were greatly outnumbered by men.
- On average in 1987, 27% of deans in academic areas were women. This percentage ranged from 97% women Deans of Nursing to 8% of Deans of Law.
- In 1987, women held more than one-half of the senior positions in academic administration only in the areas of Deans of Nursing (97%) and Deans of Home Economics (77%).
- Other positions listed in the major College and University Personnel Association (CUPA) categories of administration that have a high percentage of women include; Director of Affirmative Action (59%), Manager of Payroll (71%), Director of Publications (59%), and Director of Student Placement (53%).
- The proportion of women administrators increases at lower levels of an organization. For example, in 1987 in Admissions' offices, women held 28% of the Director of Admission positions, 50% of the Associate Director positions, and 66% of the Assistant Director positions.

NOTE: The College and University Personnel Association divides positions in administration into five major families—executive, academic affairs, administrative affairs, external affairs, and student affairs. It currently defines an "administrator" as a person holding one of 168 different position titles within one of these major categories in a college or university. The number of positions included in CUPA data has increased during the past decade.

SOURCE: College and University Personnel Association, "1987–88 Administrative Compensation Survey," 1988, special tabulations.

See Tables 96 and 97.

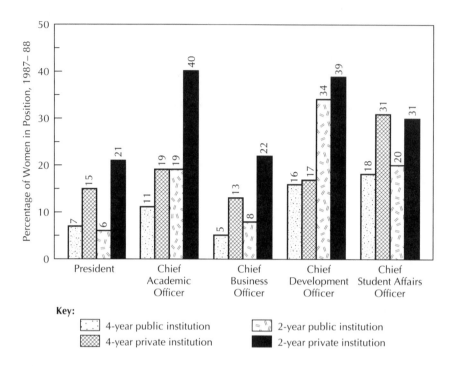

Key:
- 4-year public institution
- 4-year private institution
- 2-year public institution
- 2-year private institution

- Overall in 1987, women were more likely to hold high-level positions as administrators in private institutions than in public institutions.
- Of all positions in administration listed in 1987, women held 41% in private 4-year institutions, and only 30% in public 4-year institutions. In public 2-year institutions, women held 36% of the administrative positions; and in private 2-year institutions, they held 48%.
- In 1987, in 4-year public institutions, 10% of the Deans of Arts and Sciences were women. The percentage was 23% in 4-year private institutions and 18% in 2-year public institutions (data not available for 2-year private institutions).
- In 1987, in 4-year public institutions, the only major positions in which women held more than one-half of the positions were Dean of Home Economics (82%) and Director of Affirmative Action/Equal Employment (58%).

NOTE: The College and University Personnel Administration divides administration into five major families—executive, academic affairs, administrative affairs, external affairs, and student affairs. It currently defines an "administrator" as a person holding one of 168 administrative titles within one of these major categories in a college or university. The number of positions included in CUPA data has increased during the past decade.

SOURCE: College and University Personnel Association, "1987–88 Administrative Compensation Survey," 1988, special tabulations.

See Tables 98, 99, 100, and 101.

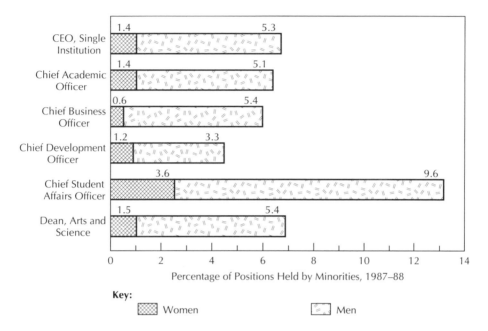

Percentage of Positions Held by Minorities, 1987–88

Key:

Women   Men

- In 1987, minority women and men combined held only 8% of all positions in administration.
- Minority women represented 10% of all women administrators in 1987, whereas minority men represented 7% of all men administrators.
- Of all minority administrators in 1987, 44% were women. Of all majority administrators, 35% were women.
- Minority women held only 2% of all deans positions in 1987.
- Minority women were most likely to be found as Director of Affirmative Action/Equal Employment (they held 24% of all such positions in 1987), and next most likely to be found as Director of Financial Aid or Director of Student Counseling (they held 7% each of those positions).

NOTE: The College and University Personnel Association (CUPA) divides administration into five major families—executive, academic affairs, administrative affairs, external affairs, and student affairs. It defines an "administrator" as a person holding one of 168 different administrative position titles within one of these major categories in a college or university. The number of positions included in CUPA data has increased during the past decade. The definition of minority used in the CUPA survey is determined at the institutional level.

SOURCE: College and University Personnel Association, "1987–88 Administrative Compensation Survey," 1988, special tabulations.

See Tables 102 and 103.

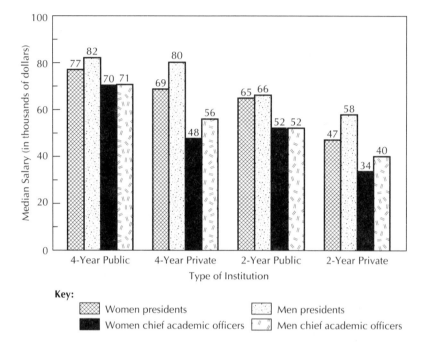

Key:

▨ Women presidents   ⬚ Men presidents
■ Women chief academic officers   ▨ Men chief academic officers

- Overall, in most major positions in administration, women have lower median salaries than men in the same position, but the differences vary by sector. In 1987, for the CEO of a single institution, there was a 6% differential between the median salaries of women and men in a 4-year public institution. The comparable differential in 4-year private institutions was 16%; in 2-year public institutions, 2%; and in 2-year private institutions, 22%.

- For both women and men in chief officer positions (chief executive, academic, business, development, and student affairs officers), median salaries in 1987 were higher in 4-year public institutions than in any other sector.

- In 1987, the median salaries of women and men in chief academic officer positions were almost the same in 4- and 2-year public institutions. In private institutions, both 4- and 2-year, men made notably more than women in these positions.

NOTE: The College and University Personnel Association (CUPA) divides administration into five major families—executive, academic affairs, administrative affairs, external affairs, student affairs. It currently defines an "administrator" as a person holding one of 168 different administrative position titles within one of these major categories in a college or university. The number of positions included in CUPA data has increased over the past decade.

SOURCE: College and University Personnel Association, 1987–88 Administrative Compensation Survey, 1988, special tabulations.

See Tables 98, 99, 100, and 101.

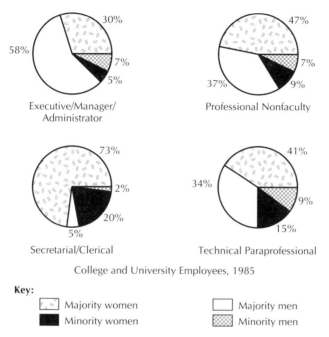

Executive/Manager/
Administrator

Professional Nonfaculty

Secretarial/Clerical

Technical Paraprofessional

College and University Employees, 1985

Key:

[illustration] Majority women   [illustration] Majority men

[illustration] Minority women   [illustration] Minority men

- In 1985, 43,698 women (35% of a total of 124,374) were full-time executives, managers, or administrators in higher education institutions. Of these women administrators, 86% were white, non-Hispanic; 10% were black, non-Hispanic; 2% were Hispanic; 2% were Asian/Pacific Islander; and less than 1% were American Indian.

- In 1985, there were 2.1 million full- and part-time employees in institutions of higher education. Part-time employees constituted 23% of this total. More of the part-time faculty were men, and more of the part-time secretarial/clerical and technical paraprofessionals were women.

- In 1985, minorities made up 12% of the full-time executives/administrators/managers in higher education. Minorities also constituted 16% of the skilled craft workers, 22% of the secretarial/clerical staff, 24% of the technical paraprofessionals, and 43% of the service maintenance workers.

NOTE: The executive/administrative/managerial category includes all persons whose assignments require *primary* responsibility for management of the institution, or a customarily recognized department thereof. The professional nonfaculty category includes persons employed for the primary purpose of performing academic support, student service, and institutional support activities, assignments requiring a college education or comparable background. The technical/paraprofessional category includes persons whose assignments require specialized knowledge or skills acquired through experience or academic work, such as that offered by many 2-year technical institutes or junior colleges. Other categories included in this report are secretarial/clerical, skilled crafts, and service/maintenance.

SOURCE: Equal Employment Opportunity Commission, "1985 EEO-6 Summary Report," preliminary tables.

See Table 85.

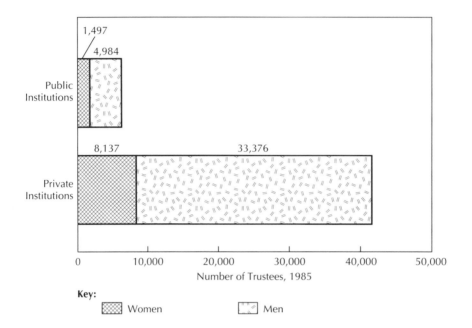

- In 1985, women constituted 23% of the voting members of governing boards in public institutions and 20% of the members in independent institutions.
- Of the women and men serving as voting members of governing boards in higher education in 1985, 90% were white, 6% black, 1% Hispanic, and 3% other. Public institutions had slightly higher percentages of black and Hispanic members than private institutions.
- Only 7% of college and university trustees in 1985 had less than a college education. Of the total trustees, 40% had a bachelor's degree as their highest degree, 23% a master's degree, and 30% either a professional or doctoral degree.
- Of those serving on governing boards in 1985, 70% were age 50 or older, and almost one-third (32%) were over age 60. In public institutions, a larger percentage of trustees were under age 50 than in private institutions.

NOTE: These data were not disaggregated by sex and race/ethnicity. Voting members do not include ex-officio members.

SOURCE: Association of Governing Boards of Colleges and Universities, *Composition of Governing Boards 1985*, 1986, Table III.

See Table 104.

Student Aid

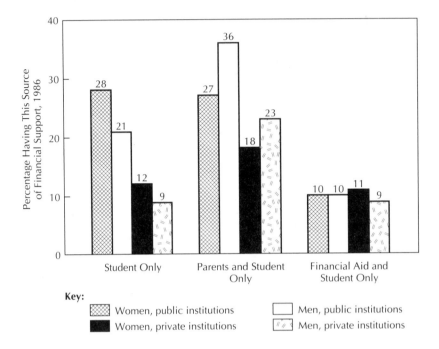

Key:

- ▨ Women, public institutions
- ■ Women, private institutions
- ☐ Men, public institutions
- ▨ Men, private institutions

- In all types of institutions, women are more likely than men to be financing their own educations.
- Three out of 5 undergraduates reported using no outside source of financial aid. These women (60%) and men (61%) reported using their own and their families' money to finance their education.
- Of all undergraduate women attending 2- and 4-year public and private institutions, 1 in 4 (25%) women were solely responsible for financing their higher education; another 25% indicated that they and their parents together were their only sources of financial support. In the case of men, 18% indicated they were solely responsible for their higher education, and 33% indicated that they and their parents together were the only sources of financial support.
- Students in 2-year public institutions were more likely to provide the sole financing for their own education than students in any other type of institution (41% of women and 31% of men).

NOTE: The total of undergraduates includes only those who reported their sources of financial support; it does not include enrollments at less than 2-year institutions. The graph includes students at both 2- and 4-year institutions.

SOURCE: ACE, special tabulations from the National Center for Education Statistics, 1987 National Postsecondary Student Aid Study database.

See Table 105.

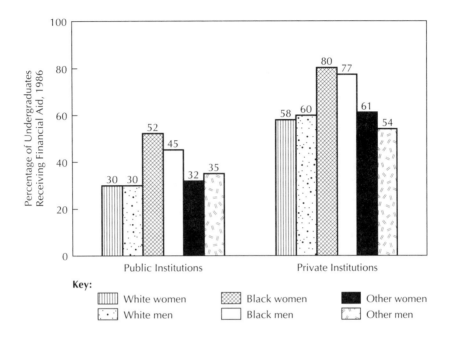

Key:
- White women
- Black women
- Other women
- White men
- Black men
- Other men

- Black students, both women and men, are more likely than other students to receive some form of financial aid. In fall 1986, of the total enrollment in higher education, 57% of black women received financial aid, compared to 36% of white women and 36% of all other women; and 50% of black men received financial aid, compared to 36% of white men and 37% of all other men. In that year, blacks made up 9% of the total enrollment in higher education, and "other" ethnic minority students and nonresident aliens made up 7%.

- Younger students, both women and men, are more likely than older students to receive some form of financial aid. Of women age 23 and younger enrolled in higher education in the fall of 1986, 46% received financial aid; of those age 24–29, 31% received aid; and of those age 30 and older, 24% received aid. For men, 43% of the (18–23) students, 31% of those age 24–29, and 25% of those age 30 and older received financial aid.

- Students in private institutions are more likely to receive some form of financial aid than students in public institutions. In 1986, among the (18–23) students in public institutions, 39% of the women and 36% of the men received financial aid. In private institutions, comparable figures were 68% for women and 66% for men.

NOTE: The NPSAS survey collected data from all postsecondary institutions. Only data from higher education institutions were used in this analysis.

SOURCE: ACE, special tabulations from the National Center for Education Statistics, 1987 National Postsecondary Student Aid Study database.

See Table 106.

PERCENTAGE OF UNDERGRADUATES AWARDED FEDERAL
FINANCIAL AID, BY SEX, TYPE OF AID, AND TYPE
AND CONTROL OF INSTITUTION, 1986

84

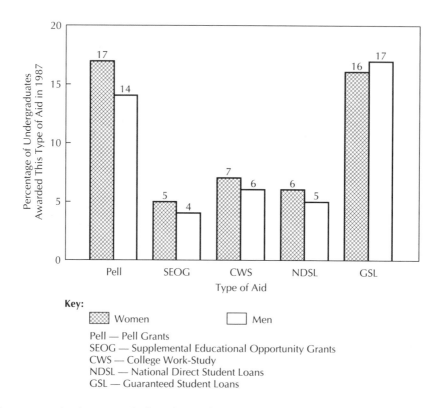

Key:

▨ Women   ▢ Men

Pell — Pell Grants
SEOG — Supplemental Educational Opportunity Grants
CWS — College Work-Study
NDSL — National Direct Student Loans
GSL — Guaranteed Student Loans

- Almost one-third (31%) of all undergraduates enrolled in 1986 received some form of federal financial aid.
- Undergraduate students in private institutions are more likely to receive some form of federal financial aid than students in public institutions. In private institutions, 48% of women and men undergraduate students received financial aid, compared to 27% of women and men in public institutions.
- Women students attending 2-year private institutions (51%), and both women and men attending 4-year nondoctoral institutions (51%), together make up the highest percentage of those persons receiving any federal aid.
- Undergraduate students attending public 4-year institutions were four times as likely as those attending public 2-year institutions to receive guaranteed student loans.
- Of all students enrolled in any type of higher education institution in fall 1986, women in private 2-year institutions were most likely to be awarded Pell grants; 28% of the women in this type of institution received Pell grants, compared to 21% of the men.

SOURCE: ACE, special tabulations from the National Center for Education Statistics, 1987 National Postsecondary Student Aid Study database.

See Table 107.

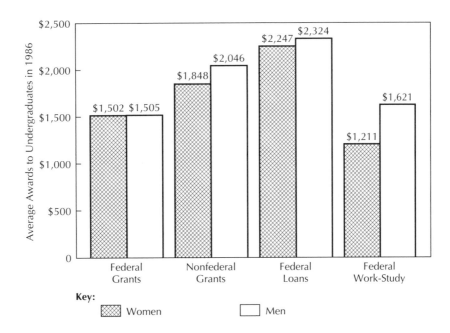

- In all categories in which aid was awarded in fall 1986, women received on average fewer dollars than men. The greatest discrepancy was in federal work-study awards, where men received an average of 134% of what women received ($1,621 for men compared to $1,211 for women).
- In fall 1986, an undergraduate man received an average of 7% more in total financial aid than an undergraduate woman ($3,996 compared to $3,740).
- Women and men undergraduates received about the same average amount in federal grants in fall 1986 (just over $1,500), but the average nonfederal grant for a man was 11% higher than that for a woman ($2,046 compared to $1,848).

SOURCE: ACE, special tabulations from the National Center for Education Statistics, 1987 National Postsecondary Student Aid Study database.

See Table 108.

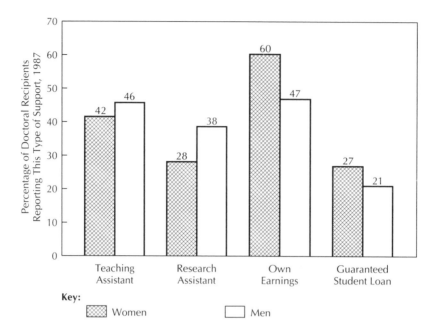

- Between 1974 and 1987, almost 20% of all doctoral recipients, both women and men, had received a university fellowship. The highest percentage achieved by women over this period was in 1974, when 23% received university fellowships. By 1987, the proportion of women who received these fellowships had dropped to 18%.
- Between 1974 and 1987, from 40% to 50% of the doctoral recipients had teaching assistantships; women had a slightly smaller percentage of this type of support than men, ranging from 2.5% to 4.5% fewer in any given year.
- The greatest overall discrepancy between women and men in sources of support for doctoral studies between 1974 and 1987 occurred in the awarding of research assistantships. In 1974, women received 12% fewer of these awards than men; in 1985, they received 15% fewer; and in 1987, 10% fewer.
- From 1978 on, a higher proportion of women than men used their own earnings, spouse's earnings, family contributions, and borrowings to support doctoral studies.
- Between 1974 and 1987, education funds from industry have increased slightly for men doctoral students (from 4% to 5% of the men reporting this source of support), but they have increased substantially for women (from 2% to 5% of the women reporting this source of support).

SOURCES: Vetter, B. M., & Babco, E. L., *Professional Women and Minorities: A Manpower Data Resource Service*, 1987, Tables 2–8. National Research Council, "Summary Report 1987: Doctorate Recipients From United States Universities," preliminary tables, Table 3.

See Tables 109 and 110.

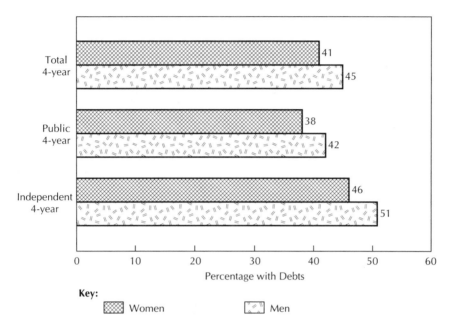

- Women are nearly as likely as men to have borrowed money to help finance their educations (41% compared to 45%). This tendency prevailed for women graduating from public as well as independent 4-year colleges.
- There were no significant differences in the size of the debts incurred by women and men during their undergraduate years.
- One year after graduation, women college graduates on average earned less than men. In 1985, women graduates who were employed full-time averaged $16,300 compared to $28,000 for men.
- Although men and women had borrowed about the same amount of money while in college, the ability of women to repay their debts differed from that of their male colleagues because of the differences in average starting salaries. For example, 13% of women college graduates with debts faced a loan burden of 10% or more of their first-year's earnings, compared to 6% for men.

SOURCE: Henderson, Cathy, "College Debts of Recent Graduates" (ACE), 1987.

See Table 113.

III

Data Issues and Sources

Guide to Sources

The information presented in the *Fact Book on Women in Higher Education* was obtained from many sources, including federal and state agencies, private research organizations, and professional associations. These agencies and organizations used a variety of research methods in collecting their data, including surveys of a "universe" (e.g., all colleges) or sample population (e.g., high school graduates) and statistical projections. Users of the *Fact Book* should be cautious in comparing the data from different sources, since differences in procedures, timing, phrasing of questions, interviewer training, and other specifics render the results from the different sources not strictly comparable.

In compiling data to be included in this book, we gave priority to primary sources as opposed to secondary sources, with the exception of the ACE's *1989–90 Fact Book on Higher Education*. Because tables for the *1989–90 Fact Book* had been updated just prior to the collection of data for this book, we decided to use those tables wherever applicable. In other cases we sought longitudinal data, preferably with a breakdown by race and ethnicity as well as simply by sex.

Readers should take care in reviewing the data on racial and ethnic minorities because the data are collected and reported in different ways by various organizations. Data on minorities have increased substantially since the mid-1970s, when Hispanic, Asian/Pacific Islander, and American Indian data were first reported, but regrettably these data have not always been collected or reported. Even when such data were available, we often found the number of Asian/Pacific Islanders and American Indians was so small in comparison to other groups that their data could not be meaningfully included in some graphical presentations.

We also wish to alert readers to the fact that, in some cases, categories are not mutually exclusive. For example, Hispanics have a number of national origins (for example, Cuban, Puerto Rican, Mexican, and so forth) and are sometimes reported by both race and ethnicity in the same table. Users of this book are urged to read tables and footnotes carefully. In general, they will find that the National Center for Education Statistics reports data on Hispanics separately, as a mutually exclusive category, and that the U.S. Census Bureau reports Hispanics both as "Hispanic" and as "black" or "white," as appropriate. We have attempted to add a note indicating that "Hispanics may be of any race" on all tables and charts where this statement seems to apply.

Several kinds of issues arise when using statistics, particularly when the data are obtained from multiple sources. Some of these issues are the representativeness of data, comparability of data, definitional differences, timeliness of data, and lack of data in certain areas. Each issue is discussed below, with relevant examples from this book.

Representativeness

The representativeness of data is determined by adding the effects of "sampling" and "nonsampling" errors. Sampling errors occur to the extent that the group used for a study differs from the population of which it is a part. Nonsampling errors are those resulting from errors in design, reporting, processing, and adjustments to cover nonrespondents. Adjustments, referred to as "imputations," are often made for nonresponse errors. Imputation methods differ, but they usually involve substituting an "average" response in place of the missing data, or in the case of item nonresponse, substituting a response from a similar respondent. A population study is not subject to sampling error if response rates are sufficiently high. Both population and sampling studies are subject to nonsampling errors, however, and their effects are much more difficult to ascertain than those of sampling errors.

Two examples from the *Fact Book on Women* point out the problems of representativeness. In the *Administrative Compensation Survey*, published by the College and University Personnel Association, data are usually received from 50% to 55% of the higher education institutions in a given year, but from year to year, the institutions reporting are not always the same ones. It is reasonable to question whether the data accurately represent the population of colleges and universities, but the data provide very useful indicators. CUPA is the only organization that provides such data, and many individuals and organizations make extensive use of it. The experience of the Office of Women in Higher Education at ACE is that the CUPA data are consistent with other studies of particular groups of administrators. In addition, many educational organizations find that the CUPA data reflect their experience in the field. Minority data, almost always gathered as a secondary item, often involve reasonably large numbers of nonresponses. Because institutions are not permitted to require students to report race or ethnicity, but are required to report that information to state and federal agencies, the handling of such nonresponses can greatly affect the representativeness of the data.

Comparability

Data comparability can be an issue either when using longitudinal data from the same source or when using data from multiple sources. An example of the former are some census data, when revisions have been made between one decennial census and the next. An example of comparability from multiple sources can be found in doctoral degree data, which are gathered by both the National Center for Education Statistics and the National Research Council. Because the methods for gathering data differ in the two organizations and because the NCES uses imputations for nonrespondents and the NRC does not, the NRC numbers are routinely somewhat smaller than, and different from, those of the NCES.

Timeliness

Timeliness of data reporting is an important issue to all data users. In general, statistics included in the *Fact Book on Women* are the latest available in fall 1988. In some cases, 1987–88 data was available (CUPA,

College Board, the Cooperative Institutional Research Program, and labor force data). In some cases, preliminary but unpublished data were available (Equal Employment Opportunity Commission's EEO-6 and some 1986–87 degree data). In other cases the most recent data were 1985–86 figures. The data on women presidents were updated in 1989.

Definitions

Definitional questions are among the most serious issues that must be considered in both data reporting and data usage. In compiling this book, the meaning of "administrator" became one of the most troublesome. The Bureau of Labor Statistics uses only one definition for general administrators, but the EEOC and CUPA use different definitions for college and university administrators. Another example concerns minority data. Before 1970, "black" often meant all nonwhites and included other racial groups that have only recently been disaggregated in statistical studies. More recently, the trend is toward disaggregation by major racial group (white, black, Hispanic, Asian/Pacific Islander, and American Indian), with further disaggregation at times within groups (e.g., Mexican Americans, Cuban Americans). Even the United States is defined in several ways—as the continental United States, the 50 states and the District of Columbia, and the 50 states and outlying territories. Users of this book will find it helpful to consult the original source tables in the Appendix when questions arise.

Lack of Data

Although data collection increases each year, some areas remain in which there are insufficient or no statistics. Some of the notable gaps in information on women in higher education concern women who serve as trustees of colleges and universities, who sit on state boards and commissions of higher education, and who function in other academic leadership roles, such as department heads or chairs of faculty senates. It would be interesting to know how many women have been Rhodes scholars or Fulbright fellows. In certain areas, such information is not available for men or women (for example, department heads and faculty senate chairs), and in others it is not disaggregated by sex (for example, Rhodes scholars). Persistent attention to data collection and to disaggregating data by sex and racial and ethnic group is needed.

For the reasons given above, readers are urged to be thoughtful when using the data presented. Compilers of the *Fact Book on Women* have tried to anticipate some of the questions readers may have. Accordingly, explanatory notes, particularly those describing the population being discussed, have been included where appropriate; some source tables in the Appendix also contain useful notes.

Major Data Sources

The following is a description of the major data collection mechanisms and publications, both primary and secondary, that were used in preparing this book. Sources are arranged alphabetically by the name of the organization that produced the surveys or publications used. The Bibliography gives complete citations for these resources and the Appendix source lines cite the applicable works for each table.

American Council on Education

One Dupont Circle, Suite 800
Washington, D.C. 20036

Fact Book on Higher Education (biennial). A secondary source, this book draws on a variety of resources, including federal and state agencies, professional associations, and private research organizations, to present information on many facets of higher education, both historically and currently.

Minorities in Higher Education (annual). A status report, this brief publication presents tabular data from several sources, together with highlights and trend analyses. The publication includes data on minority high-school graduation rates, college enrollment rates, and degrees conferred, and features a special topic that changes each year.

Cooperative Institutional Research Program (a joint project of ACE and the University of Cal-

ifornia, Los Angeles). Since 1966, CIRP has surveyed a national sample of first-time, full-time freshmen during the first few weeks of their attendance at an institution of higher education. Data are weighted to provide a normative picture of the American college freshman and are reported in *The American Freshman: National Norms. The American Freshman: Twenty Year Trends* summarizes data from 1966–1985.

College and University Personnel Association

1233 20th Avenue, N.W., Suite 503
Washington, D.C. 20036

Administrative Compensation Survey (annual). All accredited colleges and universities are surveyed for administrative salaries and years of service in selected positions. Positions surveyed are those common to most institutions, and the list currently contains 99 first-line (primary) positions (for example, president, registrar) and 69 second-line (secondary) positions (for example, assistant to the president, associate registrar). Response rates are approximately 50% to 55%, and only actual results are reported.

The College Board

45 Columbus Avenue
New York, N.Y. 10023

Scholastic Aptitude Test. High school sophomores, juniors, and seniors participate in this test, often more than once. (If they take the test more than once, only the most recent results are used.) Results are not representative of all high school students or of all college-bound students, since the sample is self-selected by students needing the scores for entrance to certain colleges. About one million students annually have taken the exam in recent years. An annual publication, *Profiles, College-Bound Seniors*, presents test data as well as other information gathered from students taking the test.

*Commission on Professionals
in Science and Technology*

1500 Massachusetts Ave., N.W., Suite 831
Washington, D.C. 20005

Professional Women and Minorities: A Manpower Data Resource Service. A secondary source, this book provides current and historical statistics about the professional segment of the U.S. population and particularly the participation and availability of women and minorities in those areas that generally require formal education to at least the baccalaureate level. Because more information is available in some fields than in others, the comprehensiveness of coverage varies. The editors have provided information from a number of sources, allowing readers to evaluate which data are more useful for their needs.

Equal Employment Opportunity Commission

2401 E St., N.W.
Washington, D.C. 20507

Higher Education Staff Information Report (EEO-6) (biennial). All institutions of higher education employing 15 or more persons are required to keep records and file biennial reports on the sex, racial/ethnic category, and salary range of all employees (full-time, part-time, and new hires). Response rates are 90% or more. An "EEO-6 Detail Summary Report" is prepared.

National Academy of Science/National Research Council

2101 Constitution Ave., N.W.
Washington, D.C. 20418

Survey of Earned Doctorates (annual). Questionnaires are distributed with the cooperation of graduate deans in U.S. universities and are filled out by graduates as they complete their doctoral degrees (institutions often make the return of the questionnaire a requirement for graduation). All types of doctoral degrees are included, but first-professional degrees such as J.D. and M.D. are excluded. Information collected includes field of study, sources of support for graduate work, and employment plans, as well as demographic data such as sex, age, race/ethnicity, citizenship, and marital status. Response rates exceed 90%.

U.S. Department of Commerce, Bureau of the Census

Washington, D.C. 20233

Current Population Survey (monthly). Sixty-thousand households throughout the 50 states and District of Columbia are surveyed monthly. The survey deals primarily with labor force data for the noninstitutional population. Each October, supplemental questions are added addressing the enrollment status of those age 3 and older. Each March, questions on educational attainment are included in the survey. A variety of *Current Population Reports* are produced from the survey. Of most interest for higher education are the Series P-20 publications, Population Characteristics, particularly "School Enrollment—Social and Economic Characteristics of Students" (based on October data) and "Educational Attainment in the United States" (based on March data). Other important resources are the Series P-23 publications, Special Studies, and the Series P-25 publications, Population Estimates and Projections.

Statistical Abstract of the United States (annual). A comprehensive compendium of statistical data on the social, political, and economic organization of the United States, this secondary source includes statistics, primarily on a national level, from both governmental and private sources. One of the 31 sections of the book contains education statistics.

U.S. Department of Education, National Center for Education Statistics

555 New Jersey Ave., N.W.
Washington, D.C. 20208

Higher Education General Information Survey (annual, 1966–1985). A population survey of all higher education institutions recognized by the Department of Education, the HEGIS survey system acquired data on the characteristics and operations of all colleges and universities. Separate surveys were conducted on institutional characteristics, fall enrollment, instructional faculty, earned degrees, and financial statistics. Reponse rates exceeded 90%. Data were reported in monographs and "Bulletins" (Ed Tabs have been used in recent years) and annually in the *Digest of Education Statistics* and the *Condition of Education*.

Integrated Postsecondary Education Data System (annual since 1986). Replacing the HEGIS survey system, the IPEDS system is a population survey of all postsecondary institutions, including colleges and universities as well as institutions providing occupational and technical education beyond the secondary level. All colleges and universities are surveyed annually, and all postsecondary institutions complete an institutional characteristics form annually, but for other survey forms, postsecondary institutions other than colleges and universities are sampled. The system contains 10 surveys, including those categories previously covered by HEGIS, as well as surveys on enrollment in occupationally specific programs, institutional activity, residence of first-time students, and libraries. Response rates in the first year (1986) varied by institutional type from 40% to 85%. Data from this survey are reported in the same publications as those in which HEGIS data were previously published.

High School and Beyond (1980, 1982, 1984, and 1986). A longitudinal study of an initial sample of nearly 60,000 1980 high school sophomores and seniors, the HSB follow-up surveys involved approximately 22,000 of the original respondents. In addition to demographic, economic, and family background data, the surveys gathered data on postsecondary plans, attendance patterns, persistence, and completion in various types of postsecondary institutions. Response rates for the follow-ups were about 90%. Some data from these surveys have been included in the *Digest of Education Statistics,* and more than 80 data tabulations are available from the Longitudinal Studies Branch.

National Postsecondary Student Aid Study (1986). A special study, the NPSAS survey sampled 1,310 institutions, about 58,000 students from those institutions, and included a subsample of 27,000 students' parents. The study focused on the costs of postsecondary education, sources of support for that education, and, in particular, how postsecondary student financial aid is targeted, received, and used. Overall student response rates were 67%; parents' response rates were 58%. A first report from the survey was available in May, 1988.

U.S. Department of Labor, Bureau of Labor Statistics

General Accounting Office Building
441 G St., N.W.
Washington, D.C. 20212

Geographic Profile of Employement and Unemployment (annual). Using data from the Current Population Survey, this publication presents an annual analysis of the labor force status, both nationally and by state and selected metropolitan region.

TABLES

Projections of U.S. Population by Sex, Race, And Ethnicity, 1985–2050

1

(Numbers in thousands.)

	Total		White		Black		Hispanic	
Year	Men	Women	Men	Women	Men	Women	Men	Women
1985	116,145	122,485	99,192	103,920	13,802	15,273	8,640	8,648
1990	121,518	128,139	102,979	107,811	14,926	16,485	9,947	9,940
1995	126,368	133,191	106,266	111,146	16,013	17,638	11,285	11,265
2000	130,491	137,464	108,879	113,775	17,040	18,714	12,627	12,596
2010	138,029	145,209	113,334	118,205	19,145	20,888	15,419	15,376
2020	144,457	152,140	116,805	121,934	21,176	22,999	18,274	18,258
2030	147,905	156,902	117,755	123,892	22,818	24,780	20,907	20,992
2040	149,118	159,442	116,891	124,057	24,107	26,223	23,229	23,485
2050	149,419	160,070	115,500	122,814	25,051	27,246	25,177	25,612

Source:
   U.S. Bureau of the Census, *Current Population Reports,* Ser. P-25, No. 952, Table 6; No. 995, Table 2, Part 13.

	U.S. Population[a] (in thousands)				Percentage of Total Population			
Year	Both Sexes	Men	Women	Black[b]	Age 65 and Older	Men	Women	Black[b]	Age 65 and Older
1900	76,094	38,867	37,227	9,194	3,099	51	49	12	4
1910	92,407	47,554	44,853	10,270	3,986	51	49	11	4
1920	106,461	54,291	52,170	10,951	4,929	51	49	10	5
1930	123,077	62,297	60,780	12,518	6,705	51	49	10	5
1940	132,122	66,352	65,770	13,494	9,031	50	50	10	7
1950	152,271	75,849	76,422	16,288	12,397	50	50	11	8
1960	180,671	89,320	91,352	20,648	16,675	49	51	11	9
1965	194,303	95,609	98,694	23,098	18,451	49	51	12	9
1970[c]	205,052	100,354	104,698	22,801	20,107	49	51	11	10
1975[c]	215,973	105,366	110,607	24,778	22,696	49	51	11	10
1980	227,757	110,888	116,869	26,903	25,704	49	51	12	11
1981	230,138	112,064	118,074	27,328	26,236	49	51	12	11
1982	232,520	113,245	119,275	27,759	26,827	49	51	12	12
1983	234,799	114,385	120,414	28,178	27,428	49	51	12	12
1984	237,001	115,494	121,507	28,580	27,973	49	51	12	12
1985	239,283	116,649	122,634	29,002	28,536	49	51	12	12
1986	241,596	117,820	123,776	29,427	29,173	49	51	12	12
Middle Series Projection[d]									
1987	243,084	118,309	124,774	30,007	29,925	49	51	12	12
1988	245,302	119,390	125,911	30,477	30,529	49	51	12	12
1989	247,498	120,463	127,035	30,946	31,115	49	51	13	13
1990	249,657	121,518	128,139	31,412	31,697	49	51	13	13
1995	259,559	126,368	133,191	33,651	33,888	49	51	13	13
2000	267,955	130,491	137,464	35,753	34,921	49	51	13	13
2010	283,238	138,029	145,209	40,033	39,195	49	51	14	14
2020	296,597	144,457	152,140	44,175	51,422	49	51	15	17
2030	304,807	147,905	156,902	47,598	64,581	49	51	16	21
2040	308,559	149,118	159,442	50,329	66,988	48	52	16	22
2050	309,488	149,419	160,070	52,297	67,411	48	52	17	22

a Except as noted otherwise, figures are estimates and projections of the total population as of July 1. The population of Alaska and Hawaii is excluded before 1950; armed forces overseas are excluded before 1940.

b Figures from 1900 to 1950 are for "nonwhite" population; figures for 1960 and 1965 are for "Negro" population; figures beginning 1970 are for "black" population. In 1960, the "Negro" population represented 9 % of the total nonwhite population.

c Figures reflect revisions based on the 1980 census.

d Middle series projections are based on a fertility rate of 1.9 lifetime births per woman.

Sources:
1 U.S. Bureau of the Census, *Current Population Reports,* Ser. P-25, No. 311; No. 519, Table 1; No. 917, Table 1; No. 952, Table 6; No. 1000, Table 1.

2 ACE/Macmillan, *1989–90 Fact Book on Higher Education,* Table 1.

	Population, Age 18–24[a] (in thousands)								
	All Races			**Black and Other Minority Races**			**Black**		
Year	Total	Men	Women	Total	Men	Women	Total	Men	Women
1950	16,075	8,009	8,067	1,889	898	992	[b]	[b]	[b]
1960	16,128	8,093	8,034	1,959	946	1,013	1,798	863	935
1970	24,712	12,451	12,261	3,180	1,551	1,630	2,829	1,374	1,455
1975	28,005	14,137	13,868	4,015	1,964	2,051	3,510	1,711	1,799
1976	28,645	14,465	14,180	4,162	2,039	2,122	3,622	1,768	1,854
1977	29,174	14,733	14,441	4,318	2,120	2,199	3,747	1,831	1,916
1978	29,662	14,961	14,661	4,459	2,191	2,268	3,858	1,886	1,972
1979	30,048	15,186	14,861	4,592	2,260	2,332	3,956	1,936	2,019
1980	30,350	15,327	15,022	4,750	2,339	2,410	4,029	1,972	2,058
1981	30,428	15,371	15,057	4,842	2,391	2,451	4,069	1,992	2,076
1982	30,283	15,301	14,981	4,902	2,426	2,476	4,084	2,002	2,083
1983	29,942	15,128	14,815	4,936	2,445	2,490	4,093	2,007	2,086
1984	29,391	14,853	14,538	4,933	2,448	2,485	4,068	1,996	2,072
1985	28,749	14,529	14,220	4,907	2,438	2,469	4,021	1,974	2,047
1986	27,973	14,139	13,834	4,865	2,420	2,446	3,956	1,943	2,013
	Series II Projections[c]								
1987	27,246	13,864	13,381	4,782	2,397	2,384	3,989	1,998	1,991
1988	26,783	13,625	13,157	4,724	2,365	2,357	3,921	1,963	1,958
1989	26,375	13,419	12,956	4,691	2,348	2,342	3,875	1,940	1,935
1990	25,794	13,127	12,667	4,625	2,315	2,310	3,798	1,901	1,897
1995	23,702	12,072	11,631	4,434	2,223	2,212	3,542	1,778	1,764
2000	24,601	12,531	12,071	4,795	2,403	2,392	3,773	1,894	1,879
2025	25,465	12,980	12,484	5,886	2,960	2,926	4,559	2,296	2,263
2050	25,683	13,092	12,591	6,453	3,250	3,203	4,815	2,426	2,390

a Total population, including armed forces overseas as of July 1.

b Source shows estimates for "nonwhite" only.

c Series II projections use a fertility assumption of 1.9 lifetime births per woman. Projections reflect results of the 1980 census.

Sources:

1 U.S. Bureau of the Census, *Current Population Reports,* Ser. P-25, No. 311; No. 519, Table 1; No. 704, Table 8; No. 870, Table 1; No. 880, Table 1; No. 917, Table 1; No. 952, Tables 5 and 6; No. 1000, Table 1.

2 ACE/Macmillan, *1989–90 Fact Book on Higher Education,* Table 3.

Expectation of Years of Life at Birth, 1920–1986

(Data before 1960 excludes Alaska and Hawaii. Data before 1940 is for death registration states only. Beginning 1970, data excludes deaths of non-U.S. residents. See also Historical Statistics, Colonial Times to 1970, ser. B, 107–115.)

Year	Total	Total Men	Total Women	White Total	White Men	White Women	Black and Other Total	Black and Other Men	Black and Other Women	Black Total	Black Men	Black Women
1920	54.1	53.6	54.6	54.9	54.4	55.6	45.3	45.5	45.2	NA	NA	NA
1930	59.7	58.1	61.6	61.4	59.7	63.5	48.1	47.3	49.2	NA	NA	NA
1940	62.9	60.8	65.2	64.2	62.1	66.6	53.1	51.5	54.9	NA	NA	NA
1950	68.2	65.6	71.1	69.1	66.5	72.2	60.8	59.1	62.9	NA	NA	NA
1955	69.6	66.7	72.8	70.5	67.4	73.7	63.7	61.4	66.1	NA	NA	NA
1960	69.7	66.6	73.1	70.6	67.4	74.1	63.6	61.1	66.3	NA	NA	NA
1965	70.2	66.8	73.7	71.0	67.6	74.7	64.1	61.1	67.4	NA	NA	NA
1970	70.8	67.1	74.7	71.7	68.0	75.6	65.3	61.3	69.4	64.1	60.0	68.3
1971	71.1	67.4	75.0	72.0	68.3	75.8	65.6	61.6	69.8	64.6	60.5	68.9
1972	71.2	67.4	75.1	72.0	68.3	75.9	65.7	61.5	70.1	64.7	60.4	69.1
1973	71.4	67.6	75.3	72.2	68.5	76.1	66.1	62.0	70.3	65.0	60.9	69.3
1974	72.0	68.2	75.9	72.8	69.0	76.7	67.1	62.9	71.3	66.0	61.7	70.3
1975	72.6	68.8	76.6	73.4	69.5	77.3	68.0	63.7	72.4	66.8	62.4	71.3
1976	72.9	69.1	76.8	73.6	69.9	77.5	68.4	64.2	72.7	67.2	62.9	71.6
1977	73.3	69.5	77.2	74.0	70.2	77.9	68.9	64.7	73.2	67.7	63.4	72.0
1978	73.5	69.6	77.3	74.1	70.4	78.0	69.3	65.0	73.5	68.1	63.7	72.4
1979	73.9	70.0	77.8	74.6	70.8	78.4	69.8	65.4	74.1	68.5	64.0	72.9
1980	73.7	70.0	77.4	74.4	70.7	78.1	69.5	65.3	73.6	68.1	63.8	72.5
1981	74.2	70.4	77.8	74.8	71.1	78.4	70.3	66.1	74.4	68.9	64.5	73.2
1982	74.5	70.9	78.1	75.1	71.5	78.7	71.0	66.8	75.0	69.4	65.1	73.7
1983	74.6	71.0	78.1	75.2	71.7	78.7	71.1	67.2	74.9	69.6	65.4	73.6
1984	74.7	71.2	78.2	75.3	71.8	78.7	71.3	67.4	75.0	69.7	65.6	73.7
1985	74.7	71.2	78.2	75.3	71.9	78.7	71.2	67.2	75.0	69.5	65.3	73.5
1986[a]	74.9	71.3	78.3	75.4	72.0	78.9	71.4	67.6	75.1	69.6	65.5	73.6

NA = not available

a   Preliminary data.

Sources:
1   U.S. National Center for Health Statistics, *Vital Statistics of the United States,* various years; and unpublished data.
2   U.S. Bureau of the Census, *Statistical Abstract of the United States, 1988,* Table 106.

Years of School Completed, by Race, Hispanic Origin, and Sex, 1960–1986

5

(Persons age 25 or older. Hispanic persons may be of any race. See also Historical Statistics, Colonial Times to 1970, *ser. H, 602–617.)*

Year, Race, Hispanic, and Sex	Popula-tion (in thousands)	Elementary School			High School		College		Median School Years Completed
		0–4 Years	5–7 Years	8 Years	1–3 Years	4 Years	1–3 Years	4 Years or More	
1960, all races	**99,438**	**8.3**	**13.8**	**17.5**	**19.2**	**24.6**	**8.8**	**7.7**	**10.6**
White	89,581	6.7	12.8	18.1	19.3	25.8	9.3	8.1	10.9
Men	43,259	7.4	13.7	18.7	18.9	22.2	9.1	10.3	10.7
Women	46,322	6.0	11.9	17.8	19.6	29.2	9.5	6.0	11.2
Black	9,054	23.8	24.2	12.9	19.0	12.9	4.1	3.1	8.0
Men	4,240	28.3	23.9	12.3	17.3	11.3	4.1	2.8	7.7
Women	4,814	19.8	24.5	13.4	20.5	14.3	4.1	3.3	8.6
1970, all races	**109,899**	**5.5**	**10.0**	**12.8**	**19.4**	**31.1**	**10.6**	**10.7**	**12.1**
White	98,246	4.5	9.1	13.0	18.8	32.2	11.1	11.3	12.1
Men	46,527	4.8	9.7	13.3	18.2	28.5	11.1	14.4	12.1
Women	51,718	4.1	8.6	12.8	19.4	35.5	11.1	8.4	12.1
Black	10,375	14.6	18.7	10.5	24.8	21.2	5.9	4.4	9.8
Men	4,714	17.7	19.1	10.2	22.9	20.0	6.0	4.2	9.4
Women	5,661	12.0	18.3	10.8	26.4	22.2	5.8	4.6	10.1
Hispanic	3.946	19.5	18.6	11.5	18.2	21.1	6.5	4.5	9.1
Men	1,897	19.1	18.0	11.3	18.1	19.9	7.6	5.9	9.3
Women	2,050	19.9	19.2	11.6	18.3	22.3	5.4	3.2	8.9
1980, all races	**132,836**	**3.6**	**6.7**	**8.0**	**15.3**	**34.6**	**15.7**	**16.2**	**12.5**
White	114,290	2.6	5.8	8.2	14.6	35.7	16.0	17.1	12.5
Men	53,941	2.8	6.0	8.0	13.6	31.8	16.4	21.3	12.5
Women	60,349	2.5	5.6	8.4	15.5	39.1	15.6	13.3	12.6
Black	13,195	8.2	11.7	7.1	21.8	29.3	13.5	8.4	12.0
Men	5,895	10.0	12.0	6.7	20.5	28.3	14.0	8.4	12.0
Women	7,300	6.7	11.6	7.3	22.9	30.0	13.2	8.3	12.0
Hispanic	6,739	15.5	16.6	8.1	15.8	24.4	12.0	7.6	10.8
Men	3,247	15.2	16.2	7.7	15.5	22.6	13.4	9.4	11.1
Women	3,493	15.8	17.1	8.4	16.1	26.0	10.6	6.0	10.6
1986, all races	**146,606**	**2.7**	**4.7**	**6.0**	**11.9**	**38.4**	**16.9**	**19.4**	**12.6**
White	127,269	2.2	4.2	6.1	11.3	39.0	17.1	20.1	12.7
Men	60,770	2.4	4.2	6.1	10.8	35.2	17.3	24.0	12.8
Women	66,500	2.1	4.2	6.1	11.8	42.5	16.9	16.4	12.6
Black	15,234	5.4	8.3	5.6	18.5	35.6	15.8	10.9	12.3
Men	6,779	6.6	8.9	5.2	17.7	34.3	16.0	11.2	12.3
Women	8,455	4.3	7.8	5.9	19.0	36.6	15.6	10.7	12.4
Hispanic	9,030	12.9	15.9	8.1	14.7	28.4	11.6	8.4	11.7
Men	4,397	13.3	15.5	7.3	14.7	27.4	12.3	9.5	11.8
Women	4,633	12.5	16.2	8.9	14.7	29.4	11.0	7.4	11.5

Sources:
U.S. Bureau of the Census, *U.S. Census of Population, 1960,* vol. 1; *1970,* vols. 1, 2; *1980,* vol. 1; *Current Population Reports,* Ser. P-20, No. 403; *Statistical Abstract of the United States, 1988,* Table 202.

Years of School Completed by Persons Age 25 and Older, by Age and Sex, Selected Years, 1940–1987

6

(In thousands, noninstitutional population.)

Years of School Completed, Sex and Age		1987	1980[a]	1960	1940
Age 25 and Older					
Both Sexes					
Total		149,144	130,409	99,465	74,776[b]
Elementary:	0–4 years	3,640	4,390	8,303	10,105
	5–7 years	6,713	7,791	13,754	13,656
	8 years	8,588	10,635	17,464	20,757
High school:	1–3 years	17,417	18,086	19,140	11,182
	4 years	57,669	47,934	24,440	10,552
College:	1–3 years	25,479	19,379	8,747	4,075
	4 years or more	29,637	22,193	7,617	3,407
Median		12.7	12.5	10.6	8.6
Men					
Total		70,677	61,389	47,997	37,463[b]
Elementary:	0–4 years	1,794	2,212	4,522	5,550
	5–7 years	3,261	3,663	7,022	7,008
	8 years	3,998	4,964	8,540	10,631
High school:	1–3 years	7,909	8,046	8,988	5,333
	4 years	24,998	20,080	10,175	4,507
College:	1–3 years	12,062	9,593	4,127	1,824
	4 years or more	16,654	12,832	4,626	2,021
Median		12.7	12.6	10.3	8.6
Women					
Total		78,467	69,020	51,468	37,313[b]
Elementary:	0–4 years	1,846	2,178	3,781	4,554
	5–7 years	3,452	4,129	6,732	6,643
	8 years	4,590	5,671	8,924	10,125
High school:	1–3 years	9,508	10,040	10,151	5,849
	4 years	32,671	27,854	14,267	6,044
College:	1–3 years	13,417	9,786	4,620	2,251
	4 years or more	12,983	9,362	2,991	1,386
Median		12.6	12.4	10.9	8.7

Years of School Completed by Persons Age 25 and Older, by Age and Sex, Selected Years, 1940–1987

6 *Continued*

(In thousands, noninstitutional population.)

Years of School Completed, Sex and Age		1987	1980[a]	1960	1940
Age 25–34					
Both Sexes					
Total		42,635	36,615	22,821	21,339[b]
Elementary:	0–4 years	390	362	709	1,377
	5–7 years	720	705	1,689	3,123
	8 years	640	719	2,049	4,553
High school:	1–3 years	3,995	3,571	5,135	4,553
	4 years	17,539	14,481	8,166	4,702
College:	1–3 years	9,157	7,942	2,572	1,554
	4 years or more	10,196	8,836	2,499	1,288
Median		12.9	12.9	12.2	10.0
Men					
Total		21,142	18,051	11,184	10,521[b]
Elementary:	0–4 years	223	198	420	779
	5–7 years	372	342	926	1,579
	8 years	326	357	1,100	2,353
High school:	1–3 years	2,030	1,639	2,441	2,220
	4 years	8,544	6,393	3,356	2,049
College:	1–3 years	4,384	4,166	1,316	692
	4 years or more	5,263	4,957	1,624	744
Median		12.9	13.1	12.2	9.7
Women					
Total		21,494	18,565	11,637	10,818[b]
Elementary:	0–4 years	168	164	289	598
	5–7 years	348	363	763	1,544
	8 years	314	362	949	2,200
High school:	1–3 years	1,965	1,932	2,694	2,333
	4 years	8,995	8,087	4,810	2,653
College:	1–3 years	4,772	3,777	1,256	862
	4 years or more	4,932	3,879	875	544
Median		12.9	12.8	12.2	10.3

a   Controlled to 1980 census base.

b   Total includes persons who did not report on years of school completed.

Source:
   U.S. Bureau of the Census, *Current Population Reports,* Ser. P-20, No. 428, Table 11.

Years of School Completed, by Race, Sex, and Age, 1986

(Persons age 25 and older, as of March 1986.)

Race, Sex and Age	Popula-tion (in thousands)	Percentage of Population Completing—							Median School Years Completed
		Elementary School			High School		College		
		0–4 Years	5–7 Years	8 Years	1–3 Years	4 Years	1–3 Years	4 Years or More	
All Races	**146,606**	**2.7**	**4.7**	**6.0**	**11.9**	**38.4**	**16.9**	**19.4**	**12.6**
Men	69,503	2.8	4.7	6.0	11.3	34.9	17.1	23.2	12.7
Women	77,102	2.5	4.6	6.0	12.5	41.6	16.7	16.1	12.6
Age 25–29	21,619	.9	1.6	1.6	9.8	42.2	21.6	22.4	12.9
Age 30–34	20,434	.9	1.7	1.6	8.2	40.1	21.7	25.7	12.9
Age 35–44	32,508	1.2	2.5	2.6	9.0	38.9	20.5	25.5	12.9
Age 45–54	22,662	2.3	4.0	4.7	12.6	42.0	15.2	19.1	12.6
Age 55 and older	49,383	5.3	9.0	12.7	16.0	34.2	11.2	11.7	12.2
Black	**15,234**	**5.4**	**8.3**	**5.6**	**18.5**	**35.6**	**15.8**	**10.9**	**12.3**
Age 25–29	2,684	.5	.8	1.2	14.1	47.0	24.5	11.8	12.7
Age 30–34	2,417	.7	1.4	2.5	15.2	44.1	20.4	15.6	12.7
Age 35–44	3,408	1.0	3.1	2.4	17.7	40.6	20.5	14.6	12.6
Age 45–54	2,403	3.2	7.4	6.9	23.6	36.0	13.2	9.6	12.2
Age 55 and older	4,323	15.6	21.2	11.9	20.7	19.5	5.5	5.6	9.2
Hispanic Origin[a]	**9,030**	**12.9**	**15.9**	**8.1**	**14.7**	**28.4**	**11.6**	**8.4**	**11.7**
Age 25–29	1,882	5.6	12.0	6.4	17.0	33.7	16.3	9.0	12.3
Age 30–34	1,594	6.5	14.5	5.0	16.1	33.6	13.6	10.9	12.2
Age 35–44	2,209	10.2	15.2	7.7	14.2	29.2	13.8	9.8	12.1
Age 45–54	1,453	13.8	17.3	8.1	15.5	28.7	9.1	7.4	11.0
Age 55 and older	1,891	27.8	20.6	13.0	11.2	17.7	4.8	4.9	8.1

a Hispanic persons may be of any race.

Source:
U.S. Bureau of the Census, *Statistical Abstract of the United States, 1988,* Table 203; unpublished data.

8

Civilian Labor Force and Participation Rates by Sex, Age, Race, and Hispanic Origin, Actual 1972, 1979, and 1986, and Moderate Growth Projections 2000

Group	Participation Rate — Actual 1972	Actual 1979	Actual 1986	Projected 2000	Level (in thousands) — Actual 1972	Actual 1979	Actual 1986	Projected 2000	Change (in thousands) 1972–1986	1986–2000	Percentage change 1972–1986	1986–2000	Growth Rate 1972–1986	1986–2000
Total, Age 16 and Older	60.4	63.7	65.3	67.8	87,037	104,960	117,837	138,775	30,800	20,938	35.4	17.8	2.2	1.2
Men, Age 16 and Older	79.0	77.8	76.3	74.7	53,556	60,727	65,423	73,136	11,867	7,713	22.2	11.8	1.4	.8
16–19	58.1	61.5	56.4	60.2	4,478	5,111	4,102	4,501	−376	399	−8.4	9.7	−0.6	.7
20–24	83.9	86.4	85.8	87.5	6,765	8,534	8,149	7,005	1,384	−1,144	20.5	−14.0	1.3	−1.1
25–34	95.7	95.3	94.6	93.6	12,349	16,386	19,383	16,559	7,034	−2,824	57.0	−14.6	3.3	−1.1
35–44	96.4	95.7	94.8	93.9	10,372	11,532	15,029	20,133	4,657	5,104	44.9	34.0	2.7	2.1
45–54	93.2	91.4	91.0	90.1	10,412	10,008	9,994	16,332	−418	6,338	−4.0	63.4	−0.3	3.6
55–64	80.4	72.8	67.3	63.2	7,155	7,213	6,954	7,238	−201	284	−2.8	4.1	−0.2	.3
65 and older	24.3	19.9	16.0	9.9	2,025	1,943	1,812	1,368	−213	−444	−10.5	−24.5	−0.8	−2.0
Women, Age 16 and Older	43.9	50.9	55.3	61.5	33,481	44,233	52,414	65,639	18,933	13,225	56.5	25.2	3.3	1.6
16–19	45.8	54.2	52.9	59.2	3,578	4,527	3,824	4,379	246	555	6.9	14.5	.5	1.0
20–24	59.1	69.0	72.4	78.4	5,365	7,233	7,293	6,746	1,928	−547	35.9	−7.5	2.2	−0.6
25–34	47.8	63.9	71.6	82.3	6,609	11,550	15,209	15,098	8,600	−111	130.1	−0.7	6.1	−0.1
35–44	52.0	63.6	73.1	84.2	6,028	8,153	12,204	18,438	6,176	6,234	102.5	51.1	5.2	3.0
45–54	53.9	58.4	65.9	75.4	6,555	6,891	7,746	14,220	1,191	6,474	18.2	83.6	1.2	4.4
55–64	42.1	41.7	42.3	45.8	4,257	4,718	4,940	5,732	683	792	16.0	16.0	1.1	1.1
65 and older	9.3	8.3	7.4	5.4	1,089	1,161	1,198	1,026	109	−172	10.0	−14.4	.7	−1.1
Whites, Age 16 and Older	60.4	63.9	65.5	68.2	77,275	91,922	101,801	116,701	24,526	14,900	31.7	14.6	2.0	1.0
Men	79.6	78.6	76.9	75.3	48,118	53,857	57,216	62,252	9,098	5,036	18.9	8.8	1.2	.6
Women	43.2	50.5	55.0	61.5	29,157	38,065	44,585	54,449	15,428	9,864	52.9	22.1	3.1	1.4
Blacks, Age 16 and Older	60.2	61.4	63.5	66.0	8,748	10,665	12,684	16,334	3,936	3,650	45.0	28.8	2.7	1.8
Men	73.9	71.6	71.2	70.7	4,855	5,556	6,373	7,926	1,518	1,553	31.3	24.4	2.0	1.6
Women	48.8	53.2	57.2	62.1	3,893	5,109	6,311	8,408	2,418	2,097	62.1	33.2	3.5	2.1
Asian and Other[a], Age 16 and Older	NA	65.9	64.9	65.8	NA	2,373	3,352	5,740	NA	2,388	NA	71.2	NA	3.9
Men	NA	76.7	74.9	72.4	NA	1,314	1,834	2,958	NA	1,124	NA	61.3	NA	3.5
Women	NA	56.0	55.9	60.1	NA	1,059	1,518	2,782	NA	1,264	NA	83.3	NA	4.5
Hispanics[b], Age 16 and Older	NA	63.5	65.4	68.7	NA	5,215	8,076	14,086	NA	6,010	NA	74.4	NA	4.1
Men	NA	81.2	81.0	80.4	NA	3,182	4,948	8,303	NA	3,355	NA	67.8	NA	3.8
Women	NA	47.4	50.1	56.9	NA	2,033	3,128	5,783	NA	2,655	NA	84.9	NA	4.5

NA = not available

a The "Asian and other" group includes American Indians, Alaskan Natives, Asians, and Pacific Islanders. The historic data are derived by subtracting "black" from the "black and other" group. Projections are made directly.

b Persons of Hispanic origin may be of any race. Labor force data for Hispanics are not available before 1976.

Source:
U.S. Bureau of Labor Statistics, *Monthly Labor Review,* Sept. 1987, Table 5.

(In years and percentages. For the civilian noninstitutional population.)

Index and Age	Total	Men				
		Race		Educational Attainment		
		White	Black and Other	Less Than High School	High School to 14 Years	15 Years or More
Life Expectancy:						
At birth	70.0	70.7	65.3	70.0	70.0	70.0
At age 25	47.3	47.9	43.3	47.3	47.3	47.3
At age 60	17.5	17.6	16.5	17.5	17.5	17.5
At age 65	14.2	14.3	13.8	14.2	14.2	14.2
Worklife Expectancy:						
At birth	38.8	39.8	32.9	34.6	39.9	41.1
At age 25	33.1	33.8	28.6	29.2	33.8	36.1
At age 60	4.4	4.5	3.3	3.3	4.7	6.3
At age 65	2.3	2.3	1.8	1.8	2.4	3.6
Percentage of Life Economically Active:[a]						
From birth	55.4	56.3	50.4	49.4	57.0	58.7
From age 25	70.0	70.6	66.1	61.7	71.5	76.3
From age 60	25.1	25.6	20.0	18.9	26.9	36.0
From age 65	16.2	16.1	13.0	12.7	16.9	25.4
Number of Times Person Enters Labor Force per:						
Person born	3.9	3.9	4.3	4.3	3.7	4.6
Person age 25	1.5	1.5	1.8	2.0	1.5	1.4
Expected Duration per Entry Remaining:[b]						
From birth	9.9	10.2	7.7	8.0	10.8	8.9
From age 25	22.1	22.5	15.9	14.6	22.5	25.8
Number of Times Person Voluntarily Leaves Labor Force:						
From birth	3.6	3.6	3.9	4.0	3.6	4.5
From age 25	2.3	2.3	2.4	2.7	2.3	2.2

Selected Worklife Indices by Sex, Race, and Educational Attainment, 1979–1980

9 *Continued*

(In years and percentages. For the civilian noninstitutional population.)

Index and Age	Women Total	Race White	Race Black and Other	Educational Attainment Less Than High School	Educational Attainment High School to 14 Years	Educational Attainment 15 Years or More
Life Expectancy:						
At birth	77.6	78.3	73.9	77.6	77.6	77.6
At age 25	54.2	54.7	51.0	54.2	54.2	54.2
At age 60	22.4	22.6	21.0	22.4	22.4	22.4
At age 65	18.5	18.7	17.7	18.5	18.5	18.5
Worklife Expectancy:						
At birth	29.4	29.7	27.4	22.3	30.1	34.9
At age 25	24.0	24.1	23.5	17.9	24.4	27.9
At age 60	3.0	3.0	3.0	2.3	3.3	3.5
At age 65	1.5	1.5	1.5	1.2	1.8	1.8
Percentage of Life Economically Active:[a]						
From birth	37.9	37.9	37.1	28.7	38.8	45.0
From age 25	44.3	44.1	46.1	33.0	45.0	51.5
From age 60	13.4	13.3	14.3	10.3	14.7	15.6
From age 65	8.1	8.0	8.5	6.5	9.7	9.7
Number of Times Person Enters Labor Force per:						
Person born	5.5	5.6	5.4	5.8	5.6	5.6
Person age 25	3.0	3.0	3.1	3.3	3.2	2.7
Expected Duration per Entry Remaining:[b]						
From birth	5.3	5.3	5.1	3.8	5.4	6.2
From age 25	8.0	8.0	7.6	5.4	7.6	10.3
Number of Times Person Voluntarily Leaves Labor Force:						
From birth	5.4	5.5	5.4	5.7	5.7	4.7
From age 25	3.8	3.8	3.7	3.8	4.0	3.6

a Ratio of worklife expectancy to life expectancy.

b Worklife expectancy divided by number of times person enters labor force.

Sources:
1 U.S. Bureau of Labor Statistics, *Monthly Labor Review,* Aug. 1985.

2 U.S. Bureau of the Census, *Statistical Abstract of the United States, 1988,* Table 606.

Civilian Labor Force and Participation Rates by Sex, Age, Race, and Hispanic Origin, Actual 1972, 1979, and 1986, and Moderate Growth Projections 2000

Group	Participation Rate — Actual 1972	Actual 1979	Actual 1986	Projected 2000	Level (in thousands) — Actual 1972	Actual 1979	Actual 1986	Projected 2000	Change (in thousands) 1972–1986	Change 1986–2000	Percentage change 1972–1986	Percentage change 1986–2000	Growth Rate 1972–1986	Growth Rate 1986–2000
Total, Age 16 and Older	60.4	63.7	65.3	67.8	87,037	104,960	117,837	138,775	30,800	20,938	35.4	17.8	2.2	1.2
Men, Age 16 and Older	79.0	77.8	76.3	74.7	53,556	60,727	65,423	73,136	11,867	7,713	22.2	11.8	1.4	.8
16–19	58.1	61.5	56.4	60.2	4,478	5,111	4,102	4,501	−376	399	−8.4	9.7	−0.6	.7
20–24	83.9	86.4	85.8	87.5	6,765	8,534	8,149	7,005	1,384	−1,144	20.5	−14.0	1.3	−1.1
25–34	95.7	95.3	94.6	93.6	12,349	16,386	19,383	16,559	7,034	−2,824	57.0	−14.6	3.3	−1.1
35–44	96.4	95.7	94.8	93.9	10,372	11,532	15,029	20,133	4,657	5,104	44.9	34.0	2.7	2.1
45–54	93.2	91.4	91.0	90.1	10,412	10,008	9,994	16,332	−418	6,338	−4.0	63.4	−0.3	3.6
55–64	80.4	72.8	67.3	63.2	7,155	7,213	6,954	7,238	−201	284	−2.8	4.1	−0.2	.3
65 and older	24.3	19.9	16.0	9.9	2,025	1,943	1,812	1,368	−213	−444	−10.5	−24.5	−0.8	−2.0
Women, Age 16 and Older	43.9	50.9	55.3	61.5	33,481	44,233	52,414	65,639	18,933	13,225	56.5	25.2	3.3	1.6
16–19	45.8	54.2	52.9	59.2	3,578	4,527	3,824	4,379	246	555	6.9	14.5	.5	1.0
20–24	59.1	69.0	72.4	78.4	5,365	7,233	7,293	6,746	1,928	−547	35.9	−7.5	2.2	−0.6
25–34	47.8	63.9	71.6	82.3	6,609	11,550	15,209	15,098	8,600	−111	130.1	−0.7	6.1	−0.1
35–44	52.0	63.6	73.1	84.2	6,028	8,153	12,204	18,438	6,176	6,234	102.5	51.1	5.2	3.0
45–54	53.9	58.4	65.9	75.4	6,555	6,891	7,746	14,220	1,191	6,474	18.2	83.6	1.2	4.4
55–64	42.1	41.7	42.3	45.8	4,257	4,718	4,940	5,732	683	792	16.0	16.0	1.1	1.1
65 and older	9.3	8.3	7.4	5.4	1,089	1,161	1,198	1,026	109	−172	10.0	−14.4	.7	−1.1
Whites, Age 16 and Older	60.4	63.9	65.5	68.2	77,275	91,922	101,801	116,701	24,526	14,900	31.7	14.6	2.0	1.0
Men	79.6	78.6	76.9	75.3	48,118	53,857	57,216	62,252	9,098	5,036	18.9	8.8	1.2	.6
Women	43.2	50.5	55.0	61.5	29,157	38,065	44,585	54,449	15,428	9,864	52.9	22.1	3.1	1.4
Blacks, Age 16 ond Older	60.2	61.4	63.5	66.0	8,748	10,665	12,684	16,334	3,936	3,650	45.0	28.8	2.7	1.8
Men	73.9	71.6	71.2	70.7	4,855	5,556	6,373	7,926	1,518	1,553	31.3	24.4	2.0	1.6
Women	48.8	53.2	57.2	62.1	3,893	5,109	6,311	8,408	2,418	2,097	62.1	33.2	3.5	2.1
Asian and Other[a], Age 16 and Older	NA	65.9	64.9	65.8	NA	2,373	3,352	5,740	NA	2,388	NA	71.2	NA	3.9
Men	NA	76.7	64.9	72.4	NA	1,314	1,834	2,958	NA	1,124	NA	61.3	NA	3.5
Women	NA	56.0	55.9	60.1	NA	1,059	1,518	2,782	NA	1,264	NA	83.3	NA	4.5
Hispanics[b], Age 16 and Older	NA	63.5	65.4	68.7	NA	5,215	8,076	14,086	NA	6,010	NA	74.4	NA	4.1
Men	NA	81.2	81.0	80.4	NA	3,182	4,948	8,303	NA	3,355	NA	67.8	NA	3.8
Women	NA	47.4	50.1	56.9	NA	2,033	3,128	5,783	NA	2,655	NA	84.9	NA	4.5

NA = not available

a The "Asian and other" group includes American Indians, Alaskan Natives, Asians, and Pacific Islanders. The historic data are derived by subtracting "black" from the "black and other" group. Projections are made directly.

b Persons of Hispanic origin may be of any race. Labor force data for Hispanics are not available before 1976.

Source:
U.S. Bureau of Labor Statistics, *Monthly Labor Review*, Sept. 1987, Table 5.

Marital Status of Women in the Civilian Labor Force, 1940–1986

(As of March, except as indicated. Persons age 14 and older through 1965; age 16 and older thereafter. Data before 1960 excludes Alaska and Hawaii. Figures for 1940 based on complete census revised for comparability with intercensal series. See also Historical Statistics, Colonial Times to 1970, ser. D 49–62.)

Year	Total	Female Labor Force (in thousands)				Percentage Distribution, Female Labor Force			Female Labor Force as Percentage of Female Population				
		Single	Married		Widowed or Divorced	Single	Married[a]	Widowed or Divorced	Total	Single	Married		Widowed or Divorced
			Total[a]	Husband Present							Total[a]	Husband Present	
1940	13,840	6,710	5,040	4,200[b]	2,090	48.5	36.4	15.1	27.4	48.1	16.7	14.7	32.0
1944[b]	18,449	7,542	8,433	6,226	2,474	40.9	45.7	13.4	35.0	58.6	25.6	21.7	35.7
1947[b]	16,323	6,181	7,545	6,676	2,597	37.9	46.2	15.9	29.8	51.2	21.4	20.0	34.6
1950	17,795	5,621	9,273	8,550	2,901	31.6	52.1	16.3	31.4	50.5	24.8	23.8	36.0
1955[b]	20,154	5,087	11,839	10,423	3,227	25.2	58.7	16.0	33.5	46.4	29.4	27.7	36.0
1960	22,516	5,401	13,485	12,253	3,629	24.0	59.9	16.1	34.8	44.1	31.7	30.5	37.1
1965	25,952	5,912	16,154	14,708	3,886	22.8	62.2	15.0	36.7	40.5	35.7	34.7	35.7
1969	29,898	6,501	19,100	17,595	4,297	21.7	63.9	14.4	41.6	51.2	40.4	39.6	35.8
1970	31,233	6,965	19,799	18,377	4,469	22.3	63.4	14.3	42.6	53.0	41.4	40.8	36.2
1971	31,778	7,220	20,034	18,573	4,524	22.7	63.0	14.2	42.5	52.8	41.4	40.8	35.7
1972	33,132	7,543	20,845	19,336	4,744	22.8	62.9	14.3	43.7	55.0	42.2	41.5	37.2
1973	34,195	7,838	21,487	19,951	4,870	22.9	62.8	14.2	44.2	55.9	42.8	42.2	36.7
1974	35,708	8,362	22,202	20,541	5,144	23.4	62.2	14.4	45.3	57.4	43.8	43.1	37.8
1975	36,981	8,599	23,037	21,360	5,345	23.2	62.3	14.5	46.0	57.0	45.1	44.4	37.7
1976	38,399	9,282	23,643	21,814	5,474	24.2	61.6	14.3	46.8	59.2	45.8	45.1	37.3
1977	40,053	9,702	24,429	22,681	5,922	24.2	61.0	14.8	48.0	59.2	47.2	46.6	39.0
1978	41,747	10,487	24,976	23,136	6,284	25.1	59.8	15.1	49.2	60.7	48.1	47.5	39.9
1979	43,844	11,304	26,073	24,223	6,467	25.8	59.5	14.8	50.8	62.9	49.9	49.3	40.0
1980	44,934	11,242	26,828	24,900	6,864	25.0	59.7	15.3	51.1	61.5	50.7	50.1	41.0
1981	46,415	11,628	27,536	25,460	7,251	25.0	59.3	15.6	52.0	62.3	51.7	51.0	41.9
1982	47,095	11,801	27,843	25,756	7,451	25.1	59.1	15.8	52.1	62.2	51.8	51.2	42.1
1983	47,779	12,282	28,140	26,227	7,357	25.7	58.9	15.4	52.3	62.6	52.3	51.8	41.2
1984	49,240	12,581	28,883	26,855	7,775	25.6	58.7	15.8	53.2	63.1	53.3	52.8	42.1
1985	50,891	12,925	29,755	27,716	8,211	25.4	58.5	16.1	54.5	65.2	54.7	54.2	42.8
1986	51,732	13,127	30,274	28,197	8,332	25.4	58.5	16.1	54.7	65.3	55.0	54.6	43.1

a Includes married, spouse absent.

b As of April

Sources:

1 U.S. Bureau of the Census, *Current Population Reports*, Ser. P-50 (for 1940–1955); *Statistical Abstract of the United States, 1987*, Table 653.

2 U.S. Bureau of Labor Statistics, Bulletin 2096; unpublished data.

Married, Separated, and Divorced Women—Labor Force Status, By Presence and Age of Children, 1960–1987

(As of March. For 1960, civilian noninstitutional persons age 14 and older; thereafter age 16 and older.)

Item	Total			No Children Under Age 18			Children Age 6–17 Only			Children Under Age 6		
	Married[a]	Separated	Divorced	Married[a]	Separated	Divorced	Married[a]	Separated	Divorced	Married[a]	Separated	Divorced
In Labor Force (in millions)												
1960	12.3	NA	NA	5.7	NA	NA	4.1	NA	NA	2.5	NA	NA
1970	18.4	1.4	1.9	8.2	.7	1.1	6.3	.4	.6	3.9	.3	.3
1980	24.9	1.9	4.4	11.2	.9	2.3	8.4	.6	1.6	5.2	.4	.5
1982	25.8	2.1	5.2	11.8	1.0	2.7	8.3	.7	1.8	5.7	.5	.6
1983	26.2	1.9	5.2	12.1	.8	2.8	8.3	.6	1.8	5.9	.5	.6
1984	26.9	2.0	5.5	12.3	.9	3.0	8.3	.7	1.9	6.2	.4	.6
1985	27.7	2.0	5.9	12.8	1.0	3.3	8.5	.7	2.0	6.4	.4	.6
1986	28.2	2.1	6.2	12.9	1.0	3.5	8.8	.6	2.0	6.6	.5	.7
1987	29.2	2.1	6.1	13.2	1.0	3.4	9.0	.7	2.0	7.0	.4	.7
Participation rate[b]												
1960	30.5	NA	NA	34.7	NA	NA	39.0	NA	NA	18.6	NA	NA
1970	40.8	52.1	71.5	42.2	52.3	67.7	49.2	60.6	82.4	30.3	45.4	63.3
1980	50.1	59.4	74.5	46.0	58.9	71.4	61.7	66.3	82.3	45.1	52.2	68.3
1982	51.2	60.0	74.9	46.2	57.5	71.6	63.2	68.4	83.6	48.7	55.2	67.2
1983	51.8	58.7	74.6	46.6	55.6	71.7	63.8	68.7	82.2	49.9	53.8	68.7
1984	52.8	60.9	74.3	47.2	59.1	70.5	65.4	70.1	84.1	51.8	53.9	67.7
1985	54.2	61.3	75.0	48.2	60.0	72.1	67.8	70.9	83.4	53.4	53.2	67.5
1986	54.6	62.2	76.0	48.2	60.4	72.1	68.4	70.6	84.7	53.8	57.4	73.8
1987	55.8	61.4	75.4	48.4	57.9	71.9	70.6	72.6	84.5	56.8	55.1	70.5

Employment (in millions)

Year												
1960	11.6	NA	NA	5.4	NA	NA	3.9	NA	NA	2.3	NA	NA
1970	17.5	1.3	1.8	7.9	.7	1.0	6.0	.4	.5	3.6	.3	.2
1980	23.6	1.7	4.2	10.7	.8	2.2	8.1	.6	1.5	4.8	.4	.5
1982	23.9	1.8	4.7	11.1	.8	2.5	7.7	.6	1.7	5.1	.4	.5
1983	24.3	1.5	4.7	11.4	.7	2.6	7.7	.5	1.5	5.2	.3	.5
1984	25.3	1.7	5.0	11.7	.8	2.8	7.9	.6	1.7	5.7	.3	.5
1985	26.1	1.8	5.4	12.2	.9	3.1	8.1	.6	1.8	5.9	.3	.5
1986	26.7	1.9	5.7	12.3	.9	3.3	8.3	.5	1.9	6.1	.4	.6
1987	27.8	1.9	5.7	12.7	.9	3.2	8.6	.6	1.9	6.5	.3	.3

Unemployment Rate[c]

Year												
1960	5.4	NA	NA	4.8	NA	NA	4.9	NA	NA	7.8	NA	NA
1970	4.8	6.8	5.4	3.3	4.2	4.7	4.8	5.9	6.5	7.9	13.3	5.2
1980	5.3	9.9	6.4	4.5	8.3	4.5	4.4	10.6	6.7	8.3	12.3	13.6
1982	7.1	14.5	8.9	5.7	11.7	7.6	7.0	14.6	9.2	10.1	20.1	13.5
1983	7.2	19.1	10.2	5.7	13.8	7.1	6.7	20.0	12.8	10.9	27.6	16.8
1984	5.7	13.9	8.6	4.6	9.0	6.6	5.0	13.1	9.7	8.9	25.0	14.3
1985	5.7	13.7	7.7	4.7	9.0	6.2	5.5	14.6	9.0	8.0	22.9	12.1
1986	5.4	10.8	7.5	4.6	7.2	6.1	4.8	11.7	8.2	7.6	16.5	12.9
1987	4.5	11.8	6.8	3.5	8.1	5.9	4.9	14.8	6.1	5.9	15.7	13.8

NA = not available

a Husband present.

b Percentage of women in each specific category in the labor force.

c Unemployed as a percentage of civilian labor force in specified group.

Sources:

1 U.S. Bureau of Labor Statistics, *Special Labor Force Reports*, Nos. 13, 130, and 134; Bulletin 2163; unpublished data.

2 U.S. Bureau of the Census, *Statistical Abstract of the United States, 1988*, Table 624.

Employed Civilians by Occupational Group, Sex, Race, and Educational Attainment, 1987

(As of March 1987. For civilian noninstitutional population age 25 and older.)

Sex, Race, and Years of School Completed	Total Employed	Managerial/ Professional	Technical/ Sales/ Administrative	Service[a]	Precision Production[b]	Operators Fabricators[c]	Farming, Forestry, Fishing
Number (in thousands)							
Men, Total:							
Less than 4 years of high school	8,306	476	703	943	2,350	3,050	783
4 years of high school only	18,551	2,120	3,453	1,784	5,534	4,801	860
1–3 years of college	9,539	2,352	2,810	937	1,905	1,277	259
4 years of college or more	14,166	9,470	3,058	437	627	403	171
White:							
Less than 4 years of high school	6,975	431	610	701	2,088	2,453	690
4 years of high school only	16,367	1,980	3,108	1,388	5,098	4,010	784
1–3 years of college	8,417	2,164	2,491	746	1,732	1,043	241
4 years of college or more	12,875	8,717	2,767	366	542	320	163
Black:							
Less than 4 years of high school	1,154	26	86	193	233	538	80
4 years of high school only	1,823	107	273	325	356	712	51
1–3 years of college	822	137	213	144	122	196	9
4 years of college or more	625	354	135	46	45	41	4
Women, Total:							
Less than 4 years of high school	4,932	245	1,033	1,973	228	1,327	128
4 years of high school only	17,538	2,190	9,392	3,361	532	1,876	188
1–3 years of college	8,344	2,345	4,569	919	136	311	65
4 years of college or more	9,315	6,392	2,357	331	87	119	29
White:							
Less than 4 years of high school	3,804	223	906	1,337	189	1,038	111
4 years of high school only	15,279	2,022	8,497	2,675	441	1,469	175
1–3 years of college	7,098	2,075	3,865	752	109	234	64
4 years of college or more	8,097	5,639	1,998	267	78	85	28
Black:							
Less than 4 years of high school	948	13	113	568	24	219	11
4 years of high school only	1,886	130	768	577	59	348	4
1–3 years of college	992	200	574	127	21	69	1
4 years of college or more	716	484	184	31	6	11	—

Percentage Distribution

Men, Total:							
Less than 4 years of high school	100.0	5.7	8.5	11.4	28.3	36.7	9.4
4 years of high school only	100.0	11.4	18.6	9.6	29.8	25.9	4.6
1–3 years of college	100.0	24.7	29.5	9.8	20.0	13.4	2.7
4 years of college or more	100.0	66.9	21.6	3.1	4.4	2.8	1.2
White:							
Less than 4 years of high school	100.0	6.2	8.7	10.1	29.9	35.2	9.9
4 years of high school only	100.0	12.1	19.0	8.5	31.1	24.5	4.8
1–3 years of college	100.0	25.7	29.6	8.9	20.5	12.4	2.9
4 years of college or more	100.0	67.7	21.5	2.8	4.2	2.5	1.3
Black:							
Less than 4 years of high school	100.0	2.2	7.4	16.7	20.2	46.5	6.9
4 years of high school only	100.0	5.9	15.0	17.8	19.5	39.0	2.8
1–3 years of college	100.0	16.7	25.9	17.5	14.9	23.9	1.1
4 years of college or more	100.0	56.6	21.6	7.4	7.2	6.6	.6
Women, Total:							
Less than 4 years of high school	100.0	5.0	20.9	40.0	4.6	26.9	2.6
4 years of high school only	100.0	12.5	53.5	19.2	3.0	10.7	1.1
1–3 years of college	100.0	28.1	54.8	11.0	1.6	3.7	.8
4 years of college or more	100.0	68.6	25.3	3.6	.9	1.3	.3
White:							
Less than 4 years of high school	100.0	5.9	23.8	35.1	5.0	27.3	2.9
4 years of high school only	100.0	13.2	55.6	17.5	2.9	9.6	1.1
1–3 years of college	100.0	29.2	54.4	10.6	1.5	3.3	.9
4 years of college or more	100.0	69.7	24.7	3.3	1.0	1.1	.3
Black:							
Less than 4 years of high school	100.0	1.4	11.9	59.9	2.5	23.1	1.2
4 years of high school only	100.0	6.9	40.7	30.6	3.1	18.5	.2
1–3 years of college	100.0	20.2	57.9	12.8	2.1	7.0	.1
4 years of college or more	100.0	67.6	25.7	4.3	.8	1.5	—

— = zero

a Includes private household workers.

b Includes craft and repair.

c Includes laborers.

Sources:

1 U.S. Bureau of Labor Statistics, unpublished data.

2 U.S. Bureau of the Census, *Statistical Abstract of the United States, 1988*, Table 628.

(In thousands. Household data not seasonally adjusted.)

Occupation	Total	Men		Women	
	Age 16 and Older	Age 16 and Older	Age 20 and Older	Age 16 and Older	Age 20 and Older
Total	117,066	65,164	60,622	51,902	47,783
Managerial and Professional Specialty	29,006	16,181	16,023	12,824	12,675
Executive, administrative, and managerial	14,541	8,837	8,768	5,704	5,655
Officials and administrators, public administration	555	328	329	227	228
Other executive, administrative, and managerial	10,134	6,602	6,540	3,532	3,489
Management-related occupations	3,851	1,907	1,899	1,944	1,938
Professional specialty	14,465	7,344	7,255	7,121	7,021
Engineers	1,850	1,723	1,717	127	126
Mathematical and computer scientists	793	517	514	276	276
Natural scientists	410	315	315	96	96
Health diagnosing occupations	797	651	651	146	144
Health assessment and treating occupations	2,210	349	344	1,861	1,858
Teachers, college and university	594	347	345	247	247
Teachers, except college and university	3,034	752	724	2,282	2,239
Lawyers and judges	720	594	593	126	124
Other professional specialty occupations	4,056	2,096	2,053	1,960	1,910
Technical, Sales and Administrative Support	35,880	12,632	11,876	23,248	21,153
Technicians and related support	3,659	1,960	1,917	1,699	1,673
Health technologists and technicians	1,246	225	225	1,022	1,010
Engineering and science technicians	1,173	930	903	243	234
Technicians, except health, engineering, and science	1,240	805	790	435	429
Sales occupations	13,926	7,070	6,605	6,856	5,711
Supervisors and proprietors	3,680	2,369	2,326	1,311	1,274
Sales representatives, finance and business services	2,407	1,423	1,396	984	951
Sales representatives, commodities, except retail	1,580	1,273	1,262	307	294
Sales workers, retail and personal services	6,195	1,985	1,601	4,210	3,152
Sales-related occupations	65	20	20	45	40
Administrative support, including clerical	18,295	3,602	3,354	14,693	13,770
Supervisors	832	369	365	463	462
Computer equipment operators	849	300	284	549	507
Secretaries, stenographers, and typists	4,916	95	87	4,822	4,561

(In thousands. Household data not seasonally adjusted.)

Occupation	Total Age 16 and Older	Men Age 16 and Older	Men Age 20 and Older	Women Age 16 and Older	Women Age 20 and Older
Financial records processing	2,464	220	211	2,244	2,194
Mail and message distributing	893	564	524	328	308
Other administrative support, including clerical	8,341	2,054	1,883	6,287	5,739
Service Occupations	15,635	6,230	5,121	9,405	7,918
Private household	992	39	32	953	719
Protective service	2,028	1,672	1,588	356	272
Service, except private household and protective	12,615	4,519	3,502	8,096	6,928
Food service	5,269	2,007	1,287	3,262	2,464
Health service	1,987	192	179	1,795	1,699
Cleaning and building service	3,189	1,840	1,643	1,348	1,248
Personal service	2,170	480	393	1,690	1,517
Precision Production, Craft, and Repair	14,134	12,899	12,472	1,235	1,190
Mechanics and repairers	4,623	4,505	4,376	119	117
Construction trades	5,364	5,235	5,000	129	120
Other precision production, craft, and repair	4,146	3,159	3,096	987	953
Operators, Fabricators, and Laborers	18,432	13,869	12,310	4,563	4,281
Machine operators, assemblers, and inspectors	8,211	4,942	4,703	3,269	3,141
Manufacturing industries	6,920	4,106	3,932	2,814	2,720
Durable goods	3,787	2,635	2,550	1,152	1,116
Nondurable goods	3,133	1,471	1,382	1,662	1,604
Nonmanufacturing industries	1,291	836	771	455	421
Transportation and material moving occupations	4,900	4,505	4,298	395	383
Motor vehicle operators	3,661	3,306	3,123	354	347
Other transportation and material moving occupations	1,239	1,199	1,175	40	36
Handlers, equipment cleaners, helpers, and laborers	5,321	4,422	3,308	899	757
Construction laborers	971	929	738	42	34
Other handlers, equipment cleaners, helpers, and laborers	4,350	3,492	2,571	857	723
Farming, Forestry, and Fishing	3,979	3,352	2,819	627	564
Farm operators and managers	1,360	1,146	1,129	214	212
Other farming, forestry, and fishing occupations	2,619	2,206	1,691	413	352

Source:
U.S. Bureau of Labor Statistics, *Employment and Earnings,* Aug. 1988, Table A-22.

(Percentage distribution. Household data not seasonally adjusted.)

Occupation and Race	Total	Men	Women
Total			
Total, age 16 and older (in thousands)	117,066	65,164	51,902
Percentage	100.0	100.0	100.0
Managerial and professional specialty	24.8	24.8	24.7
Executive, administrative, and managerial	12.4	13.6	11.0
Professional specialty	12.4	11.3	13.7
Technical, sales, and administrative support	30.6	19.4	44.8
Technicians and related support	3.1	3.0	3.3
Sales occupations	11.9	10.8	13.2
Administrative support, including clerical	15.6	5.5	28.3
Service occupations	13.4	9.6	18.1
Private household	.8	.1	1.8
Protective service	1.7	2.6	.7
Service, except private household and protective	10.8	6.9	15.6
Precision production, craft, and repair	12.1	19.8	2.4
Operators, fabricators, and laborers	15.7	21.3	8.8
Machine operators, assemblers, and inspectors	7.0	7.6	6.3
Transportation and material moving occupations	4.2	6.9	.8
Handlers, equipment cleaners, helpers, and laborers	4.5	6.8	1.7
Farming, forestry, and fishing	3.4	5.1	1.2
White			
Total, age 16 and older (in thousands)	101,432	57,125	44,307
Percentage	100.0	100.0	100.0
Managerial and professional specialty	25.8	25.8	25.7
Executive, administrative, and managerial	13.1	14.3	11.5
Professional specialty	12.7	11.5	14.2
Technical, sales, and administrative support	31.0	19.6	45.7
Technicians and related support	3.0	3.0	3.1
Sales occupations	12.5	11.5	13.8
Administrative support, including clerical	15.5	5.2	28.8

(Percentage distribution. Household data not seasonally adjusted.)

Occupation and Race	Total	Men	Women
Service occupations	12.2	8.6	16.8
Private household	.7	.1	1.6
Protective service	1.6	2.4	.6
Service, except private household and protective	9.8	6.1	14.6
Precision production, craft, and repair	12.5	20.4	2.3
Operators, fabricators, and laborers	15.0	20.3	8.2
Machine operators, assemblers, and inspectors	6.6	7.3	5.8
Transportation and material moving occupations	4.0	6.6	.7
Handlers, equipment cleaners, helpers, and laborers	4.4	6.4	1.7
Farming, forestry, and fishing	3.6	5.3	1.3
Black			
Total, age 16 and older (in thousands)	12,031	6,029	6,002
Percentage	100.0	100.0	100.0
Managerial and professional specialty	15.9	13.8	18.1
Executive, administrative, and managerial	7.4	7.0	7.8
Professional specialty	8.5	6.8	10.2
Technical, sales, and administrative support	27.0	16.4	37.6
Technicians and related support	3.1	2.9	3.3
Sales occupations	6.8	5.1	8.4
Administrative support, including clerical	17.1	8.3	25.8
Service occupations	23.0	17.9	28.1
Private household	2.0	.1	3.9
Protective service	2.8	4.2	1.2
Service, except private household and protective	18.2	13.6	22.9
Precision production, craft, and repair	8.9	15.4	2.4
Operators, fabricators, and laborers	23.1	32.8	13.2
Machine operators, assemblers, and inspectors	10.4	11.0	9.9
Transportation and material moving occupations	6.1	11.1	1.1
Handlers, equipment cleaners, helpers, and laborers	6.5	10.8	2.2
Farming, forestry, and fishing	2.2	3.8	.6

Source:
U.S. Bureau of Labor Statistics, *Employment and Earnings,* Aug. 1988, Table A-23.

Unemployment Rates, by Sex and Age Group, Selected Years, 1950–1987

| | Annual Average Unemployment Rates for | | | | | |
| | Men | | | Women | | |
Year	All (Age 16 and Older)	Age 16–19	Age 20 and Older	All (Age 16 and Older)	Age 16–19	Age 20 and Older
1950	5.1	12.7	4.7	5.7	11.4	5.1
1955	4.2	11.6	3.8	4.9	10.2	4.4
1960	5.4	15.3	4.7	5.9	13.9	5.1
1961	6.4	17.2	5.7	7.2	16.3	6.3
1962	5.2	14.7	4.6	6.2	14.6	5.4
1963	5.2	17.2	4.5	6.5	17.2	5.4
1964	4.6	15.8	3.9	6.2	16.7	5.2
1965	4.0	14.1	3.2	5.5	15.7	4.5
1966	3.2	11.7	2.5	4.8	14.1	3.8
1967	3.1	12.3	2.3	5.2	13.5	4.2
1968	2.9	11.6	2.2	4.8	14.0	3.8
1969	2.8	11.4	2.1	4.7	13.3	3.7
1970	4.4	15.0	3.5	5.9	15.6	4.8
1971	5.3	16.6	4.4	6.9	17.2	5.7
1972	4.9	15.9	4.0	6.6	16.7	5.4
1973	4.1	13.9	3.2	6.0	15.2	4.8
1974	4.8	15.5	3.8	6.7	16.5	5.5
1975	7.9	20.1	6.7	9.3	19.7	8.0
1976	7.0	19.2	5.9	8.6	18.7	7.4
1977	6.2	17.3	5.2	8.2	18.3	7.0
1978	5.2	15.7	4.2	7.2	17.0	6.0
1979	5.1	15.8	4.1	6.8	16.4	5.7
1980	6.9	18.2	5.9	7.4	17.2	6.3
1981	7.4	20.1	6.3	7.9	19.0	6.8
1982	9.9	24.4	8.8	9.4	21.9	8.3
1983	9.9	23.3	8.9	9.2	21.3	8.1
1984	7.4	19.6	6.6	7.6	18.0	6.8
1985	7.0	19.5	6.2	7.4	17.6	6.6
1986	6.9	19.0	6.1	7.1	17.6	6.2
1987	6.2	17.8	5.4	6.2	15.9	5.4

Sources:

1 U.S. Bureau of Labor Statistics, *Economic Report of the President,* 1977, Table B-28; *Monthly Labor Review,* Sept. 1979; May 1981; March 1983; Aug. 1985; Jan. 1988; *Employment and Earnings,* Jan. 1988.

2 ACE/Macmillan, *1989–90 Fact Book on Higher Education,* Table 41.

Unemployment Rate by Sex, Race, and Educational Attainment, 1970–1987

(Percentage as of March. Civilian noninstitutional population age 18 and older for 1970; age 16 and older for 1975 and later years.)

Item	1970	1975	1977	1978	1979	1980	1981	1982	1983	1984	1985	1986	1987
Men: Total[a]	3.7	9.0	7.5	6.3	5.8	6.8	8.1	10.3	11.9	8.6	7.8	7.8	7.4
High school: 1–3 years	5.6	14.7	13.4	12.1	11.9	12.8	15.6	19.4	21.4	17.6	16.2	15.3	15.4
4 years	3.4	9.1	7.2	5.9	5.5	6.9	8.8	11.3	13.6	9.4	8.3	8.6	7.5
College: 1–3 years	3.8	6.6	5.5	4.3	4.3	5.0	5.2[c]	7.5	9.3	5.7	5.0	5.4	5.7
4 years or more	1.3	2.5	2.8	2.2	1.9	1.8	2.1	3.2	3.6	2.8	2.6	2.5	2.7
Women: Total[a]	4.9	9.5	8.5	7.0	6.6	6.7	7.6	8.9	9.7	7.7	7.4	7.2	6.6
High school: 1–3 years	7.4	15.9	14.3	12.9	12.7	13.3	15.0	16.0	19.6	16.2	15.5	15.5	14.0
4 years	4.6	9.1	7.8	6.6	6.1	6.4	7.4	9.2	9.7	7.6	7.7	7.6	6.8
College: 1–3 years	4.0	7.4	6.8	5.1	4.3	4.9	5.0	6.1	6.8	6.1	5.3	5.1	4.9
4 years or more	2.0	3.6	4.2	3.0	3.0	2.5	3.0	3.3	4.0	2.7	2.5	2.4	2.4
White: Total[a]	3.9	8.5	7.2	5.8	5.4	6.0	7.0	8.6	9.7	7.2	6.6	6.6	6.1
High school: 1–3 years	5.7	14.0	12.7	10.7	10.9	11.6	13.5	17.0	19.0	15.2	14.2	13.5	13.1
4 years	3.6	8.4	6.8	5.5	5.0	5.9	7.2	9.1	10.3	7.4	7.0	7.0	6.2
College: 1–3 years	3.7	6.6	5.5	4.1	3.8	4.4	4.4	5.8	7.0	5.1	4.2	4.5	4.5
4 years or more	1.5	2.8	3.2	2.3	2.1	1.9	2.3	2.9	3.4	2.5	2.3	2.3	2.3
Black: Total[a,b]	6.7	14.7	14.7	13.2	12.6	13.4	15.9	18.9	21.0	17.1	15.6	15.0	14.5
High school: 1–3 years	9.5	22.0	20.0	21.6	19.6	20.5	24.7	24.1	29.5	27.1	24.7	24.7	23.2
4 years	7.2	15.2	14.4	12.7	12.8	13.1	16.4	20.7	22.8	18.3	16.2	16.1	14.3
College: 1–3 years	6.1	10.1	12.5	10.4	8.8	10.8	11.8	15.8	17.3	12.0	12.3	10.5	11.6
4 years or more	1.4	3.9	5.0	4.7	4.2	4.4	4.0	8.3	8.5	6.3	5.8	3.6	5.3
Hispanic origin:[c] Total[a]	NA	12.8	11.4	9.5	8.7	9.2	11.2	13.4	16.3	11.7	11.3	10.6	10.2
High school: 1–3 years	NA	18.4	17.2	14.0	14.6	14.3	17.0	21.8	23.9	18.4	15.7	17.1	14.8
4 years	NA	10.5	10.0	7.4	8.2	7.1	9.7	11.4	14.4	9.7	9.5	8.9	9.4
College: 1–3 years	NA	7.9	8.2	7.3	6.5	5.9	6.3	7.1	10.9	7.6	7.4	6.8	7.2
4 years or more	NA	3.6	5.0	7.3	3.6	3.7	2.8	4.9	6.8	3.6	3.1	3.2	2.6

NA = not available

a   Includes persons reporting no school years completed and elementary completed.

b   For 1970 and 1975, data refer to black and other workers.

c   Hispanic persons may be of any race.

Sources:

1   U.S. Bureau of Labor Statistics, *Handbook of Labor Statistics*; unpublished data.

2   U.S. Bureau of the Census, *Statistical Abstract of the United States, 1988*, Table 634.

(Persons age 15 and older)	Number With Income (in thousands)	Median Income (in dollars)
Women		
All Women	29,844	$17,504
United States		
All races	29,844	17,504
White	25,235	17,775
Black	3,668	16,211
Hispanic	1,866	14,893
Educational attainment		
Total, age 25 and older	26,409	18,531
Elementary: Total	935	10,952
Less than 8 years	518	9,927
8 years	417	12,174
High school: Total	13,160	15,952
1–3 years	1,864	12,940
4 years	11,296	16,461
College: Total	12,313	22,554
1–3 years	5,706	19,843
4 years or more	6,607	25,645
4 years	4,024	23,406
5 years or more	2,583	29,694
Men		
All Men	47,094	26,722
United States		
All races	47,094	26,722
White	41,788	27,468
Black	3,972	19,385
Hispanic	3,416	17,872
Educational attainment		
Total, age 25 and older	42,849	28,313
Elementary: Total	2,526	16,442
Less than 8 years	1,484	14,903
8 years	1,042	18,939
High school: Total	19,336	26,660
1–3 years	3,605	21,269
4 years	15,731	25,394
College: Total	20,987	34,380
1–3 years	8,088	29,536
4 years or more	12,899	37,854
4 years	7,096	35,244
5 years or more	5,803	41,691

Note: Hispanics may be of any race.

Source:
U.S. Bureau of the Census, *Current Population Reports,* Ser. P-60, No. 161, Table 7.

Median Annual Income of Year-Round, Full-Time Workers Age 25 and Older, by Years of School Completed and Sex, 1970–1985

19

Sex and Year	Total	Elementary School		High School		College		
		Less Than 8 Years	8 Years	1–3 Years	4 Years	1–3 Years	4 Years	5 Years or More
1	2	3	4	5	6	7	8	9
Men								
1970	$ 9,521	$ 6,043	$ 7,535	$ 8,514	$ 9,567	$11,183	$13,264	$14,747
1971	10,038	6,310	7,838	8,945	9,996	11,701	13,730	15,300
1972	11,148	7,042	8,636	9,462	11,073	12,428	14,879	16,877
1973	12,088	7,521	9,406	10,401	12,017	13,090	15,503	17,726
1974	12,786	7,912	9,891	11,225	12,642	13,718	16,240	18,214
1975	13,821	8,647	10,600	11,511	13,542	14,989	17,477	19,658
1976	14,732	8,991	11,312	12,301	14,295	15,514	18,236	20,597
1977	15,726	9,419	12,083	13,120	15,434	16,235	19,603	21,941
1978	16,882	10,474	12,965	14,199	16,396	17,411	20,941	23,578
1979	18,711	10,993	14,454	15,198	18,100	19,367	22,406	25,860
1980	20,297	11,753	14,674	16,101	19,469	20,909	24,311	27,690
1981	21,689	12,866	16,084	16,938	20,598	22,565	26,394	30,434
1982	22,857	12,386	16,376	17,496	21,344	23,633	28,030	32,325
1983	23,891	14,093	16,438	17,685	21,823	24,613	29,892	34,643
1984	25,497	14,624	16,812	19,120	23,269	25,831	31,487	36,836
1985	26,365	14,766	18,645	18,881	23,853	26,960	32,822	39,335
Women								
1970	5,616	3,798	4,181	4,655	5,580	6,604	8,156	9,581
1971	5,872	3,946	4,400	4,889	5,808	6,815	8,451	10,581
1972	6,331	4,221	4,784	5,253	6,166	7,020	8,736	11,036
1973	6,791	4,369	5,135	5,513	6,623	7,593	9,057	11,340
1974	7,370	5,022	5,606	5,919	7,150	8,072	9,523	11,790
1975	8,117	5,109	5,691	6,355	7,777	9,126	10,349	13,138
1976	8,728	5,644	6,433	6,800	8,377	9,475	11,010	13,569
1977	9,257	6,074	6,564	7,387	8,894	10,157	11,605	14,338
1978	10,121	6,648	7,489	7,996	9,769	10,634	12,347	15,310
1979	11,071	7,414	7,788	8,555	10,513	11,854	13,441	16,693
1980	12,156	7,742	8,857	9,676	11,537	12,954	15,143	18,100
1981	13,259	8,419	9,723	10,043	12,332	14,343	16,322	20,148
1982	14,477	8,424	10,112	10,661	13,240	15,594	17,405	21,449
1983	15,292	9,385	10,337	11,131	13,787	16,536	18,452	22,877
1984	16,169	9,828	10,848	11,843	14,569	17,007	20,257	25,076
1985	17,124	9,736	11,377	11,836	15,481	17,989	21,389	25,928

Sources:
1 U.S. Bureau of the Census, *Current Population Reports,* Ser. P-60 (various years); No. 154.

2 National Center for Education Statistics, *Digest of Education Statistics, 1988,* Table 237.

Educational Attainment and Monthly Income

Highest Degree Earned	All		Men		Women		White		Black	
	Percentage of Adults	Monthly Income	Percentage of Adults	Monthly Income	Percentage of Adults	Monthly Income	Percentage of Adults	Monthly Income	Percentage of Adults	Monthly Income
Doctorate	0.5%	$3,265	0.7%	$3,667	0.2%	a	0.5%	$3,342	0.02%	a
Professional	1.0	3,871	1.8	4,309	0.3	1,864	1.1	3,927	0.3	a
Master's	3.4	2,288	3.8	2,843	3.0	1,645	3.6	2,287	1.5	1,966
Bachelor's	10.6	1,841	11.9	2,455	9.5	1,148	11.1	1,881	5.2	1,388
Associate	3.4	1,346	3.5	1,755	3.3	959	3.5	1,367	2.6	1,158
Vocational	1.8	1,219	1.3	1,822	2.3	923	1.9	1,248	1.4	860
Some college, no degree	17.8	1,169	19.1	1,534	16.6	789	17.8	1,213	17.5	862
High school diploma	35.5	1,045	32.7	1,510	38.0	684	36.1	1,080	32.7	765
No high school diploma	26.0	693	25.3	973	26.7	453	24.4	734	38.6	513
Average monthly income	100.0	1,155	100.0	1,620	100.0	734	100.0	1,208	100.0	754
Population total	170,232,000		80,834,000		89,398,000		147,147,000		18,475,000	

a Insufficient data.

Source:
Chronicle of Higher Education, Oct. 14, 1987.

	Bachelor's Degree	Advanced Degree		Bachelor's Degree	Advanced Degree
Agriculture, forestry	$1,945	a	Liberal arts, humanities	$1,400	$1,720
Biology	1,559	a	Mathematics, statistics	2,116	a
Business, management	2,381	3,564	Medicine, dentistry	a	4,234
Economics	2,846	a	Nursing, pharmacy, health technologies	1,424	1,804
Education	1,290	2,062	Physical science, earth science	2,529	2,913
Engineering	2,833	3,308	Psychology	1,251	2,282
English, journalism	1,477	1,945	Religion, theology	a	1,584
Home economics	1,065	a	Social studies	1,610	2,124
Law	a	4,060	**All fields**	**$1,841**	**$2,711**

Note: The figures are based on a survey of 19,000 households conducted in the spring of 1984 as part of the U.S. Census Bureau's Survey of Income and Program Participation. They cover the civilian, resident U.S. population of adults age 18 and older.

a Insufficient data.

Source:
Chronicle of Higher Education, Oct. 14, 1987.

High School Dropouts Among Persons Age 14–34, by Age, Race/Ethnicity, and Sex, October 1970, 1975, 1980, and 1985

21

Total, Age 14–34

Race/Ethnicity and Sex	October, 1970	October, 1975	October, 1980	October, 1985
All races				
Total	17.0	14.1	13.0	12.0
Men	16.2	13.2	13.2	12.3
Women	17.7	15.0	12.8	11.7
White				
Total	15.2	12.8	12.1	11.5
Men	14.4	12.1	12.4	11.8
Women	16.0	13.5	11.8	11.1
Black				
Total	30.0	23.4	18.8	15.5
Men	30.4	21.9	19.0	15.6
Women	29.5	24.7	18.7	15.4
Hispanic origin[a]				
Total		33.0	35.2	31.4
Men		29.9	35.6	32.1
Women		35.7	34.9	30.8

a   Persons of Hispanic origin are also included, as appropriate, in the white and black categories.

Note: Dropouts are persons who are not enrolled in school and who are not high school graduates. People who have received GED credentials are counted as graduates. Data are based upon sample surveys of the civilian noninstitutional population.

Sources:

1   U.S. Bureau of the Census, *Current Population Reports*, Ser. P-20, Nos. 222, 303, 362, 392, 409.

2   National Center for Education Statistics, *Digest of Educational Statistics 1987*, Table 72.

Population and High School Graduates, Age 18–34, by Sex, Race, Hispanic Origin, and Mexican Origin, 1976 and 1986

22

(Numbers in thousands. Civilian noninstitutional population.)

	Total Population		High School Graduates	
	Women	Men	Women	Men
All Races				
1976	30,100	28,263	24,570	22,989
1986	34,913	33,499	29,943	28,048
White				
1976	25,817	24,775	21,434	20,575
1986	28,994	28,433	25,185	24,060
Black				
1976	3,661	2,970	2,638	1,965
1986	4,747	3,981	3,791	3,064
Hispanic				
1976	1,858	1,544	980	833
1986	2,912	3,151	1,797	1,843
Mexican				
1976	1,101	971	532	458
1986	1,766	2,223	1,022	1,181

Note: Persons of Hispanic and Mexican origin may be of any race.

Source:
U.S. Bureau of the Census, *Current Population Reports,* Ser. P-20, No. 319, Table 1; No. 429, Table 1.

Overall High School Grade Average[a]	Percentage — Women	Percentage — Men
3.75–4.00	15.6	13.3
3.50–3.74	12.3	10.1
3.25–3.49	13.2	11.8
3.00–3.24	17.6	17.0
2.75–2.99	12.4	12.4
2.50–2.74	12.3	13.2
2.25–2.49	7.7	9.5
2.00–2.24	5.5	7.6
Under 2.00	3.4	5.1
Mean Grade Point Average	3.07	2.98
Number Responding[b]	476,311	425,217
High School Rank		
Top tenth	21.9	20.2
Second tenth	20.8	20.5
Second fifth	25.6	26.8
Third fifth	27.7	27.8
Fourth fifth	3.4	3.9
Lowest fifth	0.5	0.7
Median Percentile Rank	74.2	73.0
Number Responding[c]	455,745	415,368

a   Calculated by weighting the latest self-reported grade in each of the 6 subject areas (English, mathematics, foreign languages, biological sciences, physical sciences, and social studies) by the number of years of study in the subject, and dividing by the total number of years of study in all 6 subjects. If a grade was not reported in a subject, that subject was not used in the calculation of overall grade average.

b   The number who responded to SDQ Questions 6-17 for whom a weighted GPA could be calculated.

c   The number who responded to SDQ Question 5.

Source:
The College Board, *Profiles, College-Bound Seniors, 1985,* Table 7.

	Verbal			Mathematics		
	Men	Women	Total	Men	Women	Total
1967	463	468	466	514	467	492
1968	464	466	466	512	470	492
1969	459	466	463	513	470	493
1970	459	461	460	509	465	488
1971	454	457	455	507	466	488
1972	454	452	453	505	461	484
1973	446	443	445	502	460	481
1974	447	442	444	501	459	480
1975	437	431	434	495	449	472
1976	433	430	431	497	446	472
1977	431	427	429	497	445	470
1978	433	425	429	494	444	468
1979	431	423	427	493	443	467
1980	428	420	424	491	443	466
1981	430	418	424	492	443	466
1982	431	421	426	493	443	467
1983	430	420	425	493	445	468
1984	433	420	426	495	449	471
1985	437	425	431	499	452	475
1986	437	426	431	501	451	475
1987	435	425	430	500	453	476
1988	435	422	428	498	455	476

a The average for 1967–1971 are estimates. College-Bound Seniors reports were not prepared in those years.

Source:
The College Board, *College-Bound Seniors: 1988 Profile of SAT and Achievement Test Takers,* Table A.

Percentage of 1980 High School Seniors Beginning Postsecondary Education During Academic Year 1980–81, by Type of Institution Attended and Selected Student and High School Characteristics

	Never in Postsecondary	Delayed Entry	Part-Timer	Proprietary School	Private Technical Junior College	Public Technical Junior College	Public 2-Year Junior College	Private 4-Year University	Public 4-Year University
Total	36.4	8.3	6.1	2.1	1.0	1.7	13.5	10.5	20.5
Sex									
Men	39.6	8.5	5.6	1.3	0.5	1.9	12.8	10.2	19.7
Women	33.3	8.1	6.6	2.8	1.5	1.5	14.1	10.9	21.2
Race/Ethnicity									
Hispanic	44.3	10.3	8.4	1.8	0.4	1.4	16.4	4.8	12.1
American Indian	37.4	18.6	5.9	1.5	1.6	4.3	14.6	3.8	12.3
Asian	12.2	5.5	12.1	1.1	0.0	0.7	22.3	13.3	32.6
Black	40.7	9.7	3.9	2.8	0.9	1.5	11.3	8.6	20.6
White	35.2	7.8	6.2	2.0	1.0	1.8	13.5	11.3	21.1
Hispanic Subgroups									
Mexican	45.4	11.6	8.9	2.4	0.1	1.8	17.0	2.7	10.0
Cuban	17.3	9.3	9.5	1.1	0.0	0.0	31.6	17.3	13.9
Puerto Rican	48.5	11.6	2.3	1.8	0.3	0.0	5.5	8.5	21.4
Other Hispanic	45.9	7.3	9.3	0.5	1.3	1.2	16.0	5.5	13.0
Socioeconomic Status Quartile									
Low	53.2	9.7	5.2	1.7	0.8	1.6	11.9	4.7	11.2
25%–49%	43.3	8.0	6.1	2.4	0.9	1.2	14.6	8.1	15.2
50%–75%	28.4	8.9	7.5	2.4	1.4	1.6	15.3	9.3	25.2
High	12.2	6.7	6.1	1.5	1.1	2.6	14.0	21.9	33.9

Note: Socioeconomic status was measured by a composite score of parental education, family income, father's occupation, and household characteristics in 1980.

Source:
National Center for Education Statistics, "The Timing of Abnormal Progression Among 1980 High School Seniors Entering Postsecondary Education in October 1980," Table 1, unpublished tabulations from *High School and Beyond: Senior Second Follow-up,* July 1986. See Guide to Sources.

College Enrollment and Percent of High School Graduates Enrolled in, or Completed One or More Years of College, by Sex and Race, 1960–1986

26

(As of October, unless noted. Civilian noninstitutional population, age 14–24.)

Item and Year	All Persons			Men			Women		
	Total[a]	White	Black	Total[a]	White	Black	Total[a]	White	Black
College Enrollment (in thousands):									
1960[b]	2,279	2,138	141[c]	1,365	1,297	68[c]	914	841	73[c]
1970	6,065	5,535	437	3,461	3,213	202	2,604	2,322	236
1975	7,228	6,368	699	3,821	3,437	308	3,407	2,931	392
1980	7,475	6,546	718	3,700	3,303	292	3,778	3,243	426
1985	7,799	6,729	755	3,880	3,374	355	3,917	3,357	400
1986	7,613	6,426	820	3,739	3,206	350	3,874	3,221	471
Percentage of High School Graduates Enrolled:									
1960[b]	23.8	24.3	18.7[c]	30.4	31.1	21.1[c]	18.0	18.1	16.9[c]
1970	33.3	33.9	26.7	41.8	42.9	29.5	26.3	26.3	24.7
1975	33.1	33.0	32.5	36.7	36.9	33.4	29.9	29.4	32.0
1980	32.3	32.5	28.3	33.8	34.3	27.0	30.9	30.9	29.2
1985	34.3	35.0	26.5	36.0	36.6	28.2	32.8	33.6	25.1
1986	34.4	34.6	28.8	35.7	36.1	28.2	33.3	33.3	29.4
Percentage of High School Graduates Enrolled in College or Completed 1 or More Years of College:									
1960[b]	40.4	41.0	32.5[c]	46.1	47.1	33.5[c]	35.3	35.6	31.8[c]
1970	52.3	53.4	40.0	59.2	60.8	41.2	46.5	47.1	39.0
1975	52.5	52.7	48.0	56.1	56.6	50.3	49.2	49.1	46.4
1980	51.1	51.4	46.2	51.4	51.8	44.4	51.0	51.0	47.5
1985	54.3	55.3	43.8	54.6	55.5	43.5	54.0	55.2	43.9
1986	54.8	55.3	47.4	54.2	55.0	43.7	55.3	55.6	50.2

a Includes other races, not shown separately.

b As of April

c Black and other races.

Source:
U.S. Bureau of the Census, *U.S. Census of Population: 1960,* vol. I; *Characteristics of the Population,* part 1; *Current Population Reports,* Ser. P-20, No. 409 and earlier reports; *Statistical Abstract of the United States, 1988,* Table 233; unpublished data.

Weighted National Norms for All Women

Degree, Major and Career Plans	1966	1967	1968	1969	1970	1971	1972	1973	1974	1975	1976	1977	1978	1979	1980	1981	1982	1983	1984	1985	1987
Highest Academic Degree Planned at Any College																					
None	4.8	4.4	4.1	2.3	2.7	3.2	3.6	3.8	3.9	3.7	3.3	2.3	2.3	1.8	2.3	2.3	1.7	1.9	1.5	2.1	2.0
Vocational certificate[a]	–	–	–	–	–	–	–	–	–	–	–	–	–	–	–	–	–	1.4	0.9	1.0	1.4
Associate or equivalent	7.3	9.3	8.4	10.9	10.3	10.2	10.1	10.5	10.9	9.4	9.7	10.2	9.3	8.9	9.5	9.5	9.8	8.2	8.1	7.1	6.2
Bachelor's degree (B.A., B.S., etc.)	46.1	43.7	44.2	44.0	43.6	42.5	41.3	40.3	39.2	37.0	37.2	36.4	38.5	37.5	38.1	38.2	38.8	36.6	37.4	38.1	34.7
Master's degree (M.A., M.S., etc.)	32.3	32.9	33.1	32.6	30.8	29.9	28.9	28.5	28.0	29.6	29.4	30.8	29.9	32.1	30.1	31.2	30.2	30.7	31.2	31.7	34.5
Ph. D. or Ed. D.	5.2	5.7	6.1	6.1	6.5	6.7	6.8	6.9	6.9	7.6	7.6	8.0	8.1	8.0	7.3	7.2	7.6	8.0	8.7	8.6	10.0
M.D., D.D.S., D.V.M., or D.O.	1.9	1.9	1.7	1.8	2.2	3.3	4.3	4.8	5.3	5.5	5.7	5.2	5.6	5.5	5.9	5.6	5.7	6.0	6.1	6.0	5.4
LL.B. or J.D.	*	*	*	*	0.9	1.5	2.1	2.4	2.6	3.1	3.5	3.7	3.6	3.5	3.7	3.5	3.8	3.9	3.7	3.4	4.2
B.D. or M.Div.	0.1	0.1	0.2	0.2	0.1	0.2	0.2	0.2	0.1	0.4	0.4	0.4	0.3	0.4	0.4	0.3	0.3	0.6	0.5	0.3	0.2
Other	1.8	1.8	2.1	1.9	2.9	2.8	2.7	2.9	3.0	3.7	3.3	3.0	2.4	2.3	2.6	2.3	2.1	2.7	2.0	1.7	1.4

a Item not shown for years 1966–1982.

* Data not compatible to other years due to change in question, response option, or processing.

Sources:

1 Astin, A. W., Green, K. C. & Korn, W. S., *The American Freshman: Twenty Year Trends*, 1987.

2 Astin, A. W., Green, K. C., Korn, W. S. & Schalit, M., *The American Freshman: National Norms for Fall 1987*, 1987.

Weighted National Norms for All Men

Degree, Major and Career Plans	1966	1967	1968	1969	1970	1971	1972	1973	1974	1975	1976	1977	1978	1979	1980	1981	1982	1983	1984	1985	1987
Highest Academic Degree Planned at Any College																					
None	6.1	4.1	4.1	1.9	1.6	2.4	3.2	3.5	3.8	3.8	3.1	2.3	2.1	1.7	2.4	2.0	2.0	2.2	1.6	2.0	2.0
Vocational certificate[a]	–	–	–	–	–	–	–	–	–	–	–	–	–	–	–	–	–	1.7	1.2	1.4	1.6
Associate or equivalent	4.1	5.6	5.4	7.1	5.4	6.0	6.5	6.4	6.3	6.3	6.7	6.6	6.0	5.6	6.9	7.2	6.8	5.8	5.3	5.2	4.4
Bachelor's degree (B.A., B.S., etc.)	32.5	32.3	33.7	33.7	33.9	33.9	33.9	34.3	34.6	32.7	34.2	34.8	35.8	35.4	37.2	37.5	37.8	36.4	37.8	38.3	35.9
Master's degree (M.A., M.S., etc.)	31.2	32.1	32.1	33.2	31.5	28.8	26.0	26.2	26.4	27.1	27.9	29.4	30.2	32.4	29.3	30.9	30.8	30.1	31.2	31.5	34.1
Ph. D. or Ed. D.	13.7	14.1	14.0	13.4	12.3	11.5	10.6	10.3	10.0	10.4	9.8	10.2	9.8	9.4	8.5	8.7	8.8	9.0	9.6	9.9	10.7
M.D., D.D.S., D.V.M., or D.O.	7.4	7.0	6.1	5.9	6.7	8.2	9.7	9.6	9.4	8.8	8.3	7.2	7.6	7.0	7.0	6.3	6.3	6.7	6.4	5.9	5.1
LL.B. or J.D.	*	*	*	*	5.6	6.1	6.5	6.3	6.0	6.2	6.0	5.8	5.5	5.2	4.9	4.5	4.7	4.3	4.3	3.8	4.2
B.D. or M.Div.	0.5	0.5	0.4	0.5	0.6	0.6	0.6	0.7	0.7	0.9	0.7	0.7	0.6	0.8	0.6	0.6	0.6	0.8	0.7	0.4	0.4
Other	2.1	1.8	2.0	2.1	2.4	2.9	2.9	2.9	2.7	3.9	3.3	2.9	2.4	2.4	3.1	2.3	2.2	2.9	2.3	1.6	1.5

a Item not shown for years 1966–1982.

* Data not compatible to other years due to change in question, response option, or processing.

Sources:

1 Astin, A. W., Green, K. C. & Korn, W. S., *The American Freshman: Twenty Year Trends*, 1987.

2 Astin, A. W., Green, K. C., Korn, W. S. & Schalit, M., *The American Freshman: National Norms for Fall 1987*, 1987.

Student Characteristics	Percentage of Freshmen[a] in All Institutions					
	Men			Women		
	1966	1977	1987	1966	1977	1987
Highest Degree Planned						
None	6.1	2.3	2.0	4.8	2.3	2.0
Vocational Certificate	—	—	1.6	—	—	1.4
Associate Degree	4.1	6.6	4.4	7.3	10.2	6.2
Bachelor's	32.5	34.8	35.9	46.1	36.4	34.7
Master's	31.2	29.4	34.1	32.3	30.8	34.5
Ph.D. or Ed.D.	13.7	10.2	10.7	5.2	8.0	10.0
M.D., D.O., D.D.S., or D.V.M.	7.4	7.2	5.1	1.9	5.2	5.4
L.L.B. or J.D.	2.5	5.8	4.2	0.3	3.7	4.2
B.D. or M.Div.	0.5	0.7	0.4	0.1	0.4	0.2
Other	2.1	2.9	1.5	1.8	3.0	1.4
Racial Background						
White/Caucasian	90.9	87.9	87.6	90.5	86.0	84.5
Black/Negro/Afro-American	4.5	7.8	7.2	5.6	9.8	10.0
American Indian	0.5	0.8	0.9	0.6	0.7	0.9
Asian American/Oriental	0.8	1.2	2.6	0.7	1.0	2.1
Mexican-American/Chicano	—	1.4	0.9	—	1.4	1.1
Puerto Rican-American	—	0.9	0.9	—	1.0	1.5
Other	3.3	1.9	1.6	2.7	1.6	1.7
Concern about Financing Education						
No concern	34.9	37.3	42.7	35.3	30.4	32.3
Some concern	57.0	47.6	45.9	55.5	51.3	51.8
Major concern	8.1	15.1	11.3	9.2	18.3	15.9
Average Grade in High School						
A−, A, A+	11.3	15.8	18.6	20.2	23.5	23.8
B−, B, B+	49.5	60.2	56.8	59.6	62.9	60.4
C, C+	37.9	23.4	23.9	19.9	13.5	15.6
D	1.3	0.6	0.6	0.3	0.2	0.2
Objectives Considered to Be Essential or Very Important						
Help others in difficulty	59.2	57.3	50.0	79.5	73.0	66.5
Be an authority in my field	70.3	77.5	78.1	60.8	72.1	76.4
Be very well off financially	54.1	65.6	79.5	31.6	50.7	72.1

Student Characteristics	Percentage of Freshmen[a] in All Institutions					
	Men			Women		
	1966	1977	1987	1966	1977	1987
Raise a family	NA	58.8	55.9	NA	58.9	59.5
Obtain recognition from colleagues	48.0	51.8	59.5	36.3	44.9	57.3
Probable Major Field of Study						
Agriculture (includes forestry)	3.4	3.3	2.1	0.1	1.4	0.7
Biological sciences	4.2	4.8	3.8	3.1	4.5	3.7
Business	17.3	23.8	28.6	10.9	21.1	26.0
Education	4.7	3.8	4.0	17.5	13.6	13.3
Engineering	17.9	17.0	17.0	0.3	1.8	2.7
English	1.9	0.6	0.9	7.3	1.3	1.5
Fine and Applied Arts	6.8	3.6	4.7	10.3	5.5	5.7
Health professional (non-M.D.)	1.5	2.3	1.9	9.8	15.5	9.4
History, political science	7.8	3.6	3.7	5.7	2.4	3.1
Humanities (other)	2.4	2.3	2.0	7.4	3.8	3.1
Mathematics or statistics	4.6	1.0	0.6	4.5	0.7	0.6
Physical science	5.0	3.5	2.3	1.2	1.3	0.9
Preprofessional	11.3	3.8	1.3	2.3	2.8	2.5
Social science[b]	5.2	3.2	3.0	11.7	8.0	7.9
Other fields	4.0	19.4	17.4	6.1	11.2	11.1
Undecided	1.9	4.0	5.4	1.8	5.3	7.6
Probable Career Occupation						
Artists (includes performer)	4.6	2.2	3.0	8.9	2.9	3.3
Businessman	18.5	22.7	28.0	3.3	18.7	24.2
Clergy or religious worker[c]	1.2	0.8	0.4	0.8	0.2	0.1
Doctor (M.D. or D.D.S.)[d]	7.4	5.3	4.2	1.7	3.0	3.8
Educator (college teacher)	2.1	0.3	0.4	1.5	0.3	0.3
Educator (secondary ed.)	10.5	2.3	2.7	18.4	3.5	3.5
Educator (elementary ed.)	0.8	0.6<	0.7	15.7	7.5	8.8
Engineer	16.3	15.1	15.2	0.2	1.5	2.6
Farmer or forester[e]	3.2	4.9	1.9	0.2	1.5	0.4
Health professional (non-M.D.)	3.1	4.2	2.7	6.6	10.8	9.2
Lawyer	6.7	5.5	4.5	0.7	3.4	4.5
Nurse	0.1	0.3	0.2	5.3	8.8	4.0
Research scientist	4.9	2.8	1.8	1.9	1.6	1.2
Other occupation	15.8	24.1	24.2	31.0	25.1	21.7
Undecided	5.0	8.8	9.9	3.6	10.7	12.6

NA = not available

— = item not shown in report

a Weighted national norms for first-time, full-time freshmen based on data from a sample of over 150,000 students each year.

b Listed as "psychology, sociology, anthropology" in 1966.

c Listed as "clergyman" in 1966.

d Listed as "doctor (M.D.)" in 1966.

e Listed as "farmer" in 1966.

Sources:

1 Astin, A. W., Panos, R. J., & Creager, J. A., *National Norms for Entering College Freshmen, Fall 1966*, 1966.

2 Astin, A. W., King, M. R., & Richardson, G. T., *The American Freshman: National Norms for Fall 1977*, 1977.

3 Astin, A. W., Green, K. C., Korn, W. S. & Shalit, M., *The American Freshman: National Norms for Fall 1987*, 1987.

4 ACE/Macmillan, *1989–90 Fact Book on Higher Education*, Table 121.

29a

Attitudes and Values	1967	1970	1977	1980	1987
Objectives Considered to be Essential or Very Important					
Become accomplished in one of the performing arts					
(acting, dancing, etc.)[a]	14.6	14.8	15.6	13.2	14.0
Become an authority in my field	63.7	60.8	72.1	71.7	76.4
Obtain recognition from colleagues for contributions					
to my special field[a]	34.9	33.4	44.9	52.5	59.3
Become an expert in finance and commerce	4.0	8.6	NA	NA	21.5
Have administrative responsibility for					
the work of others[a]	17.7	14.7	30.9	37.0	43.4
Be very well-off financially	30.0	28.0	50.7	57.8	72.1
Help others who are in difficulty	73.6	74.0	73.0	72.7	66.5
Participate in an organization like the Peace Corps					
or Vista[a]	28.0	26.1	NA	NA	NA
Become a community leader	18.9	11.5	NA	NA	NA
Make a theoretical contribution to science[a]	6.1	6.2	10.7	11.5	9.3
Write original works (poems, novels, etc.)	16.7	15.9	15.8	13.8	12.7
Never be obligated to people	23.2	20.8	NA	NA	NA
Create artistic work (painting, sculpture, decorating, etc.)	22.1	21.4	19.2	16.5	13.9
Help promote racial understanding	NA	NA	39.7	35.8	30.2
Keep up to date with political affairs	49.1	50.6	35.2	35.0	NA
Be successful in my own business[a]	32.8	31.9	38.6	43.6	46.4
Develop a meaningful philosophy of life	87.6	79.1	61.5	52.1	39.2
Influence the political structure	NA	14.0	12.2	12.6	13.6
Influence social values	NA	36.2	32.7	34.8	38.8
Raise a family	NA	72.4	58.9	63.6	59.5
Participate in a community action program	NA	32.3	32.4	30.3	21.6
Become involved in programs to clean up the environment	NA	NA	27.8	25.4	14.9

NA = not available

a   Text or format of question differs slightly in different years.

Sources:
1   Astin, A. W., Green, K. C., & Korn, W. S., *The American Freshman: Twenty Year Trends,* 1987.
2   Astin, A. W., Green, K. C., Korn, W. S., & Shalit, M., *The American Freshman: National Norms for Fall 1987,* 1987.

Attitudes and Values	1967	1970	1977	1980	1987
Objectives Considered to be Essential or Very Important					
Become accomplished in one of the performing arts					
(acting, dancing, etc.)[a]	8.7	11.1	11.3	10.7	11.1
Become an authority in my field	71.0	71.7	77.5	74.7	78.1
Obtain recognition from colleagues for contributions					
to my special field[a]	46.2	45.3	51.8	56.4	59.5
Become an expert in finance and commerce	17.5	21.7	NA	NA	34.5
Have administrative responsibility for					
the work of others[a]	30.6	27.4	37.9	40.5	47.0
Be very well-off financially	54.2	48.3	65.6	69.4	79.5
Help others who are in difficulty	52.3	57.4	57.3	56.0	56.0
Participate in an organization like the Peace Corps					
or Vista[a]	11.6	14.3	NA	NA	NA
Become a community leader	27.7	18.3	NA	NA	NA
Make a theoretical contribution to science[a]	15.8	13.4	17.4	18.5	15.9
Write original works (poems, novels, etc.)	11.5	12.4	11.7	11.1	12.8
Never be obligated to people	26.2	24.2	NA	NA	NA
Create artistic work (painting, sculpture, decorating, etc.)	10.2	11.9	12.3	12.1	12.6
Help promote racial understanding	NA	NA	31.9	30.1	27.6
Keep up to date with political affairs	51.8	54.7	44.5	45.4	NA
Be successful in my own business[a]	57.3	53.9	55.5	55.4	55.4
Develop a meaningful philosophy of life	79.1	72.6	56.4	48.7	39.6
Influence the political structure	NA	21.8	19.2	20.1	19.5
Influence social values	NA	32.3	29.0	29.4	32.8
Raise a family	NA	63.5	58.8	62.5	55.9
Participate in a community action program	NA	27.0	26.5	24.1	17.7
Become involved in programs to clean up the environment	NA	NA	31.1	28.1	20.8

NA = not available

a Text or format of question differs slighty in different years.

Sources:

1 Astin, A. W., Green, K. C., & Korn, W. S., *The American Freshman: Twenty Year Trends*, 1987, p. 49.

2 Astin, A. W., Green, K. C., Korn, W. S., & Shalit, M., *The American Freshman: National Norms for Fall 1987*, 1987, p. 28.

Percentage of 1980 High School Seniors Who Entered Higher Education in Fall 1980 and Persisted Through First Year of College in 1980–81

30

	4-Year		2-Year	
	Public	Private	Public	Private
Total	89.9	93.6	76.9	89.0
Sex				
Men	90.6	94.5	78.0	76.4
Women	89.3	92.8	75.9	93.1
Race/Ethnicity				
Hispanic	85.1	89.5	81.2	a
American Indian	a	a	73.7	a
Asian	99.6	99.4	85.4	a
Black	88.0	89.5	69.7	a
White	90.1	94.0	77.0	92.6

a Too few people in sample to provide estimates.

Source:
   National Center for Education Statistics, "The Timing of Abnormal Progression Among 1980 High School Seniors Entering Postsecondary Education in October 1980," Tables 3A and 3B, unpublished tabulations from *High School and Beyond: Senior Second Follow-up,* July 1986. See Guide to Sources.

Percentage of 1980 High School Seniors Who Were Dropouts, Stopouts, Transferred to Another Institution, or Remained in Same Institution Following Completion of One Year of Higher Education, by Sex and Type of Institution

31

Type of Institution	Dropouts		Stopouts		Transfer		Same Institution	
	Men	Women	Men	Women	Men	Women	Men	Women
4-year public	2.4	3.5	.7	.7	17.9	17.8	79.1	78.1
4-year private	2.1	2.7	1.3	.6	18.2	15.1	78.4	81.6
2-year public	8.3	9.4	.6	2.2	12.6	15.7	78.6	72.7
2-year private	a	1.5	a	.5	a	7.6	a	90.4

a Too few men in sample to provide estimates.

Note: "Dropping out" means no return to any postsecondary education during 1981–1984.

Source:
   National Center for Education Statistics, "The Timing of Abnormal Progression Among 1980 High School Seniors Entering Postsecondary Education in October 1980," Table 2, unpublished tabulations from *High School and Beyond: Senior Second Follow-up,* July 1986. See Guide to Sources.

Opening Fall Enrollment of All Students in All Institutions, by Sex, Selected Years, 1950–1987

32

	Opening Fall Enrollment in All Institutions[a]							
	Number			Percentage Distribution		Indexes (1965 = 100)		
Year	Total	Men	Women	Men	Women	Total	Men	Women
1950	2,296,592	1,569,322	727,270	68	32	38	43	31
1955	2,678,623	1,747,429	931,194	65	35	45	48	40
1960	3,610,007	2,270,640	1,339,367	63	37	60	62	58
1965[b]	5,967,411	3,652,675	2,314,736	61	39	100	100	100
1966	6,438,477	3,880,557	2,557,920	60	40	108	106	111
1967	6,963,687	4,158,557	2,805,130	60	40	117	114	121
1968	7,571,636	4,505,833	3,065,803	60	40	127	123	132
1969	8,066,233	4,775,622	3,290,611	59	41	135	131	142
1970	8,649,368	5,076,023	3,573,345	59	41	145	139	154
1971	9,025,031	5,242,740	3,782,291	58	42	151	144	163
1972	9,297,787	5,275,902	4,021,885	57	43	156	144	174
1973	9,694,297	5,414,164	4,280,133	56	44	162	148	185
1974	10,321,539	5,667,053	4,654,486	55	45	173	155	201
1975	11,290,719	6,198,623	5,092,096	55	45	189	170	220
1976	11,121,426	5,860,215	5,261,211	53	47	186	160	227
1977	11,415,020	5,846,098	5,568,922	51	49	191	160	241
1978	11,391,950	5,697,834	5,694,116	50	50	191	156	246
1979	11,707,126	5,740,551	5,966,575	49	51	196	157	258
1980[c]	12,096,895	5,874,374	6,222,521	49	51	203	161	269
1981	12,371,672	5,975,056	6,396,616	48	52	207	164	276
1982	12,425,780	6,031,384	6,394,396	49	51	209	165	276
1983	12,464,661	6,023,725	6,440,936	48	52	209	165	278
1984	12,241,940	5,863,574	6,378,366	48	52	205	161	276
1985	12,247,055	5,818,450	6,428,605	48	52	205	159	278
1986[d]	12,500,798	5,885,445	6,615,353	47	53	209	161	286
1987[e]	12,544,000	5,881,000	6,663,000	47	53	210	161	288

a Before 1980, data are for the 50 states, the District of Columbia, Canal Zone, Guam, Puerto Rico, the Virgin Islands, and Trust Territories of the Pacific.

b Data before 1965 show enrollment of degree-credit students only. Figures for all other years are for degree-credit *and* non-degree-credit students.

c Beginning in 1980, data show totals for the 50 states and the District of Columbia only; data for independent institutions have been disaggregated to show both the nonprofit and the proprietary sector.

d Preliminary data.

e Estimate.

Sources:

1 USOE, *Opening (Fall) Enrollment in Higher Education, 1960: Analytic Report* (Washington: GPO), 1961, p. 10.

2 USOE, *Opening (Fall) Enrollment in Higher Education, 1962: Institutional Data* (Washington: GPO), 1962, p. 3.

3 NCES, *Fall Enrollment in Higher Education* (Washington: GPO), *1971*, p. 13; *1977* p. 27; *1979*, pp. 12, 13.

4 CES, *Fall Enrollment in Colleges and Universities, 1984*, November 1986; Fall enrollment surveys, 1985, 1986, unpublished tabulations; *Early Estimates*, December 1987. See Guide to Sources.

5 ACE/Macmillan, *1989–90 Fact Book on Higher Education*, Table 46.

Fact File: College and University Enrollment Projections, 1988–1997

	1988	1989	1990	1991	1992	1993	1994	1995	1996	1997
Total enrollment	**12,560,000**	**12,570,000**	**12,585,000**	**12,529,000**	**12,408,000**	**12,300,000**	**12,201,000**	**12,151,000**	**12,142,000**	**12,173,000**
One-year change	+0.1%	+0.1%	+0.1%	−0.4%	−1.0%	−0.9%	−0.8%	−0.4%	−0.1%	+0.3%
Men	5,880,000	5,890,000	5,905,000	5,884,000	5,845,000	5,798,000	5,744,000	5,705,000	5,688,000	5,688,000
Women	6,680,000	6,680,000	6,680,000	6,645,000	6,563,000	6,502,000	6,457,000	6,446,000	6,454,000	6,485,000
Public institutions										
4-year	5,346,000	5,320,000	5,323,000	5,303,000	5,250,000	5,197,000	5,148,000	5,120,000	5,113,000	5,127,000
2-year	4,411,000	4,444,000	4,454,000	4,432,000	4,389,000	4,361,000	4,338,000	4,329,000	4,333,000	4,342,000
Private institutions										
4-year	2,532,000	2,537,000	2,539,000	2,528,000	2,506,000	2,482,000	2,457,000	2,443,000	2,437,000	2,443,000
2-year	268,000	269,000	269,000	266,000	263,000	260,000	258,000	259,000	259,000	261,000
Full-time students	7,157,000	7,116,000	7,095,000	7,013,000	6,916,000	6,819,000	6,743,000	6,708,000	6,711,000	6,750,000
Part-time students	5,403,000	5,454,000	5,490,000	5,516,000	5,492,000	5,481,000	5,458,000	5,443,000	5,431,000	5,423,000
Undergraduate	10,919,000	10,926,000	10,937,000	10,875,000	10,757,000	10,647,000	10,561,000	10,526,000	10,530,000	10,570,000
Graduate	1,363,000	1,368,000	1,372,000	1,378,000	1,377,000	1,379,000	1,369,000	1,358,000	1,349,000	1,343,000
First-professional	278,000	276,000	276,000	276,000	274,000	274,000	271,000	267,000	263,000	260,000
Full-time equivalent	9,068,000	9,088,000	9,080,000	9,008,00	8,903,000	8,803,000	8,718,000	8,678,000	8,677,000	8,713,000

Source:
Chronicle of Higher Education, Nov. 30, 1988.

	Opening Fall Enrollment in 4-Year Institutions[a]							
	Number			Percentage Distribution		Indexes (1965 = 100)		
Year	Total	Men	Women	Men	Women	Total	Men	Women
1950	2,079,020	1,429,349	649,671	69	31	43	49	35
1955	2,369,647	1,550,474	819,173	65	35	49	53	44
1960	3,156,390	1,987,348	1,169,042	63	37	66	68	62
1965	4,790,559	2,917,314	1,873,245	61	39	100	100	100
1970	6,422,154	3,757,222	2,664,932	59	41	134	129	142
1971	6,533,611	3,791,169	2,742,442	58	42	136	130	146
1972[b]	6,525,973	3,725,393	2,800,580	57	43	136	128	150
1973	6,660,536	3,751,703	2,908,833	56	44	139	129	155
1974	6,892,897	3,824,202	3,068,695	55	45	144	131	164
1975	7,288,749	4,018,105	3,270,644	55	45	152	138	175
1976	7,204,813	3,865,863	3,338,950	54	46	150	133	178
1977	7,336,036	3,865,857	3,470,179	53	47	153	133	185
1978	7,327,118	3,797,072	3,530,046	52	48	153	130	188
1979	7,457,099	3,804,577	3,652,522	51	49	156	130	195
1980	7,577,763	3,831,299	3,746,464	51	49	158	131	200
1981	7,655,461	3,850,591	3,804,870	50	50	160	132	203
1982	7,654,074	3,861,222	3,792,852	50	50	160	132	202
1983	7,741,195	3,892,616	3,848,579	50	50	162	133	205
1984	7,711,167	3,846,974	3,964,193	50	50	161	132	206
1985	7,715,978	3,816,216	3,899,762	49	51	161	131	208
1986[c]	7,826,036	3,825,903	4,000,133	49	51	163	131	214
1987[d]	7,816,000	3,802,000	4,013,000	49	51	163	130	214

a   Before 1963, enrollment figures were for bachelor's and higher degree-credit only. Data for all other years reflect *total* enrollment. Beginning in 1981, data show total enrollment in 4-year institutions for the 50 states and the District of Columbia only; data for independent institutions have been disaggregated to show both the nonprofit and proprietary institutions.

b   Before 1972, the National Center for Education Statistics counted data from 2-year branch campuses of 4-year institutions with the parent institution's totals. Beginning in 1972, enrollment at 2-year branch campuses is counted with other 2-year institutions.

c   Preliminary data.

d   Estimate.

Sources:

1   USOE, *Opening (Fall) Enrollment in Higher Education, 1960: Analytic Report* (Washington: GPO), 1961, p. 10.

2   USOE, *Opening Fall Enrollment in Higher Education* (Washington: GPO), *1965*, p. 7.

3   NCES, *Fall Enrollment in Higher Education* (Washington: GPO), *1971*, p. 3; *1972*, pp. 3, 738; *1975*, p. 3; *1977*, p. 2; *1979*, pp. 12, 13.

4   CES, *Fall Enrollment in Colleges and Universities, 1984*, November 1986; fall enrollment surveys, 1985, 1986, unpublished tabulations; see Guide to Sources.

5   ACE/Macmillan, *1989–90 Fact Book on Higher Education*, Table 59.

	Opening Fall Enrollment in 2-Year Institutions[a]							
	Number			Percentage Distribution		Indexes (1965 = 100)		
Year	Total	Men	Women	Men	Women	Total	Men	Women
1950	217,572	139,973	77,599	64	36	**18**	19	18
1955	308,976	196,955	112,021	64	36	**26**	27	25
1960	453,617	283,292	170,325	62	38	**39**	39	39
1965	1,176,852	735,361	441,491	62	38	**100**	100	100
1970	2,227,214	1,318,810	908,413	59	41	**189**	179	206
1971	2,491,420	1,451,571	1,039,849	58	42	**212**	197	236
1972[b]	2,771,814	1,550,509	1,221,305	56	44	**236**	211	277
1973	3,033,761	1,662,461	1,371,300	55	45	**258**	226	311
1974	3,428,642	1,842,851	1,585,791	54	46	**291**	251	359
1975	4,001,970	2,180,518	1,821,452	54	46	**340**	297	413
1976	3,916,613	1,994,352	1,922,261	51	49	**333**	271	435
1977	4,078,984	1,980,241	2,098,743	49	51	**347**	269	475
1978	4,064,832	1,900,762	2,164,070	47	53	**345**	258	490
1979	4,250,027	1,935,974	2,314,053	46	54	**361**	263	524
1980	4,519,132	2,043,075	2,476,057	45	55	**384**	278	561
1981	4,716,211	2,124,465	2,591,746	45	55	**401**	289	561
1982	4,771,706	2,170,162	2,601,544	45	55	**405**	295	589
1983	4,723,466	2,131,109	2,592,357	45	55	**401**	290	587
1984	4,530,273	2,016,600	2,514,173	44	56	**385**	274	569
1985	4,531,077	2,002,234	2,528,843	44	56	**385**	272	573
1986[c]	4,674,762	2,059,542	2,615,220	44	56	**397**	280	592
1987[d]	4,728,000	2,078,000	2,650,000	44	56	**402**	283	600

a   Before 1963, enrollment figures were for bachelor's and higher degree-credit only. Data for all other years reflect total enrollment. Beginning in 1981, data show total enrollment in 2-year institutions for the 50 states and the District of Columbia only; data for independent institutions have been disaggregated to show both the nonprofit and proprietary institutions.

b   Before 1972, the National Center for Education Statistics counted data from 2-year branch campuses of 4-year institutions with the parent institution's totals. Beginning in 1972, enrollment at 2-year branch campuses is counted with other 2-year institutions.

c   Preliminary data.

d   Estimate.

Sources:

1   USOE, *Opening (Fall) Enrollment in Higher Education, 1960: Analytic Report* (Washington: GPO), 1961, p. 10.

2   USOE, *Opening (Fall) Enrollment in Higher Education* (Washington: GPO), 1962, p. 3; 1963, p. 6; 1964, p. 5; 1965, p. 7.

3   NCES, *Fall Enrollment in Higher Education* (Washington: GPO), *1971*, p. 3; *1972*, pp. 4, 738; *1975*, p. 3; *1977*, p. 2; *1979*, pp. 12, 13.

4   CES, *Fall Enrollment in Colleges and Universities, 1984*, November 1986; fall enrollment surveys, 1985, 1986, unpublished tabulations; *Early Estimates*, December 1987. See Guide to Sources.

5   ACE/Macmillan, *1989–90 Fact Book on Higher Education*, Table 61.

Total Undergraduate Enrollment[a] in Institutions of Higher Education, by Sex of Student, Attendance Status, and Control of Institution, Fall 1969–Fall 1986

36

(In thousands.)

Year	Total	Full-Time	Part-Time	Men Full-Time	Men Part-Time	Women Full-Time	Women Part-Time	Men Public	Men Private	Women Public	Women Private
1969	6,884	4,991	1,893	2,952	1,056	2,039	837	2,997	1,011	2,162	714
1970	7,376	5,280	2,096	3,097	1,157	2,183	939	3,241	1,013	2,387	735
1971	7,743	5,512	2,231	3,201	1,217	2,311	1,014	3,427	991	2,580	745
1972	7,941	5,488	2,453	3,121	1,308	2,367	1,145	3,467	962	2,756	756
1973	8,261	5,580	2,681	3,135	1,403	2,445	1,278	3,579	959	2,943	780
1974	8,798	5,726	3,072	3,191	1,574	2,535	1,498	3,799	966	3,232	801
1975	9,679	6,169	3,510	3,459	1,798	2,710	1,712	4,245	1,012	3,581	841
1976	9,429	6,030	3,399	3,242	1,660	2,788	1,739	3,949	953	3,668	859
1977	9,714	6,093	3,621	3,188	1,708	2,905	1,913	3,937	959	3,905	913
1978	9,691	5,967	3,724	3,072	1,694	2,895	2,030	3,812	954	3,974	951
1979	9,998	6,080	3,919	3,087	1,734	2,993	2,185	3,865	956	4,181	995
1980	10,475	6,362	4,113	3,227	1,773	3,135	2,340	4,014	985	4,427	1,048
1981	10,755	6,449	4,306	3,261	1,848	3,188	2,458	4,090	1,018	4,558	1,088
1982	10,825	6,484	4,341	3,299	1,871	3,184	2,470	4,140	1,031	4,573	1,081
1983	10,846	6,514	4,332	3,304	1,854	3,210	2,478	4,117	1,042	4,580	1,107
1984	10,618	6,348	4,270	3,195	1,812	3,153	2,459	3,990	1,017	4,504	1,107
1985	10,597	6,320	4,277	3,156	1,806	3,163	2,471	3,953	1,010	4,525	1,110
1986[b]	10,797	6,348	4,449	3,145	1,873	3,203	2,576	4,007	1,011	4,665	1,114

a Includes unclassified undergraduate students.

b Preliminary data.

Note: Because of rounding, details may not add to totals.

Source:
National Center for Education Statistics, *Projections of Education Statistics to 1988–89; Projections of Education Statistics to 1990–91;* "Fall Enrollment in Colleges and Universities" surveys, 19; *Digest of Education Statistics,* 1988, Table 125. See Guide to Sources.

	First-Time Freshmen in All Institutions[a]				
	Number			Percentage Distribution	
Year	Total	Men	Women	Men	Women
1950	516,836	319,733	197,103	62	38
1955	675,060	418,363	256,697	62	38
1960	929,823	542,774	387,049	58	42
1965	1,642,000	947,000	695,000	58	42
1970	2,080,244	1,159,393	920,851	56	44
1971	2,135,947	1,178,399	957,548	55	45
1972	2,171,268	1,166,197	1,055,071	54	46
1973	2,248,100	1,192,464	1,005,636	53	47
1974	2,392,869	1,255,985	1,136,884	52	48
1975	2,543,552	1,340,621	1,202,931	53	47
1976	2,377,242	1,183,745	1,193,497	50	50
1977	2,431,600	1,172,147	1,259,453	48	52
1978	2,422,398	1,155,747	1,266,651	48	52
1979	2,538,119	1,194,534	1,343,585	47	53
1980	2,625,138	1,233,446	1,391,692	47	53
1981	2,636,231	1,233,157	1,403,074	47	53
1982[a]	2,505,466	1,199,237	1,306,229	48	52
1983	2,443,703	1,159,049	1,284,654	47	53
1984	2,356,898	1,112,303	1,244,595	47	53
1985	2,292,222	1,075,736	1,216,486	47	53
1986	2,213,652	1,044,612	1,169,040	47	53

Note: Before 1973, data include all "first-time *students*" who had not previously attended any institution of higher education. Beginning in 1973, data include "first-time freshmen" only.

a Data are opening fall enrollments of first-time students for the 50 states and the District of Columbia, Canal Zone, Puerto Rico, the Pacific Islands, and the Virgin Islands. Data before 1965 are bachelor's and higher degree-credit enrollments only. For 1965 and later, they are total enrollments. Beginning in 1982, data show opening fall enrollments of first-time freshmen for the 50 states and the District of Columbia only.

Sources:

1 USOE, *Opening (Fall) Enrollment in Higher Education, 1960 Analytic Report* (Washington: GPO), 1961, p. 11.

2 USOE, *Opening (Fall) Enrollment in Higher Education* (Washington: GPO), 1965, p. 7.

3 NCES, *Fall Enrollment in Higher Education* (Washington: GPO), *1970, Supplementary Information, Summary Data,* p. 15; *1971,* pp. 390, 391; *1972,* pp. 20, 21; *1973,* pp. 209, 214, 219; *1974,* pp. 5, 194, 199, 204; *1975,* pp. 30, 31; *1977,* pp. 23; *1979,* pp. 12, 13.

4 CES, *Fall Enrollment in Colleges and Universities, 1984,* November 1986; fall enrollment surveys, 1985, 1986, unpublished tabulations. See Guide to Sources.

5 ACE/Macmillan, *1989–90 Fact Book on Higher Education,* Table 75.

Enrollment of First-Time Freshmen in 4-Year Institutions, by Sex, Selected Years, 1950–1986

38

	First-Time Freshmen in 4-Year Institutions[a]				
	Number			Percentage Distribution	
Year	Total	Men	Women	Men	Women
1950	410,325	254,413	155,912	62	28
1955	534,800	332,024	202,776	62	38
1960	714,440	413,497	300,943	58	42
1965[b]	1,082,000	609,000	473,000	56	44
1970	1,166,391	630,970	535,421	54	46
1971	1,138,418	608,190	530,228	53	47
1972[c]	1,073,427	563,848	509,579	53	47
1973	1,091,143	568,567	522,576	52	48
1974	1,147,158	593,726	553,432	52	48
1975	1,182,945	607,518	575,427	51	49
1976	1,146,781	577,838	568,942	50	50
1977	1,163,004	575,273	587,731	49	51
1978	1,163,685	572,368	591,317	49	51
1979	1,197,571	584,152	613,419	49	51
1980	1,209,451	588,146	621,305	49	51
1981	1,201,264	581,312	619,952	48	52
1982[d]	1,135,027	557,181	577,846	49	51
1983	1,132,126	552,030	580,096	49	51
1984	1,116,749	541,590	575,159	48	52
1985	1,115,755	538,271	577,484	48	52
1986[e]	1,112,655	534,285	578,370	48	52

a   Before 1973, data are opening enrollments of first-time *students*. Beginning in 1973, data are opening fall enrollments only for first-time *freshmen.*

b   Estimate.

c   Before 1972, the National Center for Education Statistics counted data from 2-year branch campuses of 4-year institutions with the parent institution's totals. Beginning in 1972, enrollment at 2-year branch campuses is counted with other 2-year institutions.

d   Beginning in 1982, the data reflected opening fall enrollments of first-time freshmen in the 50 states and the District of Columbia only; the data for independent institutions have been disaggregated to show both nonprofit and proprietary institutions.

e   Preliminary data.

Sources:

1   USOE, *Opening (Fall) Enrollment in Higher Education, 1960 Analytic Report* (Washington: GPO), 1961, p. 11.

2   USOE, *Opening (Fall) Enrollment in Higher Education* (Washington: GPO), 1965, p. 7.

3   NCES, *Fall Enrollment in Higher Education* (Washington: GPO), *1970, Supplementary Information, Summary Data,* p. 15; *1971,* pp. 390, 391; *1972,* pp. 20, 21; *1973,* pp. 209, 214, 219; *1974,* pp. 5, 194, 199, 204; *1975,* pp. 30, 31; *1977,* p. 23; *1979,* p. 12.

4   NCES, *Fall Enrollment in Colleges and Universities, 1980, Preliminary Estimates,* NCES Early Release, October 31, 1980, table B.

5   CES, *Fall Enrollment in Colleges and Universities, 1984,* November 1986; fall enrollment surveys, 1985, 1986; unpublished tabulations. See Guide to Sources.

6   ACE/Macmillan, *1989–90 Fact Book on Higher Education,* Table 80.

Enrollment of First-Time Freshmen in 2-Year Institutions, by Sex, Selected Years, 1950–1986

39

Year	First-Time Freshmen in 2-Year Institutions[a]				
	Number			Percentage Distribution	
	Total	Men	Women	Men	Women
1950	106,511	65,320	41,191	61	39
1955	140,260	86,339	53,921	62	38
1960	215,383	129,277	83,106	60	40
1965[b]	560,000	338,000	222,000	60	40
1970	913,853	528,423	385,430	58	42
1971	997,529	570,209	427,320	57	43
1972[c]	1,097,841	602,349	495,492	55	45
1973	1,156,957	623,897	533,060	54	46
1974	1,245,711	662,259	583,452	53	47
1975	1,360,607	733,103	627,504	54	46
1976	1,230,461	605,907	624,554	49	51
1977	1,268,596	596,874	671,722	47	53
1978	1,258,713	583,379	675,334	46	54
1979	1,340,548	610,382	730,166	46	54
1980	1,404,312	640,735	763,577	46	54
1981[a]	1,422,157	646,756	775,401	45	55
1982	1,370,439	642,056	728,383	47	53
1983	1,311,577	607,019	704,558	46	54
1984	1,240,149	570,713	669,436	46	54
1985	1,176,467	537,465	639,002	46	54
1986[d]	1,100,997	510,327	590,670	46	54

a   Data are opening fall enrollments of first-time students for the 50 states and the District of Columbia, Canal Zone, Puerto Rico, the Pacific Islands, and the Virgin Islands. Data before 1965 are bachelor's and higher degree-credit enrollments only. For 1965 and later, they are *total* enrollments. Beginning in 1981, the data reflect opening fall enrollments of first-time freshmen for the 50 states and the District of Columbia only, and the data for independent institutions have been disaggregated to show both nonprofit and proprietary institutions.

b   Estimate.

c   Before 1972, the National Center for Education Statistics counted data from 2-year branch campuses of 4-year institutions with the parent institution's totals. Beginning in 1972, enrollment at 2-year branch campuses is counted with 2-year institutions.

d   Preliminary data.

Sources:

1   USOE, *Opening (Fall) Enrollment in Higher Education, 1960 Analytic Report* (Washington: GPO), 1961, p. 11.

2   USOE, *Opening Fall Enrollment in Higher Education* (Washington: GPO), 1965, p. 7.

3   NCES, *Fall Enrollment in Higher Education* (Washington: GPO), *1970, Supplementary Information, Summary Data,* p. 15; *1971,* pp. 390, 391; *1972,* pp. 20, 21; *1973,* pp. 209, 214, 219; *1974,* pp. 5, 194, 199, 204; *1975,* pp. 30, 31; *1977,* p. 23; *1979,* p. 12.

4   NCES, *Fall Enrollment in Colleges and Universities, 1980, Preliminary Estimates,* NCES Early Release, October 31, 1980, table B.

5   CES, *Fall Enrollment in Colleges and Universities, 1984,* November 1986; fall enrollment surveys, 1985, 1986, unpublished tabulations. See Guide to Sources.

6   ACE/Macmillan, *1989–90 Fact Book on Higher Education,* Table 82.

Year	Number of Women at 4-Year Institutions			Percentage	
	Total	**Full-Time**	**Part-Time**	**Full-Time**	**Part-Time**
1963[a]	**1,499,480**	1,052,367	447,113	70	30
1964[a]	**1,663,400**	1,172,091	490,309	71	29
1965[a]	**1,851,985**	1,327,649	524,336	72	28
1966	**2,038,251**	1,448,672	589,579	71	29
1967	**2,204,316**	1,585,000	619,316	72	28
1968	**2,361,478**	1,709,081	652,397	72	28
1969	**2,502,091**	1,800,491	701,600	72	28
1970	**2,664,932**	1,901,408	763,524	71	29
1971	**2,742,442**	1,977,989	764,453	72	28
1972[b]	**2,800,580**	1,993,207	807,373	71	29
1973	**2,908,833**	2,041,993	866,840	70	30
1974	**3,068,695**	2,116,564	952,131	69	31
1975	**3,270,644**	2,217,890	1,052,754	68	32
1976	**3,338,950**	2,284,212	1,054,738	68	32
1977	**3,470,179**	2,379,744	1,090,435	69	31
1978	**3,530,046**	2,408,512	1,121,534	68	32
1979	**3,652,522**	2,491,814	1,160,708	68	32
1980	**3,746,464**	2,536,804	1,209,660	68	32
1981	**3,804,870**	2,570,169	1,259,413	68	32
1982[c]	**3,792,852**	2,558,519	1,234,333	67	33
1983	**3,848,579**	2,589,166	1,234,701	67	33
1984	**3,864,193**	2,588,438	1,275,755	67	33
1985	**3,899,762**	2,603,202	1,296,560	67	33
1986[d]	**4,000,133**	2,650,751	1,349,382	66	34
1987[e]	**4,013,000**	NA	NA	NA	NA

NA = not available

For footnotes, see Table 41.

Sources:
1 National Center for Education Statistics, "Opening Fall Enrollment in Higher Education" surveys, 1965, 1966, 1967, 1968, 1969, 1970, 1972, 1975, 1977; "Fall Enrollment in Higher Education" (analytic report), 1974, 1976; "Fall Enrollment in Colleges and Universities" surveys, 1984, 1986; Unpublished tabulations from the fall enrollment surveys, 1985, 1986; "Early Estimates," December 1987.
2 ACE/Macmillan, *1989–90 Fact Book on Higher Education,* Table 70.

Year	Number of Men at 4-Year Institutions			Percentage	
	Total	Full-Time	Part-Time	Full-Time	Part-Time
1963[a]	2,401,230	1,708,354	692,876	71	29
1964[a]	2,611,191	1,870,670	740,521	72	28
1965[a]	2,873,042	2,111,933	761,109	74	26
1966	3,069,370	2,281,219	788,151	74	26
1967	3,241,292	2,418,630	822,662	75	25
1968	3,413,732	2,562,803	850,929	75	25
1969	3,582,992	2,680,827	902,165	75	25
1970	3,757,222	2,795,167	962,055	74	26
1971	3,791,169	2,858,919	932,250	75	25
1972[b]	3,725,393	2,785,400	939,993	75	25
1973	3,751,703	2,765,024	986,679	74	26
1974	3,824,202	2,796,337	1,027,864	73	27
1975	4,018,105	2,916,385	1,101,720	73	27
1976	3,865,863	2,825,936	1,039,927	73	27
1977	3,865,857	2,829,920	1,035,927	73	27
1978	3,797,072	2,772,161	1,024,911	73	27
1979	3,804,577	2,789,505	1,015,072	73	27
1980	3,831,299	2,812,797	1,018,502	73	27
1981[c]	3,850,591	2,815,107	1,035,484	73	27
1982	3,861,222	2,822,274	1,038,948	73	27
1983	3,892,616	2,845,083	1,047,533	73	27
1984	3,846,974	2,806,161	1,040,813	73	27
1985	3,816,216	2,781,412	1,034,804	73	27
1986[d]	3,825,903	2,776,856	1,049,047	73	27
1987[e]	3,802,000	NA	NA	NA	NA

NA = Not available

Note: Unless otherwise noted, data show opening fall enrollment of all students (degree-credit and non-degree-credit) in 4-year institutions of higher education in the 50 states, the District of Columbia, Canal Zone, Guam, Puerto Rico, the Virgin Islands, and the Trust Territories of the Pacific.

a   Bachelor's and higher degree-credit only.

b   Before 1972, the National Center for Education Statistics counted data from 2-year branch campuses of 4-year institutions with the parent institution's totals. Beginning in 1972, enrollment at 2-year branch campuses is counted with other 2-year institutions.

c   Beginning in 1982, data show enrollment for the 50 states and the District of Columbia.

d   Preliminary data.

e   Estimate.

For sources, see Table 40.

Enrollment of Women in 2-Year Institutions, by Attendance Status, 1963–1987

42

	Number of Women at 2-Year Institutions			Percentage	
Year	Total	Full-Time	Part-Time	Full-Time	Part-Time
1963[a]	239,509	123,270	116,239	51	49
1965[a]	321,712	175,644	146,068	55	45
1966	519,669	272,689	246,980	52	48
1967	600,814	301,003	299,811	50	50
1968	704,325	353,360	350,965	50	50
1969	788,520	384,971	403,549	49	51
1970	908,413	436,652	471,761	48	52
1971	1,039,849	499,228	540,621	48	52
1972[b]	1,221,305	554,472	666,833	45	55
1973	1,371,300	604,492	766,808	44	56
1974	1,585,791	646,170	939,621	41	49
1975	1,821,452	739,846	1,081,606	41	59
1976	1,922,261	776,828	1,145,433	40	60
1977	2,098,743	820,304	1,278,439	39	61
1978	2,164,070	790,384	1,373,686	37	63
1979	2,314,053	821,417	1,492,636	35	65
1980	2,476,057	871,910	1,604,147	35	65
1981[c]	2,591,746	898,244	1,693,502	35	65
1982	2,601,544	909,144	1,692,400	35	65
1983	2,592,357	912,097	1,680,260	35	65
1984	2,514,173	862,441	1,651,732	34	66
1985	2,528,843	864,299	1,664,544	34	66
1986[d]	2,615,220	866,917	1,748,303	33	67
1987[e]	2,650,000	NA	NA	NA	NA

NA = Not available

For footnotes, see Table 43.

Sources:
1 National Center for Education Statistics, "Fall Enrollment in Higher Education" surveys, 1965, 1966, 1967, 1968, 1969, 1970, 1972, 1975, 1977, 1979; "Fall Enrollment in Higher Education" (analytic report), 1974, 1976; "Fall Enrollment in Colleges and Universities" surveys, 1984, 1986; unpublished tabulations from the fall enrollment surveys, 1985, 1986; "Early Estimates," Dec. 1987. See Guide to Sources.
2 ACE/Macmillan, *1989–90 Fact Book on Higher Education*, Table 74.

Year	Number of Men at 2-Year Institutions			Percentage	
	Total	**Full-Time**	**Part-Time**	**Full-Time**	**Part-Time**
1963[a]	**388,297**	205,623	182,674	53	47
1965[a]	**523,532**	322,029	201,503	62	38
1966	**811,187**	467,191	343,996	58	42
1967	**917,265**	522,358	394,907	57	43
1968	**1,092,101**	625,236	466,865	57	43
1969	**1,192,630**	675,332	517,298	57	43
1970	**1,318,801**	732,248	586,553	56	44
1971	**1,451,571**	796,018	655,553	55	45
1972[b]	**1,550,509**	798,328	752,181	51	49
1973	**1,662,461**	845,176	817,285	51	49
1974	**1,842,851**	883,397	959,454	48	52
1975	**2,180,518**	1,048,775	1,131,743	48	52
1976	**1,994,352**	916,113	1,078,239	46	54
1977	**1,980,241**	865,841	1,114,400	44	56
1978	**1,900,762**	799,554	1,101,208	42	58
1979	**1,935,974**	798,690	1,137,284	41	59
1980	**2,043,075**	876,447	1,166,628	43	57
1981[c]	**2,124,465**	897,730	1,226,735	42	58
1982	**2,170,162**	930,681	1,239,481	43	57
1983	**2,131,109**	914,704	1,216,405	43	57
1984	**2,016,600**	841,348	1,175,252	42	58
1985	**2,002,234**	826,308	1,175,926	41	59
1986[d]	**2,059,542**	821,979	1,237,563	40	60
1987[e]	**2,078,000**	NA	NA	NA	NA

NA = Not available

a Bachelor's and higher degree-credit only.

b Before 1972, the National Center for Education Statistics counted data from 2-year branch campuses of 4-year institutions with the parent institution's totals. Beginning in 1972, enrollment at 2-year branch campuses is counted with 2-year institutions.

c Beginning in 1981, data show total enrollment in 2-year institutions for the 50 states and the District of Columbia only; data for independent institutions have been disaggregated to show both nonprofit and proprietary institutions.

d Preliminary data.

e Estimate.

For sources, see Table 42.

Fall Enrollment in Institutions of Higher Education, by Attendance Status and Race/Ethnicity of Students and by Institutional Type, Control, and Sex of Student, Fall 1986.

Institutional Type, Control, and Sex of Student	All Students			White, Non-Hispanic			Black, Non-Hispanic		
	Total	Full-Time	Part-Time	Total	Full-Time	Part-Time	Total	Full-Time	Part-Time
All Institutions	12,500,798	7,116,503	5,384,295	9,914,183	5,609,470	4,304,713	1,080,899	636,344	444,555
4-year	7,826,036	5,427,607	2,398,429	6,339,593	4,363,959	1,975,634	615,249	433,237	182,012
Men	3,825,903	2,776,856	1,049,047	3,080,438	2,223,750	856,688	251,679	185,407	66,272
Women	4,000,133	2,650,751	1,349,382	3,259,155	2,140,209	1,118,946	363,570	247,830	115,740
2-year	4,674,762	1,688,896	2,985,866	3,574,590	1,245,511	2,329,079	465,650	203,107	262,543
Men	2,059,542	821,979	1,237,563	1,566,048	613,471	952,577	184,149	84,894	99,255
Women	2,615,220	866,917	1,748,303	2,008,542	632,040	1,376,502	281,501	118,213	163,288
Public	9,721,574	5,168,400	4,553,174	7,649,824	4,053,086	3,596,738	854,544	466,899	387,645
4-year	5,303,482	3,661,309	1,642,173	4,273,827	2,941,527	1,332,300	424,233	293,447	130,786
Men	2,574,923	1,868,743	706,180	2,064,048	1,496,561	567,487	171,196	124,456	46,740
Women	2,728,559	1,792,566	935,993	2,209,779	1,444,966	764,813	253,037	168,991	84,046
2-year	4,418,092	1,507,091	2,911,001	3,375,997	1,111,559	2,264,438	430,311	173,452	256,859
Men	1,936,997	742,550	1,194,447	1,467,930	554,252	913,678	171,038	73,839	97,199
Women	2,481,095	764,541	1,716,554	1,908,067	557,307	1,350,760	259,273	99,613	159,660
Private	2,779,224	1,948,103	831,121	2,264,359	1,556,384	707,975	226,355	169,445	56,910
4-year	2,522,554	1,766,298	756,256	2,065,766	1,422,432	643,334	191,016	139,790	51,226
Men	1,250,980	908,113	342,867	1,016,390	727,189	289,201	80,483	60,951	19,532
Women	1,271,574	858,185	413,389	1,049,376	695,243	354,133	110,533	78,839	31,694
2-year	256,670	181,805	74,865	198,593	133,952	64,641	35,339	29,655	5,684
Men	122,545	79,429	43,116	98,118	59,219	38,899	13,111	11,055	2,056
Women	134,125	102,376	31,749	100,475	74,733	25,742	22,228	18,600	3,628

Source:
National Center for Education Statistics, "Trends in Minority Enrollment in Higher Education, Fall 1976 – Fall 1986," April 1988, Table 3.

Total Enrollment in Institutions of Higher Education, by Control of Institution, Level of Enrollment, and Race/Ethnicity and Sex of Student, Fall 1976 and 1984

Year, Race/Ethnicity, and Sex of Student	Enrollment, by Control of Institution			Enrollment, by Level			
	Total	Public	Private	Undergraduate	Graduate	First-Professional	Unclassified
1976 Total	**10,985,614**	**8,641,037**	**2,344,577**	**8,432,240**	**1,081,858**	**244,121**	**1,227,395**
Men	5,794,390	4,499,541	1,294,849	4,420,228	599,778	189,642	584,742
Women	5,191,224	4,141,496	1,049,728	4,012,012	482,080	54,479	642,653
White, non-Hispanic	9,076,131	7,094,521	1,981,610	6,899,743	907,583	220,003	1,048,802
Men	4,813,717	3,714,567	1,099,150	3,645,423	496,260	172,422	499,612
Women	4,262,414	3,379,954	882,460	3,254,320	411,323	47,581	549,190
Black, non-Hispanic	1,033,025	831,212	201,813	866,147	65,352	11,181	90,345
Men	469,881	375,389	94,492	397,084	27,016	7,234	38,547
Women	563,144	455,823	107,321	469,063	38,336	3,947	51,798
Hispanic	383,790	336,818	46,972	323,540	20,274	4,547	35,429
Men	209,714	183,881	25,833	175,940	11,359	3,498	18,917
Women	174,076	152,937	21,139	147,600	8,915	1,049	16,512
Asian or Pacific Islander	197,878	165,716	32,162	152,533	18,487	4,075	22,783
Men	108,434	89,423	19,011	82,558	11,600	2,933	11,343
Women	89,444	76,293	13,151	69,975	6,887	1,142	11,440
American Indian/Alaskan Native	76,110	67,500	8,610	61,267	3,887	1,253	9,703
Men	38,543	34,236	4,307	30,809	2,193	1,032	4,509
Women	37,567	33,264	4,303	30,458	1,694	221	5,194
Nonresident alien	218,880	145,270	73,410	129,010	66,275	3,062	20,333
Men	154,101	102,045	52,056	88,414	51,350	2,523	11,814
Women	64,579	43,225	21,354	40,596	14,925	539	8,519

1984[a] Total	12,161,778	9,424,911	2,736,867	9,451,066	1,100,353	276,364	1,333,995
Men	5,824,388	4,448,502	1,375,886	4,518,645	569,469	183,626	552,648
Women	6,337,390	4,976,409	1,360,981	4,932,421	530,884	92,738	781,347
White, non-Hispanic	9,706,845	7,524,802	2,242,043	7,549,607	882,253	241,597	1,093,388
Men	4,667,606	3,542,374	1,125,232	3,620,973	436,893	162,537	447,203
Women	5,099,239	3,982,428	1,116,811	3,928,634	445,360	79,060	646,185
Black, non-Hispanic	1,069,885	841,338	228,549	897,185	52,834	13,243	106,623
Men	434,515	340,030	94,485	368,089	19,961	7,017	39,448
Women	635,370	501,306	134,064	529,096	32,873	6,226	67,175
Hispanic	528,786	452,514	76,272	436,814	24,402	7,913	59,857
Men	251,030	213,705	37,325	206,337	11,676	5,152	27,865
Women	277,756	238,809	38,947	230,277	12,726	2,761	31,992
Asian or Pacific Islander	381,746	317,454	64,292	301,167	28,543	9,240	42,796
Men	205,542	169,568	35,974	160,564	17,865	5,786	21,327
Women	176,204	147,886	28,318	140,603	10,678	3,454	21,469
American Indian/Alaskan Native	82,672	71,642	11,030	68,815	3,634	980	9,243
Men	37,056	32,262	4,794	30,842	1,706	616	3,892
Women	45,616	39,380	6,236	37,973	1,928	364	5,351
Nonresident alien	331,844	217,163	114,681	197,678	108,687	3,391	22,088
Men	228,639	150,563	78,076	131,840	81,368	2,518	12,913
Women	103,205	66,600	36,605	65,838	27,319	873	9,175

a Some 214 institutions did not report the racial/ethnic status of their student body. Data for 195 of these nonreporting institutions, representing about 5% of total enrollment, were imputed. For those institutions that reported race data in 1982, data have been estimated by applying their 1982 race distribution to their total enrollment reported in 1984.

Note: Because of underreporting and nonreporting of racial/ethnic data, totals in this table may be slightly smaller than totals appearing in other tables. Because of rounding, details may not add to totals.

Source:
National Center for Education Statistics, "Fall Enrollment in Colleges and Universities, 1984" (survey); *Digest of Education Statistics, 1987*, Table 131.

Total Enrollment in Institutions of Higher Education, by Control of Institution, Sex, Level of Enrollment, and Attendance Status, Fall 1985

Level of Enrollment and Attendance Status	All Institutions			Public Institutions			Private Institutions		
	Total	Men	Women	Total	Men	Women	Total	Men	Women
All Students	**12,247,055**	**5,818,450**	**6,428,605**	**9,479,273**	**4,437,488**	**5,041,785**	**2,767,782**	**1,380,962**	**1,386,820**
Full-time	7,075,221	3,607,720	3,467,501	5,120,246	2,606,362	2,513,884	1,954,975	1,001,358	953,617
Part-time	5,171,834	2,210,730	2,961,104	4,359,027	1,831,126	2,527,901	812,807	379,604	433,203
Total undergraduate students[a]	10,596,674	4,962,080	5,634,594	8,477,125	3,952,548	4,524,577	2,119,549	1,009,532	1,110,017
Undergraduate students	9,414,074	4,470,074	4,944,000	7,443,611	3,516,141	3,927,470	1,970,463	953,933	1,016,530
Full-time	6,162,391	3,076,720	3,085,671	4,549,901	2,286,260	2,263,641	1,612,490	790,460	822,030
Part-time	3,251,683	1,393,354	1,858,329	2,893,710	1,229,881	1,663,829	357,973	163,473	194,500
Unclassified students below the baccalaureate	1,182,600	492,006	690,594	1,033,514	436,407	597,107	149,086	55,599	93,487
Full-time	157,201	79,726	77,475	137,875	70,157	67,718	19,326	9,569	9,757
Part-time	1,025,399	412,280	613,119	895,639	366,250	529,389	129,760	46,030	83,730
Total postbaccalaureate students	1,650,381	856,370	794,011	1,002,148	484,940	517,208	648,233	371,430	276,803
First-professional students	274,200	179,792	94,408	111,808	71,373	40,435	162,392	108,419	53,973
Full-time	246,619	162,368	84,251	106,693	68,392	38,301	139,926	93,976	45,950
Part-time	27,581	17,424	10,157	5,115	2,981	2,134	22,466	14,443	8,023
Graduate students	1,129,538	577,224	552,314	703,076	341,863	361,213	426,462	235,361	191,101
Full-time	470,967	269,819	201,148	297,023	167,860	129,163	173,944	101,959	71,985
Part-time	658,571	307,405	351,166	406,053	174,003	232,050	252,518	133,402	119,116
Unclassified postbaccalaureate students	246,643	99,354	147,289	187,264	71,704	115,560	59,379	27,650	31,729
Full-time	38,043	19,087	18,956	28,754	13,693	15,061	9,289	5,394	3,895
Part-time	208,600	80,267	128,333	158,510	58,011	100,499	50,090	22,256	27,834

a Includes students enrolled for an undergraduate degree and also unclassified students below the baccalaureate level.

Source:
National Center for Education Statistics, "Fall Enrollment in Colleges and Universities, 1985" (survey); *Digest of Education Statistics, 1988*, Table 120.

College Enrollment, by Sex, Age, and Race, 1972 – 1986

(In thousands, as of October. Covers civilian noninstitutional population age 14 and older. Degree credit enrollment only.)

Sex, Age, and Race	1972	1975	1978	1979	1980	1981[a]	1981[b]	1982	1983	1984	1985	1986
Total	**9,095**	**10,880**	**11,140**	**11,380**	**11,387**	**11,814**	**12,127**	**12,309**	**12,320**	**12,304**	**12,524**	**12,402**
Men[c]	5,218	5,911	5,581	5,480	5,430	5,636	5,825	5,899	6,010	5,989	5,905	5,848
Age 18–24	3,534	3,693	3,621	3,508	3,604	3,724	3,833	3,837	3,820	3,929	3,749	3,649
Age 25–34	1,178	1,521	1,396	1,356	1,325	1,375	1,442	1,460	1,576	1,464	1,464	1,508
Age 35 and older	365	569	457	487	405	443	453	490	506	476	561	600
Women[c]	3,877	4,969	5,559	5,900	5,957	6,178	6,303	6,410	6,310	6,317	6,616	6,554
Age 18–24	2,724	3,243	3,373	3,482	3,625	3,680	3,741	3,841	3,657	3,662	3,788	3,747
Age 25–34	581	947	1,173	1,319	1,378	1,431	1,485	1,528	1,510	1,522	1,599	1,483
Age 35 and older	418	614	845	914	802	934	940	900	989	970	1,100	1,197
White	8,147	9,547	9,662	9,956	9,926	10,166	10,352	10,550	10,566	10,521	10,782	10,497
Men	4,723	5,263	4,913	4,823	4,804	4,900	5,011	5,078	5,162	5,111	5,101	4,987
Women	3,427	4,285	4,748	5,132	5,123	5,265	5,342	5,474	5,404	5,410	5,680	5,510
Black and other races	949	1,333	1,479	1,424	1,461	1,648	1,775	1,758	1,754	1,784	1,742	1,905
Men	496	648	668	657	626	735	814	821	848	878	805	861
Women	450	684	811	768	834	913	961	936	906	906	938	1,044

a Population controls based on 1970 census.

b Population controls based on 1980 census.

c Includes persons 14 to 17 years old, not shown separately.

Sources:
U.S. Bureau of the Census, *Current Population Reports,* Ser. P-20, No. 409 and earlier reports; *Statistical Abstract of the United States, 1988,* Table 234; and unpublished data.

College Enrollment by Sex, Age, and Race, 1987

(In thousands. Covers civilian noninstitutional population, age 14 and older. Degree credit enrollment only.)

Age	All Races			White			Black			Hispanic[a]		
	Total	Male	Female	Total	Male	Female	Total	Male	Female	Total	Male	Female
18–24	7,693	3,867	3,826	6,483	3,289	3,192	823	377	445	455	247	208
25–34	2,985	1,421	1,564	2,468	1,176	1,293	341	136	205	204	119	85
35 and older	1,802	625	1,176	1,584	541	1,044	155	62	93	73	21	51
Total	12,480	5,914	6,566	10,535	5,006	5,529	1,319	575	743	732	387	344

a Hispanics may be of any race.

Note: Totals are not exact because of rounding.

Source:
U.S. Bureau of the Census, unpublished data, 1989.

Total Enrollment in Institutions of Higher Education, by Control of Institution, and Race/Ethnicity and Sex of Student, Biennially, Fall 1976 – Fall 1986

49

Control of Institution and Race/Ethnicity of Student	Number (in thousands)						Percentage Distribution					
	1976	1978	1980	1982	1984	1986	1976	1978	1980	1982	1984	1986
All Institutions												
Total	10,986	11,231	12,087	12,388	12,235	12,501	100.0	100.0	100.0	100.0	100.0	100.0
White, non-Hispanic	9,076	9,194	9,833	9,997	9,815	9,914	82.6	81.9	81.4	80.7	80.2	79.3
Black, non-Hispanic	1,033	1,054	1,107	1,101	1,076	1,081	9.4	9.4	9.2	8.9	8.8	8.6
Hispanic	384	417	472	519	535	624	3.5	3.7	3.9	4.2	4.4	5.0
Asian or Pacific Islander	198	235	286	351	390	448	1.8	2.1	2.4	2.8	3.2	3.6
American Indian/Alaskan Native	76	78	84	88	84	90	0.7	0.7	0.7	0.7	0.7	0.7
Nonresident alien	219	253	305	331	335	344	2.0	2.2	2.5	2.7	2.7	2.7
Public												
Total	8,641	8,770	9,456	9,695	9,458	9,722	78.7	78.1	78.2	78.3	77.3	77.8
White, non-Hispanic	7,095	7,136	7,656	7,785	7,543	7,650	64.6	63.5	63.3	62.8	61.6	61.2
Black, non-Hispanic	831	840	876	873	844	855	7.6	7.5	7.2	7.0	6.9	6.8
Hispanic	337	363	406	446	456	539	3.1	3.2	3.4	3.6	3.7	4.3
Asian or Pacific Islander	166	195	240	296	323	372	1.5	1.7	2.0	2.4	2.6	3.0
American Indian/Alaskan Native	68	68	74	77	72	79	0.6	0.6	0.6	0.6	0.6	0.6
Nonresident alien	145	167	204	219	219	226	1.3	1.5	1.7	1.8	1.8	1.8
Private												
Total	2,345	2,461	2,630	2,693	2,777	2,779	21.3	21.9	21.8	21.7	22.7	22.2
White, non-Hispanic	1,982	2,058	2,177	2,212	2,272	2,264	18.0	18.3	18.0	17.9	18.6	18.1
Black, non-Hispanic	202	215	231	228	232	226	1.8	1.9	1.9	1.8	1.9	1.8
Hispanic	47	55	66	74	79	84	0.4	0.5	0.5	0.6	0.6	0.7
Asian or Pacific Islander	32	40	47	55	67	76	0.3	0.4	0.4	0.4	0.5	0.6
American Indian/Alaskan Native	9	9	10	10	11	11	0.1	0.1	0.1	0.1	0.1	0.1
Nonresident alien	73	85	101	113	116	118	0.7	0.8	0.8	0.9	0.9	0.9
Men												
Total	5,794	5,621	5,868	5,999	5,859	5,885	52.7	50.1	48.5	48.4	47.9	47.1
White, non-Hispanic	4,814	4,613	4,773	4,830	4,690	4,646	43.8	41.1	39.5	39.0	38.3	37.2
Black, non-Hispanic	470	453	464	458	437	436	4.3	4.0	3.8	3.7	3.6	3.5
Hispanic	210	213	232	252	254	292	1.9	1.9	1.9	2.0	2.1	2.3
Asian or Pacific Islander	105	126	151	189	210	239	1.0	1.1	1.3	1.5	1.7	1.9
American Indian/Alaskan Native	39	37	38	40	38	40	0.4	0.3	0.3	0.3	0.3	0.3
Nonresident alien	154	180	211	230	231	232	1.4	1.6	1.7	1.9	1.9	1.9
Women												
Total	5,191	5,609	6,219	6,389	6,376	6,615	47.3	49.9	51.5	51.6	52.1	52.9
White, non-Hispanic	4,262	4,581	5,060	5,167	5,125	5,268	38.8	40.8	41.9	41.7	41.9	42.1
Black, non-Hispanic	563	601	643	644	639	645	5.1	5.4	5.3	5.2	5.2	5.2
Hispanic	174	205	240	267	281	332	1.6	1.8	2.0	2.2	2.3	2.7
Asian or Pacific Islander	89	109	135	162	180	209	0.8	1.0	1.1	1.3	1.5	1.7
American Indian/Alaskan Native	38	41	46	48	46	51	0.3	0.4	0.4	0.4	0.4	0.4
Nonresident alien	65	73	94	101	104	111	0.6	0.7	0.8	0.8	0.9	0.9

Note: Because of underreporting and nonreporting of racial/ethnic data, data was estimated when possible. Also, due to rounding, detail may not add to totals.

Source:
National Center for Education Statistics, "Trends in Minority Enrollment in Higher Education, Fall 1976 – Fall 1986," Table 1.

	1975–76	1980–81	1985–86
Total	105,808	111,206	104,454
Women	98,803	105,185	97,142
Men	7,005	6,021	7,312
Full-Time	82,593	79,520	69,134
Women	79,021	77,655	66,758
Men	3,572	1,865	2,376
Part-Time	23,215	31,686	35,320
Women	19,782	27,530	30,384
Men	3,433	4,156	4,936
Public: Total	11,041	10,014	8,194
Full-time	7,315		
Part-time	3,726		
Public: Women	10,674	9,462	7,579
Full-time	7,122		
Part-time	3,552		
Public: Men	367	552	615
Full-time	193		
Part-time	174		
Private: Total	94,767	101,192	96,260
Full-time	75,278		
Part-time	19,489		
Private: Women	88,129	95,723	89,563
Full-time	71,899		
Part-time	16,230		
Private: Men	6,638	5,469	6,697
Full-time	3,379		
Part-time	3,259		

Note: Women's colleges are those that reported their institutions as such on the Higher Education General Information Survey (HEGIS) forms.

Source:
ACE, Special 1988 tabulations of the National Center for Education's HEGIS tapes. See Guide to Sources.

Total Enrollment in Selected Major Fields of Study in 4-Year Institutions of Higher Education, by Sex, Fall 1976 – Fall 1986

51

Selected Major Fields of Study	1976			1986		
	Total	Men	Women	Total	Men	Women
Total Enrollment	**7,126,515**	**3,828,893**	**3,297,622**	**7,832,698**	**3,827,529**	**4,005,169**
Percentage	**100.0**	**53.7**	**46.3**	**100.0**	**48.9**	**51.1**
Agriculture and natural resources						
Enrollment	124,903	92,370	32,533	NA	NA	NA
Percentage	100.0	74.0	26.0	NA	NA	NA
Architecture and environmental design						
Enrollment	58,149	44,207	13,942	56,756	36,878	19,878
Percentage	100.0	76.0	24.0	100.0	65.0	35.0
Business and management						
Enrollment	951,945	679,795	272,150	1,270,424	690,705	579,719
Percentage	100.0	71.4	28.6	100.0	54.4	45.6
Dentistry						
Enrollment	20,272	18,049	2,223	17,773	12,916	4,857
Percentage	100.0	89.0	11.0	100.0	72.7	27.3
Engineering						
Enrollment	374,815	346,023	28,792	486,180	414,974	71,206
Percentage	100.0	92.3	7.7	100.0	85.4	14.6
Law						
Enrollment	119,581	88,679	30,902	106,212	62,913	43,299
Percentage	100.0	74.2	25.8	100.0	59.2	40.8
Life sciences						
Enrollment	289,906	175,379	114,527	218,007	108,046	109,961
Percentage	100.0	60.5	39.5	100.0	49.6	50.4
Mathematics						
Enrollment	NA	NA	NA	89,473	51,109	38,364
Percentage	NA	NA	NA	100.0	57.1	42.9
Medicine						
Enrollment	58,085	45,145	12,940	65,711	43,836	21,875
Percentage	100.0	77.7	22.3	100.0	66.7	33.3
Physical sciences						
Enrollment	146,025	115,137	30,888	128,981	92,483	36,498
Percentage	100.0	78.8	21.2	100.0	71.7	28.3
Veterinary medicine						
Enrollment	6,126	4,425	1,701	8,849	4,163	4,686
Percentage	100.0	72.2	27.8	100.0	47.0	53.0
All other						
Enrollment	4,976,708	2,219,684	2,757,024	5,384,332[a]	2,309,506[a]	3,074,826[a]
Percentage	100.0	44.6	55.4	100.0	42.9	57.1

NA = not available

a Includes students whose major field of study was not reported.

Source:
National Center for Education Statistics, "Fall Enrollment in Colleges and Universities" surveys; *Digest of Education Statistics,* 1988, Table 142.

Total Graduate Enrollment[a] in Institutions of Higher Education, by Sex of Student, Attendance Status, and Control of Institution, Fall 1969 – Fall 1985

(In thousands.)

Year	Total Enrollment	Men Full-Time	Men Part-Time	Women Full-Time	Women Part-Time	Men Public	Men Private	Women Public	Women Private
1969	955	252	338	111	255	393	197	273	93
1970	1,031	264	366	115	285	423	207	301	99
1971	1,012	269	346	119	275	415	200	296	100
1972	1,066	268	358	126	313	427	199	330	109
1973	1,123	273	375	137	340	442	206	358	119
1974	1,190	276	387	151	375	454	209	398	128
1975	1,263	290	410	163	400	481	219	425	138
1976	1,333	287	427	176	443	477	237	454	165
1977	1,318	289	411	183	434	457	242	443	174
1978	1,312	280	402	188	442	441	241	453	177
1979	1,309	280	389	196	444	427	242	457	182
1980	1,343	281	394	204	466	426	247	474	195
1981	1,343	277	397	207	462	419	255	468	201
1982	1,322	280	390	205	447	417	253	453	200
1983	1,340	286	391	211	452	418	259	454	209
1984	1,345	286	386	215	459	411	261	459	215
1985	1,376	289	388	220	479	414	263	477	223

a   Includes unclassified postbaccalaureate students.

Note: Because of rounding, details may not add to totals.

Source:
National Center for Education Statistics, *Projections of Education Statistics to 1988–89; Projections of Education Statistics to 1990–91;* "Fall Enrollment in Colleges and Universities" surveys; *Digest of Education Statistics,* 1987, Table 111.

53

| Year | Graduate Enrollment[a] | | | | |
| | Number | | | Percentage Distribution | |
	Total	Men	Women	Men	Women
1929–30	**47,255**	29,070	18,185	62	38
1939–40	**105,748**	67,417	38,331	64	36
1949–50	**237,572**	172,310	65,262	73	27
1955	**250,771**	177,163	73,608	71	29
1960[c]	**356,000**	253,000	103,000	71	29
1965[c]	**697,000**	465,000	232,000	67	33
1970	**1,031,000**	632,000	399,000	61	39
1975	**1,263,000**	700,000	563,000	55	45
1976	**1,333,000**	714,000	619,000	54	46
1977	**1,318,000**	700,000	617,000	53	47
1978	**1,319,000**	688,000	632,000	52	48
1979	**1,309,000**	669,000	640,000	51	49
1980[d]	**1,099,652**	571,617	528,035	52	48
1981	**1,101,272**	571,363	529,909	52	48
1982	**1,089,962**	570,606	519,356	52	48
1983	**1,104,808**	577,448	527,360	52	48
1984	**1,114,184**	576,609	537,575	52	48
1985	**1,129,538**	577,224	552,314	51	49
1986[e]	**1,433,862**	693,487	740,375	48	52
1987[c]	**1,377,000**	662,000	715,000	48	52
Projections[b]					
1988	**1,363,000**	690,000	673,000	51	49
1989	**1,368,000**	694,000	674,000	51	49
1990	**1,372,000**	695,000	677,000	51	49
1995	**1,358,000**	684,000	674,000	50	50
1997	**1,343,000**	674,000	669,000	50	50

a Strict comparability of data is limited due to changes in the survey definition of "graduate student." The data shown for 1980 through 1985 exclude unclassified postbaccalaureate students. The estimates and projections for 1986 and later *include* unclassified postbaccalaureate students. See Guide to Sources.

b National Center for Education Statistics middle alternative projections.

c Estimate.

d Beginning in 1980, data for independent institutions have been disaggregated to show both the nonprofit and proprietary institutions.

e Preliminary data.

Sources:

1 USOE, *Statistics of Higher Education* (Washington: GPO), *1947-48,* pp. 72-77; *1949-50,* pp. 56,61; *1955-56,* pp. 124,135.

2 CES, *Projections of Education Statistics* (Washington: GPO), *to 1979-80,* p. 34; *to 1986-87,* table 9; *to 1997-98,* prepublication data.

3 CES, *Fall Enrollment in Colleges and Universities, 1984,* November 1986; fall enrollment surveys, 1985, 1986, unpublished tabulations. See Guide to Sources.

4 ACE/Macmillan, *1989–90 Fact Book on Higher Education,* Table 84.

Total First-Professional Enrollment in Institutions of Higher Education, by Sex of Student, Attendance Status, and Control of Institution, Fall 1969 – Fall 1986

54

Year	Total	Full-Time	Part-Time	Men Full-Time	Men Part-Time	Women Full-Time	Women Part-Time	Men Public	Men Private	Women Public	Women Private
1969	164,737	143,081	21,656	131,368	17,558	11,713	4,098	64,241	84,685	8,354	7,457
1970	173,411	157,384	16,027	144,270	14,379	13,114	1,648	68,956	89,693	6,501	8,261
1971	192,668	176,224	16,444	159,386	14,672	16,838	1,772	98,233	75,825	9,430	9,180
1972	206,659	190,039	16,620	168,990	14,453	21,049	2,167	79,723	103,720	10,842	12,374
1973	218,990	201,663	17,327	171,731	14,566	29,932	2,761	81,811	104,486	16,138	16,555
1974	235,452	216,329	19,123	178,926	15,153	37,403	3,970	84,271	109,808	20,085	21,288
1975	242,267	219,886	22,381	177,117	14,983	42,769	7,398	79,240	112,860	23,557	26,610
1976	244,292	220,124	24,168	171,967	17,843	48,157	6,325	77,873	111,937	23,468	31,014
1977	251,357	226,318	25,039	173,165	18,286	53,153	6,753	78,189	113,262	24,901	35,005
1978	256,904	232,540	24,364	174,906	17,315	57,634	7,049	77,748	114,473	26,839	37,844
1979	263,404	238,949	24,455	176,394	16,969	62,555	7,486	77,122	116,241	29,026	41,015
1980	277,767	251,359	26,408	181,448	17,896	69,911	8,512	81,022	118,322	33,415	45,008
1981	274,595	248,328	26,267	175,414	17,522	72,914	8,745	77,562	115,374	34,177	47,482
1982	278,425	252,108	26,317	173,941	17,259	78,167	9,058	76,273	114,927	37,183	50,042
1983	278,529	249,636	28,893	169,071	19,025	80,565	9,868	74,938	113,158	38,484	51,949
1984	278,598	249,708	28,890	166,286	18,663	83,422	10,227	73,722	111,227	40,186	53,463
1985	274,200	246,619	27,581	162,368	17,424	84,251	10,157	71,373	108,419	40,435	53,973
1986[a]	269,970	245,596	24,374	158,533	15,168	87,063	9,206	70,268	103,433	41,538	54,731

a Preliminary data.

Note: Because of rounding, details may not add to totals.

Source:
National Center for Education Statistics, *Projections of Education Statistics to 1988–89; Projections of Education Statistics to 1990–91;* "Fall Enrollment in Colleges and Universities" surveys; *Digest of Education Statistics,* 1988, Table 128.

Year	Degrees Conferred, All Levels[a]				
	Total	Men	Women	Public	Independent
1947–48	318,749	208,581	110,168	155,456	163,293
1949–50	498,373	376,860	121,513	246,249	252,124
1954–55	354,445	230,356	124,089	184,255	170,190
1959–60	479,215	315,242	163,973	262,809	216,406
1964–65	667,592	410,573	257,019	384,802	282,790
1965–66	714,624	440,427	274,197	420,595	294,029
1969–70	1,072,581	638,987	433,594	692,715	379,866
1970–71	1,147,985	680,344	467,641	751,785	396,200
1971–72	1,224,027	722,832	501,195	812,929	411,098
1972–73	1,280,022	751,936	528,086	856,072	423,950
1973–74	1,320,739	765,529	555,210	888,250	432,489
1974–75	1,315,659	746,588	569,071	881,276	434,383
1975–76	1,344,581	755,777	588,804	895,863	448,718
1976–77	1,344,493	745,149	599,344	893,508	450,985
1977–78	1,342,137	728,996	613,141	883,953	458,184
1978–79	1,335,393	711,630	623,763	868,701	466,692
1979–80	1,330,244	700,019	630,225	860,133	470,111
1980–81	1,335,792	692,429	643,364	860,859	474,934
1981–82	1,353,283	693,343	659,940	869,270	464,013
1982–83	1,365,336	697,045	668,291	873,506	491,830
1983–84	1,366,188	699,312	666,876	867,433	498,755
1984–85	1,373,734	698,073	675,661	873,735	499,999
1985–86	1,383,953	700,511	683,442	879,490	504,463
1986–87[b]	1,386,000	687,000	698,000	879,000	506,000
Projections					
1987–88	1,386,900	685,700	701,200	NA	NA
1988–89	1,386,900	682,700	704,200	NA	NA
1989–90	1,382,000	680,900	701,100	NA	NA
1994–95	1,352,300	665,600	686,700	NA	NA
1997–98	1,314,400	645,000	669,400	NA	NA

NA = not available

Note: Data before 1979–80 are for the aggregate United States (50 states, the District of Columbia, and outlying parts). For 1979–80 and later, the figures are for the 50 states and District of Columbia.

a Figures include bachelor's, master's, doctor's, and first-professional degrees.

b Estimate.

Sources:
1 National Center for Education Statistics, "Degrees and Other Formal Awards Conferred" surveys; "Projections of Education Statistics to 1997–98," 1988 (prepublication copy).

2 ACE/Macmillan, *1989–90 Fact Book on Higher Education,* Table 123.

Percentage Distribution of Bachelor's and Higher Degrees, by Level of Degree and Sex of Student, Selected Years, 1948 – 1998

56

	Percentage Distribution of Conferred Degrees									
	All Degrees		Bachelor's[a]		First-Professional[ab]		Master's[b]		Doctor's	
Year	Men	Women	Men	Women	Men	Women	Men	Women	Men	Women
1947–48	65	35	65	35	NA	NA	68	32	88	12
1949–50	76	24	76	24	NA	NA	71	29	90	10
1954–55	65	35	64	36	NA	NA	67	33	91	9
1959–60	66	34	65	35	NA	NA	68	32	90	10
1964–65	62	38	57	43	87	13	68	32	89	11
1965–66	62	38	57	43	95	5	66	34	88	12
1969–70	60	40	57	43	95	5	60	40	87	13
1970–71	59	41	57	43	94	6	60	40	86	14
1971–72	59	41	56	44	94	6	59	41	84	16
1972–73	59	41	56	44	93	7	59	41	82	18
1973–74	58	42	56	44	90	10	57	43	81	19
1974–75	57	43	55	45	88	12	55	45	79	21
1975–76	56	44	54	46	84	16	54	46	77	23
1976–77	55	45	54	46	81	19	53	47	76	24
1977–78	54	46	53	47	78	22	52	48	74	26
1978–79	53	47	52	48	76	24	51	49	72	28
1979–80	53	47	51	49	75	25	51	49	70	30
1980–81	52	48	50	50	74	27	50	50	69	31
1981–82	51	49	50	50	72	28	49	51	68	32
1982–83	51	49	49	51	70	30	50	50	67	33
1983–84	51	49	50	50	69	31	51	49	64	36
1984–85	51	49	49	51	67	33	50	50	66	34
1985–86	51	49	49	51	67	33	50	50	65	35
1986–87[c]	50	50	48	52	65	35	49	51	65	35
Projections										
1987–88	49	51	48	52	65	35	49	51	63	37
1988–89	49	51	48	52	64	36	49	51	62	38
1989–90	49	51	48	52	64	36	49	51	61	39
1994–95	49	51	48	52	60	40	48	52	57	43
1997–98	49	51	49	51	57	43	48	52	54	46

NA = not available

a   Before 1961–62, reports combined bachelor's and first-professional degrees. Figures for 1947–48 to 1959–60 are based on the combined total of both types of degrees.

b   For 1964–65 and earlier, master's degrees that were considered to be first-professional degrees, such as a master of library science, were counted as first-professional degrees. Beginning in 1965–1966, all master's degrees are included in the count of master's degrees; none are counted as first-professional degrees.

c   Estimate.

Sources:
1   USOE/NCES/CES "Degrees and Other Formal Awards Conferred" surveys; *Projections of Education Statistics to 1997–98* (Washington: GPO), 1988, prepublication copy.

2   ACE/Macmillan, *1989–90 Fact Book on Higher Education*, Table 128.

Highest Degree Earned, by Race, Sex, and Age, for Persons Age 18 and Older

(Numbers in thousands.)

Race, Age, and Sex	Total	Doctorate	Professional	Master's	Bachelor's	Associate	Vocational	Some College, No Degree	High School Graduate Only	Not a High School Graduate
All Persons										
Total	170,232	768	1,744	5,795	18,069	5,768	3,105	30,301	60,358	44,324
Men	80,834	585	1,432	3,110	9,581	2,804	1,023	15,444	26,407	20,448
Women	89,398	183	312	2,685	8,488	2,964	2,082	14,857	33,951	23,876
White										
Total	147,147	705	1,634	5,353	16,339	5,108	2,769	26,255	53,129	35,855
Men	70,276	558	1,355	2,923	8,703	2,498	919	13,444	23,270	16,606
Women	76,871	147	279	2,430	7,636	2,610	1,850	12,811	29,859	19,249
Black										
Total	18,475	32	53	286	963	482	254	3,229	6,043	7,133
Men	8,274	14	35	101	416	197	70	1,589	2,589	3,263
Women	10,201	18	18	185	547	285	184	1,640	3,454	3,870
Age										
18–24	28,494	5		63	1,968	978	389	8,698	11,048	5,346
25–34	40,474	147	509	1,585	6,353	2,099	806	8,231	14,973	5,770
35–44	30,480	255	538	1,947	4,318	1,366	678	5,428	10,883	5,067
45–54	22,264	123	249	993	2,109	662	455	2,832	8,959	5,883
55–64	22,060	125	256	681	1,750	422	385	2,675	7,789	7,977
65 and older	26,458	114	193	526	1,570	241	391	2,436	6,706	14,281
Percentage Distribution										
All Persons										
Total	1.000	0.005	0.010	0.034	0.106	0.034	0.018	0.178	0.355	0.260
Men	1.000	0.007	0.018	0.038	0.119	0.035	0.013	0.191	0.327	0.253
Women	1.000	0.002	0.003	0.030	0.095	0.033	0.023	0.166	0.380	0.267
White										
Total	1.000	0.005	0.011	0.036	0.111	0.035	0.019	0.178	0.361	0.244
Men	1.000	0.008	0.019	0.042	0.124	0.036	0.013	0.191	0.331	0.236
Women	1.000	0.002	0.004	0.032	0.099	0.034	0.024	0.167	0.388	0.250
Black										
Total	1.000	0.002	0.003	0.015	0.052	0.026	0.014	0.175	0.327	0.386
Men	1.000	0.002	0.004	0.012	0.050	0.024	0.008	0.192	0.313	0.394
Women	1.000	0.002	0.002	0.018	0.054	0.028	0.018	0.161	0.339	0.379
Age										
18–24	1.000	0.000	0.000	0.002	0.069	0.034	0.014	0.305	0.388	0.188
25–34	1.000	0.004	0.013	0.039	0.157	0.052	0.020	0.203	0.370	0.143
35–44	1.000	0.008	0.018	0.064	0.142	0.045	0.022	0.178	0.357	0.166
45–54	1.000	0.006	0.011	0.045	0.095	0.030	0.020	0.127	0.402	0.264
55–64	1.000	0.006	0.012	0.031	0.079	0.019	0.017	0.121	0.353	0.362
65 and older	1.000	0.004	0.007	0.020	0.059	0.009	0.015	0.092	0.253	0.540

Source:
U.S. Bureau of the Census, *Current Population Reports*, Ser. P-70, No. 11, "What It's Worth: Educational Background and Economic Status, Spring 1984," Table 1.

Number and Percentage Distribution of Degrees Conferred by All Institutions of Higher Education, by Race/Ethnicity, Level of Degree, and Sex of Recipient, 1984–85

Degree Level and Sex of Recipient	Generated Total		Minority					
			Total		American Indian/ Alaskan Native		Black Non-Hispanic	
	Number	Percentage	Number	Percentage	Number	Percentage	Number	Percentage
Associate	429,823	100	68,073	15,8	2,953	0.7	35,799	8.3
Women	239,406	100	38,630	16.1	1,755	0.7	21,607	9.0
Men	190,417	100	29,443	15.5	1,198	0.6	14,192	7.5
Bachelor's	968,311	100	112,988	11.7	4,246	0.4	57,473	5.9
Women	492,163	100	62,016	12.6	2,248	0.5	34,455	7.0
Men	476,148	100	50,972	10.7	1,998	0.4	23,018	4.8
Master's	280,421	100	29,841	10.6	1,256	0.4	13,939	5.0
Women	141,004	100	16,157	11.5	673	0.5	8,739	6.2
Men	139,417	100	13,684	9.8	583	0.4	5,200	3.7
Doctor's	32,307	100	3,056	9.5	119	0.4	1,154	3.6
Women	11,011	100	1,198	10.9	55	0.5	593	5.4
Men	21,296	100	1,858	8.7	64	0.3	561	2.6
First-Professional	71,057	100	6,977	9.8	248	0.3	3,029	4.3
Women	23,556	100	2,787	11.8	72	0.3	1,406	6.0
Men	47,501	100	4,190	8.8	176	0.4	1,623	3.4

Number and Percentage Distribution of Degrees Conferred by All Institutions of Higher Education, by Race/Ethnicity, Level of Degree, and Sex of Recipient, 1984–85

58 *Continued*

Degree Level and Sex of Recipient	Minority Asian/Pacific Islander		Hispanic		White Non-Hispanic		Nonresident Alien	
	Number	Percentage	Number	Percentage	Number	Percentage	Number	Percentage
Associate	9,914	2.3	19,407	4.5	355,343	82.7	6,407	1.5
Women	4,422	1.8	10,846	4.5	198,065	82.7	2,711	1.1
Men	5,492	2.9	8,561	4.5	157,278	82.6	3,696	1.9
Bachelor's	25,395	2.6	25,874	2.7	826,106	85.3	29,217	3.0
Women	11,841	2.4	13,472	2.7	421,021	85.5	9,126	1.9
Men	13,554	2.8	12,402	2.6	405,085	85.1	20,091	4.2
Master's	7,782	2.8	6,864	2.4	223,628	79.7	26.952	9.6
Women	2,940	2.1	3,805	2.7	117,569	83.4	7,278	5.2
Men	4,842	3.5	3,059	2.2	106,059	76.1	19,674	14.1
Doctor's	1,106	3.4	677	2.1	23,934	74.1	5,317	16.5
Women	304	2.8	246	2.2	8.917	81.0	896	8.1
Men	802	3.8	431	2.0	15,017	70.5	4,421	20.8
First-Professional	1,816	2.6	1,884	2.7	63,219	89.0	861	1.2
Women	664	2.8	645	2.7	20,589	87.4	180	0.8
Men	1,152	2.4	1,239	2.6	42,630	89.7	681	1.4

Note: Generated totals may not agree with previously published total degree data, which were not based on race/ethnicity, because of the new schools for which racial/ethnic data were not imputed.

Sources:
National Center for Education Statistics, "Degrees and Other Formal Awards Conferred Between July 1, 1984 and June 30, 1985," tabulations from final file with imputations for racial/ethnic nonresponses; Ed Tabs, "Earned Degree Data," Jan. 1988, Table 7.

Percentage of Highest Educational Degree Attained by 1980 High School Seniors, by Selected Student and School Characteristics, Spring 1986

59

Student and School Characteristics	Degree Status of 1980 High School Seniors in 1986						
	Total	No High School Diploma[a]	High School Diploma	License[b]	Associate Degree	Bachelor's Degree	Graduate or Professional Degree
Total	100.0	0.9	61.8	11.9	6.5	18.2	0.7
Sex							
Men	100.0	1.0	64.0	10.5	5.9	17.6	0.9
Women	100.0	0.8	59.6	13.3	7.0	18.8	0.6
Race/Ethnicity							
White	100.0	0.8	60.0	11.5	6.6	20.2	0.9
Black	100.0	1.2	69.4	13.9	5.3	9.9	0.2
Hispanic	100.0	1.7	70.2	13.8	7.3	6.8	0.1
Asian	100.0	c	49.6	12.6	8.7	27.3	1.7
American Indian	100.0	c	61.3	18.6	9.3	10.8	c
Socioeconomic Status group[d]							
Low	100.0	1.2	74.1	12.3	5.5	6.6	0.2
Low-middle	100.0	0.5	66.7	13.6	8.0	11.1	0.2
High-middle	100.0	0.1	58.4	12.9	7.7	20.4	0.6
High	100.0	c	45.7	8.7	6.3	37.1	2.2
High School Programs[e]							
General	100.0	0.8	69.7	12.6	6.5	10.2	0.2
Academic	100.0	0.1	45.6	8.8	7.2	36.6	1.8
Vocational	100.0	0.6	72.8	16.2	6.9	3.6	0.0
Postsecondary Education Plans[f]							
No plans	100.0	1.4	83.5	12.7	2.1	0.2	c
Attend vocational/ technical school	100.0	0.3	72.5	17.7	8.4	1.1	c
Attend college less than 4 years	100.0	0.2	65.5	14.4	13.1	6.8	c
Earn bachelor's degree	100.0	c	48.3	8.2	6.9	35.8	0.7
Earn advanced degree	100.0	0.1	43.5	7.9	4.9	40.6	3.0
Type of High School							
Public	100.0	1.0	63.2	12.1	6.6	16.4	0.7
Catholic	100.0	c	47.4	11.9	6.4	32.8	1.6
Other private	100.0	c	52.3	7.0	3.9	36.7	0.1

a   Seniors who dropped out of high school after spring 1980 survey.

b   Persons who earned a certificate for completing a program of study.

c   Less than .05%.

d   Socioeconomic status was measured by a composite score on parental education, family income, father's occupation, and household characteristics in 1980.

e   Student's self-reported high school program.

f   During their senior year of high school, students were asked about the highest level of education they planned to attain. Students who planned to get less than a high school education or a high school education only were classified as having no postsecondary education plans.

Note: Because of rounding, percentages may not add to 100.0.

Source:

National Center for Education Statistics, "High School and Beyond" survey; *Digest of Educational Statistics, 1988,* Table 214.

Highest Degrees Attained by 1980 High School Seniors by Spring 1986, by Fall 1980 Enrollment Status and Sex of Student

60

	Total % Receiving Postsecondary Degrees	Associate	Bachelor's	Graduate or Professional
Total[b]	25.4%	6.5%	18.2%	.7%
Men	24.4	5.9	17.6	.9
Women	26.4	7.0	18.8	.6
Women[c]				
Full-time, private 4-year	62.0	5.4	54.6	2.0
Full-time, public 4-year	50.1	4.6	44.2	1.3
Full-time, public 2-year	23.9	21.7	16.6	.6
Part-time, total[a]	36.6	13.3	22.9	.4
Not enrolled directly after high school	6.6	3.1	3.4	.1
Men[c]				
Full-time, private 4-year	57.6	4.7	48.5	4.4
Full-time, public 4-year	51.4	4.4	45.7	1.3
Full-time, public 2-year	38.5	19.5	18.6	.4
Part-time, total[a]	60.7	10.4	49.6	.7
Not enrolled directly after high school	7.8	4.0	3.6	.2

a Excludes private 2-year institutions.

b Total is all 1980 high-school seniors.

c Students by enrollment status in fall 1980.

Source:
National Center for Education Statistics, "Highest Degree Attained by 1980 High School Seniors by Sex, Race, Type of Community and Type of High School as of Spring, 1986," unpublished tabulations, Tables 2 and 3.

Associate Degrees Conferred in Institutions of Higher Education, by Sex and Field of Study: 50 States and Washington, D.C., Academic Years 1983 – 1985

61

Field of Study	1983–1984			1985–1986		
	Total	Men	Women	Total	Men	Women
Total	456,441	207,141	249,300	446,047	196,166	249,881
Agricultural and natural resources, total	7,760	5,228	2,532	5,741	3,975	1,766
Agricultural business and production	4,779	3,397	1,382	3,651	2,620	1,031
Agricultural science	1,506	660	846	1,096	526	570
Renewable natural resources	1,475	1,171	304	994	829	165
Architecture and environmental design	1,689	333	1,356	1,432	211	1,221
Area and ethnic studies	23	10	13	33	10	23
Business and management	120,236	44,018	76,218	117,358	38,429	78,929
Accounting	6,146	1,968	4,178	5,094	1,517	3,577
Business and management, general	13,956	6,725	7,231	12,163	5,132	7,031
Business administration and management	19,717	9,877	9,840	18,988	8,448	10,540
Business and management, other	11,711	7,028	4,683	11,268	5,933	5,335
Business data processing	16,307	7,307	9,000	15,926	7,065	8,861
Secretarial and related programs	20,830	235	20,595	21,095	283	20,872
Business and office, other	15,079	5,396	9,683	15,373	4,641	10,732
Marketing and distribution	15,622	5,113	10,509	16,553	5,022	11,531
Consumer and personal services	868	369	499	898	388	510
Communications	2,049	1,023	1,026	2,055	1,164	891
Communications technologies	1,821	1,100	721	1,929	1,156	773
Computer and information sciences	10,065	4,996	5,069	10,704	5,506	5,198
Education	7,653	2,393	5,260	7,391	2,256	5,135
Engineering	3,699	3,313	386	5,256	4,597	659
Engineering technologies	58,898	53,576	5,322	58,083	52,880	5,203
Mechanics and repairers	9,177	8,780	397	10,996	10,204	792
Construction trades	2,407	2,231	176	2,131	2,041	90
Engineering technologies, other	47,314	42,565	4,749	44,956	40,635	4,321
Foreign languages	355	168	187	437	239	198
Health sciences	66,448	7,725	58,723	66,559	7,884	58,675
Dental assisting	4,560	407	4,153	4,051	357	3,694
Emergency medical technician—ambulance	500	357	143	88	62	26
Emergency medical technician—paramedic	201	139	62	267	189	78
Medical lab technician	2,712	478	2,234	2,609	439	2,170
Medical assisting	1,835	33	1,802	2,004	39	1,965
Nursing assisting	97	21	76	33	10	23

Associate Degrees Conferred in Institutions of Higher Education, by Sex and Field of Study: 50 States and Washington, D.C., Academic Years 1983 – 1985

61 *Continued*

Field of study	1983–1984			1985–1986		
	Total	Men	Women	Total	Men	Women
Practical nursing	1,622	118	1,504	991	76	915
Nursing, general	37,395	2,529	34,866	38,610	2,818	35,792
Health sciences, other	17,526	3,643	13,883	17,906	3,894	14,012
Home economics	9,369	2,303	7,066	9,469	2,698	6,771
Law	1,742	267	1,475	2,259	280	1,979
Letters	638	233	405	548	198	350
Liberal and general studies	109,619	49,365	60,254	107,672	46,971	60,701
Library and archival sciences	218	29	189	126	15	111
Life sciences	1,109	548	561	998	424	574
Mathematics	809	502	307	602	370	232
Military sciences	88	86	2	30	29	1
Multi- and interdisciplinary studies	10,339	4,767	5,572	9,586	4,371	5,215
Parks and recreation	1,022	466	556	634	323	311
Philosophy and religion	193	117	76	114	79	35
Theology	677	372	305	705	432	273
Physical sciences	3,142	2,046	1,096	2,107	1,255	852
Science technologies	1,438	911	527	1,054	641	413
Physical sciences, other	1,704	1,135	569	1,053	614	439
Psychology	1,031	363	668	939	294	645
Protective services	13,163	9,950	3,213	12,096	8,932	3,164
Criminal justice administration and studies	5,996	4,289	1,707	5,579	3,873	1,706
Law enforcement and security services	4,074	3,007	1,067	4,167	3,061	1,106
Fire control and safety	2,150	2,072	78	1,666	1,607	59
Protective services, other	943	582	361	684	391	293
Public affairs	4,344	1,822	2,522	3,649	1,559	2,090
Transportation and material moving				1,338	1,039	299
Public affairs, other				2,311	520	1,791
Social sciences	2,958	1,385	1,573	2,540	1,045	1,495
Visual and performing arts	15,284	8,637	6,647	13,961	8,166	5,795
Fine arts, general	1,422	537	885	924	322	602
Graphic arts technician	2,131	619	1,512	1,855	592	1,263
Precision production	8,691	6,176	2,515	9,104	6,341	2,763
Visual and performing arts, other	3,040	1,305	1,735	2,078	911	1,167
Undistributed				1,034	418	616

Note: At the associate degree level, data were imputed by field of study for 103 institutions for 1983 that did not report data. Data for the 18 nonrespondents in 1985 were imputed at the total levels only, so field of study data do not add to grand totals by: 2,537 (total), 1,025 (men), and 1,512 (women).

Sources:
National Center for Education Statistics, unpublished tabulations from "Associate Degrees and Other Awards Below the Baccalaureate, 1983 to 1985," Table 1.1; "Degrees and Other Formal Awards Conferred, 1985–86"; *Digest of Education Statistics, 1988,* Table 170.

Bachelor's Degrees Conferred to Women, by Field of Study and Year, 1974–1975 to 1985–1986

Field of Study	1974–75	1975–76	1976–77	1977–78	1978–79	1979–80	1980–81	1981–82	1982–83	1983–84	1984–85	1985–86
Women, Total	418,092	420,821	424,004	433,857	444,046	455,806	465,257	479,634	490,370	491,990	496,949	501,900
Agriculture and natural resources	2,467	3,557	4,777	5,581	6,280	6,757	6,732	6,586	6,824	6,111	5,630	5,279
Architecture and environmental design	1,435	1,750	1,973	2,196	2,397	2,536	2,655	2,903	3,420	3,291	3,306	3,295
Area and ethnic studies	1,907	1,965	1,914	1,895	1,741	1,715	1,739	1,830	1,871	1,695	1,768	1,800
Business and management	21,599	28,112	35,438	43,608	52,537	62,464	73,543	84,333	95,175	100,122	105,319	108,889
Communications	7,450	8,465	9,787	11,347	12,554	14,200	16,245	18,481	21,636	22,812	24,040	24,779
Communications technologies	343	359	495	573	637	760	858	824	781	706	805	665
Computer and information sciences	953	1,118	1,531	1,852	2,447	3,372	4,919	7,049	8,904	11,926	14,299	14,966
Education	122,458	112,737	103,781	98,657	92,290	87,247	81,233	76,711	74,321	70,167	66,897	66,235
Engineering	822	1,295	2,022	3,464	4,847	5,915	7,024	8,231	9,601	10,668	11,195	11,049
Engineering technologies	192	165	196	245	327	490	675	875	1,353	1,467	1,457	1,532
Foreign languages	13,485	11,807	10,573	9,656	8,971	8,402	7,799	7,447	7,200	6,939	7,304	7,318
Health sciences	38,003	42,401	45,235	47,620	50,658	52,271	52,884	53,321	54,410	54,259	54,727	54,852
Home economics	16,092	16,689	16,717	16,836	17,410	17,550	17,454	16,856	15,751	15,300	14,539	14,231
Law	62	100	154	187	274	311	388	430	642	739	708	778
Letters	30,267	26,543	24,160	22,820	21,979	21,800	21,664	22,573	21,547	22,232	22,428	23,269
Liberal and general studies	5,858	7,197	8,523	9,800	10,316	10,680	10,103	10,142	10,019	10,097	10,620	10,604
Library and archival sciences	989	785	710	613	528	378	353	264	230	222	176	140
Life sciences	17,129	18,755	19,387	19,797	19,655	19,542	19,067	18,885	18,418	18,082	18,381	18,531
Mathematics	7,595	6,509	5,893	5,171	4,907	4,816	4,736	5,006	5,458	5,845	6,982	7,581
Military sciences	0	2	1	9	12	10	12	21	29	16	26	21
Multi- and interdisciplinary studies	5,992	7,348	7,404	7,028	6,724	6,596	7,504	8,510	8,577	8,512	8,204	8,195
Parks and recreation	1,951	2,334	2,625	2,859	3,406	3,352	3,506	3,329	3,272	2,987	2,854	2,770
Philosophy and religion	2,601	2,532	2,406	2,448	2,252	2,267	2,220	2,101	2,142	2,136	2,156	2,078
Theology	1,319	1,511	1,575	1,526	1,563	1,582	1,483	1,537	1,642	1,548	1,636	1,475
Physical sciences	3,786	4,112	4,501	4,896	5,222	5,546	5,888	6,186	6,389	6,537	6,637	5,962
Psychology	26,798	27,076	26,820	26,211	25,997	26,543	26,538	27,408	27,259	27,080	27,117	27,943
Protective services	1,672	2,311	2,984	3,964	4,496	5,020	5,004	4,752	4,969	4,850	4,816	4,741
Public affairs	9,265	9,975	10,922	11,936	12,873	12,772	13,044	13,006	11,380	9,804	9,203	9,208
Social sciences	50,352	47,664	45,873	45,683	45,157	45,085	44,306	44,434	42,380	41,110	40,289	41,049
Visual and performing arts	25,250	25,647	25,627	25,379	25,589	25,827	25,681	25,603	24,770	24,730	23,430	22,665

Note: Beginning in 1982–83, the taxonomy used to collect data on earned degrees by major field of study was revised. The figures for earlier years have been reclassified when necessary to make them conform to the new taxonomy. Data for 1982–83 are subject to slight revision.

Marketing and distribution to business and management.

Military technologies to military science.

Transportation and material moving to public affairs.

Science technologies to physical sciences.

Construction trades to engineering technology.

Mechanics and repairers to engineering technology.

Sources:
National Center for Education Statistics, "Degrees and Other Formal Awards Conferred," surveys, 1974–75 to 1984–85; "Trends in Bachelor's and Higher Degrees, 1975–1985," Table 28; "Bachelor's and Higher Degrees Conferred in 1985–86" (bulletin), Table 2.

Bachelor's Degrees Conferred to Men, by Field of Study and Year, 1974–1975 to 1985–1986

Field of Study	1974–75	1975–76	1976–77	1977–78	1978–79	1979–80	1980–81	1981–82	1982–83	1983–84	1984–85	1985–86
Men, Total	504,841	504,925	495,545	487,347	477,344	473,611	469,883	473,364	479,140	482,319	482,528	485,923
Agriculture and natural resources	15,061	15,845	16,690	17,069	16,854	16,045	15,154	14,443	14,085	13,206	12,477	11,544
Architecture and environmental design	6,791	7,396	7,249	7,054	6,876	6,596	6,800	6,825	6,403	5,895	6,019	5,824
Area and ethnic studies	1,637	1,612	1,536	1,362	1,265	1,125	1,148	1,032	1,100	1,184	1,099	1,260
Business and management	111,411	114,267	115,526	116,579	119,227	122,897	125,795	129,668	131,718	129,909	128,032	129,271
Communications	10,706	11,580	11,911	12,526	12,352	12,727	13,183	13,947	15,318	15,774	16,318	16,887
Communications technologies	749	878	1,021	954	914	929	996	970	867	873	920	760
Computer and information sciences	4,080	4,534	4,876	5,349	6,272	7,782	10,202	13,218	15,606	20,246	24,579	26,923
Education	44,557	42,070	39,941	37,484	33,819	30,922	27,076	24,402	23,670	22,215	21,264	20,986
Engineering	38,566	37,093	38,914	43,405	48,174	52,487	56,263	58,790	62,647	65,064	65,959	65,284
Engineering technologies	7,272	7,778	8,151	8,540	9,027	10,001	11,038	12,109	15,669	17,245	17,494	18,088
Foreign languages	4,121	3,664	3,371	3,074	2,854	2,731	2,520	2,394	2,485	2,540	2,650	2,784
Health sciences	10,855	11,412	11,887	11,548	11,161	11,336	10,464	10,204	10,204	10,079	9,786	9,683
Home economics	680	720	722	785	890	861	916	1,016	954	1,016	1,016	1,057
Law	374	431	405	466	404	372	388	416	457	533	449	419
Letters	18,267	16,476	14,689	13,545	12,578	11,697	11,544	11,761	11,196	11,507	11,663	12,165
Liberal and general studies	7,174	7,539	8,240	9,894	9,208	9,389	8,493	8,003	8,505	8,718	8,571	8,644
Library and archival sciences	80	58	71	80	30	20	22	43	28	33	26	17
Life sciences	34,612	35,520	34,218	31,705	29,191	26,828	24,149	22,754	21,564	20,558	20,064	19,993
Mathematics	10,586	9,475	8,303	7,398	6,899	6,562	6,342	6,593	6,995	7,366	8,164	8,725
Military sciences	340	1,175	932	377	335	241	293	262	238	179	273	235
Multi- and interdisciplinary studies	9,193	10,359	9,745	8,916	7,906	7,808	8,391	9,141	8,705	8,222	7,523	7,505
Parks and recreation	2,567	2,848	2,889	2,764	2,575	2,401	2,223	2,006	1,926	1,765	1,739	1,663
Philosophy and religion	6,396	5,915	5,752	5,459	5,095	4,802	4,556	4,208	4,341	4,299	4,244	4,161
Theology	3,490	4,009	4,534	4,793	4,528	4,625	4,358	4,461	4,411	4,366	4,403	4,127
Physical sciences	16,992	17,353	17,996	18,090	17,985	17,864	18,064	17,866	17,016	17,134	17,095	15,769
Psychology	24,190	22,832	20,553	18,348	16,464	15,419	14,295	13,623	13,105	12,792	12,694	12,578
Protective services	8,284	10,196	11,546	10,921	10,307	9,995	8,703	7,686	7,610	7,804	7,694	7,963
Public affairs	5,465	6,776	6,705	6,146	6,009	5,650	5,670	5,733	4,910	4,592	4,635	4,670
Social sciences	84,813	78,623	71,006	67,144	62,765	58,434	56,039	55,111	52,708	52,102	51,172	52,654
Visual and performing arts	15,532	16,491	16,166	15,572	15,380	15,065	14,798	14,819	14,699	15,103	14,506	14,284

Note: Beginning in 1982–83, the taxonomy used to collect data on earned degrees by major field of study was revised. The figures for earlier years have been reclassified when necessary to make them conform to the new taxonomy. Data for 1982–83 are subject to slight revision.

Marketing and distribution to business and management.
Military technologies to military science.
Transportation and material moving to public affairs.
Science technologies to physical sciences.
Construction trades to engineering technology.
Mechanics and repairers to engineering technology.

Sources:
National Center for Education Statistics, "Degrees and Other Formal Awards Conferred," surveys, 1974–75 to 1984–85; "Trends in Bachelor's and Higher Degrees, 1975–1985," Table 2A; "Bachelor's and Higher Degrees Conferred in 1985–86" (bulletin), Table 2A. See Guide to Sources.

Bachelor's Degrees Conferred, Selected Fields, by Race/Ethnicity, 1975–76 and 1984–85[a]

	Minorities					Hispanic				
	1975–76 Total	Percentage	1984–85 Total	Percentage	Percentage Change	1975–76 Total	Percentage	1984–85 Total	Percentage	Percentage Change
Education										
Total	18,558	12.0[b]	9,242	10.5	−50.2[e]	2,831	1.8	2,533	2.9	−10.5[e]
Men	5,179	12.3[c]	2,571	12.2	−50.4	948	2.2	597	2.8	−37.0
Women	13,379	11.9[d]	6,671	10.0	−50.1	1,883	1.7	1,936	2.9	2.8
Business										
Total	14,211	10.0	25,871	11.6	82.0	2,467	1.7	5,616	2.5	127.6
Men	9,522	8.3	12,299	9.9	29.2	1,998	1.7	2,928	2.4	46.5
Women	4,689	16.7	13,572	13.7	189.4	469	1.7	2,688	2.7	473.1
Social Sciences										
Total	15,911	12.6	11,427	12.6	−28.2	3,032	2.4	2,846	3.1	−6.1
Men	8,764	11.2	5,566	11.0	−36.5	1,953	2.5	1,557	3.1	−20.3
Women	7,147	15.0	5,861	14.7	−18.0	1,079	2.3	1,289	3.2	19.5
Health Professions										
Total	4,655	8.7	6,969	11.0	49.7	901	1.7	1,550	2.4	72.0
Men	924	8.1	1,844	12.0	99.6	242	2.1	309	3.2	27.7
Women	3,731	8.8	5,849	10.8	56.8	659	1.6	1,241	2.3	88.3
Biological/Life Sciences										
Total	4,559	8.4	5,397	14.2	18.4	873	1.6	1,241	3.3	42.2
Men	2,574	7.3	2,598	13.1	0.9	564	1.6	681	3.4	20.7
Women	1,985	10.6	2,799	15.4	41.0	309	1.7	560	3.1	81.2
Engineering										
Total	3,332	7.3	8,505	11.2	155.3	841	1.8	1,775	2.3	111.1
Men	3,184	7.2	6,790	10.5	113.3	809	1.8	1,501	2.3	85.5
Women	148	10.2	1,715	15.6	1,058.8	32	2.2	274	2.5	756.3

Bachelor's Degrees Conferred, Selected Fields, by Race/Ethnicity, 1975–76 and 1984–85[a]

	Black					White				
	1975–76 Total	Percentage	1984–85 Total	Percentage	Percentage Change	1975–76 Total	Percentage	1984–85 Total	Percentage	Percentage Change
Education										
Total	14,209	9.2	5,456	6.2	−61.6[e]	135,464	87.5	77,531	88.3	−42.8[e]
Men	3,700	8.8	1,569	7.4	−57.6	36,653	86.9	18,119	85.7	−50.6
Women	10,509	9.3	3,887	5.8	−63.0	98,811	87.7	59,412	89.2	−39.9
Business										
Total	9,489	6.7	14,157	6.3	49.2	125,251	87.9	190,249	85.2	51.9
Men	5,877	5.1	6,279	5.1	6.8	102,514	89.6	106,795	86.1	4.2
Women	3,612	12.9	7,878	7.9	118.1	22,737	81.1	83,454	84.0	267.0
Social Sciences										
Total	10,978	8.7	6,100	6.7	−44.4	108,090	85.9	77,117	84.9	−28.7
Men	5,713	7.3	2,778	5.5	−51.4	68,013	87.1	43,787	86.2	−35.6
Women	5,265	11.0	3,322	8.3	−36.9	40,077	83.9	33,330	83.3	−16.8
Health Professions										
Total	2,741	5.1	3,836	6.1	39.9	48,462	90.1	55,501	87.7	14.5
Men	397	3.5	484	5.1	21.9	10,196	89.5	8,114	85.1	−20.4
Women	2,344	5.5	3,352	6.2	43.0	38,266	90.3	47,387	88.2	23.8
Biological/Life Sciences										
Total	2,326	4.3	2,045	5.4	−12.1	48,603	89.8	31,807	83.5	−34.6
Men	1,163	3.3	806	4.0	−30.7	32,142	90.8	16,805	84.4	−47.7
Women	1,163	6.2	1,239	6.8	6.5	16,461	88.0	15,002	82.4	−8.9
Engineering										
Total	1,370	3.0	2,039	2.7	48.8	38,970	85.7	60,992	80.6	56.5
Men	1,303	3.0	1,479	2.3	13.5	37,729	85.7	52,167	80.7	38.3
Women	67	4.6	560	5.1	735.8	1,241	85.1	8,825	80.1	611.1

a Some institutions did not report the racial/ethnic data for earned degrees. Data for some of these nonreporting institutions were imputed. Because of underreporting and nonreporting of racial/ethnic data, totals on this table may be slightly smaller than totals appearing on other tables. Because of rounding, details may not add to totals.

b Degrees awarded to this group as a percentage of all degrees in this field.

c Degrees awarded to men in this group as a percentage of all degrees awarded to men in this field.

d Degrees awarded to women in this group as a percentage of all degrees awarded to women in this field.

e Percentage change reflects the difference between the 1975–76 total and the 1984–85 total.

Sources:

1 Equal Employment Opportunity Commission, "Data on Earned Degrees Conferred from Institutions of Higher Education by Race/Ethnicity, 1975–76."

2 National Center for Education Statistics, "Degrees and Other Formal Awards Conferred" surveys, 1985.

3 ACE, "Minorities in Higher Education: Sixth Annual Status Report 1987," Table 4A.

Bachelor's Degrees Conferred, Selected Fields, by Race/Ethnicity, 1975–76 and 1984–85[a]

	Asian/Pacific Islander					American Indian				
	1975–76 Total	Percentage	1984–85 Total	Percentage	Percentage Change	1975–76 Total	Percentage	1984–85 Total	Percentage	Percentage Change
Education										
Total	776	0.5	770	0.9	−0.8	742	0.5	483	0.6	−34.9
Men	292	0.7	240	1.1	−17.8	239	0.6	165	0.8	−31.0
Women	484	0.4	530	0.8	9.5	503	0.4	318	0.5	−36.8
Business										
Total	1,829	1.3	5,199	2.3	184.3	426	0.3	899	0.4	111.0
Men	1,297	1.1	2,605	2.1	100.8	350	0.3	487	0.4	39.1
Women	532	1.9	2,594	2.6	387.6	76	0.3	412	0.4	442.1
Social Sciences										
Total	1,388	1.1	2,034	2.2	46.5	513	0.4	447	0.5	−12.9
Men	787	1.0	1,002	2.0	27.3	311	0.4	229	0.5	−26.4
Women	601	1.3	1,032	2.6	71.7	202	0.4	218	0.5	7.9
Health Professions										
Total	847	1.6	1,310	2.1	54.7	166	0.3	273	0.4	64.5
Men	247	2.2	298	3.1	20.6	38	0.3	49	0.5	28.9
Women	600	1.4	1,012	1.9	68.7	128	0.3	224	0.4	75.0
Biological/Life Sciences										
Total	1,217	2.2	1,950	5.1	60.2	143	0.3	161	0.4	12.6
Men	757	2.1	1,022	5.1	35.0	90	0.3	89	0.4	−1.1
Women	460	2.5	928	5.1	101.7	53	0.3	72	0.4	35.8
Engineering										
Total	971	2.1	4,482	5.9	361.6	150	0.3	209	0.3	39.3
Men	924	2.1	3,641	5.6	294.0	148	0.3	169	0.3	14.2
Women	47	3.2	841	7.6	1,689.4	2	0.1	40	0.4	1,900.0

Bachelor's Degrees Conferred, Selected Fields, by Race/Ethnicity, 1975–1976 and 1984–1985[a]

	Nonresident Alien				
	1975–1976 Total	Percentage	1984–1985 Total	Percentage	Percentage Change
Education					
Total	746	0.5	1,015	1.2	36.1
Men	325	0.8	456	2.2	40.3
Women	421	0.4	559	0.8	32.8
Business					
Total	2,970	2.1	7,250	3.2	144.1
Men	2,374	2.1	4,980	4.0	109.8
Women	596	2.1	2,270	2.3	280.9
Social Sciences					
Total	1,819	1.4	2,251	2.5	23.7
Men	1,293	1.7	1,436	2.8	11.1
Women	526	1.1	815	2.0	54.9
Health Professions					
Total	649	1.2	819	1.3	26.2
Men	276	2.4	280	2.9	1.4
Women	373	0.9	539	1.0	44.5
Biological/Life Sciences					
Total	938	1.7	911	2.4	−2.9
Men	677	1.9	502	2.5	−25.8
Women	261	1.4	409	2.2	56.7
Engineering					
Total	3,171	7.0	6,185	8.2	95.0
Men	3,102	7.0	5,703	8.8	83.8
Women	69	4.7	482	4.4	598.6

a   Some institutions did not report the racial/ethnic data for earned degrees. Data for some of these nonreporting institutions were imputed. Because of underreporting and nonreporting of racial/ethnic data, totals on this table may be slightly smaller than totals appearing on other tables. Because of rounding, details may not add to totals.

b   Degrees awarded to this group as a percentage of all degrees in this field.

c   Degrees awarded to men in this group as a percentage of all degrees awarded to men in this field.

d   Degrees awarded to women in this group as a percentage of all degrees awarded to women in this field.

e   Percentage change reflects the difference between the 1975–76 total and the 1984–85 total.

Sources:

1   Equal Employment Opportunity Commission, "Data on Earned Degrees Conferred from Institutions of Higher Education by Race/Ethnicity, 1975–76."

2   National Center for Education Statistics, "Degrees and Other Formal Awards Conferred" surveys, 1985.

3   ACE, "Minorities in Higher Education: Sixth Annual Status Report 1987," Table 4A.

Bachelor's Degrees by Race/Ethnicity for Selected Years[a]

	1975–76		1980–81		1984–85		Percent Change 1975–76 to 1984–85
	Total	Percent	Total	Percent	Total	Percent	
All	918,388	100.0	934,800	100.0	968,311	100.0	5.4
Men	499,602	54.4[b]	469,625	50.2	476,148	50.8	−4.7
Women	418,786	45.6[c]	465,175	49.8	492,163	49.2	17.5
Minority	91,777	10.0[d]	104,892	11.2	112,988	11.7	23.1
Men	44,039	8.8[e]	47,128	10.0	50,972	10.7	15.7
Women	47,738	11.4[f]	57,764	12.4	62,016	12.6	29.9
Hispanic	17,964	2.0	21,832	2.3	25,874	2.7	44.0
Men	10,171	2.0	10,810	2.3	12,402	2.5	21.9
Women	7,793	1.9	11,022	2.4	13,472	2.8	72.9
Black	59,122	6.4	60,673	6.5	57,473	5.9	−2.8
Men	25,634	5.1	24,511	5.2	23,018	4.7	−10.2
Women	33,488	8.0	36,162	7.8	34,455	7.2	2.9
White	811,599	88.4	807,319	86.4	826,106	85.3	1.8
Men	444,682	89.0	406,173	86.5	405,085	82.3	−8.9
Women	366,917	87.6	401,146	86.2	421,021	88.4	14.7
Asian/Pacific Islander	11,193	1.2	18,794	2.0	25,395	2.6	126.9
Men	6,318	1.3	10,107	2.2	13,554	2.8	114.5
Women	4,875	1.2	8,687	1.9	11,841	2.5	142.9
American Indian	3,498	0.4	3,593	0.4	4,246	0.4	21.4
Men	1,916	0.4	1,700	0.4	1,998	0.4	4.3
Women	1,582	0.4	1,893	0.4	2,248	0.5	42.1
Nonresident Alien	15,012	1.6	22,589	2.4	29,217	3.0	94.6
Men	10,881	2.2	16,324	3.5	20,091	4.1	84.6
Women	4,131	1.0	6,265	1.3	9,126	1.9	120.6

Notes:

a Some institutions did not report the racial/ethnic data for earned degrees. Data for some of these nonreporting institutions were imputed. Because of underreporting and nonreporting of racial/ethnic data, totals on this table may be slightly smaller than totals appearing on other tables. Because of rounding, details may not add to totals.

b Degrees awarded to men as a percentage of all bachelor's degrees awarded that year.

c Degrees awarded to women as a percentage of all bachelor's degrees awarded that year.

d Degrees awarded to this group as a percentage of all bachelor's degrees awarded that year.

e Degrees awarded to men in this group as a percentage of all bachelor's degrees awarded to men that year.

f Degrees awarded to women in this group as a percentage of all bachelor's degrees awarded to women that year.

Sources:

1 U.S. Department of Education, Equal Employment Opportunity Commission "Data on Earned Degrees Conferred from Institutions of Higher Education by Race/Ethnicity 1975–76."

2 U.S. Department of Education, Center for Education Statistics, *Digest of Education Statistics, 1983–84*, p. 121.

3 U.S. Department of Education, Center for Education Statistics "Degrees Conferred" surveys, 1985.

4 ACE, *Minorites in Higher Education: Sixth Annual Status Report, 1987*, Table 3A.

Distribution of Bachelor's Degrees in Women's Colleges	Percentage	
White women	88	
Black women	7	
Hispanic women	3	
Asian women	2	
American Indian women	< 1	
Total women	100	$(N^a = 14{,}646)$
Women	97	
Men	3	
Total	100	$(N^a = 15{,}576)$
Majority students (Men and women)	88	
Minority students (Men and women)	12	
Total	100	$(N^a = 15{,}181)$

a   N is the total number on which the percentages are based.

Women's Colleges	Field of Study	All Institutions[b]
15%	Business and management	24%
7	Education	9
18	Health/life sciences	11
7	Letters	3
4	Engineering, mathematics, physical sciences	12
7	Psychology	4
16	Social sciences	9
7	Visual and performing arts	4
3	Foreign languages	1
16	Other	23
100	Total	100
(N[a] = 15,576)		(N[a] = 979,477)

a N is the total number on which the percentages are based.

b Includes degrees awarded to both women and men.

Sources:

1 ACE, unpublished tabulations from the National Center for Education Statistics, HEGIS tapes.

2 National Center for Education Statistics, *Digest of Education Statistics, 1987,* Table 154.

67

Year	Master's Degrees[a]				
	Total	Men	Women	Public	Independent
1947–48	42,449	28,939	13,510	17,696	24,753
1949–50	58,219	41,237	16,982	26,192	32,027
1954–55	58,204	38,740	19,464	32,291	25,913
1959–60	74,497	50,937	23,560	42,991	31,506
1964–65	112,195	76,211	35,984	68,199	43,996
1965–66	140,772	93,184	47,588	84,313	56,459
1969–70	209,387	126,146	83,241	135,351	74,036
1970–71	231,486	138,590	92,896	152,305	79,181
1971–72	252,774	150,085	102,689	167,949	84,825
1972–73	264,525	155,000	109,525	175,220	89,305
1973–74	278,259	158,344	119,915	185,504	92,755
1974–75	293,651	162,115	131,536	194,666	98,985
1975–76	313,001	167,745	145,256	207,209	105,792
1976–77	318,241	168,210	150,031	209,689	108,552
1977–78	312,816	161,708	151,108	202,891	109,925
1978–79	302,075	153,772	148,303	192,683	109,392
1979–80	298,081	150,749	147,332	187,499	110,582
1980–81	295,739	147,013	148,696	184,384	111,358
1981–82	295,546	145,532	150,014	182,295	113,251
1982–83	289,921	144,697	145,224	176,246	113,675
1983–84	284,263	143,595	140,668	170,693	113,570
1984–85	286,251	143,390	142,861	170,000	116,251
1985–86	288,567	143,508	145,059	169,903	118,664
1986–87[b]	291,000	142,000	148,000	171,000	119,000
Projections					
1987–88	290,000	142,000	148,000	NA	NA
1988–89	290,000	142,000	148,000	NA	NA
1989–90	290,000	142,000	148,000	NA	NA
1994–95	290,000	140,000	150,000	NA	NA
1997–98	290,000	139,000	151,000	NA	NA

NA = not available

Note: Data before 1979–80 are for the aggregate United States (the 50 states, the District of Columbia, and outlying parts). For 1979–80 and later, the figures shown are for the 50 states and the District of Columbia.

a Figures for 1947–48 to 1964–65 generally exclude those master's degrees that are considered first-professional degrees, such as master of library science and master of social work. Data for 1965–66 and later include all master's degrees.

b Estimate.

Sources:
1 National Center for Education Statistics, "Degrees and Other Formal Awards Conferred" surveys; "Projections of Education Statistics to 1997–98," 1988 (prepublication copy).

2 ACE/Macmillan, *1989–90 Fact Book on Higher Education,* Table 126.

	1975–76		1980–81		1984–85		Percentage Change 1975–76 to 1984–85
	Total	Percentage	Total	Percentage	Total	Percentage	
All	309,263	100.0	294,183	100.0	280,421	100.0	−9.3
Men	165,474	53.5[b]	145,666	49.5	139,419	49.7	−15.7
Women	143,789	46.5[c]	148,517	50.5	141,004	50.3	1.9
Minority	30,418	9.8[d]	30,910	10.5	29,841	10.4	−1.9
Men	13,595	8.2[e]	13,517	9.3	13,684	9.5	0.7
Women	16,823	11.7[f]	17,393	11.7	16,157	11.3	−4.0
Hispanic	5,299	1.7	6,461	2.2	6,864	2.4	29.5
Men	2,868	1.7	3,085	2.1	3,059	2.1	6.7
Women	2,431	1.7	3,376	2.3	3,805	2.7	56.5
Black	20,345	6.6	17,133	5.8	13,939	4.9	−31.5
Men	7,809	4.7	6,158	4.2	5,200	3.6	−33.4
Women	12,536	8.7	10,975	7.4	8,739	6.1	−30.3
White	262,771	85.0	241,216	82.0	223,628	78.1	−14.9
Men	139,507	84.3	115,562	79.3	106,059	74.0	−24.0
Women	123,264	85.7	125,654	84.6	117,569	82.3	−4.6
Asian/Pacific Islander	3,910	1.3	6,282	2.1	7,782	2.7	99.0
Men	2,409	1.5	3,773	2.6	4,842	3.4	101.0
Women	1,501	1.0	2,509	1.7	2,940	2.1	95.9
American Indian	783	0.3	1,034	0.4	1,256	0.4	60.4
Men	428	0.3	501	0.3	583	0.4	36.2
Women	355	0.2	533	0.4	673	0.5	89.6
Nonresident Alien	16,074	5.2	22,057	7.5	26,952	9.4	67.7
Men	12,372	7.5	16,587	11.4	19,674	13.7	59.0
Women	3,702	2.6	5,470	3.7	7,278	5.1	96.6

a   Some institutions did not report the racial/ethnic data for earned degrees. Data for some of these nonreporting institutions were imputed. Because of underreporting and nonreporting of racial/ethnic data, totals on this table may be slightly smaller than totals appearing on other tables. Because of rounding, details may not add to totals.

b   Degrees awarded to men as a percentage of all master's degrees awarded that year.

c   Degrees awarded to women as a percentage of all master's degrees awarded that year.

d   Degrees awarded to this group as a percentage of all master's degrees awarded that year.

e   Degrees awarded to men in this group as a percentage of all master's degrees awarded to men that year.

f   Degrees awarded to women in this group as a percentage of all master's degrees awarded to women that year.

Sources:
1   Equal Employment Opportunity Commission, "Data on Earned Degrees Conferred from Institutions of Higher Education by Race/Ethnicity, 1975–76."

2   National Center for Education Statistics, *Digest of Education Statistics, 1983–84;* "Degrees and Other Formal Awards Conferred," surveys, 1985.

3   ACE, "Minorites in Higher Education: Sixth Annual Status Report, 1987," Table 3B.

Master's Degrees Conferred on Women by Field of Study and Year, 1974–75 to 1984–86

Field of Study	1974–75	1975–76	1976–77	1977–78	1978–79	1979–80	1980–81	1981–82	1982–83	1983–84	1984–85	1985–86
Women, Total	130,880	144,523	149,381	150,408	147,709	147,332	148,696	150,014	145,224	140,668	142,861	145,059
Agriculture and natural resources	364	478	547	755	807	894	942	1,049	1,125	1,189	1,082	1,100
Architecture and environmental design	595	670	724	811	887	894	919	1,085	1,133	1,026	1,127	1,131
Area and ethnic studies	503	452	498	465	416	410	406	399	415	425	415	438
Business and management	3,062	4,953	6,654	8,176	9,671	12,284	14,504	17,056	18,862	20,088	20,903	20,849
Communications	1,090	1,253	1,279	1,549	1,292	1,489	1,544	1,654	1,891	2,002	2,013	2,095
Communications technologies	86	55	93	74	107	66	113	95	52	54	80	118
Computer and information sciences	338	377	466	567	575	764	971	1,310	1,508	1,811	2,037	2,412
Education	74,748	82,621	83,537	80,625	76,852	72,931	70,682	67,804	61,621	55,606	55,192	55,634
Engineering	371	568	697	840	933	1,122	1,323	1,573	1,746	2,096	2,242	2,396
Engineering technologies	4	14	23	25	18	20	39	55	51	61	66	97
Foreign languages	2,549	2,353	2,182	1,931	1,687	1,570	1,410	1,399	1,155	1,202	1,165	1,212
Health sciences	6,191	7,930	8,413	9,629	10,558	10,937	11,853	12,099	12,836	13,174	13,248	14,164
Home economics	1,698	1,993	2,127	2,401	2,288	2,456	2,318	2,154	2,184	2,146	2,104	2,017
Law	100	173	208	261	255	286	326	383	488	415	419	483
Letters	6,215	5,804	5,424	5,315	4,658	4,311	4,190	4,165	3,753	3,760	3,870	4,122
Liberal and general studies	1,006	993	799	766	728	833	675	668	543	756	731	706
Library and archival sciences	6,372	6,296	6,026	5,530	4,747	4,370	4,018	3,707	3,244	3,039	3,135	2,905
Life sciences	1,963	2,085	2,396	2,406	2,566	2,412	2,324	2,448	2,482	2,410	2,412	2,397
Mathematics	1,422	1,310	1,299	1,145	1,051	1,032	875	906	979	950	1,008	1,112
Military sciences	0	0	1	1	0	0	0	1	1	1	1	2
Multi- and inter-disciplinary studies	697	769	872	915	1,051	1,258	1,123	1,470	1,254	1,283	1,339	1,310
Parks and recreation	191	214	222	247	394	350	340	250	301	301	303	261
Philosophy and religion	475	445	454	542	473	485	501	464	424	412	466	450
Theology	998	1,058	1,137	1,015	1,140	1,217	1,419	1,414	1,494	1,698	1,506	1,598
Physical sciences	838	818	881	941	990	971	1,084	1,196	1,133	1,308	1,344	1,432
Psychology	3,022	3,640	3,988	4,241	4,331	4,430	4,640	4,582	5,140	5,041	5,364	5,370
Protective services	139	202	288	391	383	392	398	362	349	318	385	326
Public affairs	6,863	7,696	8,666	9,308	9,753	10,152	10,734	10,902	10,133	9,504	10,107	10,192
Social sciences	5,066	4,993	5,055	4,827	4,507	4,355	4,452	4,484	4,196	3,969	3,980	4,089
Visual and performing arts	3,914	4,310	4,425	4,709	4,591	4,641	4,573	4,880	4,731	4,623	4,817	4,641

Note: Beginning in 1982–83, the taxonomy used to collect data on earned degrees by major field of study was revised. The figures for earlier years have been reclassified when necessary to make them conform to the new taxonomy. Data for 1982–83 are subject to slight revision.

Marketing and distribution to business and management.
Military technologies to military science.
Transportation and material moving to public affairs.
Science technologies to physical sciences.
Construction trades to engineering technology.
Mechanics and repairers to engineering technology.

Sources:

1 National Center for Education Statistics, "Degrees and Other Formal Awards Conferred," surveys, 1974–75 to 1984–85.
2 National Center for Education Statistics, "Trends in Bachelor's and Higher Degrees, 1975–1985," Table 3B; "Bachelor's and Higher Degrees Conferred in 1985–86" (bulletin), Table 3B.

Master's Degrees Conferred on Men by Field of Study and Year, 1974–75 to 1985–86

Field of Study	1974–75	1975–76	1976–77	1977–78	1978–79	1979–80	1980–81	1981–82	1982–83	1983–84	1984–85	1985–86
Men, Total	161,570	167,248	167,783	161,212	153,370	150,749	147,043	145,532	144,697	143,595	143,390	143,508
Agriculture and natural resources	2,703	2,862	3,177	3,268	3,187	3,082	3,061	3,114	3,129	2,989	2,846	2,701
Architecture and environmental design	2,343	2,545	2,489	2,304	2,226	2,245	2,234	2,242	2,224	2,197	2,148	2,129
Area and ethnic studies	663	543	554	516	437	442	398	410	411	463	464	489
Business and management	33,185	37,559	39,766	40,150	40,701	42,722	43,394	44,243	46,457	46,565	46,624	46,288
Communications	1,554	1,708	1,591	1,528	1,362	1,422	1,352	1,450	1,611	1,511	1,447	1,405
Communications technologies	64	110	128	145	121	105	96	128	50	89	129	205
Computer and information sciences	1,961	2,226	2,332	2,471	2,480	2,883	3,247	3,625	3,813	4,379	5,064	5,658
Education	45,421	45,796	43,288	38,143	35,143	31,020	28,256	25,953	23,232	21,581	20,945	20,719
Engineering	14,756	15,446	15,264	15,198	14,294	14,782	15,063	15,953	17,084	17,998	18,684	18,663
Engineering technologies	217	314	261	335	250	319	284	358	469	506	565	505
Foreign languages	1,258	1,178	965	795	739	666	694	609	604	571	559	509
Health sciences	3,710	3,955	3,910	3,990	4,223	4,131	4,151	3,843	4,232	4,269	4,135	4,460
Home economics	203	186	207	212	222	234	252	201	222	276	279	281
Law	1,145	1,269	1,366	1,525	1,392	1,531	1,506	1,510	1,603	1,387	1,377	1,441
Letters	3,853	3,664	3,277	2,991	2,631	2,496	2,325	2,256	2,014	2,058	2,064	2,169
Liberal and general studies	624	765	693	621	523	540	410	426	346	417	449	448
Library and archival sciences	1,719	1,741	1,546	1,384	1,159	1,004	841	799	735	766	758	721
Life sciences	4,587	4,497	4,718	4,400	4,265	4,098	3,654	3,426	3,214	2,996	2,647	2,616
Mathematics	2,905	2,547	2,396	2,228	1,985	1,828	1,692	1,821	1,858	1,791	1,874	2,047
Military sciences	0	0	42	44	38	46	43	48	109	126	118	81
Multi- and inter-disciplinary studies	1,241	1,264	2,134	2,185	2,284	2,321	2,311	2,414	1,676	1,865	1,845	1,794
Parks and recreation	413	357	387	327	361	297	303	276	264	254	241	234
Philosophy and religion	927	911	846	707	670	719	728	688	667	741	701	713
Theology	2,230	2,232	2,488	2,314	2,418	2,705	2,801	2,650	3,288	3,408	2,846	2,869
Physical sciences	4,969	4,648	4,450	4,620	4,461	4,248	4,200	4,318	4,157	4,268	4,452	4,470
Psychology	4,044	4,171	4,313	3,919	3,672	3,376	3,358	3,209	3,238	2,961	3,044	2,923
Protective services	854	995	1,393	1,511	1,346	1,413	1,140	974	951	901	850	748
Public affairs	7,747	8,421	9,251	9,033	8,547	8,261	7,790	7,314	6,112	5,869	5,938	6,108
Social sciences	11,826	10,831	10,340	9,751	8,300	7,746	7,403	7,408	6,916	6,496	6,400	6,339
Visual and performing arts	4,448	4,507	4,211	4,327	3,933	4,067	4,056	3,866	4,011	3,897	3,897	3,775

Note: Beginning in 1982–83, the taxonomy used to collect data on earned degrees by major field of study was revised. The figures for earlier years have been reclassified when necessary to make them conform to the new taxonomy. Data for 1982–83 are subject to slight revision.

Marketing and distribution to business and management.
Military technologies to military science.
Transportation and material moving to public affairs.
Science technologies to physical sciences.
Construction trades to engineering technology.
Mechanics and repairers to engineering technology.

Sources:

1 National Center for Education Statistics, "Degrees and Other Formal Awards Conferred," surveys, 1974–75 to 1984–85.

2 National Center for Education Statistics, "Trends in Bachelor's and Higher Degrees, 1975–1985," Table 3A; "Bachelor's and Higher Degrees Conferred in 1985–86" (bulletin), Table 3.

	First-Professional Degrees[a]				
Year	Total	Men	Women	Public	Independent
1960–61	36,447	32,473	3,974	12,846	23,601
1964–65	45,946	39,893	6,053	18,111	27,835
1966–67	32,493	31,064	1,429	13,278	19,215
1968–69	35,681	34,069	1,612	15,038	20,643
1969–70	35,252	33,344	1,908	14,733	20,519
1970–71	38,276	35,797	2,479	16,341	21,935
1971–72	43,774	41,021	2,753	18,727	25,047
1972–73	50,435	46,827	3,608	22,104	28,331
1973–74	54,278	48,904	5,374	23,474	30,804
1974–75	56,259	49,230	7,029	23,907	32,352
1975–76	63,061	53,210	9,851	26,092	36,969
1976–77	64,780	52,668	12,112	26,669	38,111
1977–78	66,964	52,553	14,411	27,408	39,556
1978–79	69,222	52,909	16,313	28,103	41,119
1979–80	70,131	52,716	17,415	27,942	42,189
1980–81	71,956	52,792	19,164	29,128	42,828
1981–82	72,032	52,223	19,809	29,611	42,421
1982–83	73,136	51,310	21,826	29,757	43,379
1983–84	74,407	51,334	23,073	29,586	44,821
1984–85	75,063	50,455	24,608	30,152	44,911
1985–86	73,910	49,261	24,649	29,568	44,342
1986–87[b]	74,000	48,000	26,000	30,000	44,000
Projections					
1987–88	74,400	48,600	25,800	NA	NA
1988–89	74,300	47,900	26,400	NA	NA
1989–90	74,300	47,300	27,000	NA	NA
1994–95	73,900	44,100	29,800	NA	NA
1997–98	73,700	42,200	31,500	NA	NA

NA = not available

Note: Data before 1979–80 are for the aggregate United States (50 states, the District of Columbia, and outlying parts) except where noted. For 1979–80 and later, the figures shown are for the 50 states and the District of Columbia.

a   For 1960–61 to 1964–65, data for first-professional degrees that required 5 or more years of study, and master's degrees that were considered first-professional degrees, such as master's degrees in library science, social work, and public administration; for 1965–66 and later, data show only those first-professional degrees that required at least 2 years of college work for admission and a total of 6 or more years of work for the degree.

b   Estimate.

Sources:
1   National Center for Education Statistics, "Degrees and Other Formal Awards Conferred" surveys; "Projections of Education Statistics to 1997–98," 1988 (prepublication copy). See Guide to Sources.
2   ACE/Macmillan, *1989–90 Fact Book on Higher Education,* Table 125.

First-Professional Degrees Conferred, by Field and Sex, Selected Years, 1947–48 to 1985-86

Year		Medicine Number	Percentage	Dentistry Number	Percentage	Optometry Number	Percentage	Osteopathy Number	Percentage	Podiatry Number	Percentage
1947–48	Total	6,714		1,625		1,425		NA		NA	
	Women	744	11.1	37	2.3	40	2.8				
1949–50	Total	5,612		2,579		1,801		346		NA	
	Women	584	10.4	18	0.7	19	1.1	19	5.5		
1953–54	Total	6,757		3,102		706		499		NA	
	Women	343	9.1	39	0.8	20	2.8	10	2.2		
1957–58	Total	6,861		3,065		264		466		NA	
	Women	351	5.1	34	0.9	1	0.4	6	1.3		
1959-60	Total	7,074		3,247		339		423		NA	
	Women	394	5.9	26	0.8	4	1.2	8	1.9		
1963–64	Total	7,342		3,196		305		352		NA	
	Women	432	6.3	14	0.4	5	1.7	4	1.1		
1965–66	Total	7,720		3,264		380		360		136	
	Women	516	7.2	35	1.1	3	0.8	5	1.4	2	1.5
1970–71	Total	8,986		3,777		531		472		241	
	Women	829	9.2	46	1.2	13	2.4	11	2.3	5	2.0
1972–73	Total	10,398		5,086		771		523		259	
	Women	939	9.0	58	1.4	20	2.6	15	2.9	1	0.4
1974–75	Total	12,550		4,809		792		665		353	
	Women	1,654	13.2	149	3.1	40	5.1	35	5.3	4	1.1
1976–77	Total	13,599		5,138		953		852		486	
	Women	2,611	19.2	374	7.3	105	11.0	75	8.8	16	3.3
1978–79	Total	14,925		5,488		1,046		1,065		572	
	Women	3,452	23.1	652	11.9	136	13.0	167	15.7	41	7.2
1979–80	Total	15,046		5,321		1,085		1,011		580	
	Women	3,523	23.4	719	13.5	170	15.7	159	15.7	73	12.6
1980–81	Total	15,505		5,460		1,097		1,145		597	
	Women	3,833	24.7	788	14.4	207	18.9	188	16.4	69	11.6
1981–82	Total	15,985		5,550		1,113		1,017		599	
	Women	3,991	25.0	825	14.9	224	20.0	186	18.3	63	10.5
1982–83	Total	15,728		5,371		1,120		1,317		631	
	Women	4,193	26.7	838	15.6	246	22.0	261	19.8	79	12.5
1983–84	Total	16,343		5,274		1,171		1,287		607	
	Women	4,632	28.3	1,089	20.6	285	24.3	262	20.4	77	12.7
1984–85	Total	16,318		5,337		1,117		1,489		582	
	Women	4,904	30.1	1,063	19.9	306	27.4	353	23.7	118	20.3
1985–86	Total	16,117		4,958		NA		NA		NA	
	Women	4,957	30.8	1,094	22.1						

Year	Veterinary Medicine Number	Percentage	Law Number	Percentage	Theology Number	Percentage	Architecture Number	Percentage	Pharmacy Number	Percentage
1947–48 Total	242		10,990		NA		1,074		2,104	
Women	13	5.4	420	3.8			131	12.2	449	21.3
1949–50 Total	803		14,312		3,221		2,563		5,751	
Women	12	1.5	421	3.0	211	6.6	122	4.8	441	7.7
1953–54 Total	803		9,298		4,463		1,623		3,885	
Women	10	1.2	322	3.5	119	2.7	92	5.7	343	8.8
1957–58 Total	809		9,394		4,989		1,612		3,782	
Women	13	1.6	272	2.9	61	1.2	76	4.7	391	10.3
1959–60 Total	825		9,240		5,184		1,801		3,492	
Women	18	2.2	230	2.5	87	1.6	57	3.3	416	13.5
1963–64 Total	852		10,679		4,423		2,059		2,207	
Women	32	3.9	307	2.9	65	1.5	78	3.9	254	11.5
1965–66 Total	922		13,246		4,124		2,599		3,763	
Women	52	6.0	470	3.5	74	1.8	103	4.6	536	16.6
1970–71 Total	1,252		17,652		5,055		5,578		4,593	
Women	98	7.8	1,293	7.3	118	2.3	667	12.0	951	25.2
1972–73 Total	1,299		27,484		5,291		6,980		5,079	
Women	133	10.2	2,224	8.1	182	3.4	923	13.2	1,277	25.1
1974–75 Total	1,415		29,497		5,098		8,238		6,487	
Women	225	15.9	4,455	15.1	348	6.8	1,435	17.4	1,821	28.1
1976–77 Total	1,586		34,104		5,861		9,222		7,495	
Women	362	22.8	7,657	22.5	554	9.5	1,973	21.4	2,434	32.5
1978–79 Total	1,714		35,387		6,607		9,297		6,919	
Women	496	28.9	10,084	28.5	866	13.1	2,401	25.8	2,759	39.9
1979–80 Total	1,852		35,855		7,012		9,176		7,122	
Women	615	33.2	10,828	30.2	1,009	14.4	2,548	27.8	2,919	41.0
1980–81 Total	1,922		36,331		6,898		9,455		6,640	
Women	677	35.2	11,768	32.1	962	13.9	2,645	28.1	2,910	43.8
1981–82 Total	1,886		35,543		6,091		9,728		6,448	
Women	668	35.4	11,607	32.7	1,084	15.7	2,903	29.9	3,031	47.0
1982–83 Total	2,012		36,540		6,494		9,823		5,919	
Women	822	40.9	13,218	36.2	1,099	16.9	3,420	34.8	2,925	49.4
1983–84 Total	2,138		37,012		6,878		9,186		5,393	
Women	887	41.5	13,630	36.8	1,205	17.5	3,291	35.9	2,657	49.3
1984–85 Total	2,178		37,451		7,221		9,325		5,011	
Women	1,043	47.9	14,421	38.5	1,335	18.5	3,306	35.5	2,668	53.2
1985–86 Total	2,104		NA		NA		NA		6,010	
Women	1,021	48.5							3,265	54.3

NA = not available

Sources:

1 National Center for Education Statistics, "Earned Degrees Conferred" surveys, 1947–48 to 1984–85. American Medical Association, *Journal of the American Medical Association,* Mar. 1980; Dec. 25, 1981; Dec. 24 and 31, 1982. American Bar Association, *A Review of Legal Education in the United States,* Fall 1979 – Fall 1986.

2 Personal communication from the Association of American Medical Colleges, American Veterinary Association, American Dental Association, American Podiatry Association, and the American Association of Colleges of Pharmacy, 1987.

3 Vetter, B. M. & Babco, E. L., *Professional Women and Minorities: A Manpower Data Resource Service,* 1987, Table 3-2.

First-Professional Degrees Conferred in Dentistry, Medicine, and Law, by Sex, 1949–50 to 1985–86

Year	Dentistry (D.D.S. or D.M.D.)				Medicine (M.D.)				Law (LL.B. or J.D.)			
	Number of Institutions Conferring Degrees	Degrees Conferred			Number of Institutions Conferring Degrees	Degrees Conferred			Number of Institutions Conferring Degrees	Degrees Conferred		
		Total	Men	Women		Total	Men	Women		Total	Men	Women
1949–50	40	2,579	2,561	18	72	5,612	5,028	584	a	a	a	a
1951–52	41	2,918	2,895	23	72	6,201	5,871	330	a	a	a	a
1953–54	42	3,102	3,063	39	73	6,712	6,377	335	a	a	a	a
1955–56	42	3,009	2,975	34	73	6,810	6,464	346	131	8,262	7,974	288
1957–58	43	3,065	3,031	34	75	6,816	6,469	347	131	9,394	9,122	272
1959–60	45	3,247	3,221	26	79	7,032	6,645	387	134	9,240	9,010	230
1961–62	46	3,183	3,166	17	81	7,138	6,749	389	134	9,364	9,091	273
1963–64	46	3,180	3,168	12	82	7,303	6,878	425	133	10,679	10,372	307
1965–66	47	3,178	3,146	32	84	7,673	7,170	503	136	13,246	12,776	470
1967–68	48	3,422	3,375	47	85	7,944	7,318	626	138	16,454	15,805	649
1969–70	48	3,718	3,684	34	86	8,314	7,615	699	145	14,916	14,115	801
1970–71	48	3,745	3,703	42	89	8,919	8,110	809	147	17,421	16,181	1,240
1971–72	48	3,862	3,819	43	92	9,253	8,423	830	147	21,764	20,266	1,498
1972–73	51	4,047	3,992	55	97	10,307	9,388	919	152	27,205	25,037	2,168
1973–74	52	4,440	4,355	85	99	11,356	10,093	1,263	151	29,326	25,986	3,340
1974–75	52	4,773	4,627	146	104	12,447	10,818	1,629	154	29,296	24,881	4,415
1975–76	56	5,425	5,187	238	107	13,426	11,252	2,174	166	32,293	26,085	6,208
1976–77	57	5,138	4,764	374	109	13,461	10,891	2,570	169	34,104	26,447	7,657
1977–78	57	5,189	4,623	566	109	14,279	11,210	3,069	169	34,402	25,457	8,945
1978–79	58	5,434	4,794	640	109	14,786	11,381	3,405	175	35,206	25,180	10,026
1979–80	58	5,258	4,558	700	112	14,902	11,416	3,486	179	35,647	24,893	10,754
1980–81	58	5,460	4,672	788	116	15,505	11,672	3,833	176	36,331	24,563	11,768
1981–82	59	5,282	4,467	815	119	15,814	11,867	3,947	180	35,991	23,965	12,026
1982–83	59	5,585	4,631	954	118	15,484	11,350	4,134	177	36,853	23,550	13,303
1983–84	60	5,353	4,302	1,051	119	15,813	11,359	4,454	179	37,012	23,382	13,630
1984–85	59	5,339	4,233	1,106	120	16,041	11,167	4,874	181	37,491	23,070	14,421
1985–86	59	5,046	3,907	1,139	120	15,938	11,022	4,916	181	35,844	21,874	13,970

a   Data before 1955–56 are not shown because they lack comparability with the figures for subsequent years.

Source:
National Center for Education Statistics, "Degrees and Other Formal Awards Conferred" surveys, various years; *Digest of Educational Statistics, 1988*, Table 180.

74

First-Professional Degrees Conferred by Field, Sex of Recipient, and Year, 1974–75 to 1985–86

Field	1974–75	1975–76	1976–77	1977–78	1978–79	1979–80	1980–81	1981–82	1982–83	1983–84	1984–85	1985–86
Total	55,916	62,649	64,359	66,581	68,848	70,131	71,956	72,032	73,136	74,407	75,063	73,910
Dentistry	4,773	5,425	5,138	5,189	5,434	5,258	5,460	5,282	5,585	5,353	5,339	5,046
Medicine	12,447	13,426	13,461	14,279	14,786	14,902	15,505	15,814	15,484	15,813	16,041	15,938
Optometry	792	975	953	1,014	1,046	1,085	1,097	1,110	1,116	1,086	1,115	1,029
Osteopathic medicine	665	818	852	944	1,065	1,011	1,145	1,047	1,319	1,515	1,489	1,547
Pharmacy	NA	439	527	547	639	637	664	625	705	709	861	903
Podiatry	351	428	486	543	572	580	597	598	631	607	582	612
Veterinary medicine	1,415	1,532	1,586	1,635	1,714	1,835	1,922	2,038	2,060	2,269	2,178	2,270
Chiropractic	NA	1,577	1,368	1,661	1,779	2,061	2,337	2,626	2,889	3,105	2,661	3,395
Law	29,296	32,293	34,104	34,402	35,206	35,647	36,331	35,991	36,853	37,012	37,491	35,844
Theological professions	5,095	5,706	5,861	6,367	6,607	7,115	6,898	6,901	6,494	6,878	7,221	7,283
Other	1,082	30	23	0	0	0	0	0	0	60	85	43
Men, Total	48,956	52,892	52,374	52,270	52,652	52,716	52,792	52,223	51,310	51,334	50,455	49,261
Dentistry	4,627	5,187	4,764	4,623	4,794	4,558	4,672	4,467	4,631	4,302	4,233	3,907
Medicine	10,818	11,252	10,891	11,210	11,381	11,416	11,672	11,867	11,350	11,359	11,167	11,022
Optometry	752	900	848	881	910	915	890	889	869	824	812	744
Osteopathic medicine	630	759	777	826	898	852	957	860	1,063	1,185	1,136	1,159
Pharmacy	NA	309	382	382	409	398	381	365	376	332	430	432
Podiatry	347	417	470	517	531	507	528	535	552	530	464	488
Veterinary medicine	1,190	1,255	1,224	1,234	1,218	1,233	1,245	1,301	1,216	1,309	1,135	1,191
Chiropractic	NA	1,430	1,252	1,495	1,590	1,811	1,948	2,157	2,308	2,401	2,072	2,554
Law	24,881	26,085	26,447	25,457	25,180	24,893	24,563	23,965	23,550	23,382	23,070	21,874
Theological professions	4,748	5,271	5,307	5,645	5,741	6,133	5,936	5,817	5,395	5,673	5,886	5,865
Other	963	27	12	0	0	0	0	0	0	37	50	25
Women, Total	6,960	9,757	11,985	14,311	16,196	17,415	19,164	19,809	21,826	23,073	24,608	24,649
Dentistry	146	238	374	566	640	700	788	815	954	1,051	1,106	1,139
Medicine	1,629	2,174	2,570	3,069	3,405	3,486	3,833	3,947	4,134	4,454	4,874	4,916
Optometry	40	75	105	133	136	170	207	221	247	262	303	285
Osteopathic medicine	35	59	75	118	167	159	188	187	256	330	353	388
Pharmacy	NA	130	145	165	230	239	283	260	329	377	431	471
Podiatry	4	11	16	26	41	73	69	63	79	77	118	124
Veterinary medicine	225	277	362	401	496	602	677	737	844	960	1,043	1,079
Chiropractic	NA	147	116	166	189	250	389	469	581	704	589	841
Law	4,415	6,208	7,657	8,945	10,026	10,754	11,768	12,026	13,303	13,630	14,421	13,970
Theological professions	347	435	554	722	866	982	962	1,084	1,099	1,205	1,335	1,418
Other	119	3	11	0	0	0	0	0	0	23	35	18

NA = not available

Sources:
National Center for Education Statistics, "Degrees and Other Formal Awards Conferred," surveys, 1974–75 to 1984–85; "Trends in Bachelor's and Higher Degrees: 1975–1985," 1987, Table 5; "Bachelor's and Higher Degrees Conferred in 1985–86" (bulletin), Table 5.

Year	Doctor's Degrees[a]				
	Total	Men	Women	Public	Independent
1947–48	3,989	3,496	493	1,580	2,409
1949–50	6,420	5,804	616	2,668	3,752
1954–55	8,840	8,014	826	4,560	4,280
1959–60	9,829	8,801	1,028	5,098	4,731
1964–65	16,467	14,692	1,775	9,472	6,995
1965–66	18,239	16,121	2,118	10,774	7,465
1969–70	29,872	25,892	3,980	19,189	10,683
1970–71	32,113	27,534	4,579	20,794	11,319
1971–72	33,369	28,095	5,274	21,782	11,587
1972–73	34,790	28,575	4,215	22,370	12,420
1973–74	33,826	27,374	6,452	21,817	12,009
1974–75	34,086	26,819	7,267	22,179	11,907
1975–76	34,076	26,273	7,803	21,763	12,313
1976–77	32,244	25,150	8,094	21,241	12,003
1977–78	32,156	23,669	8,487	20,471	11,685
1978–79	32,756	23,555	9,201	20,831	11,925
1979–80	32,615	22,943	9,672	20,608	12,007
1980–81	32,958	22,711	10,247	20,895	12,063
1981–82	32,707	22,224	10,483	20,889	11,818
1982–83	32,775	21,902	10,873	21,186	11,589
1983–84	33,209	22,064	11,145	21,141	12,068
1984–85	32,943	21,700	11,243	21,337	11,606
1985–86	33,653	21,819	11,834	21,433	12,220
1986–87[b]	34,200	22,100	12,100	22,000	12,000
Projections					
1987–88	33,500	21,100	12,400	NA	NA
1988–89	33,600	20,800	12,800	NA	NA
1989–90	33,700	20,600	13,100	NA	NA
1994–95	34,400	19,500	14,900	NA	NA
1997–98	34,700	18,800	15,900	NA	NA

NA = not available

Note: Data before 1979–80 are for the aggregate United States (the 50 states, the District of Columbia, and outlying parts). For 1979–80 and later, data are for the 50 states and the District of Columbia.

a   In addition to the Ph.D., figures include degrees such as Ed.D., S.T.D., and Sc.D. Honorary doctorates and first-professional degrees such as M.D., D.D.S., and D.V.M. are excluded.

b   Estimate.

Sources:
1   National Center for Education Statistics, "Degrees and Other Formal Awards Conferred" surveys, various years; "Projections of Education Statistics to 1997–98," 1988 (prepublication copy).

2   ACE/Macmillan, *1989–90 Fact Book on Higher Education,* Table 127.

Discipline	Percentage of Doctorates Awarded to Women					
	1949–50	1959–60	1969–70	1974–75	1984–85	1985–86
All Disciplines	**10**	**10**	**13**	**21**	**34**	**35**
Humanities						
English	21	21	31	41	55	58
French	28	38	46	65	68	74
German	20	33	30	44	59	52
Philosophy	17	18	12	15	18	23
Spanish	24	35	39	47	65	64
Education	**16**	**19**	**20**	**31**	**52**	**53**
Social Sciences						
Anthropology	21	17	27	35	49	51
Economics	4	4	5	8	16	20
History	11	9	13	22	35	33
Political science	8	8	11	16	26	26
Psychology	15	15	22	31	49	52
Sociology	18	16	19	30	52	45
Biological Sciences						
Bacteriology/microbiology	19	14	21	26	37	35
Biochemistry	15	13	15	22	30	35
Biology, general	15	11	20	28	34	33
Botany	8	7	9	13	27	26
Zoology	18	14	10	24	30	31
Physical Sciences						
Chemistry	4	5	8	11	20	21
Mathematics	6	6	8	11	16	17
Physics	1	2	3	5	9	9

Sources:

1 National Center for Education Statistics, "Degrees and Other Formal Awards Conferred" surveys.

2 ACE/Macmillan, *1989–90 Fact Book on Higher Education*, Table 130.

Doctor's Degrees Conferred to Women, by Field of Study and Year, 1974–75 to 1985–86

Field of Study	1974–75	1975–76	1976–77	1977–78	1978–79	1979–80	1980–81	1981–82	1982–83	1983–84	1984–85	1985–86
Women, Total	7,266	7,797	8,090	8,473	9,189	9,672	10,247	10,483	10,873	11,145	11,243	11,834
Agriculture and natural resources	33	61	62	62	73	112	127	154	145	171	177	192
Architecture and environmental design	11	13	11	16	22	13	20	22	23	22	23	17
Area and ethnic studies	38	63	49	45	50	52	59	44	63	49	51	68
Business and management	41	52	54	72	100	115	125	151	136	202	148	210
Communications	44	49	38	51	52	70	73	58	85	87	90	101
Communications technologies	2	1	3	2	2	2	2	6	3	1	1	6
Computer and information sciences	14	23	19	15	30	27	25	21	34	26	25	45
Education	2,299	2,599	2,774	2,961	3,264	3,522	3,736	3,730	3,787	3,770	3,732	3,795
Engineering	66	66	73	57	83	95	104	138	125	165	207	228
Engineering technologies	0	0	0	0	0	0	0	2	0	0	1	1
Foreign languages	402	414	387	355	345	315	314	294	278	254	253	263
Health sciences	172	166	172	245	258	347	358	411	506	590	634	637
Home economics	105	127	123	145	148	146	169	174	171	209	198	233
Law	0	3	8	5	7	4	4	2	17	21	17	6
Letters	773	804	747	727	691	690	698	686	607	658	667	672
Liberal and general studies	5	11	11	14	71	24	13	15	26	21	25	12
Library and archival sciences	23	32	40	24	36	38	40	53	31	36	48	35
Life sciences	743	729	726	798	906	946	1,052	1,089	1,075	1,056	1,125	1,129
Mathematics	110	94	109	124	122	100	114	94	116	126	109	124
Military sciences	0	0	0	0	0	0	0	0	0	0	0	0
Multi- and interdisciplinary studies	69	77	82	82	134	94	96	136	155	138	108	121
Parks and recreation	3	2	3	1	6	8	12	7	10	8	13	13
Philosophy and religion	74	83	89	76	93	77	82	77	98	112	91	104
Theology	33	42	42	54	57	77	101	103	89	78	104	117
Physical sciences	301	299	319	312	350	384	376	451	458	491	552	588
Psychology	754	819	991	966	1,065	1,166	1,274	1,262	1,487	1,456	1,416	1,591
Protective services	0	0	2	5	1	3	8	10	8	5	6	4
Public affairs	71	100	106	129	111	131	162	179	163	190	218	211
Social sciences	877	895	835	870	866	872	845	824	889	881	918	985
Visual and performing arts	203	173	215	260	246	242	258	290	288	322	286	326

Note: Beginning in 1982–83, the taxonomy used to collect data on earned degrees by major field of study was revised. The figures for earlier years have been reclassified when necessary to make them conform to the new taxonomy. Data for 1982–83 are subject to slight revision.

Marketing and distribution to business and management.
Military technologies to military science.
Transportation and material moving to public affairs.
Science technologies to physical sciences.
Construction trades to engineering technology.
Mechanics and repairers to engineering technology.

Sources:
National Center for Education Statistics, "Degrees and Other Formal Awards Conferred" surveys, 1974–75 to 1984–85; "Trends in Bachelor's and Higher Degrees, 1975–1985," Table 4B; "Bachelor's and Higher Degrees Conferred in 1985–86" (bulletin), Table 4.

Doctor's Degrees Conferred to Men, by Field of Study and Year, 1974–75 to 1985–86

Field of Study	1974–75	1975–76	1976–77	1977–78	1978–79	1979–80	1980–81	1981–82	1982–83	1983–84	1984–85	1985–86
Men, Total	26,817	26,267	25,142	23,658	23,541	22,943	22,711	22,224	21,902	22,064	21,700	21,819
Agriculture and natural resources	958	867	831	909	877	879	940	925	1,004	1,001	1,036	966
Architecture and environmental design	58	69	62	57	74	66	73	58	74	62	66	56
Area and ethnic studies	127	125	104	100	85	99	103	58	90	90	86	89
Business and management	968	901	809	794	760	677	717	704	673	775	718	759
Communications	118	147	124	128	130	112	98	124	120	128	138	111
Communications technologies	1	7	6	10	8	9	9	12	6	3	5	5
Computer and information sciences	199	221	197	181	206	213	227	230	228	225	223	299
Education	5,147	5,179	5,189	4,634	4,472	4,419	4,164	3,950	3,764	3,703	3,419	3,315
Engineering	3,040	2,753	2,510	2,380	2,417	2,407	2,447	2,483	2,697	2,814	3,014	3,172
Engineering technologies	2	2	3	3	6	5	10	13	9	2	8	9
Foreign languages	455	450	365	294	296	234	274	242	210	208	184	185
Health sciences	437	411	366	393	447	424	469	499	649	573	565	604
Home economics	51	51	37	58	71	46	78	73	84	70	78	78
Law	21	73	52	34	39	36	56	20	55	100	88	48
Letters	1,178	1,080	976	889	813	810	682	627	569	557	572	543
Liberal and general studies	11	25	22	41	193	82	10	20	29	27	28	26
Library and archival sciences	33	39	35	43	34	35	31	31	21	38	39	27
Life sciences	2,641	2,663	2,671	2,511	2,636	2,690	2,666	2,654	2,266	2,381	2,307	2,229
Mathematics	865	762	714	681	608	624	614	587	582	569	590	618
Military sciences	0	0	0	0	0	0	0	0	0	0	0	0
Multi- and interdisciplinary studies	185	160	189	164	311	201	160	222	232	240	177	198
Parks and recreation	11	13	12	9	19	13	30	26	23	19	23	26
Philosophy and religion	470	471	379	368	322	297	328	287	306	330	377	373
Theology	839	991	1,083	1,106	1,175	1,242	1,175	1,185	1,119	1,124	1,036	1,066
Physical sciences	3,325	3,132	3,022	2,821	2,752	2,705	2,765	2,835	2,811	2,815	2,851	2,963
Psychology	1,688	1,762	1,770	1,621	1,597	1,602	1,681	1,518	1,621	1,517	1,492	1,497
Protective services	11	9	8	12	14	15	13	14	30	26	27	17
Public affairs	200	198	210	256	233	241	226	210	184	231	213	174
Social sciences	3,332	3,259	2,949	2,713	2,492	2,347	2,269	2,237	2,042	2,030	1,933	1,970
Visual and performing arts	446	447	447	448	454	413	396	380	404	406	407	396

Note: Beginning in 1982–83, the taxonomy used to collect data on earned degrees by major field of study was revised. The figures for earlier years have been reclassified when necessary to make them conform to the new taxonomy. Data for 1982–83 are subject to slight revision.

Marketing and distribution to business and management.
Military technologies to military science.
Transportation and material moving to public affairs.
Science technologies to physical sciences.
Construction trades to engineering technology.
Mechanics and repairers to engineering technology.

Sources:

National Center for Education Statistics, "Degrees and Other Formal Awards Conferred" surveys, 1974–75 to 1984–85; "Trends in Bachelor's and Higher Degrees, 1975–1985," Table 4A; "Bachelor's and Higher Degrees Conferred in 1985–86" (bulletin); Table 4.

Characteristic	Women	Men
Doctorates awarded	11,370	20,908
Percentage married	52	60
Median age at doctorate	35.4 years	32.8 years
Percentage with baccalaureate in same field as doctorate	51	57
Median time lapse from baccalaureate to doctorate	12 years	10 years
Primary employment activity anticipated after doctorate		
Research and development	16	35
Teaching	42	34
Administration	16	12
Professional services	17	11
Other	3	2
Unknown	6	6
Total	100	100
Field of Study		
Physical Sciences		
Physics and astronomy	120	1,116
Chemistry	406	1,568
Earth, atmospheric and marine sciences	114	513
Engineering	242	3,474
Computer sciences	65	385
Mathematics	125	615
Total	1,072	7,671
Life Sciences		
Biochemistry	198	374
Other biosciences	1,152	2,100
Health sciences	477	329
Agricultural sciences	193	919
Total	2,020	3,722
Social Sciences		
Psychology	1,652	1,446
Economics	140	683
Anthropology and sociology	349	426
Political science and International relations	126	363
Other social sciences	182	351
Total	2,449	3,269
Humanities		
History	202	385
English and American language and literature	375	294
Foreign languages and literature	262	182
Other humanities	735	1,069
Total	1,574	1,930
Business and Management	229	751
Education	3,550	2,897
Other Professional Fields	450	633
Other or Unspecified	26	35

Source:
National Research Council, "Summary Report 1987: Doctorate Recipients From United States Universities," preliminary tabulations, Table 2.

Total Doctor's Degrees by Race/Ethnicity, Selected Years[a]

	1975–76		1980–81		1984–85		Percentage Change 1975–76 to 1984–85
	Total	Percentage	Total	Percentage	Total	Percentage	
All	33,787	100.0	32,839	100.0	32,307	100.0	−4.4
Men	26,010	77.0[b]	22,595	68.8	21,296	65.9	−18.1
Women	7,777	23.0[c]	10,244	31.2	11,011	34.1	41.6
Minority	2,285	6.8[d]	2,728	8.3	3,056	9.5	33.7
Men	1,617	6.2[e]	1,721	7.6	1,858	8.7	14.9
Women	668	8.6[f]	1,007	9.8	1,198	10.9	79.3
Hispanic	396	1.2	456	1.4	677	2.1	71.1
Men	289	1.1	277	1.2	431	2.0	49.1
Women	107	1.4	179	1.7	246	2.2	130.0
Black	1,213	3.6	1,265	3.9	1,154	3.6	−4.9
Men	771	3.0	694	3.1	561	2.6	−27.2
Women	442	5.7	571	5.6	593	5.4	34.1
White	27,434	81.2	25,908	78.9	23,934	74.1	−12.8
Men	20,852	80.2	17,310	76.6	15,017	41.9	−27.9
Women	6,582	84.6	8,598	83.9	8,917	81.0	35.5
Asian/Pacific Islander	583	1.7	877	2.7	1,106	3.4	89.7
Men	480	1.8	655	2.9	802	3.8	67.1
Women	103	1.3	222	2.2	304	2.8	195.1
American Indian	93	0.3	130	0.4	119	0.4	28.0
Men	77	0.3	95	0.4	64	0.3	−16.9
Women	16	0.2	35	0.3	55	0.5	243.8
Nonresident Alien	4,068	12.0	4,203	12.8	5,317	16.5	30.7
Men	3,541	13.6	3,564	15.8	4,421	20.8	24.9
Women	527	6.8	639	6.2	896	8.1	70.0

a   Some institutions did not report the racial/ethnic data for earned degrees. Data for some of these nonreporting institutions were imputed. Because of underreporting and nonreporting of racial/ethnic data, totals on this table may be slightly smaller than totals appearing on other tables. Because of rounding, details may not add to totals.

b   Degrees awarded to men as a percentage of all doctorate degrees awarded that year.

c   Degrees awarded to women as a percentage of all doctorate degrees awarded that year.

d   Degrees awarded to this group as a percentage of all doctorate degrees awarded that year.

e   Degrees awarded to men in this group as a percentage of all doctorate degrees awarded to men that year.

f   Degrees awarded to women in this group as a percentage of all doctorate degrees awarded to women that year.

Sources:

1   Equal Employment Opportunity Commission, "Data on Earned Degrees Conferred from Institutions of Higher Education by Race/Ethnicity, 1975–76."

2   National Center for Education Statistics, *Digest of Education Statistics, 1983–84;* "Degrees and Other Formal Awards Conferred" surveys, 1985.

3   ACE, "Minorites in Higher Education: Sixth Annual Status Report, 1987," Table 3C.

Year	Total Institutions	Total Faculty	Men	Women	Percentage of Women
1869–1870	563	5,553	4,887	666	12.0
1879–1880	811	11,522	7,328	4,194	36.4
1889–1890	998	15,809	12,704	3,105	19.6
1899–1900	977	23,868	19,151	4,717	19.8
1909–1910	951	36,480	29,132	7,348	20.1
1919–1920	1,041	48,615	35,807	12,808	26.3
1929–1930	1,409	82,386	60,017	22,369	27.2
1939–1940	1,708	146,929	106,328	40,601	27.6
1949–1950	1,851	246,722	186,189	60,533	24.5
1959–1960	2,008	380,554	296,773	83,781	22.0
1969–1970	2,525	450,000	346,000	104,000	23.1
1979–1980	3,152	675,000	486,000	189,000	28.0
1981–1982	3,253	696,000	496,000	200,000	28.7
1983–1984	3,284	723,000	511,000	212,000	29.3

Note: "Faculty" is defined as the total number of different persons, not reduced to full-time equivalents. Part-time as well as full-time faculty are included. Numbers before 1900 are estimates and from 1970 on are estimates of senior instructional staff, excluding graduate assistants.

Sources:

1   National Center for Education Statistics, *Digest of Education Statistics*, 1973 to 1983–84.

2   Vetter, B. M. & Babco, E. L., *Professional Women and Minorities: A Manpower Data Resource*, Table 5-17.

Type of Institution and Year	Women as a Percentage of Full-Time Instructional Faculty[a] With Rank of						
	All Ranks	Professor	Associate Professor	Assistant Professor	Instructor	Lecturer	No Rank
All Institutions							
1972–73	22.3	9.8	16.3	23.8	39.9	34.9	32.8
1982–83	26.9	10.7	22.0	36.1	51.7	47.5	36.5
1985–86	28.0	11.9	24.3	38.0	52.0	48.8	38.2
All Public Institutions							
1972–73	22.7	10.0	15.8	23.7	39.2	35.1	32.3
1982–83	27.1	10.7	21.9	35.9	52.2	47.4	36.2
1985–86	28.1	12.0	23.9	37.7	51.9	48.9	37.8
Public universities							
1972–73	17.1	6.7	12.3	20.0	44.4	30.3	23.4
1982–83	19.0	6.3	17.9	30.7	54.6	46.1	37.3
1985–86	19.8	7.1	19.6	32.6	57.0	48.3	41.0
Public, Other 4-year							
1972–73	23.2	12.7	17.4	24.7	44.0	40.2	38.8
1982–83	26.4	12.7	22.0	37.7	52.1	47.2	36.3
1985–86	26.5	12.6	23.3	38.6	52.2	48.3	39.9
Public 2-year							
1972–73	32.3	21.2	24.3	31.3	35.1	51.2	32.4
1982–83	36.6	23.6	33.0	41.6	50.8	57.7	36.2
1985–86	38.0	26.3	36.0	43.6	48.9	58.0	37.8
All Independent Institutions							
1972–73	21.2	9.5	17.2	24.1	42.5	34.2	34.7
1982–83	26.6	10.6	22.3	36.5	50.6	47.7	38.7
1985–86	27.9	11.7	25.3	38.6	52.5	48.4	41.8
Independent universities							
1972–73	14.5	5.4	12.9	19.0	41.0	29.1	10.0
1982–83	20.2	7.0	19.4	32.2	50.6	48.5	45.5
1985–86	20.8	7.5	23.0	32.2	51.9	48.2	49.4
Independent, Other 4-year							
1972–73	23.6	12.3	19.1	25.7	41.5	38.1	30.1
1982–83	28.0	12.6	23.3	37.9	50.1	46.4	31.4
1985–86	29.0	13.3	25.8	40.0	51.6	48.1	35.1
Independent 2-Year							
1972–73	45.4	31.5	34.3	41.3	53.8	52.9	40.6
1982–83	45.2	32.9	35.8	43.2	56.9	55.6	44.6
1985–86	49.9	34.8	40.5	59.2	65.2	87.5	48.1

Note: Data are for the 50 states and the District of Columbia.

a Full-time instructional faculty on 9- or 10-month contracts; for 1982–83 and 1985–86, the figures include both 9- and 12-month contracts.

Sources:
1 National Center for Education Statistics, letter from Assistant Commissioner for Educational Statistics, February 16, 1973, unpublished tabulations; "Salaries, Tenure, and Fringe Benefits of Full-time Instructional Faculty" surveys, unpublished tabulations.
2 ACE/Macmillan, *1989–90 Fact Book on Higher Education*, Table 108.

Number of Full-Time Instructional Faculty and Percentage Tenured, by Sex, Academic Rank, and Type and Control of Institution, 1984–85

Academic Rank	Number of Faculty Members			Percentage With Tenure		
	Total	Men	Women	Total	Men	Women
Public Ph.D. Universities						
Professors	40,329	37,488	2,841	97.2	97.3	96.3
Associate professor	28,862	23,273	5,589	88.0	87.9	88.3
Assistant professor	23,220	15,649	7,571	14.6	12.5	19.0
Instructor	4,190	1,826	2,364	5.8	5.8	5.9
Lecturer	3,016	1,591	1,425	5.2	6.9	3.4
No academic rank	747	442	305	5.2	6.9	3.4
All ranks combined	100,364	80,269	20,095	68.2	73.6	46.3
Private Ph.D. Universities						
Professors	12,564	11,674	890	97.1	97.2	95.7
Associate professor	7,815	6,130	1,685	76.6	76.7	76.3
Assistant professor	7,349	5,047	2,302	7.0	6.5	8.2
Instructor	987	508	479	2.0	2.8	1.3
Lecturer	676	336	340	0.6	0.3	0.9
No academic rank	151	94	57	0.0	0.0	0.0
All ranks combined	29,542	23,789	5,753	63.4	68.9	40.6
Public 4-Year Institutions						
Professor	3,280	2,797	483	95.2	95.2	95.4
Associate professor	4,095	3,145	950	81.8	80.7	85.5
Assistant professor	4,392	2,765	1,627	34.7	35.0	34.3
Instructor	1,456	733	723	7.6	7.0	8.2
Lecturer	361	180	181	6.6	6.7	6.6
No academic rank	946	662	284	21.8	24.0	16.5
All ranks combined	14,530	10,282	4,248	66.2	71.5	51.9
Private 4-Year Institutions						
Professor	9,311	7,945	1,366	89.2	89.9	85.0
Associate professor	9,658	7,053	2,605	71.7	73.1	67.9
Assistant professor	11,077	6,510	4,567	17.5	17.4	17.7

Number of Full-Time Instructional Faculty and Percentage Tenured, by Sex, Academic Rank, and Type and Control of Institution, 1984–85

83 *Continued*

Academic Rank	Number of Faculty Members			Percentage With Tenure		
	Total	Men	Women	Total	Men	Women
Instructor	3,570	1,652	1,918	1.2	1.5	0.9
Lecturer	171	81	90	2.3	2.5	2.2
No academic rank	946	662	284	21.8	24.0	16.5
All ranks combined	34,733	23,903	10,830	50.2	57.0	35.1
Public 2-Year Institutions						
Professor	7,943	5,903	2,040	88.5	88.9	87.5
Associate professor	9,806	6,414	3,392	83.4	84.0	82.4
Assistant professor	9,701	5,534	4,167	53.5	54.6	52.1
Instructor	8,843	4,814	4,029	30.1	34.2	25.2
Lecturer	426	224	202	43.4	44.2	42.6
No academic rank	46,031	28,724	17,307	51.3	54.3	46.3
All ranks combined	82,750	51,613	31,137	56.6	60.0	51.0
Private 2-Year Institutions						
Professor	455	312	143	49.9	52.6	44.1
Associate professor	619	407	212	34.2	34.4	34.0
Assistant professor	848	422	426	13.7	14.0	13.4
Instructor	841	401	440	5.1	6.5	3.9
Lecturer	70	32	28	3.3	0.0	7.1
No academic rank	2,562	1,333	1,193	13.7	16.4	10.6
All ranks combined	5,349	2,907	2,442	17.7	20.9	13.8
All Institutions, Public and Private[a]						
Professor	114,675	101,591	13,084	94.0	94.3	91.5
Associate Professor	96,455	73,753	22,702	80.3	80.5	79.6
Assistant Professor	88,966	55,764	33,202	24.8	23.3	27.2
Instructor	30,005	14,991	15,014	13.3	15.7	10.9
Lecturer	6,929	3,652	3,277	10.6	11.2	9.9
No academic rank	53,675	33,413	20,262	45.8	48.7	41.1
All ranks combined	390,705	283,164	107,541	60.6	66.1	45.9

a   Includes comprehensive institutions and specialized institutions.

Sources:

1   National Center for Education Statistics, unpublished data on professionals in science and technology, 1985.

2   Vetter, B. M. & Babco, E. L., *Professional Women and Minorities: A Manpower Data Resource Service*, 1987, Table 5-7.

Full Professor						
	Men			Women		
	1975	1983	1985	1975	1983	1985
Total Number	88,761	114,072	117,660	9,335	14,070	15,533
Participation rate	90.4	89.0	88.3	9.6	11.0	11.7
White	84,316	106,554	109,461	8,645	12,665	14,009
Participation rate	86.1	83.2	82.2	8.8	9.9	10.5
Black	1,640	2,034	2,132	505	823	829
Participation rate	1.7	1.6	1.6	0.5	0.6	0.6
Hispanic	653	1,137	1,240	103	232	259
Participation rate	0.7	0.9	0.9	0.1	0.2	0.2
Asian	1,809	4,151	4,548	128	315	399
Participation rate	1.8	3.2	3.4	0.1	0.2	0.3
American Indian	134	196	279	18	35	37
Participation rate	0.2	0.2	0.2	0.1	a	a

Associate Professor						
	Men			Women		
	1975	1983	1985	1975	1983	1985
Total Number	82,709	87,176	87,935	16,802	24,711	26,858
Participation rate	83.1	77.9	76.6	16.9	22.1	23.4
White	77,758	80,100	79,967	15,250	22,146	23,964
Participation rate	78.1	71.6	69.7	15.3	19.8	20.9
Black	1,942	2,461	2,667	1,001	1,508	1,654
Participation rate	1.9	2.2	2.3	1.0	1.3	1.4
Hispanic	902	1,210	1,340	265	394	465
Participation rate	0.9	1.1	1.2	0.3	0.4	0.4
Asian	2,043	3,176	3,600	270	608	717
Participation rate	2.1	2.8	3.1	0.3	0.5	0.6
American Indian	155	229	361	35	55	58
Participation rate	0.2	0.2	0.3	0.2	a	0.1

Assistant Professor					
Men			**Women**		
1975	**1983**	**1985**	**1975**	**1983**	**1985**
Total Number					
87,080	74,166	73,730	34,153	39,164	41,082
Participation rate					
71.8	65.4	64.2	28.2	34.6	35.8
White					
79,944	65,692	64,486	30,499	34,484	35,968
Participation rate					
66.0	58.0	56.2	25.1	30.4	31.3
Black					
3,237	2,964	3,020	2,591	2,883	3,055
Participation rate					
2.7	2.6	2.6	2.1	2.5	2.7
Hispanic					
1,301	1,389	1,380	486	619	674
Participation rate					
1.1	1.2	1.2	0.4	0.5	0.6
Asian					
2,207	3,905	4,426	589	1,097	1,297
Participation rate					
1.8	3.4	3.9	0.5	1.0	1.1
American Indian					
201	216	418	60	81	88
Participation rate					
0.2	0.2	0.3	0.1	0.1	0.1

Instructor, Lecturer, and Other					
Men			**Women**		
1975	**1983**	**1985**	**1975**	**1983**	**1985**
Total number					
78,002	68,366	66,729	49,528	48,948	48,740
Participation rate					
61.2	58.3	57.8	38.8	41.7	42.2
White					
69,951	61,078	58,729	42,834	42,972	42,570
Participation rate					
54.9	52.1	50.9	33.6	36.6	36.9
Black					
3,982	3,081	2,976	4,690	3,697	3,517
Participation rate					
3.1	2.6	2.6	3.7	3.2	3.0
Hispanic					
1,678	1,436	1,598	888	939	1,027
Participation rate					
1.3	1.2	1.4	0.7	0.8	0.9
Asian					
1,755	2,460	3,005	920	1,156	1,433
Participation rate					
2.2	2.1	2.6	0.7	1.0	1.2
American Indian					
320	34	421	161	184	193
Participation rate					
0.2	a	0.4	0.1	0.2	0.2

Note: Details may not add to total because of rounding.

a Less than 0.05%.

Source:
Equal Employment Opportunity Commission, "EEO-6 Higher Education Staff Information" surveys, 1975, 1983, and 1985.

1985 EEO-6 U.S. Summary Report

	Total Both Sexes A	Men Total Men B	Men Non-Hispanic White C	Men Non-Hispanic Black D	Men Hispanic E	Men Asian/Pacific Islanders F	Men American Indian/Alaskan Native G	Women Total Women H	Women Non-Hispanic White I	Women Non-Hispanic Black J	Women Hispanic K	Women Asian/Pacific Islanders L	Women American Indian/Alaskan Native M	Minority Totals Men	Minority Totals Women
Full-Time Faculty															
9–10 Month contract salaries	342,566	245,064	222,385	7,938	4,048	9,784	909	97,502	86,602	6,754	1,832	2,034	280	22,679	10,900
Less than 9–10 month contracts	5,623	3,423	2,893	258	44	199	29	2,200	1,843	234	36	79	8	530	357
11–12 month contracts	140,610	105,726	95,691	2,857	1,591	5,340	247	34,844	30,353	2,242	536	1,668	85	10,035	4,531
Total	488,799	354,213	320,969	11,053	5,683	15,323	1,185	134,586	118,798	9,230	2,404	3,781	373	33,244	15,788
All Other Full-Time Employees															
Executive/administrative/managerial	124,374	80,676	72,204	5,203	1,598	1,279	392	43,698	37,768	4,243	892	641	154	8,472	5,930
Professional/nonfaculty	274,946	119,656	101,894	7,448	2,998	6,443	833	155,290	129,485	14,730	3,324	7,104	647	17,762	25,805
Secretarial/clerical	340,781	26,339	17,871	5,117	1,850	1,191	310	314,442	247,390	44,510	12,566	8,338	1,638	8,468	67,052
Technical/paraprofessional	132,694	57,519	45,480	6,334	2,977	2,372	356	75,175	54,764	14,693	2,745	2,654	319	12,039	20,411
Skilled craftsmen	59,960	56,959	47,824	5,722	2,529	474	410	3,001	2,331	514	100	45	11	9,135	670
Service maintenance	201,591	123,894	75,581	35,321	9,791	2,225	976	77,697	38,377	33,055	4,571	1,266	428	48,313	39,320
Total	1,134,346	465,043	360,854	65,185	21,743	13,984	3,277	669,303	510,115	111,745	24,198	20,048	3,197	104,189	159,188
Additional															
Executive/administrative/managerial	29,376	23,417	21,524	1,081	309	439	64	5,959	5,184	585	66	108	16	1,893	775
Soft Money	131,674	57,580	46,366	4,610	1,999	4,372	233	74,094	57,438	10,094	3,095	3,137	330	11,214	16,656
Foreign	41,198	27,700	13,165	2,051	3,116	9,210	158	13,498	5,700	1,734	1,609	4,398	57	14,535	7,798
Full-Time Faculty by Rank and Tenure															
Tenured															
Professor	120,944	107,328	100,008	1,884	1,096	4,090	250	13,616	12,336	697	234	320	29	7,320	1,280
Associate professor	86,682	66,443	61,001	1,890	971	2,302	279	20,239	18,124	1,219	372	476	43	5,442	2,110
Assistant professor	24,584	14,697	13,212	859	265	270	91	9,887	8,507	1,044	161	163	12	1,485	1,380
Instructor	22,784	14,940	13,322	688	541	296	93	7,844	6,738	582	245	235	44	1,618	1,106
Lecturer	817	448	333	65	30	19	1	369	231	97	22	18	1	115	138
Other faculty	4,730	3,077	2,727	106	51	179	14	1,653	1,317	151	44	132	9	350	336
Total	260,541	206,933	190,603	5,492	2,954	7,156	728	53,608	47,258	3,790	1,078	1,344	138	16,330	6,350
Nontenured															
Professor	3,839	3,283	2,930	125	50	169	9	556	457	61	7	27	4	353	99
Associate professor	16,970	13,066	11,440	535	220	818	53	3,904	3,415	299	56	127	7	1,626	489
Assistant professor	65,819	43,539	37,923	1,645	796	2,909	266	22,280	19,648	1,558	363	665	46	5,616	2,632
Instructor	15,930	7,914	6,842	525	219	291	37	8,016	6,947	701	186	159	23	1,072	1,069
Lecturer	936	485	377	75	11	21	1	451	331	75	23	19	3	108	120
Other faculty	2,631	1,458	1,222	58	29	133	16	1,173	1,010	97	19	44	3	236	163
Total	106,125	69,745	60,734	2,963	1,325	4,341	382	36,380	31,808	2,791	654	1,041	86	9,011	4,572

Other															
Professor	8,410	7,049	6,523	123	94	289	20	1,361	1,216	71	18	52	4	526	145
Associate professor	11,141	8,426	7,526	242	149	480	29	2,715	2,420	136	37	114	8	900	295
Assistant professor	24,409	15,494	13,351	516	319	1,247	61	8,915	7,813	453	150	469	30	2,143	1,102
Instructor	38,259	21,292	19,206	927	401	572	186	16,967	15,083	1,219	235	358	72	2,086	1,884
Lecturer	8,177	4,234	3,786	170	78	173	27	3,943	3,553	166	93	117	14	448	390
Other Faculty	21,205	12,881	10,914	362	238	1,321	46	8,324	7,360	429	160	351	24	1,967	964
Total	111,601	69,376	61,306	2,340	1,279	4,082	369	42,225	37,445	2,474	693	1,461	152	8,070	4,780
Totals	478,267	346,054	312,643	10,795	5,558	15,579	1,479	132,213	116,511	9,055	2,425	3,846	376	33,411	15,702
Part-Time Employees															
Executive/administrative/ managerial	4,214	2,070	1,832	144	38	33	23	2,144	1,944	121	38	23	18	238	200
Tenured faculty	7,761	5,672	5,339	96	84	140	13	2,089	1,952	30	31	68	8	333	137
Nontenured faculty	30,057	17,385	15,807	919	215	405	39	12,672	11,757	527	142	221	25	1,578	915
Other	232,002	135,695	121,416	5,957	3,390	4,444	488	96,307	85,328	6,093	2,315	2,208	363	14,279	10,979
Professional/nonfaculty	48,930	16,976	14,546	877	350	1,100	103	31,954	28,910	1,478	499	961	106	2,430	3,044
Secretarial/clerical	84,062	15,651	11,908	1,881	863	939	60	68,411	57,476	6,412	2,530	1,579	414	3,743	10,935
Technical/paraprofessional	35,467	13,974	10,819	1,563	611	902	79	21,493	17,469	2,388	745	756	135	3,155	4,024
Skilled craftsmen	2,829	2,048	1,678	198	105	45	22	781	677	62	22	15	5	370	104
Service maintenance	38,185	20,325	14,197	3,892	1,074	985	177	17,860	12,479	3,940	717	594	130	6,128	5,381
Total	483,507	229,796	197,542	15,527	6,730	8,993	1,004	253,711	217,992	21,051	7,039	6,425	1,204	32,254	35,719
New Hires															
Executive/administrative/ managerial	5,792	3,253	2,875	225	78	69	6	2,539	2,234	207	48	44	6	378	305
Tenured faculty	1,949	1,417	1,267	33	25	81	11	532	458	44	12	15	3	150	74
Nontenured faculty	17,276	10,984	9,516	483	222	723	40	6,292	5,566	405	116	181	24	1,468	726
Other	16,646	9,976	8,520	389	231	743	93	6,670	5,849	447	132	219	23	1,456	821
Professional/nonfaculty	25,284	10,747	9,018	644	297	748	40	14,537	12,565	1,117	355	454	46	1,729	1,972
Secretarial/clerical	27,962	2,693	1,968	442	172	93	18	25,269	20,107	3,473	1,138	413	138	725	5,162
Technical/paraprofessional	10,465	4,364	3,538	383	200	222	21	6,101	4,949	684	230	207	31	826	1,152
Skilled craftsmen	2,234	2,014	1,663	198	109	19	25	220	180	31	5	3	1	351	40
Service maintenance	13,392	8,702	5,180	2,587	714	159	62	4,690	2,764	1,493	323	78	32	3,522	1,926
Total	121,000	54,150	43,545	5,384	2,048	2,857	316	66,850	54,672	7,901	2,359	1,614	304	10,605	12,178

Total Full-Time Employment: 1,623,145

Note: The sizes of samples used in the table above are as follows: Total institutions, 2,950; total public, 1,553, total private, 1,397. Total systems, 232; system campuses, 843. Federal contractors, 848; noncontractors, 2,102.

Source:

U.S. Equal Employment Opportunity Commission, "EEO-6 Higher Education Staff Information" surveys, 1985.

Tenure Status of Academically Employed Doctoral Scientists and Engineers, by Field and Sex, 1985

Scientific and Engineering	Number Employed			Percentage Tenured		Percentage in Tenure Track		Percentage Not in Tenure Track		Number Tenured	
	Men	Women	Percentage of Women	Men	Women	Men	Women	Men	Women	Men	Women
All Scientific and Engineering Fields	171,402	32,287	15.9	62.9	37.7	15.9	23.4	13.9	31.0	107,812	12,172
Science, Mathematics, Engineering											
Chemists	14,768	1,725	10.5	63.0	36.9	11.1	14.7	14.6	39.5	9,304	636
Physicists and astronomers	14,376	512	3.4	55.2	34.0	8.0	15.6	19.3	32.6	7,935	174
Mathematical scientists	12,914	1,287	9.1	72.0	53.8	15.1	26.3	7.3	15.7	9,278	692
Computer and information specialists	1,265	157	11.0	33.3	34.4	47.7	43.3	13.6	17.8	421	54
Earth and environmental scientists	5,684	443	7.2	59.1	28.4	16.5	27.5	18.3	37.0	3,359	126
Biological scientists	33,731	9,427	21.8	61.0	30.1	15.1	18.1	18.4	41.3	20,576	2,838
Agricultural scientists	10,186	571	5.3	63.4	25.9	20.0	37.5	11.7	30.6	6,458	148
Medical scientists	6,365	2,560	28.7	55.5	37.5	20.5	33.2	17.9	22.1	3,532	960
Engineers	21,192	404	1.9	62.4	25.7	21.1	48.5	9.5	17.8	13,224	104
Total	120,481	17,086								74,107	5,732
Social Science											
Psychologists	16,210	7,081	30.4	62.3	37.3	13.8	22.6	17.6	30.9	10,099	2,641
Social scientists	34,711	8,120	19.0	68.2	46.5	16.9	26.2	9.7	23.0	23,673	3,776
Total	50,921	15,201								33,772	6,417

Source:
National Research Council, special tabulation from "1985 Survey of Doctoral Scientists and Engineers," unpublished as cited in Vetter, B. M. & Babco, E. L., *Professional Women and Minorities: A Manpower Data Resource Service*, 1987, Table 5-7.

Tenure Status of Academically Employed Ph.D.'s in the Humanities, by Field of Ph.D. and Sex, 1985

	Field of Doctorate									
	All Fields		English and American Languages and Literature		History		Other Languages and Literatures		Other Humanities	
Age and Tenure	Men	Women	Men	Women	Men	Women	Men	Women	Men	Women
Total Number										
Employed	47,000	17,900	11,700	5,800	12,600	2,200	7,900	5,000	14,800	4,900
Percentages										
Tenured	75.0	51.0	78.1	53.9	76.0	51.8	77.3	51.6	70.6	46.7
Not tenured	21.4	44.9	18.1	42.1	20.6	44.7	21.1	45.3	24.8	47.9
Tenure track	11.3	20.0	9.2	16.2	8.4	16.9	12.3	22.5	15.1	23.6
Non-tenure track	9.5	24.1	8.4	25.1	12.1	27.2	8.2	22.2	9.0	23.5

Note: "Other languages and literature" refers to classical languages and literature and modern languages and literature. "Other humanities" are art history, music, speech/theater, philosophy, and other Humanities fields. Percentages for those not reporting tenure status are not included in this table; therefore totals may not add to 100%.

Source: National Research Council, "Humanities Doctorates in the United States, 1985 Profile," as cited in Vetter, B. M. & Babco, E. L., *Professional Women and Minorities: A Manpower Data Resource Service*, 1987, Table 5-5.

Full-Time Faculty and Percentage With Tenure, by Sex, and by Region and State, Fall 1985

88

Region and State	Full-Time Faculty[a]			Percentage With Tenure	
	Both Sexes	Men	Women	Men	Women
U.S. and Outlying Parts	395,857	283,828	112,029	66	46
50 States and the District of Columbia	390,731	281,212	109,519	66	46
New England	**28,454**	**20,549**	**7,905**	**66**	**45**
Connecticut	5,630	4,185	1,445	74	55
Maine	1,809	1,260	549	55	28
Massachusetts	15,288	10,905	4,383	65	44
New Hampshire	1,933	1,414	519	61	35
Rhode Island	2,365	1,734	631	71	56
Vermont	1,429	1,051	378	60	33
Mideast	**77,266**	**54,887**	**22,379**	**69**	**48**
Delaware	1,247	853	394	61	28
District of Columbia	3,609	2,451	1,158	59	36
Maryland	6,779	4,544	2,235	67	46
New Jersey	9,132	6,399	2,733	76	61
New York	35,915	25,409	10,506	68	49
Pennsylvania	20,584	15,231	5,353	69	46
Southeast	**87,555**	**60,550**	**27,005**	**60**	**40**
Alabama	7,032	4,719	2,313	66	57
Arkansas	3,260	2,310	950	63	41
Florida	13,293	9,480	3,813	65	53
Georgia	8,278	5,741	2,537	63	43
Kentucky	5,762	4,022	1,740	71	48
Louisiana	7,077	4,885	2,192	63	43
Mississippi	4,828	3,020	1,808	42	22
North Carolina	11,867	7,931	3,936	48	26
South Carolina	5,640	3,822	1,818	53	26
Tennessee	7,540	5,374	2,166	67	47
Virginia	10,070	7,243	2,827	58	33
West Virginia	2,908	2,003	905	66	47
Great Lakes	**67,863**	**49,982**	**17,881**	**69**	**47**
Illinois	19,330	14,075	5,255	75	60
Indiana	9,287	6,853	2,434	67	41

Region and State	Full-Time Faculty[a]			Percentage With Tenure	
	Both Sexes	Men	Women	Men	Women
Michigan	13,751	10,281	3,470	71	49
Ohio	15,578	11,440	4,138	69	43
Wisconsin	9,917	7,333	2,584	57	31
Plains	**32,170**	**23,607**	**8,563**	**63**	**39**
Iowa	6,161	4,577	1,584	60	38
Kansas	5,186	3,743	1,443	64	46
Minnesota	6,744	5,035	1,709	66	40
Missouri	7,651	5,525	2,126	63	38
Nebraska	3,582	2,617	965	62	34
North Dakota	1,529	1,158	371	57	32
South Dakota	1,317	952	365	61	31
Southwest	**36,374**	**26,135**	**10,239**	**58**	**38**
Arizona	4,731	3,549	1,182	63	36
New Mexico	2,301	1,765	536	61	35
Oklahoma	5,303	3,761	1,542	58	37
Texas	24,039	17,060	6,979	57	38
Rocky Mountains	**11,604**	**9,050**	**2,554**	**66**	**41**
Colorado	5,444	4,252	1,192	64	41
Idaho	1,300	1,014	286	62	46
Montana	1,395	1,101	294	68	35
Utah	2,410	1,884	526	69	41
Wyoming	1,055	799	256	68	47
Far West	**48,993**	**36,038**	**12,955**	**78**	**64**
Alaska	776	549	227	19	10
California	34,435	25,362	9,073	81	68
Hawaii	1,767	1,257	510	70	49
Nevada	879	642	237	69	48
Oregon	4,480	3,237	1,243	70	54
Washington	6,656	4,991	1,665	76	59
U.S. Service Schools	**452**	**414**	**38**	**80**	**40**
Outlying Parts	**5,126**	**2,616**	**2,510**	**53**	**52**

a These data are based on a survey conducted to estimate salaries and fringe benefits, rather than total number of faculty. Slightly different numbers would be expected from a census of all instructional staff in institutions of higher education.

Sources:
1 National Center for Education Statistics, "Salaries, Tenure, and Fringe Benefits of Full-Time Instructional Faculty" surveys, unpublished tabulations.
2 ACE/Macmillan, *1989–90 Fact Book on Higher Education*, Table 106.

Full-Time Faculty in Higher Education, by Race/Ethnicity and Sex, 1975, 1983, and 1985

Race/Ethnicity and Sex	1975 Number	1975 Percentage	1983 Number	1983 Percentage	1985 Number	1985 Percentage	Percentage Change 1975–83	Percentage Change 1983–85	Percentage Change 1975–85
Total	446,830	100.0	485,739	100.0	488,799	100.0	8.7	0.6	9.4
Men	336,362	75.3	356,579	73.4	354,213	72.5	6.0	-0.7	5.3
Women	110,468	24.7	129,160	26.6	134,586	27.5	16.9	4.2	21.8
White	409,947	91.7	440,505	90.7	439,767	90.0	7.5	-0.2	7.3
Men	312,293	69.9	326,171	67.1	320,969	65.7	4.4	-1.6	2.8
Women	97,654	21.9	114,334	23.5	118,798	24.3	17.1	3.9	21.7
Black	19,746	4.4	19,571	4.0	20,283	4.1	-0.9	3.6	2.7
Men	10,894	2.4	10,541	2.2	11,053	2.3	-3.2	4.9	1.5
Women	8,852	2.0	9,030	1.9	9,230	1.9	2.0	2.2	4.3
Hispanic	6,323	1.4	7,456	1.5	8,087	1.7	17.9	8.5	27.9
Men	4,573	1.0	5,240	1.1	5,683	1.2	14.6	8.5	24.3
Women	1,750	0.4	2,216	0.5	2,404	0.5	26.6	8.5	37.4
Asian	9,763	2.2	16,889	3.5	19,104	3.9	73.0	13.1	95.7
Men	7,830	1.8	13,677	2.8	15,323	3.1	74.7	12.0	95.7
Women	1,933	0.4	3,222	0.7	3,781	0.8	66.7	17.3	95.6
American Indian	1,051	0.2	1,308	0.3	1,558	0.3	24.5	19.1	48.2
Men	772	0.2	950	0.2	1,185	0.2	23.1	24.7	53.5
Women	279	0.1	358	0.1	373	0.1	28.3	4.2	33.7

Note: Data include full-time faculty who are in non-tenure-earning positions, tenured faculty, and faculty who are nontenured but who are in positions that lead to consideration for tenure. Details may not add to total because of rounding.

Sources:
1 Equal Employment Opportunity Commission, "EEO-6 Higher Education Staff Information" surveys, 1975, 1983, and 1985.
2 ACE, "Minorities in Higher Education: Seventh Annual Status Report," 1988, Table 11.

	Percentage Distribution							
	1975		1984					
	All Institutions		All Institutions		2-Year Institutions		4-Year Institutions	
Characteristics	Men	Women	Men	Women	Men	Women	Men	Women
Age								
Over 60	5.7	7.8	10.4	7.5	8.8	10.3	10.8	6.3
51–60	18.8	21.1	24.9	18.8	23.3	18.2	25.4	19.0
41–50	29.0	25.7	35.8	33.3	39.3	36.9	34.8	31.8
36–40	17.2	14.3	15.3	19.4	15.3	19.3	15.3	19.4
31–35	20.4	16.3	10.7	15.0	10.4	11.6	10.7	16.5
30 or younger	8.8	14.9	2.9	6.0	2.8	3.7	3.0	7.0
Highest Degree Held								
Bachelor's or less	4.5	7.8	4.3	6.5	13.5	13.6	1.8	3.5
Master's	25.2	41.0	22.3	42.3	49.9	60.7	14.7	34.7
First-professional, law	1.7	0.5	1.2	0.7	0.5	0.6	1.3	0.7
First-professional, medicine	4.3	1.6	2.8	1.1	0.9	0.0	3.3	1.6
Ph.D. or Ed.D.	55.4	33.6	60.1	38.0	27.1	12.5	69.2	48.6
Other doctorate	4.0	2.8	0.9	1.1	0.7	0.3	1.0	1.5
Other first professional	4.5	12.5	2.9	6.6	5.8	9.9	2.1	5.2
Multiple, above master's[a]	NA[b]	NA	5.2	3.5	1.0	2.1	6.3	4.1
None	0.6	0.3	0.4	0.3	0.4	0.4	0.4	0.2
Racial Background								
White	94.3	93.0	93.3	93.0	92.1	92.5	93.6	93.2
Black	2.5	4.6	1.8	3.6	3.1	4.4	1.5	3.2
American Indian	0.1	0.2	0.0	0.0	0.0	0.0	0.0	0.0
Mexican-American, Puerto Rican, Hispanic	0.4	0.1	1.2	1.1	2.3	1.6	1.0	0.9
Asian-American	2.2	1.4	3.1	1.5	2.1	0.9	3.3	1.8
Other	0.5	0.7	0.6	0.7	0.4	0.5	0.7	0.8

	Percentage Distribution							
	1975[c]		1984					
	All Institutions		All Institutions		2-Year Institutions		4-Year Institutions	
Characteristics	Men	Women	Men	Women	Men	Women	Men	Women
Present Rank								
Professor	29.4	11.3	41.1	15.6	25.8	14.0	45.3	16.2
Associate Professor	26.4	21.4	25.6	22.5	19.3	19.1	27.3	23.9
Assistant Professor	26.2	33.2	17.3	29.6	8.2	15.1	19.7	35.8
Instructor	9.6	25.2	9.7	20.6	27.6	31.4	4.8	16.0
Lecturer	2.8	3.3	1.8	4.1	0.6	1.5	2.1	5.2
No ranks designated	4.4	3.9	3.9	5.0	17.4	14.9	0.2	0.8
Other	1.2	1.7	0.8	2.6	1.1	4.0	0.6	2.1
Major Field of Highest Degree								
Business	4.4	3.0	3.7	2.2	2.4	3.3	4.0	1.7
Education	12.4	22.7	10.6	14.6	14.6	13.3	9.4	15.1
Biological sciences	9.1	4.9	8.7	3.6	5.3	1.9	9.7	4.3
Physical sciences	13.5	5.3	15.0	6.0	11.2	9.5	16.1	4.5
Engineering	5.1	0.2	6.3	0.4	5.4	0.0	6.5	0.6
Social sciences	13.7	10.1	14.7	12.0	13.3	6.2	15.1	14.4
Fine arts	8.4	9.8	6.8	9.5	6.9	9.1	6.7	9.6
Humanities	17.8	20.9	14.0	15.7	16.9	14.0	13.2	16.4
Health sciences	4.6	1.5	4.2	14.6	2.2	17.7	4.8	13.2
Other professions[d]	0.5	0.0	2.9	7.5	1.8	6.1	3.3	8.1
All other fields[e]	8.5	18.9	2.9	2.7	3.8	2.6	2.6	2.8
None	2.0	2.8	10.2	11.3	16.3	16.4	8.5	9.1

NA = not available

a Respondent indicated more than one degree above a master's degree.

b Question not asked in 1975 survey.

c Based on 42,345 responding regular faculty from both academic departments and professional schools.

d Includes law only in 1975.

e Includes new and semi-professions in 1975.

Sources:
1 The Carnegie Foundation for the Advancement of Teaching, Carnegie Surveys, 1975; Carnegie Survey of Faculty, 1985. Used by permission.

2 ACE/Macmillan, *1986–87 Fact Book on Higher Education*, Tables 120, 121.

Science/Engineering Postdoctorates and Other Nonfaculty
Doctoral Research Staff in Doctorate-Granting Institutions,
by Field and Sex, 1985

91

	Postdoctorates			Other Nonfaculty Doctoral Research Staff		
	Total	Men	Women	Total	Men	Women
Total, all fields	22,691	17,174	5,517	5,120	3,828	1,292
Engineering	1,364	1,264	100	609	558	51
Sciences, total	21,327	15,910	5,417	4,511	3,270	1,241
Physical sciences	4,517	3,917	600	962	835	127
Environmental sciences	375	318	57	184	163	21
Mathematical sciences	231	202	29	176	153	23
Computer sciences	74	64	10	77	67	10
Life sciences	15,264	10,893	4,371	2,756	1,846	910
Agricultural	357	289	68	116	84	32
Biological	9,284	6,497	2,787	1,679	1,134	545
Health	5,623	4,107	1,516	961	628	333
Psychology	498	273	225	209	115	94
Social sciences	366	243	125	147	91	56

Source:
National Science Foundation, "Academic Science/Engineering: Postdoctorates and Other Nonfaculty Research Staff in Doctorate Institutions,"
1986, selected unpublished data as cited in Vetter, B. M. & Babco, E. L., *Professional Women and Minorities: A Manpower Data Resource
Service*, 1987, Table 5-14.

Average Salaries of Full-Time Instructional Faculty on 9- or 10-Month Contracts in Institutions of Higher Education, by Academic Rank and Sex, 1976–77 to 1985–86

92

(In current dollars.)

Academic Year and Sex	All Ranks Combined	Professor	Associate Professor	Assistant Professor	Instructor	Lecturer	Undesignated or No Academic Rank
1976–77							
Total	$17,560	$23,792	$17,905	$14,662	$11,835	$13,431	$16,634
Men	18,378	24,029	18,055	14,851	12,085	14,147	17,253
Women	15,100	21,536	17,189	14,225	11,589	12,397	15,467
1977–78							
Total	18,709	25,133	18,987	15,530	12,504	14,528	17,831
Men	19,575	25,370	19,133	15,726	12,729	15,181	18,459
Women	16,159	22,943	18,325	15,109	12,288	13,688	16,637
1978–79							
Total	19,826	26,470	20,047	16,374	13,193	15,281	18,764
Men	20,785	26,727	20,221	16,602	13,441	15,927	19,462
Women	17,080	24,143	19,300	15,914	12,966	14,465	17,482
1979–80							
Total	21,379	28,388	21,451	17,465	14,023	16,122	20,477
Men	22,438	28,672	21,651	17,720	14,323	16,932	21,245
Women	18,396	25,910	20,642	16,974	13,750	15,142	19,069
1980–81							
Total	23,365	30,813	23,254	18,915	15,219	17,482	22,368
Men	24,536	31,076	23,470	19,231	15,590	18,450	23,187
Women	20,058	28,396	22,399	18,301	14,894	16,351	20,899
1981–82							
Total	25,533	33,539	25,324	20,628	16,508	18,933	24,385
Men	26,859	33,838	25,572	21,038	16,990	19,912	25,317
Women	21,874	30,879	24,391	19,894	16,097	17,839	22,743
1982–83							
Total	27,284	35,641	26,966	22,078	17,659	20,240	25,613
Men	28,729	35,997	27,278	22,603	18,236	21,361	26,582
Women	23,338	32,620	25,851	21,157	17,150	19,010	23,926
1983–84[a]							
1984–85							
Total	30,447	39,743	29,945	24,668	19,567	22,334	27,548
Men	32,182	40,269	30,392	25,330	20,284	23,557	28,528
Women	25,941	35,824	28,517	23,575	18,942	21,004	25,929
1985–86							
Total	32,392	42,268	31,787	26,277	20,918	23,770	29,088
Men	34,294	42,833	32,273	27,094	21,693	25,238	30,267
Women	27,576	38,252	30,300	24,966	20,237	22,273	27,171

a   The data for the 1983–84 academic year were not edited; thus, they could not be analyzed.

Sources:
National Center for Education Statistics, "Salaries, Tenure, and Fringe Benefits of Full-Time Instructional Faculty" surveys (HEGIS); "College Faculty Salaries, 1976–1986," Aug. 1987, App. Table B. See Guide to Sources.

Average Salaries of Full-Time Instructional Faculty on 9- or 10-Month Contracts in Institutions of Higher Education, by Academic Rank, Sex, and Type and Control of Institution, 1976–77 and 1985–86

93

(in current dollars)

Academic Year and Type and Control of Institution	Average Salary, by Academic Rank							Average Salary by Sex	
	All Ranks Combined	Professor	Associate Professor	Assistant Professor	Instructor	Lecturer	No Academic Rank	Men	Women
1976–77									
All Institutions	$17,560	$23,792	$17,905	$14,662	$11,835	$13,431	$16,634	$18,378	$15,100
4-year	17,869	23,922	17,899	14,639	11,711	13,514	12,866	18,696	14,977
Universities	19,674	25,919	18,854	15,285	12,025	13,925	13,576	20,522	15,794
Other	16,686	22,056	17,293	14,277	11,589	12,964	12,730	17,385	14,593
2-year	16,466	20,992	17,962	14,845	12,275	11,550	16,891	17,039	15,379
Public Institutions	17,845	24,092	18,356	15,029	12,142	13,595	17,054	18,620	15,573
4-year	18,313	24,272	18,388	15,037	12,019	13,701	13,391	19,091	15,539
Universities	19,403	25,474	18,822	15,299	11,930	14,003	13,345	20,223	15,744
Other	17,509	23,075	18,078	14,871	12,061	13,317	13,428	18,186	15,425
2-year	16,685	21,355	18,119	14,983	12,445	11,636	17,126	17,235	15,628
Private Institutions	16,787	23,152	16,791	13,823	11,056	12,850	12,099	17,736	13,709
4-year	16,977	23,216	16,825	13,855	11,129	12,877	12,668	17,891	13,899
Universities	20,358	26,910	18,944	15,250	12,309	13,682	14,281	21,265	15,933
Other	15,248	20,183	15,806	13,243	10,831	11,609	12,575	15,959	13,218
2-year	11,637	14,189	13,958	11,989	9,526	a	11,409	12,193	10,850
1985–86									
All Institutions	32,392	42,268	31,787	26,277	20,918	23,770	29,088	34,294	27,576
4-year	33,270	42,803	31,940	26,335	20,383	23,805	24,055	35,174	27,696
Universities	37,145	47,323	33,656	28,242	20,626	24,129	24,923	39,151	29,354
Other	31,553	40,285	31,199	25,601	20,323	23,632	23,997	33,237	27,152
2-year	29,259	36,076	30,483	25,823	22,434	23,154	29,420	30,490	27,294
Public Institutions	32,750	42,328	32,367	26,951	21,553	23,839	29,597	34,528	28,299
4-year	34,033	43,044	32,642	27,100	20,895	23,862	25,142	35,786	28,680
Universities	36,152	45,660	33,018	27,860	20,035	23,877	24,201	38,089	28,671
Other	32,977	41,481	32,460	26,762	21,167	23,854	25,265	34,542	28,683
2-year	29,590	36,418	30,733	26,162	22,818	23,500	29,712	30,758	27,693
Private Institutions	31,402	42,118	30,400	24,891	19,314	23,477	21,577	33,656	25,523
4-year	31,732	42,260	30,486	24,987	19,483	23,574	23,394	33,900	25,889
Universities	39,751	51,682	35,387	29,165	22,581	24,866	26,602	41,929	31,174
Other	28,982	37,803	28,862	23,777	19,031	22,539	23,295	30,789	24,640
2-year	19,436	24,519	22,291	19,297	16,419	a	18,783	20,412	18,504

a   The number of faculty reported in this category were too small to yield reliable results.

Source:
National Center for Education Statistics, "Salaries, Tenure, and Fringe Benefits of Full-Time Instructional Faculty" surveys (HEGIS); "College Faculty Salaries, 1976–1986," Aug. 1987, App. Table C. See Guide to Sources.

Average Salaries of Full-Time Instructional Faculty on 9- or 10-Month Contracts in Institutions of Higher Education, by Academic Rank and Sex, 1976–77 to 1985–86

94

(in constant 1985–86 dollars)

Academic Year and Sex	All Ranks Combined	Professor	Associate Professor	Assistant Professor	Instructor	Lecturer	Undesignated or No Academic Rank
1976–77							
Total	$32,600	$44,100	$33,200	$27,200	$21,900	$24,900	$30,800
Men	34,100	44,500	33,500	27,500	22,400	26,200	32,000
Women	28,000	39,900	31,900	26,400	21,500	23,000	28,700
1977–78							
Total	32,500	43,700	33,000	27,000	21,700	25,200	31,000
Men	34,000	44,100	33,200	27,300	22,100	26,400	32,100
Women	28,100	39,900	31,800	26,200	21,300	23,800	28,900
1978–79							
Total	31,500	42,000	31,800	26,000	21,000	24,300	29,800
Men	33,000	42,400	32,100	26,400	21,300	25,300	30,900
Women	27,100	38,300	30,600	25,300	20,600	23,000	27,800
1979–80							
Total	30,000	39,800	30,100	24,500	19,700	22,600	28,700
Men	31,500	40,200	30,400	24,800	20,100	23,700	29,800
Women	25,800	36,300	28,900	23,800	19,300	21,200	26,700
1980–81							
Total	29,300	38,700	29,200	23,800	19,100	22,000	28,100
Men	30,800	39,000	29,500	24,200	19,600	23,200	29,100
Women	25,200	35,700	28,100	23,000	18,700	20,500	26,200
1981–82							
Total	29,500	38,800	29,300	23,800	19,100	21,900	28,200
Men	31,000	39,100	29,600	24,300	19,600	23,000	29,300
Women	25,300	35,700	28,200	23,000	18,600	20,600	26,300
1982–83							
Total	30,300	39,500	29,900	24,500	19,600	22,400	28,400
Men	31,900	39,900	30,300	25,100	20,200	23,700	29,500
Women	25,900	36,200	28,700	23,500	19,000	21,100	26,500
1983–84[a]							
1984–85							
Total	31,300	40,900	30,800	25,400	20,100	23,000	28,300
Men	33,100	41,400	31,300	26,100	20,900	24,200	29,400
Women	26,700	36,900	29,300	24,300	19,500	21,600	26,700
1985–86							
Total	32,400	42,300	31,800	26,300	20,900	23,800	29,100
Men	34,300	42,800	32,300	27,100	21,700	25,200	30,300
Women	27,600	38,300	30,300	25,000	20,200	22,300	27,200

a The data for the 1983–84 academic year were not edited; thus, they could not be analyzed.

Note: Salaries are in constant 1985–86 dollars, using the Consumer Price Index to adjust figures in previous years to control for inflation.

Source:
National Center for Education Statistics, "Salaries, Tenure, and Fringe Benefits of Full-Time Instructional Faculty" surveys (HEGIS); "College Faculty Salaries, 1976–1986," Aug. 1987, Table 3. See Guide to Sources.

Type of Institution	1975	1984	1987	1989
Private	**132**	**182**	**184**	**182**
4-year	98	134	156	151
2-year	34	48	28	31
Public	**16**	**104**	**112**	**146**
4-year	5	32	39	44
2-year	11	72	73	102
Total	**148**	**286**	**296**	**328**

Notes: The total number of women chief executive officers reflects both new appointments and women presidents of newly accredited institutions. For purposes of this table, only institutions accredited by, or candidates for accreditation by, the 6 major regional accrediting associations (MSA/CHE, NEASC-CIHE, NCA, NASC, SACS-Comm. on Colleges, WASC-Sr., WASC-Jr.) in the United States and outlying areas (N = 3000) are included.

a   Additional information on the presidents and their institutions, not reflected in the above table, include:

77	(23%)	are members of religious orders
43	(13%)	are members of a minority group
		(20 are black, 16 are Hispanic, 5 are Native American, 2 are Asian-Americans)
226	(69%)	have enrollments under 3,000
62	(19%)	have enrollments between 3,000 and 10,000
40	(12%)	have enrollments over 10,000

Source:
ACE, Office of Women in Higher Education, "Women Chief Executive Officers in U.S. Colleges and Universities, Table XII," 1990, and unpublished files of the Office. ACE, *Accredited Institutions of Postsecondary Education, 1989–90*, published for the Council on Postsecondary Accreditation; ACE membership database.

Position Title	Number of Men	Number of Women	Percentage of Women
Chief Executive Officer, Single Institution	1,194	137	10
Chief Academic Officer	1,144	234	17
Director, Library Services	681	521	43
Director, Institutional Research	335	193	36
Chief Health Professions Officer	71	24	25
Dean, Arts and Letters	86	21	20
Dean, Arts and Sciences	344	64	16
Dean, Business	545	80	13
Dean, Communications	74	17	19
Dean, Continuing Education	388	172	31
Dean, Education	315	91	22
Dean, Extension	70	18	20
Dean, Fine Arts	149	35	19
Dean, Graduate Programs	284	69	20
Dean, Health-Related Professions	110	95	46
Dean, Home Economics	12	40	77
Dean, Humanities	149	62	29
Dean, Instruction	31	14	31
Dean, Law	114	10	8
Dean, Library and Information Science	47	19	29
Dean, Mathematics	85	14	14
Dean, Nursing	8	272	97
Dean, Occupational Studies/Vocational Education/Technology	199	31	13
Dean, Sciences	224	38	14
Dean, Social Sciences	166	39	19
Dean, Social Work	45	26	37
Dean, Special Programs	68	36	35
Dean, Undergraduate Programs	53	33	38

Position Title	Number of Men	Number of Women	Percentage of Women
Chief Business Officer	1,230	145	10
Chief Planning Officer	163	52	24
Chief Budgeting Officer	338	97	22
Chief Personnel and Human Resources Officer	416	302	42
Director, Bookstore	382	445	54
Director, Affirmative Action/Equal Employment	128	187	59
Manager, Payroll	164	404	71
Chief Development Officer	678	168	20
Director, Annual Giving	206	221	52
Director, Corporate/Foundation Relations	144	120	45
Chief Public Relations Officer	379	347	48
Director, Alumni Affairs	356	390	52
Director, Development and Alumni Affairs	79	47	37
Director, Governmental/Legislative Relations	83	27	24
Director, Publications	177	251	59
Director, Information Office	197	201	50
Chief Student Affairs Officer	983	323	25
Director, Admissions	712	275	28
Registrar	592	510	46
Director, Student Financial Aid	700	555	44
Director, Student Housing	399	232	37
Director, Student Placement	419	467	53
Director, Student Counseling	505	356	41
Director, Athletics	807	75	8

Note: This table is a list of selected positions in each area of administration. A more complete list is shown in Table A-98.

Source:
College and University Personnel Association (CUPA), "Administrative Compensation Survey 1987–88," special tabulations, 1988.

Number and Median Salary of Administrators in All Types of Institutions, by Sex, 1987–88

Position Title	Men				Women			
	Years	Median Salary	Percentage Difference	Number	Years	Median Salary	Percentage Difference	Number
Executive								
Chief Executive Officer, System	4	$86,130	23.0	123	2	$70,000		6
Assistant to the President, System	3	54,599	41.6	42	2	38,550		28
Chief Executive Officer, Single Institution	5	75,000	8.7	1,194	3	68,967		137
Assistant to the President, Single Institution	3	47,400	42.4	280	3	33,290		289
Executive Vice President	4	62,700	17.4	269	3	53,385		23
Academic								
Chief Academic Officer	3	58,400	16.8	1,144	2	50,000		234
Director, Conferences	3	38,064	37.4	92	2	27,700		98
Chief Health Professions Officer	4	90,925	153	71	3	36,000		24
Director, Library Services	8	41,446	21.9	681	5	34,000		521
Circulation Librarian	7	28,975	28.4	111	5	22,572		367
Acquisitions Librarian	7	31,712	22.4	137	7	25,903		359
Technical Services Librarian	6	31,100	17.4	173	5	26,500		452
Public Services Librarian	5	33,723	20.9	134	5	27,900		250
Reference Librarian	7	28,976	16.8	186	5	24,800		458
Director, Institutional Research	4	42,577	18.5	335	3	35,939		193
Associate Director, Institutional Research	3	38,110	23.5	62	3	30,861		51
Director, Educational Media Services	7	32,200	34.6	435	4	23,929		96
Director, Learning Resources Center	7	39,250	34.3	247	4	29,233		224
Director, International Studies Education	4	45,263	51.4	110	4	29,904		46
Director, Computer Center Operations/ Academic	4	40,548	22.9	366	3	33,000		67
Associate Director, Computer Center Operations/Academic	3	38,400	29.0	120	3	29,772		48
Administrator, Grants and Contracts	4	47,212	45.6	271	3	32,430		165
Dean, Arts and Letters	4	51,792	3.6	86	3	50,000		21
Dean, Arts and Sciences	4	60,008	16.5	344	1	51,500		64
Dean, Business	3	59,500	43.0	545	3	41,600		80
Dean, Communications	5	53,844	20.5	74	2	44,671		17
Dean, Continuing Education	5	47,856	21.7	388	3	39,337		172
Dean, Education	4	59,000	21.1	315	3	48,725		91
Dean, Extension	5	52,531	45.9	70	3	36,000		18
Dean, Fine Arts	5	53,320	9.6	149	2	48,667		35
Dean, Graduate Programs	4	61,500	9.8	284	3	56,000		69
Dean, Health-Related Professions	6	57,680	22.8	110	4	46,979		95
Dean, Home Economics	6	63,204	5.3	12	4	60,000		40
Dean, Humanities	4	45,516	16.1	149	4	39,200		62
Dean, Instruction	2	48,944	11.2	31	3	44,000		14
Dean, Law	3	95,000	5.6	114	2	90,000		10
Dean, Library and Information Sciences	3	57,404	10.5	47	4	51,940		19
Dean, Mathematics	6	43,527	11.7	85	3	38,968		14
Dean, Nursing	8	59,122	13.7	8	5	52,000		272

Position Title	Men				Women			
	Years	Median Salary	Percentage Difference	Number	Years	Median Salary	Percentage Difference	Number
Dean, Occupational Studies/ Vocational Education/Technology	4	$47,500	8.8	199	2	$43,677		31
Dean, Sciences	5	50,000	22.5	224	3	40,813		38
Dean, Social Sciences	6	46,210	12.7	166	3	41,018		39
Dean, Social Work	7	68,917	19.5	45	6	57,648		26
Dean, Special Programs	3	42,000	15.4	68	3	36,396		36
Dean, Undergraduate Programs	4	54,875	15.5	53	3	47,500		33
Administrative								
Chief Business Officer	6	54,995	27.9	1,230	3	43,000		145
Director, Health and Safety	5	37,236	8.5	152	1	34,332		14
Director, Telecommunications	3	40,507	40.4	192	4	28,860		72
Chief Planning Officer	4	45,625	24.8	163	2	44,540		52
Chief Budgeting Officer	6	47,772	19.4	338	3	40,000		97
Associate Budget Director	4	40,008	19.4	115	2	33,508		75
Chief Planning and Budget Officer	5	55,700	16.9	82	3	47,652		14
General Counsel	6	59,804	3.8	137	5	57,589		43
Associate General Counsel	4	53,024	27.5	38	2	41,600		30
Chief Personnel/Human Resources Officer	6	46,855	35.2	416	3	34,650		302
Associate Director, Personnel/Human Resources	5	40,620	39.6	112	3	29,100		167
Manager, Benefits	5	37,284	44.3	85	3	25,830		223
Manager, Training and Development	3	36,000	15.2	50	3	31,261		94
Manager, Employee Relations	6	39,500	27.4	34	3	31,000		44
Manager, Labor Relations	3	42,550	12.1	37	3	37,944		16
Manager, Employment	4	34,956	35.5	65	3	25,800		160
Manager, Wage and Salary/ Compensation	5	34,466	15.9	77	2	29,748		93
Manager, Personnel Information Systems	3	39,432	49.9	43	4	26,308		57
Director, Affirmative Action/Equal Employment	4	42,813	9.3	128	4	39,165		187
Associate Director, Affirmative Action/ Equal Employment	4	34,172	20.6	18	4	28,329		34
Director, Personnel and Affirmative Action	6	38,376	27.2	90	4	30,181		130
Director, Computer Center	5	43,500	33.5	707	3	32,577		103
Associate Director, Computer Center	5	40,000	35.6	174	3	29,500		53
Data Base Administrator	3	39,282	15.9	132	3	33,884		49
Systems Analyst I (highest level)	4	33,075	14.2	189	4	28,970		74
Systems Analyst II (lowest level)	2	27,700	17.2	109	2	23,630		61
Programmer Analyst I (highest level)	3	28,400	12.1	233	3	25,329		129
Programmer Analyst II (lowest level)	2	22,350	1.7	142	2	21,970		143
Director, Computer Center Operations/Administrative	5	42,303	31.0	241	4	32,302		62
Associate Director, Computer Center Operations/Administrative	4	39,250	43.2	104	4	27,400		40

| Position Title | | Men | | | | Women | | |
	Years	Median Salary	Percentage Difference	Number	Years	Median Salary	Percentage Difference	Number
Director, Information Systems	4	$49,000	53.1	192	3	$32,000		44
Chief, Physical Plant/Facilities Management Officer	5	39,720	18.6	1,167	3	33,500		21
Associate Director, Physical Plant/ Facilities Management	4	33,950	55.0	456	6	21,900		13
Manager, Landscape and Grounds	5	26,160	16.6	499	3	22,436		29
Manager, Building and Maintenance Trades	5	29,400	12.7	439	5	26,088		6
Manager, Custodial Services	5	26,054	13.2	481	5	23,016		97
Comptroller	5	44,750	35.6	609	3	33,000		212
Manager, Payroll	6	33,691	43.4	164	5	23,496		404
Director, Accounting	6	37,500	32.1	342	3	28,377		231
Staff Accountant (highest level)	3	26,790	16.8	161	2	22,944		237
Staff Accountant (lowest level)	2	20,795	13.6	88	2	18,310		183
Bursar	6	35,430	35.4	175	3	26,162		187
Associate Bursar	4	28,359	14.7	38	4	24,734		55
Director, Purchasing	6	35,600	37.5	507	4	25,900		227
Associate Director, Purchasing	4	33,135	29,0	129	3	25,692		84
Director, Bookstore	8	30,100	50.5	382	6	20,000		445
Associate Director, Bookstore	5	24,003	31.3	69	4	18,277		90
Director, Internal Audit	5	42,500	34.4	221	2	31,620		84
Director, Auxiliary Services	5	42,840	38.0	275	3	31,039		58
Manager, Mail Services	5	21,205	24.0	248	5	17,100		176
Director, Campus Security	5	30,000	27.3	821	1	23,574		20
Director, Risk Management and Insurance	4	43,541	4.2	92	4	41,766		33
Administrator, Hospital Medical Center	4	102,606	25.1	42	2	82,000		8
Director, Medical Center Public Relations/Affairs	3	49,000	4.0	19	5	47,096		30
Director, Medical Center Personnel	5	48,960	15.5	17	2	42,400		11
External Affairs								
Chief Development Officer	3	51,000	24.7	678	2	40,900		168
Director, Annual Giving	2	32,352	15.5	206	2	28,000		221
Director, Corporate/Foundation Relations	2	40,500	26.6	144	2	32,000		120
Coordinator, Resource Development	1	33,751	38.9	39	2	24,300		121
Director, Estate Planning	3	41,000	12.0	112	2	36,600		27
Chief Public Relations Officer	3	40,000	31.8	379	2	30,357		347
Director, Governmental/Legislative Relations	4	60,000	25.3	83	3	47,900		27
Chief Development and Public Relations Officer	4	58,800	36.2	151	3	43,160		59
Director, Alumni Affairs	3	34,776	32.8	356	2	26,184		390
Director, Development and Alumni Affairs	2	40,935	24.2	79	2	32,968		47
Director, Special and Deferred Gifts	3	39,085	28.6	134	2	30,401		58
Director, Church Relations	2	28,900	39.3	76	1	20,750		21
Director, Community Services	6	41,088	24.5	94	3	33,000		111

	Men				Women			
Position Title	**Years**	**Median Salary**	**Percentage Difference**	**Number**	**Years**	**Median Salary**	**Percentage Difference**	**Number**
Director, Publications	4	$34,529	24.3	177	3	$27,775		251
Associate Director, Publications	3	26,412	22.8	44	2	21,504		73
Manager, Printing Services	7	28,500	33.3	317	5	21,380		99
Director, Information Office	3	35,000	23.2	197	3	28,399		201
Director, News Bureau	4	31,000	20.2	112	2	25,799		123
Student Services								
Chief Student Affairs Officer	6	48,368	15.2	983	3	42,000		323
Director, Admissions	5	38,075	15.7	712	2	32,900		275
Associate Director, Admissions	3	29,628	16.1	235	2	25,530		233
Assistant Director, Admissions	2	21,486	2.6	145	2	20,945		280
Director, Admissions and Registrar	6	43,400	22.2	184	4	35,504		68
Registrar	8	37,520	33.6	592	5	28,086		510
Associate Registrar	6	35,297	36.5	118	5	25,860		160
Assistant Registrar	5	27,092	28.4	95	3	21,100		273
Director, Admissions and Financial Aid	3	43,000	7.5	116	2	40,000		39
Director, Student Financial Aid	7	35,976	32.6	700	4	27,138		555
Associate Director, Student Financial Aid	3	27,239	18.4	168	2	23,000		362
Director, Food Services	6	34,667	27.8	236	4	27,136		107
Associate Director, Food Services	5	29,599	17.5	71	3	25,200		59
Director, Student Housing	4	31,500	30.1	399	2	24,216		232
Associate Director, Student Housing	3	28,604	30.0	120	3	22,000		89
Housing Officer/Administrative Operations	3	30,500	21.6	59	4	25,078		42
Housing Officer/Residence Life	2	24,000	8.2	95	2	22,175		125
Housing Officer/Family Housing	4	30,932	35.3	31	4	22,860		18
Director, Housing and Food Service	8	49,224	33.0	40	3	37,000		8
Director, Foreign Students	5	33,000	26.1	131	4	26,180		121
Director, Student Union	7	36,446	48.3	255	3	24,571		90
Associate Director, Student Union	3	30,450	19.9	77	2	25,400		52
Student Union Business Manager	4	29,511	30.2	50	3	22.660		24
Director, Student Activities	4	30,000	24.3	399	3	24,129		327
Director, Student Placement	6	34,344	29.6	419	3	26,500		467
Director, Student Counseling	6	38,300	28.7	505	3	29,760		356
Associate Director, Student Counseling	4	36,200	50.1	82	3	24,110		84
Director, Student Health Services (Physician Administrator)	7	64,800	16.6	204	4	55,574		80
Director, Student Health Services (Nurse Administrator)	4	25,900	10.2	10	5	23,504		505
Chaplain	4	27,000	24.3	252	2	21,723		52
Director, Athletics	5	42,181	40.0	807	3	30,120		75
Director, Sports Information	3	23,738	24.9	404	1	19,000		26
Director, Athletics/Women	8	33,380	2.9	8	6	32,443		144
Director, Campus Recreation/Intramurals	5	28,900	24.2	294	3	23,275		73

Note: Data includes responses from 1,410 institutions, including 4-year and 2-year, public and private. All positions were not applicable for each institution.

Source:
College and University Personnel Association, "Administrative Compensation Survey, 1987–88," special tabulations, 1988.

Number and Median Salary of Administrators in Selected Public Universities and 4-Year Colleges, by Sex, 1987–88

98

Position Title	Men				Women			
	Years	Median Salary	Percentage Difference	Number	Years	Median Salary	Percentage Difference	Number
Executive								
Assistant to the President, System	2	$61,000	11.9	20	5	$54,500		9
Chief Executive Officer, Single Institution	5	82,000	6.2	311	1	77,185		24
Assistant to the President, Single Institution	3	53,000	36.2	99	3	38,923		89
Academic								
Chief Academic Officer	3	71,000	1.4	327	1	70,000		39
Director, Conferences	4	40,020	30.4	47	2	30,692		41
Director, Library Services	7	50,880	0.1	228	3	50,820		104
Circulation Librarian	7	29,640	14.3	56	5	25,941		144
Acquisitions Librarian	8	33,240	15.6	77	7	28,750		148
Technical Services Librarian	6	37,290	19.8	69	7	31,128		149
Public Services Librarian	3	35,990	1.5	72	4	35,444		92
Reference Librarian	6	31,061	3.7	89	6	29,944		154
Director, Institutional Research	5	46,800	15.0	149	3	40,700		71
Associate Director, Institutional Research	4	38,655	14.6	41	3	33,741		26
Director, Educational Media Services	8	39,683	41.7	162	4	28,000		28
Director, Learning Resources Center	8	41,000	39.4	78	4	29,416		42
Director, International Studies Education	5	55,913	57.3	66	5	35,537		12
Director, Computer Center Operations /Academic	4	48,074	20.2	124	3	40,008		13
Associate Director, Computer Center Operations/Academic	5	42,756	25.8	58	4	33,984		14
Administrator, Grants and Contracts	5	50,460	39.4	154	4	36,186		59
Dean, Arts and Letters	4	62,022	8.9	46	2	56,941		11
Dean, Arts and Sciences	4	65,636	1.0	179	1	65,000		19
Dean, Business	3	66,625	9.7	269	4	60,719		11
Dean, Continuing Education	5	55,600	15.8	147	3	48,000		42
Dean, Education	4	60,719	0.2	228	2	60,622		45
Dean, Fine Arts	4	59,500		83	3	60,528	1.7	15
Dean, Graduate Programs	5	64,000	8.0	176	3	59,235		45
Dean, Health-Related Professions	6	65,540	7.7	51	2	60,856		21
Dean, Home Economics	4	64,500		7	3	66,800	3.6	31
Dean, Humanities	4	57,166		49	1	62,000	8.5	12
Dean, Library and Information Sciences	3	61,036	8.1	30	4	56,468		15
Dean, Occupational Studies/Vocational Education/Technology	4	57,449		50	4	60,768	5.8	5
Dean, Sciences	4	59,130	17.9	101	1	50,160		8

Position Title	Men				Women			
	Years	Median Salary	Percentage Difference	Number	Years	Median Salary	Percentage Difference	Number
Dean, Social Sciences	3	$53,633		55	2	$63,000	17.5	11
Dean, Social Work	8	68,896		29	6	71,000	3.1	14
Dean, Special Programs	3	53,320	18.5	14	3	45,000		8
Dean, Undergraduate Programs	6	60,000	6.3	23	4	56,433		15
Administrative								
Chief Business Officer	6	66,780	41.3	350	2	47,250		20
Director, Health and Safety	5	36,384	6.0	108	1	34,332		10
Director, Telecommunications	3	42,024	45.6	117	3	28,860		34
Chief Planning Officer	5	55,000	7.8	68	1	51,000		16
Chief Budgeting Officer	6	48,608	20.6	176	3	40,308		46
Associate Budget Director	4	41,750	17.8	54	2	35,432		36
Chief Planning and Budget Officer	5	58,000	21.3	48	3	47,796		7
General Counsel	6	58,982	5.3	86	5	56,000		18
Associate General Counsel	6	52,200	27.8	17	2	40,836		20
Chief Personnel/Human Resources Officer	7	48,318	19.8	191	4	40,324		79
Associate Director, Personnel/ Human Resources	6	40,552	28.9	70	4	31,450		64
Manager, Benefits	6	37,212	44.0	53	4	25,836		99
Manager, Training and Development	2	32,689	6.6	28	3	30,667		58
Manager, Employee Relations	6	39,900	35.2	23	3	29,508		20
Manager, Labor Relations	4	40,000	1.0	29	4	39,609		9
Manager, Employment	4	35,742	42.8	41	3	25,027		82
Manager, Wage and Salary/Manager, Compensation	6	33,365	14.8	45	2	29,063		52
Manager, Personnel Information Systems	3	35,000	29.9	23	5	26,950		26
Director, Affirmative Action/Equal Employment	4	42,800	10.3	87	3	38,800		121
Associate Director, Affirmative Action/ Equal Employment	3	33,075	20.7	11	4	27,407		21
Director, Personnel and Affirmative Action	8	37,370	23.5	29	3	30,265		27
Director, Computer Center	7	50,191	17.7	246	3	42,660		22
Associate Director, Computer Center	5	44,352	24.4	75	3	35,663		15
Data Base Administrator	3	40,200	17.0	66	2	34,354		19
Systems Analyst I (highest level)	4	34,710	11.1	78	5	31,242		31
Systems Analyst II (lowest level)	3	31,308	25.1	43	2	25,020		32
Programmer Analyst I (highest level)	4	28,765	12.5	80	4	25,578		46
Programmer Analyst II (lowest level)	2	21,661		50	3	22,830	5.4	49

Number and Median Salary of Administrators in Selected Public Universities and 4-Year Colleges, by Sex, 1987–88

98 *Continued*

Position Title	Men				Women			
	Years	Median Salary	Percentage Difference	Number	Years	Median Salary	Percentage Difference	Number
Director, Computer Center Operations/ Administrative	5	$48,480	9.9	85	4	$44,129		12
Associate Director, Computer Center Operations/Administrative	4	46,412	10.0	59	6	42,200		7
Director, Information Systems	5	52,000	22.2	76	2	42,548		11
Manager, Landscape and Grounds	5	27,924	16.0	220	3	24,072		9
Manager, Custodial Services	6	28,056	16.9	210	5	23,998		33
Comptroller	6	50,200	42.6	216	4	35,200		33
Manager, Payroll	6	37,368	43.2	88	5	26,101		154
Director, Accounting	6	41,600	24.0	148	4	33,540		67
Staff Accountant (highest level)	4	28,795	18.0	62	2	24,406		62
Staff Accountant (lowest level)	4	22,220	15.8	31	1	19,188		56
Bursar	6	37,585	34.8	92	3	27,881		61
Associate Bursar	6	31,500	19.3	19	2	26,404		24
Director, Purchasing	7	37,392	30.4	247	4	28,679		71
Associate Director, Purchasing	5	34,156	28.3	78	3	26,628		40
Director, Bookstore	9	35,106	53.7	172	6	22,844		61
Associate Director, Bookstore	7	27,092	23.2	36	5	21,982		21
Director, Internal Audit	6	43,405	30.7	120	2	33,204		51
Director, Auxiliary Services	6	45,577	14.2	136	3	39,900		10
Manager, Mail Services	6	22,969	2.2	123	4	22,470		44
Director, Risk Management and Insurance	5	42,905	8.6	49	6	39,500		14
Director, Medical Center Public Relations/Affairs	5	43,500		10	1	43,948	1.0	12
Director, Medical Center Personnel	5	47,672		10	2	50,220	5.3	7
External Affairs								
Chief Development Officer	3	57,978	14.5	179	3	50,635		35
Director, Annual Giving	2	36,000	13.4	48	2	31,746		50
Director, Corporate/ Foundation Relations	3	44,849	34.5	42	2	33,336		14
Coordinator, Resource Development	3	33,751	35.7	10	2	24,874		27
Director, Estate Planning	2	44,925	1.3	18	2	44,329		7
Chief Public Relations Officer	4	45,500	8.8	124	3	41,813		68
Director, Governmental/ Legislative Relations	4	59,943	19.0	54	1	50,384		11
Chief Development and Public Relations Officer	4	66,007	23.7	60	5	53,340		14
Director, Alumni Affairs	3	39,562	28.3	139	3	30,835		106
Director, Development and Alumni Affairs	3	43,935	8.7	31	2	40,430		15
Director, Special and Deferred Gifts	2	44,280	40.5	32	1	31,525		12

Position Title	Men				Women			
	Years	Median Salary	Percentage Difference	Number	Years	Median Salary	Percentage Difference	Number
Director, Community Services	6	$41,777	28.5	24	4	$32,508		15
Director, Publications	5	38,520	20.4	89	4	32,000		73
Associate Director, Publications	3	30,580	20.1	15	2	25,452		20
Manager, Printing Services	8	31,260	20.2	144	4	26,000		34
Director, Information Office	5	40,000	16.1	92	3	34,459		61
Director, News Bureau	5	33,300	15.8	52	2	28,764		53
Student Services								
Chief Student Affairs Officer	7	59,149		297	4	59,372	0.4	66
Director, Admissions	6	42,144	22.4	211	3	34,445		67
Associate Director, Admissions	7	35,196	16.9	82	3	30,119		61
Assistant Director, Admissions	3	27,042	14.6	49	3	23,600		81
Director, Admissions and Registrar	5	47,500	10.0	76	2	43,200		17
Registrar	9	42,900	17.8	210	4	36,430		82
Associate Registrar	7	35,796	17.4	73	6	30,500		51
Assistant Registrar	7	28,116	12.3	50	4	25,027		85
Director, Student Financial Aid	8	39,486	14.5	252	4	34,485		97
Associate Director, Student Financial Aid	4	31,000	13.7	89	2	27,255		110
Director, Food Services	6	37,370		100	3	37,800	1.2	27
Associate Director, Food Services	5	31,261		28	5	32,250	3.2	19
Director, Student Housing	6	37,116	16.0	194	3	32,000		54
Associate Director, Student Housing	5	32,941	26.0	76	4	26,148		31
Housing Officer/Administrative Operations	3	30,598	3.8	42	4	29,491		27
Housing Officer/Residence Life	3	26,000		38	3	28,073	8.0	49
Housing Officer/Family Housing	4	30,932	35.3	25	3	22,860		14
Director, Foreign Students	6	35,217	23.8	77	5	28,444		53
Director, Student Union	7	38,088	8.9	169	5	34,968		29
Associate Director, Student Union	5	32,100	24.4	55	2	25,810		30
Student Union Business Manager	4	28,800	21.5	42	3	23,712		17
Director, Student Activities	6	34,700	16.2	154	4	29,850		82
Director, Student Placement	8	39,900	30.5	175	3	30,582		128
Director, Student Counseling	7	42,204	31.6	214	3	32,076		81
Associate Director, Student Counseling	5	40,301	27.4	47	4	31,622		27
Director, Student Health Services (Physician Administrator)	6	67,224	11.9	129	3	60,060		43
Director, Athletics	4	50,378	19.9	295	4	42,000		16
Director, Sports Information	5	26,156	5.8	215	3	24,720		7
Director, Campus Recreation/Intramurals	5	31,510	13.2	160	4	27,832		35

Note: Data includes responses from 402 institutions. All positions were not applicable for each institution.

Source:
College and University Personnel Association, "Administrative Compensation Survey, 1987–88," special tabulations, 1988.

Number and Median Salary of Administrators in Selected Private Universities and 4-Year Colleges, by Sex, 1987–88

Position Title	Men				Women			
	Years	Median Salary	Percentage Difference	Number	Years	Median Salary	Percentage Difference	Number
Executive								
Assistant to the President, System	1	$44,500	96.6	8	7	$22,632		5
Chief Executive Officer, Single Institution	5	80,000	16.0	436	4	68,967		75
Assistant to the President, Single Institution	3	42,500	37.1	113	4	31,000		117
Executive Vice President	4	61,000	17.3	109	4	52,000		13
Academic								
Chief Academic Officer	3	56,000	17.8	423	3	47,540		100
Director, Conferences	2	31,400	27.6	32	2	24,607		43
Chief Health Professions Officer	3	124,000	297	16	1	31,250		7
Director, Library Services	7	36,750	24.6	286	4	29,500		225
Circulation Librarian	7	28,805	41.2	39	4	20,400		163
Acquisitions Librarian	6	28,600	26.5	40	7	22,610		163
Technical Services Librarian	7	27,375	17.5	62	5	23,300		213
Public Services Librarian	5	30,804	27.3	40	5	24,200		109
Reference Librarian	5	23,328	5.7	78	5	22,062		216
Director, Institutional Research	4	37,693	25.0	73	3	30,160		72
Associate Director, Institutional Research	1	35,257	25.5	8	2	28,100		12
Director, Educational Media Services	5	25,725	18.7	158	4	21,671		56
Director, Learning Resources Center	4	29,314	15.4	62	3	25,400		85
Director, International Studies Education	4	36,050	28.8	36	4	28,000		29
Director, Computer Center Operations/ Academic	4	36,500	14.0	177	3	32,025		35
Associate Director, Computer Center Operations/Academic	3	33,900	28.4	50	2	26,412		30
Administrator, Grants and Contracts	4	39,300	39.2	60	3	28,224		58
Dean, Arts and Sciences	3	57,378	14.4	102	2	50,174		31
Dean, Business	3	59,850	88.9	151	2	31,690		22
Dean, Continuing Education	4	44,200	33.9	100	2	33,000		61
Dean, Education	4	45,954	34.1	75	4	34,272		36
Dean, Fine Arts	6	45,500	35.9	36	2	33,491		12
Dean, Graduate Programs	3	50,828	1.7	85	2	50,000		23
Dean, Health-Related Professions	5	48,500	5.4	12	7	46,000		7
Dean, Humanities	4	35,070	27.7	46	3	27,464		17
Dean, Sciences	6	36,419	31.3	52	2	27,729		10
Dean, Social Sciences	4	33,045	7.9	37	2	30,630		14
Dean, Social Work	5	74,000	73.0	16	5	42,785		11
Dean, Special Programs	2	40,000	28.2	15	4	31,200		11
Dean, Undergraduate Programs	2	46,500	20.7	21	1	38,522		16

Position Title	Men				Women			
	Years	Median Salary	Percentage Difference	Number	Years	Median Salary	Percentage Difference	Number
Administrative								
Chief Business Officer	5	$52,100	22.0	439	3	$42,700		64
Director, Telecommunications	3	40,000	51.2	47	3	26,460		22
Chief Planning Officer	3	52,690	42.4	41	3	37,000		17
Chief Budgeting Officer	4	46,500	15.8	81	3	40,140		25
Associate Budget Director	3	36,000	17.3	34	2	30,700		24
Chief Planning and Budget Officer	4	47,700	5.1	25	3	45,370		5
General Counsel	7	72,250	14.5	29	3	63,120		11
Associate General Counsel	3	59,000	96.7	15	2	30,000		5
Chief Personnel/Human Resources Officer	5	41,600	34.2	118	4	31,000		127
Associate Director, Personnel/Human Resources	1	37,740	48.7	13	3	25,376		63
Manager, Benefits	5	41,240	70.4	20	3	24,200		84
Manager, Training and Development	4	43,703	36.6	7	3	32,000		20
Manager, Employment	2	30,000	18.9	16	2	25,221		47
Manager, Wage and Salary/Manager, Compensation	3	36,750	24.9	13	2	29,435		28
Manager, Personnel Information Systems	3	44,316	92.7	9	3	23,000		18
Director, Affirmative Action/Equal Employment	5	43,016	1.5	10	6	42,400		32
Director, Personnel and Affirmative Action	3	36,500	31.2	18	3	27,810		47
Director, Computer Center	5	39,715	41.2	243	3	28,119		53
Associate Director, Computer Center	4	32,300	40.4	63	3	23,000		29
Data Base Administrator	3	32,000	6.0	34	3	30,200		20
Systems Analyst I (highest level)	4	29,428	16.7	64	3	25,207		23
Systems Analyst II (lowest level)	2	22,932	0.1	40	2	22,900		25
Programmer Analyst I (highest level)	3	25,056	0.4	88	3	24,950		52
Programmer Analyst II (lowest level)	2	21,000	5.0	50	2	20,000		58
Director, Computer Center Operations/Administrative	5	40,150	38.4	99	3	29,000		35
Associate Director, Computer Center Operations/Administrative	5	33,610	31.8	31	4	25,500		26
Director, Information Systems	3	47,000	57.1	64	2	29,925		11
Chief, Physical Plant/Facilities Management Officer	5	36,087	22.7	439	3	29,400		10
Associate Director, Physical Plant/Facilities Management	4	30,090	70.2	163	4	17,678		8

Number and Median Salary of Administrators in Selected Private Universities and 4-Year Colleges, by Sex, 1987–88

99 *Continued*

Position Title	Men				Women			
	Years	Median Salary	Percentage Difference	Number	Years	Median Salary	Percentage Difference	Number
Manager, Landscape and Grounds	6	$25,501	29.8	186	2	$19,647		13
Manager, Custodial Services	4	24,585	25.4	173	5	19,600		48
Comptroller	5	41,500	34.0	250	3	30,959		106
Manager, Payroll	7	30,975	55.7	47	5	19,900		154
Director, Accounting	4	32,210	28.8	104	4	25,000		102
Staff Accountant (highest level)	3	25,200	22.0	43	2	20,650		99
Staff Accountant (lowest level)	2	18,564	9.2	27	1	17,000		75
Bursar	7	34,077	34.7	56	3	25,300		92
Associate Bursar	4	25,000	13.2	14	1	22,080		26
Director, Purchasing	5	33,200	48.8	143	3	22,318		71
Associate Director, Purchasing	5	33,135	73.7	27	2	19,071		24
Director, Bookstore	7	25,650	40.0	134	6	18.323		211
Associate Director, Bookstore	3	19,500	15.2	14	5	16,920		46
Director, Internal Audit	3	43,655	56.3	53	2	27,935		23
Director, Auxiliary Services	4	38,500	29.9	69	4	29,643		27
Manager, Mail Services	5	18,750	25.0	93	5	15,000		102
Director, Campus Security	4	26,292	36.0	325	2	19,330		14
Director, Risk Management and Insurance	3	43,541	33.8	30	4	32,550		9
Director, Medical Center Public Relations/ Affairs	1	50,242	4.8	6	5	47,937		8
External Affairs								
Chief Development Officer	3	51,900	29.4	366	2	40,100		76
Director, Annual Giving	2	31,000	11.4	138	1	27,830		152
Director, Corporate/Foundation Relations	2	39,000	21.9	89	2	32,000		94
Coordinator, Resource Development	1	28,232	23.8	20	2	22,800		82
Director, Estate Planning	4	40,888	24.7	88	2	32,800		20
Chief Public Relations Officer	3	37,800	40.0	156	2	27,000		163
Director, Governmental/Legislative Relations	4	65,750	56.2	21	3	42,100		10
Chief Development and Public Relations Officer	4	55,300	17.5	68	3	47,054		20
Director, Alumni Affairs	3	31,930	31.9	194	2	24,200		233
Director, Development and Alumni Affairs	1	45,000	42.9	24	1	31,500		18
Director, Special and Deferred Gifts	3	36,598	25.0	94	2	29,290		39
Director, Church Relations	2	28,900	44.5	68	1	20,000		18
Director, Community Services	3	39,500	65.1	15	3	23,920		22
Director, Publications	3	30,440	17.1	67	2	26,000		139
Associate Director, Publications	4	24,120	21.8	19	2	19,800		41

Position Title	Men				Women			
	Years	Median Salary	Percentage Difference	Number	Years	Median Salary	Percentage Difference	Number
Manager, Printing Services	6	$24,678	42.5	106	4	$17,316		44
Director, Information Office	3	32,200	22.3	66	2	26,325		73
Director, News Bureau	3	28,500	22.2	51	2	23,330		58
Student Services								
Chief Student Affairs Officer	5	42,300	14.3	358	3	37,000		157
Director, Admissions	3	36,813	10.5	332	2	33,312		121
Associate Director, Admissions	2	27,178	13.6	128	2	23,930		144
Assistant Director, Admissions	2	19,201		81	1	20,000	4.2	148
Registrar	7	33,390	25.2	254	6	26,676		259
Associate Registrar	5	30,000	34.4	34	5	22,317		80
Assistant Registrar	2	22,600	17.8	32	3	19,188		143
Director, Admissions and Financial Aid	3	45,000	3.7	72	2	43,409		24
Director, Student Financial Aid	7	32,700	31.5	253	3	24,874		260
Associate Director, Student Financial Aid	2	22,884	11.6	53	2	20,500		184
Director, Food Services	7	35,500	53.7	94	5	23,100		41
Associate Director, Food Services	5	26,562	27.7	37	3	20,800		31
Director, Student Housing	3	25,992	14.0	169	2	22,800		158
Associate Director, Student Housing	1	24,000	29.0	40	1	18,600		52
Housing Officer/Administrative Operations	3	28,750	27.2	15	2	22,600		13
Housing Officer/Residence Life	2	23,000	24.3	48	2	18,500		69
Director, Foreign Students	4	27,057	9.6	48	3	24,693		59
Director, Student Union	4	31,940	40.4	70	2	22,750		54
Associate Director, Student Union	2	22,485		18	3	22,590	0.5	17
Student Union Business Manager	5	30,000	37.7	7	2	21,794		6
Director, Student Activities	2	23,265	5.7	130	2	22,000		161
Director, Student Placement	4	31,280	25.9	147	3	24,840		246
Director, Student Counseling	4	33,624	31.0	153	3	25,666		174
Associate Director, Student Counseling	3	28,500	37.4	27	2	20,743		41
Director, Student Health Services (Physician Administrator)	7	51,600	72.0	67	5	30,000		24
Director, Student Health Services (Nurse Administrator)	4	25,907	22.1	6	5	21,210		278
Chaplain	4	27,240	26.1	230	2	21,600		45
Director, Athletics	5	37,000	42.3	362	3	26,000		46
Director, Sports Information	3	21,000	15.4	182	1	18,191		18
Director, Campus Recreation/Intramurals	3	24,675	21.4	101	2	20,325		31

Note: Data includes responses from 581 institutions. All positions were not applicable for each institution.

Source:
College and University Personnel Association, "Administrative Compensation Survey, 1987–88," special tabulations, 1988.

Position Title	Men				Women			
	Years	Median Salary	Percentage Difference	Number	Years	Median Salary	Percentage Difference	Number
Executive								
Assistant to the President, System	4	$49,657	37.2	13	2	$36,199		13
Chief Executive Officer, Single Institution	5	66,465	1.5	313	3	65,500		21
Assistant to the President, Single Institution	3	46,651	41.2	40	3	33,049		51
Academic								
Chief Academic Officer	3	51,822		284	2	52,077	0.5	68
Director, Conferences	3	37,800	57.7	8	3	23,974		9
Chief Health Professions Officer	6	48,200	37.4	5	5	35,086		12
Director, Library Services	11	38,000	8.1	99	6	35,147		128
Circulation Librarian	7	31,771	27.1	9	7	25,000		35
Acquisitions Librarian	7	31,664	26.9	8	9	24,960		32
Technical Services Librarian	6	33,896	19.7	23	6	28,325		60
Public Services Librarian	7	33,723	18.0	10	9	28,572		33
Reference Librarian	15	29,743	14.0	13	7	26,081		56
Director, Institutional Research	2	38,940	4.9	92	3	37,125		43
Associate Director, Institutional Research	3	39,040	26.5	12	1	30,861		8
Director, Educational Media Services	8	34,122	13.6	90	3	30,041		11
Director, Learning Resources Center	7	42,300	20.4	91	5	35,121		83
Director, Computer Center Operations/ Academic	5	40,038	34.4	46	4	29,800		12
Administrator, Grants and Contracts	2	39,469	24.1	33	3	31,799		42
Dean, Arts and Letters	6	43,921	2.9	23	3	42,671		8
Dean, Arts and Sciences	5	45,404	10.1	59	2	41,256		13
Dean, Business	4	43,030	3.7	113	3	41,500		46
Dean, Communications	8	44,880	30.3	16	2	34,441		9
Dean, Continuing Education	6	43,204	9.9	128	4	39,300		59
Dean, Education	6	38,190		6	3	40,749	6.7	8
Dean, Extension	6	37,500	9.6	22	3	34,213		11
Dean, Fine Arts	7	41,000	4.8	25	1	39,135		8
Dean, Health-Related Professions	8	44,782	0.4	36	4	44,612		59
Dean, Humanities	5	44,612	9.0	49	4	40,924		31
Dean, Instruction	2	48,944	13.9	30	2	42,961		9
Dean, Mathematics	6	44,100	11.0	42	3	39,720		7
Dean, Occupational Studies/Vocational Education/Technology	4	44,347	3.9	138	2	42,671		22
Dean, Sciences	8	44,371	2.0	66	6	43,492		17
Dean, Social Sciences	9	46,396	10.8	65	8	41,859		13
Dean, Special Programs	2	40,438		36	2	44,000	8.8	15
Administrative								
Chief Business Officer	6	49,860	9.2	338	4	45,640		30
Director, Telecommunications	1	35,956	34.7	20	4	26,702		8
Chief Planning Officer	3	53,152	33.2	39	3	39,900		18
Chief Budgeting Officer	5	44,520	28.4	53	3	34,686		18
Associate Budget Director	3	30,000		18	4	31,415	4.7	9
General Counsel	6	50,421		8	2	50,562	0.3	8
Chief Personnel/Human Resources Officer	6	46,686	34.9	82	3	34,613		71
Associate Director, Personnel/Human Resources	2	46,200	60.2	13	3	28,840		30
Manager, Training and Development	2	38,111	2.2	7	2	37,277		11
Manager, Employment	4	28,596	5.0	5	4	27,245		15
Manager, Wage and Salary/Manager, Compensation	2	39,228	20.4	7	6	32,587		8
Director, Affirmative Action/Equal Employment	5	43,220	15.5	19	2	37,435		25
Director, Personnel and Affirmative Action	6	38,376	22.6	36	4	31,300		48
Director, Computer Center	5	40,050	28.1	171	3	31,261		20
Associate Director, Computer Center	6	35,679	21.0	25	2	29,475		6
Data Base Administrator	3	35,102		23	3	37,225	6.0	7

Number and Median Salary of Administrators in Selected Public 2-Year Colleges and Technical Institutes, by Sex, 1987–88

Position Title	Men Years	Men Median Salary	Men Percentage Difference	Men Number	Women Years	Women Median Salary	Women Percentage Difference	Women Number
Systems Analyst I (highest level)	4	$32,800	13.1	41	3	$28,998		15
Programmer Analyst I (highest level)	4	29,942	16.7	54	2	25,663		22
Programmer Analyst II (lowest level)	2	24,941	6.4	32	2	23,440		27
Director, Computer Center Operations/ Administrative	6	36,864	56.7	42	2	23,525		6
Director, Information Systems	5	44,540	18.7	39	5	37,527		13
Chief, Physical Plant/Facilities Management Officer	6	37,270		273	1	47,700	28.0	5
Manager, Landscape and Grounds	6	25,019	11.2	60	3	22,507		6
Manager, Custodial Services	4	25,080	13.0	71	6	22,188		9
Comptroller	5	40,142	11.8	104	4	35,904		51
Manager, Payroll	3	25,871	15.2	15	5	22,453		63
Director, Accounting	8	34,720	21.5	63	3	28,566		46
Staff Accountant (highest level)	3	27,036	12.3	40	2	24,066		52
Staff Accountant (lowest level)	2	22,693	11.4	16	3	20,362		30
Bursar	5	32,960	24.9	18	7	26,395		21
Director, Purchasing	7	33,780	31.1	80	4	25,776		67
Associate Director, Purchasing	2	26,712	0.9	10	3	26,478		13
Director, Bookstore	8	29,214	35,8	57	6	21,520		129
Associate Director, Bookstore	5	23,856	33.7	16	5	17,844		15
Director, Internal Audit	3	35,584	18.6	27	1	30,000		8
Director, Auxiliary Services	5	37,775	18.3	53	3	31,920		15
Manager, Mail Services	5	18,968		17	5	20,266	6.8	14
External Affairs								
Chief Development Officer	3	44,548	15.6	67	2	38,524		35
Director, Annual Giving	1	36,050	48.3	6	2	24,309		6
Director, Corporate/Foundation Relations	1	39,000	16.5	10	1	33,479		6
Coordinator, Resource Development	2	43,000	43.3	5	2	30,000		6
Chief Public Relations Officer	3	37,000	11.9	75	3	33,064		84
Chief Development and Public Relations Officer	4	40,139	12.0	14	3	35,830		20
Director, Alumni Affairs	3	31,887	21.8	7	3	26,184		17
Director, Development and Alumni Affairs	2	36,057	15.7	11	1	31,164		10
Director, Community Services	6	41,088	19.1	54	3	34,509		65
Director, Publications	10	29,640	8.8	14	3	27,236		25
Manager, Printing Services	8	24,500	30.3	47	10	18,796		16
Director, Information Office	3	30,500	8.2	31	3	28,194		56
Student Services								
Chief Student Affairs Officer	6	47,250	7.4	258	2	44,000		65
Director, Admissions	7	37,039	14.7	117	2	32,296		50
Associate Director, Admissions	2	29,628	20.9	14	2	24,506		17
Assistant Director, Admissions	6	27,579	12.6	10	2	24,483		24
Director, Admissions and Registrar	6	42,238	26.1	78	6	33,500		40
Registrar	8	37,214	21.9	98	5	30,516		96
Associate Registrar	2	35,430	31.2	8	4	27,000		18
Assistant Registrar	5	28,918	19.7	11	4	24,157		25
Director, Admissions and Financial Aid	5	32,945	19.9	18	2	27,480		7
Director, Student Financial Aid	7	36,500	31.8	161	5	27,702		139
Associate Director, Student Financial Aid	3	25,330		19	3	25,486	0.6	48
Director, Food Services	4	27,627	23.6	29	5	22,343		26
Director, Student Housing	3	27,430	15.8	23	2	23,688		6
Director, Foreign Students	7	31,017	29.7	5	3	23,920		5
Director, Student Union	9	36,121	124	11	2	16,100		6
Director, Student Activities	7	33,696	23.5	101	4	27,284		63
Director, Student Placement	6	32,282	14.0	87	3	28,319		70
Director, Student Counseling	7	39,348	8.7	119	4	36,200		80
Associate Director, Student Counseling	8	32,309	23.4	6	2	26,190		12
Director, Athletics	8	39,060	23.7	130	4	31,583		11

Note: Data includes responses from 383 institutions. All positions were not applicable for each institution.

Source:
College and University Personnel Association, "Administrative Compensation Survey, 1987–88," special tabulations, 1988.

Number and Median Salary of Administrators in Selected Private 2-Year Colleges and Technical Institutes, by Sex, 1987–88

Position Title	Men				Women			
	Years	Median Salary	Percentage Difference	Number	Years	Median Salary	Percentage Difference	Number
Executive								
Chief Executive Officer, Single Institution	5	$57,500	22.1	34	2	$47,108		9
Academic								
Chief Academic Officer	5	40,000	17.0	26	2	34,200		17
Director, Library Services	8	28,850	31.1	11	3	22,000		25
Director, Learning Resources Center	8	22,000	22.2	6	3	18,000		8
Director, Computer Center Operations/Academic	2	20,933		6	4	22,575	7.8	5
Administrative								
Chief Business Officer	3	34,850	10.3	28	2	31,600		8
Comptroller	8	31,000	51.0	7	2	20,534		11
External Affairs								
Chief Development Officer	2	35,955	38.3	14	1	26,000		9
Student Services								
Chief Student Affairs Officer	2	26,500		24	2	29,660	11.9	11
Director, Admissions	4	27,500		18	2	27,575	0.3	13
Associate Director, Admissions	1	22,500	7.1	6	1	21,000		5
Registrar	4	28,700	31.5	8	1	21,818		23
Director, Student Financial Aid	6	27,500	44.7	7	3	19,000		24
Director, Student Housing	1	20,000	0.0	6	3	20,000		9
Director, Student Activities	1	18,725	8.8	7	1	17,208		10
Director, Student Counseling	2	25,112	10.1	7	2	22,805		13

Note: Data includes responses from 44 institutions. All positions were not applicable for each institution.

Source:
College and University Personnel Association, "Administrative Compensation Survey, 1987–88," special tabulations, 1988.

Number and Median Salary of Minority Administrators in All Types of Institutions, by Sex, 1987–88

Position Title	Men				Women			
	Years	Median Salary	Percentage Difference	Number	Years	Median Salary	Percentage Difference	Number
Executive								
Chief Executive Officer, Single Institution	5	$71,478	18.1	70	2	$60,500		19
Assistant to the President, Single Institution	2	44,688	28.9	27	2	34,680		33
Academic								
Chief Academic Officer	3	57,000	11.6	70	1	51,081		20
Director, Library Services	6	40,692	15.6	36	6	35,189		49
Circulation Librarian	2	29,616	30.1	13	4	22,770		28
Acquisitions Librarian	6	29,251	10.7	10	7	26,416		40
Technical Services Librarian	5	30,500	26.8	14	6	24,053		47
Public Services Librarian	6	28,097	8.1	12	7	26,000		27
Reference Librarian	8	29,743	23.9	15	5	24,000		39
Director, Institutional Research	2	38,504	9.1	31	2	35,300		25
Director, Educational Media Services	6	35,500	39.1	25	5	25,521		9
Director, Learning Resources Center	4	33,135	1.2	31	4	32,730		25
Director, Computer Center Operations/ Academic	3	38,191	11.6	20	3	34,224		9
Administrator, Grants and Contracts	2	40,077	28.6	22	3	31,167		23
Dean, Arts and Sciences	3	49,511		22	0	56,184	13.5	6
Dean, Business	3	53,656	16.3	31	11	46,137		7
Dean, Continuing Education	4	48,004	1.5	28	2	47,300		13
Dean, Education	3	62,520	53.4	21	1	40,749		23
Dean, Fine Arts	2	49,000		13	2	63,000	28.6	6
Dean, Graduate Programs	3	58,797	0.9	27	3	58,300		6
Dean, Health-Related Professions	6	58,432	9.2	17	3	53,489		14
Dean, Humanities	3	44,201	33.9	13	4	33,000		5
Dean, Library and Information Sciences	3	55,000	35.4	6	9	40,631		5
Dean, Sciences	3	49,924	62.9	19	2	30,648		10
Dean, Social Sciences	5	36,695		23	6	38,600	5.2	6
Dean, Social Work	6	66,000	24.5	8	6	53,000		6
Dean, Special Programs	4	44,601	1.4	16	3	44,000		9
Administrative								
Chief Business Officer	5	50,028	29.9	74	3	38,500		9
Director, Telecommunications	2	36,200	25.4	15	4	28,860		5
Chief Planning Officer	2	32,461		13	6	40,000	23.2	6
Chief Budgeting Officer	3	40,140		27	2	40,212	0.2	11
Associate Budget Director	4	28,000		8	2	33,000	17.9	8
General Counsel	4	53,000	4.8	8	3	50,562		6
Chief Personnel/Human Resources Officer	5	47,212	26.9	44	5	37,218		32
Associate Director, Personnel/Human Resources	2	38,325	32.9	20	2	28,835		21
Manager, Benefits	2	37,080	58.0	9	3	23,466		25
Manager, Training and Development	6	36,706	27.5	9	2	28,788		18
Manager, Employee Relations	4	32,000	52.4	11	3	21,000		10
Manager, Employment	2	36,708	37.1	16	3	26,775		42
Manager, Wage and Salary/Manager, Compensation	3	37,368	20.5	9	2	31,000		14
Manager, Personnel Information Systems	1	39,432	47.7	5	2	26,700		6
Director, Affirmative Action/ Equal Employment	4	42,800	0.9	114	3	42,400		76
Associate Director, Affirmative Action/ Equal Employment	3	34,172	16.7	15	2	29,285		16
Director, Personnel and Affirmative Action	5	37,860	2.3	16	4	37,000		25

Position Title	Men				Women			
	Years	Median Salary	Percentage Difference	Number	Years	Median Salary	Percentage Difference	Number
Director, Computer Center	4	$37,500	23.0	39	4	$30,500		8
Associate Director, Computer Center	4	50,400	42.8	8	4	35,300		5
Data Base Administrator	3	32,697		13	4	37,350	14.2	10
Systems Analyst I (highest level)	1	25,000		11	2	35,712	42.8	8
Programmer Analyst I (highest level)	2	24,868		29	1	25,300	1.7	13
Programmer Analyst II (lowest level)	1	22,000	8.6	24	4	20,267		20
Director, Computer Center Operations/ Administrative	3	38,902	29.2	13	6	30,100		6
Manager, Custodial Services	6	27,232	10.2	116	5	24,709		26
Comptroller	3	40,880	20.2	32	2	34,000		17
Manager, Payroll	4	25,798	11.4	18	4	23,148		47
Director, Accounting	4	39,877	37.5	33	3	29,000		29
Staff Accountant (highest level)	3	24,500	8.4	22	2	22,601		35
Staff Accountant (lowest level)	2	20,795	15.4	19	2	18,022		34
Bursar	5	32,855	22.6	16	3	26,800		23
Director, Purchasing	5	31,876	5.9	39	3	30,095		29
Associate Director, Purchasing	3	26,748	14.3	10	3	23,400		8
Director, Bookstore	8	26,316	22.4	26	6	21,500		28
Associate Director, Bookstore	2	17,894	6.2	5	5	16,848		12
Director, Internal Audit	5	43,728	24.4	21	3	35,153		6
Manager, Mail Services	6	20,835	22.7	59	6	16,980		23
External Affairs								
Chief Development Officer	2	50,496	13.7	28	3	44,419		10
Chief Public Relations Officer	2	40,000	19.8	22	2	33,390		19
Director, Alumni Affairs	3	29,680	15.7	23	5	25,662		22
Director, Community Services	5	44,688	26.7	17	2	35,267		12
Director, Publications	2	36,050	10.0	7	2	32,760		13
Manager, Printing Services	6	25,000	33.4	33	4	18,744		13
Director, Information Office	2	24,793		6	1	27,923	12.6	10
Student Services								
Chief Student Affairs Officer	5	52,632	5.3	125	2	50,000		47
Director, Admissions	3	36,400	16.7	54	3	31,200		34
Associate Director, Admissions	2	32,657	19.1	27	5	27,430		28
Assistant Director, Admissions	3	25,275	7.6	18	2	23,500		42
Director, Admissions and Registrar	7	38,900	43.5	21	3	27,102		8
Registrar	9	35,086	25.3	30	7	28,000		50
Associate Registrar	6	32,164	29.7	10	6	24,797		12
Assistant Registrar	4	21,650		12	6	24,959	15.3	24
Director, Student Financial Aid	6	36,613	21.4	93	5	30,160		88
Associate Director, Student Financial Aid	2	26,004	3.2	29	2	25,196		52
Director, Food Services	3	30,060	36.6	14	6	22,000		9
Associate Director, Food Services	4	18,863		10	2	22,050	16.9	5
Director, Student Housing	2	27,000	16.9	43	2	23,100		12
Associate Director, Student Housing	2	25,567		15	1	26,148	2.3	7
Housing Officer/Residence Life	2	21,000		9	1	26,220	24.9	10
Director, Foreign Students	5	27,881	12.2	24	4	24,840		18
Director, Student Union	5	30,000		23	4	34,968	16.6	8
Associate Director, Student Union	3	30,264	17.3	8	5	25,810		7
Director, Student Activities	3	28,848	6.0	61	3	27,204		39
Director, Student Placement	5	32,655	13.0	36	5	28,892		47
Director, Student Counseling	5	41,685	40.6	44	3	29,642		62
Associate Director, Student Counseling	4	28,500	0.7	11	2	28,291		14
Director, Student Health Services (Physician Administrator)	11	26,000	8.3	13	2	24,000		8

Note: Data includes responses from 1,410 institutions. All positions were not applicable for each institution.

Source:
College and University Personnel Association, "Administrative Compensation Survey, 1987–88," special tabulations, 1988.

Position Title	Men				Women			
	Years	Median Salary	Percentage Difference	Number	Years	Median Salary	Percentage Difference	Number
Executive								
Chief Executive Officer, System	4	$86,813	24.0	116	1	$70,000		5
Assistant to the President, System	3	54,599	41.6	38	2	38,553		23
Chief Executive Officer, Single Institution	5	75,000	8.7	1118	3	69,000		118
Assistant to the President, Single Institution	3	47,600	43.2	252	4	33,231		256
Executive Vice President	5	63,000	21.2	251	3	52,000		22
Academic								
Chief Academic Officer	3	58,580	17.2	1069	2	50,000		213
Director, Conferences	3	38,064	41.0	92	2	27,000		94
Chief Health Professions Officer	5	93,700	160	66	3	36,000		23
Director, Library Services	8	41,461	23.0	640	5	33,700		469
Circulation Librarian	7	28,896	28.4	98	5	22,500		337
Acquisitions Librarian	7	31,742	23.4	127	6	25,722		316
Technical Services Librarian	7	31,100	15.9	156	5	26,834		403
Public Services Librarian	4	34,250	22.1	122	5	28,048		221
Reference Librarian	6	28,896	15.1	170	5	25,115		417
Director, Institutional Research	4	43,260	19.5	303	3	36,186		167
Associate Director, Institutional Research	3	38,110	20.2	62	2	31,705		47
Director, Educational Media Services	7	32,069	34.0	409	4	23,929		87
Director, Learning Resources Center	7	39,799	37.2	215	4	29,000		199
Director, International Studies Education	4	45,263	46.7	103	4	30,845		43
Director, Computer Center Operations/ Academic	4	40,834	37.0	344	3	29,800		57
Associate Director, Computer Center Operations/ Academic	4	38,700	26.7	111	3	30,536		45
Administrator, Grants and Contracts	5	47,940	41.4	248	3	33,897		142
Dean, Arts and Letters	4	51,792	3.6	84	2	50,000		16
Dean, Arts and Sciences	4	60,520	17.8	319	2	51,384		58
Dean, Business	3	59,823	44.2	514	3	41,500		72
Dean, Communications	5	55,514	35.1	71	2	41,076		16
Dean, Continuing Education	5	47,853	21.8	360	3	39,280		158
Dean, Education	4	58,905	19.3	292	3	49,379		67
Dean, Extension	5	52,531	26.2	65	3	41,616		17
Dean, Fine Arts	5	53,320	11.7	136	2	47,745		29
Dean, Graduate Programs	4	62,700	12.9	257	3	55,560		63
Dean, Health-Related Professions	6	57,399	24.8	93	4	46,000		81
Dean, Home Economics	7	58,647		10	3	60,000	2.3	36
Dean, Humanities	4	45,516	13.3	136	4	40,178		57
Dean, Instruction	2	48,836	11.0	28	3	44,000		13
Dean, Law	3	96,600	1.9	109	2	94,800		8
Dean, Library and Information Sciences	3	57,404	10.5	41	4	51,940		14
Dean, Mathematics	7	43,527	10.1	75	3	39,520		10
Dean, Nursing	8	59,122	15.2	7	5	51,341		244

Position Title	Men				Women			
	Years	Median Salary	Percentage Difference	Number	Years	Median Salary	Percentage Difference	Number
Dean, Occupational Studies/								
Vocational Education/Technology	4	$47,601	9.0	176	2	$43,677		30
Dean, Sciences	6	50,369	22.3	205	3	41,188		28
Dean, Social Sciences	6	46,860	12.0	143	3	41,822		33
Dean, Social Work	8	68,917	18.2	37	5	58,300		20
Dean, Special Programs	2	40,718	19.8	52	3	34,000		26
Dean, Undergraduate Programs	5	54,875	23.1	50	4	44,575		29
Administrative								
Chief Business Officer	6	55,692	29.5	1151	3	43,000		135
Director, Health and Safety	5	37,840	10.2	142	1	34,332		13
Director, Telecommunications	3	41,500	38.2	176	4	30,025		67
Chief Planning Officer	4	56,263	25.0	148	2	45,000		46
Chief Budgeting Officer	6	48,360	26.7	310	3	38,170		86
Associate Budget Director	4	40,109	19.7	106	2	33,508		67
Chief Planning and Budget Officer	5	56,000	17.2	77	3	47,796		13
General Counsel	6	60,293	3.2	128	5	58,422		37
Associate General Counsel	4	53,024	27.5	35	2	41,600		28
Chief Personnel/Human Resources								
Officer	6	46,855	36.6	371	3	34,308		270
Associate Director, Personnel/Human								
Resources	5	40,620	39.6	92	3	29,105		146
Manager, Benefits	6	37,284	41.8	76	4	26,296		196
Manager, Training and Development	3	36,000	13.8	41	3	31,635		76
Manager, Employee Relations	7	40,080	26.4	23	3	31,700		34
Manager, Labor Relations	3	42,550	7.4	34	3	39,609		13
Manager, Employment	4	33,700	33.2	49	2	25,296		117
Manager, Wage and Salary/Manager,								
Compensation	5	34,466	16.5	67	2	29,594		78
Manager, Personnel Information								
Systems	3	40,600	56.2	37	4	26,000		51
Director, Affirmative Action/Equal								
Employment	5	46,300	21.8	14	5	37,999		111
Director, Personnel and Affirmative								
Action	7	38,376	28.2	74	4	29,930		104
Director, Computer Center	5	43,730	34.2	664	3	32,577		94
Associate Director, Computer Center	5	40,000	35.6	163	3	29,500		47
Data Base Administrator	3	39,430	24.1	118	3	31,765		39
Systems Analyst I (highest level)	4	33,075	14.6	176	4	28,863		65
Systems Analyst II (lowest level)	2	27,601	16.8	104	2	23,630		55
Programmer Analyst I (highest level)	3	29,197	15.3	200	3	25,329		116
Programmer Analyst II (lowest level)	2	22,475	2.2	117	2	22,000		123
Director, Computer Center Operations/								
Administrative	5	42,400	31.3	228	4	32,302		56
Associate Director, Computer Center								
Operations/Administrative	5	39,432	43.9	98	3	27,400		39
Director, Information Systems	4	49,000	54.0	184	3	31,827		40

Number and Median Salary of Non-Minority
Administrators in All Types of Institutions,
by Sex, 1987–88

103 *Continued*

Position Title	Men				Women			
	Years	Median Salary	Percentage Difference	Number	Years	Median Salary	Percentage Difference	Number
Chief, Physical Plant/Facilities Management Officer	6	$40,177	23.7	1085	3	$32,477		19
Associate Director, Physical Plant/Facilities Management	4	34,059	55.5	425	6	21,900		11
Manager, Landscape and Grounds	5	26,000	15.9	453	3	22,436		29
Manager, Building and Maintenance Trades	5	29,500	13.1	412	5	26,088		5
Manager, Custodial Services	4	25,800	23.6	362	5	20,868		71
Comptroller	6	44,830	37.1	576	3	32,689		194
Manager, Payroll	6	35,400	49.6	146	5	23,660		355
Director, Accounting	6	37,350	32.2	309	4	28,248		200
Staff Accountant (highest level)	3	27,000	17.4	137	2	23,000		200
Staff Accountant (lowest level)	2	21,000	16.3	67	2	18,060		145
Bursar	6	36,370	39.0	159	3	26,162		161
Associate Bursar	4	30,000	26.1	34	4	23,800		46
Director, Purchasing	6	35,850	40.1	466	4	25,584		197
Associate Director, Purchasing	4	33,809	30.3	117	2	25,956		76
Director, Bookstore	7	30,458	52.9	355	6	19,915		416
Associate Director, Bookstore	6	24,800	32.4	64	3	18,732		78
Director, Internal Audit	5	42,500	36.2	199	2	31,200		78
Director, Auxiliary Services	5	43,500	40.1	250	3	31,039		54
Manager, Mail Services	5	21,250	24.3	188	4	17,100		152
Director, Campus Security	5	30,000	27.3	701	2	23,574		18
Director, Risk Management and Insurance	4	43,852	5.0	88	4	41,766		31
Administrator, Hospital Medical Center	4	108,156	31.9	40	4	82,000		7
Director, Medical Center Public Relations/ Affairs	3	49,000	2.8	19	5	47,663		25
Director, Medical Center Personnel	4	48,960	28.4	16	2	38,131		8
External Affairs								
Chief Development Officer	3	51,100	26.8	644	2	40,300		157
Director, Annual Giving	2	32,200	15.0	202	2	28,000		213
Director, Corporate/Foundation Relations	2	41,718	30.4	134	2	32,000		118
Coordinator, Resource Development	1	34,539	42.1	37	2	24,300		115
Director, Estate Planning	3	41,000	12.0	110	2	36,600		27
Chief Public Relations Officer	3	40,000	33.3	357	2	30,000		325
Director, Governmental/Legislative Relations	4	60,294	25.9	78	2	47,900		23
Chief Development and Public Relations Officer	4	59,000	37.2	146	3	43,000		57
Director, Alumni Affairs	3	35,280	34.7	332	2	26,200		367
Director, Development and Alumni Affairs	2	40,935	24.0	78	2	33,000		43
Director, Special and Deferred Gifts	3	38,760	27.5	132	2	30,401		54
Director, Church Relations	2	29,400	41.7	72	1	20,750		21
Director, Community Services	6	39,685	22.1	76	3	32,500		99
Director, Publications	4	34,529	24.4	168	3	27,759		238

Number and Median Salary of Non-Minority
Administrators in All Types of Institutions,
by Sex, 1987–88

103 *Concluded*

Position Title	Men				Women			
	Years	Median Salary	Percentage Difference	Number	Years	Median Salary	Percentage Difference	Number
Associate Director, Publications	3	$26,412	23.4	43	2	$21,400		72
Manager, Printing Services	7	28,594	33.7	284	5	21,380		86
Director, Information Office	3	35,000	22.3	191	3	28,620		191
Director, News Bureau	4	31,261	21.2	107	2	25,799		120
Student Services								
Chief Student Affairs Officer	6	47,748	15.2	855	3	41,436		274
Director, Admissions	5	38,075	15.4	654	2	33,000		240
Associate Director, Admissions	3	28,900	15.6	206	2	25,000		205
Assistant Director, Admissions	2	20,500		126	2	20,600	0.5	238
Director, Admissions and Registrar	6	43,819	22.6	163	4	35,733		59
Registrar	8	37,550	33.5	560	5	28,125		458
Associate Registrar	6	35,297	36.0	108	4	25,961		148
Assistant Registrar	5	27,484	30.9	82	3	21,002		247
Director, Admissions and Financial Aid	4	43,249	8.1	111	2	40,000		35
Director, Student Financial Aid	7	35,830	36.0	605	3	26,338		460
Associate Director, Student Financial Aid	3	27,500	21.6	139	2	22,620		308
Director, Food Services	6	35,000	27.3	219	4	27,504		98
Associate Director, Food Services	5	29,790	18.2	60	3	25,200		53
Director, Student Housing	4	32,075	31.6	356	2	24,380		217
Associate Director, Student Housing	3.	30,000	39.5	105	3	21,500		81
Housing Officer/Administrative Operations	3	30,500	13.0	54	4	27,000		40
Housing Officer/Residence Life	2	24,276	10.1	85	2	22,050		114
Housing Officer/Family Housing	4	30,832	29.0	29	4	23,900		17
Director, Housing and Food Service	9	49,250	33.1	37	3	37,000		8
Director, Foreign Students	5	33,075	26.3	106	3	26,180		103
Director, Student Union	7	36,933	53.9	231	3	24,000		82
Associate Director, Student Union	4	30,450	22.4	69	2	24,873		45
Student Union Business Manager	5	30,000	33.3	44	2	22,500		22
Director, Student Activities	4	30,009	25.0	338	3	24,000		287
Director, Student Placement	6	34,500	31.0	381	3	26,337		419
Director, Student Counseling	6	38,274	28.6	459	3	29,760		292
Associate Director, Student Counseling	5	36,448	57.4	71	3	23,150		69
Director, Student Health Services (Physician Administrator)	7	67,110	18.0	189	4	56,889		72
Director, Student Health Services (Nurse Administrator)	4	25,900	10.7	10	5	23,400		457
Chaplain	4	27,300	24.1	238	2	22,000		49
Director, Athletics	5	42,329	40.4	757	3	30,154		71
Director, Sports Information	3	23,895	25.8	386	1	19,000		23
Director, Athletics/Women	8	33,380	2.9	8	6	32,443		141
Director, Campus Recreation/Intramurals	4	29,852	28.3	260	3	23,275		70

Note: Data includes responses from 1,410 institutions. All positions were not applicable for each institution.

Source:
College and University Personnel Association, "Administrative Compensation Survey, 1987–88," special tabulations, 1988.

Characteristics	Total Governing Boards			
			Multicampus	
	Total (N[a] = 2,237)	Single Campus (N = 2,050)	Three or Less[b] (N = 79)	More Than Three[c] (N = 76)
Total Number Serving	47,994	45,379	1,646	969
Sex:				
Men	79.9	79.8	82.9	80.7
Women	20.1	20.2	17.1	19.3
Total	100.0	100.0	100.0	100.0
Race:				
White	90.1	90.1	91.6	87.6
Black	6.3	6.2	6.0	9.1
Hispanic	0.6	0.6	2.2	1.5
Other	3.0	3.1	0.2	1.8
Total	100.0	100.0	100.0	100.0
Education:				
Less than high school	.0	.0	0.1	0.1
High school diploma	4.4	4.3	5.9	6.5
Associate's degree	2.9	3.0	2.5	3.1
Bachelor's degree	40.2	40.2	41.7	40.3
Master's degree	22.8	23.1	18.5	15.7
Professional degree	18.9	18.7	21.7	24.8
Doctoral degree	10.7	10.7	9.5	9.5
Total	100.0	100.0	99.9	100.0
Age:				
Less than 30	2.0	2.0	2.2	3.6
30–39	6.8	6.7	7.7	8.2
40–49	20.8	20.7	21.6	24.5
50–59	38.1	38.2	37.5	34.9
60–69	24.1	24.2	22.6	23.5
70 or older	8.2	8.2	8.4	5.4
Total	100.0	100.0	100.0	100.0

a   N equals the number of boards whose membership is described in the body of the tables.

b   Three or fewer boards governing 2 or 3 institutions.

c   More than 3 boards governing more than 3 institutions.

Source:
Association of Governing Boards, *Composition of Governing Boards 1985*, Table III.

Characteristics	Public				Independent		
			Multicampus				
	Total Public[a] (N = 751)	Single Campus (N = 597)	Three or Less[b] (N = 79)	More Than Three[c] (N = 75)	Total Independent[a] (N = 1,487)	Single Campus (N = 1,453)	Multicampus (N = 34)
Total Number Servings	6,481	4,879	665	937	41,513	40,500	1,013
Sex:							
Men	76.9	75.9	78.7	80.9	80.4	80.3	85.5
Women	23.1	24.1	21.3	19.1	19.6	19.7	14.5
Total	100.0	100.0	100.0	100.0	100.0	100.0	100.0
Race:							
White	85.2	84.8	84.9	87.5	90.9	90.8	96.0
Black	11.4	12.0	10.3	9.1	5.5	5.5	3.2
Hispanic	2.7	2.7	4.5	1.6	0.3	0.3	0.7
Other	0.7	0.5	0.3	1.8	3.3	3.4	0.1
Total	100.0	100.0	100.0	100.0	100.0	100.0	100.0
Education:							
Less than high school	0.0	0.0	0.2	0.1	0.0	0.0	0.0
High school diploma	9.1	9.9	7.3	6.6	3.7	3.6	4.9
Associate's degree	5.0	5.5	3.7	3.2	2.6	2.7	1.6
Bachelor's degree	38.8	38.7	38.3	40.0	40.5	40.4	44.1
Master's degree	18.2	18.5	20.4	15.3	23.5	23.6	17.6
Professional degree	21.8	20.9	23.1	25.5	18.5	18.4	20.2
Doctoral degree	6.9	6.5	6.5	9.3	11.2	11.2	11.6
Total	99.8	100.0	99.7	100.0	100.0	100.0	100.0
Age:							
Less than 30	1.8	1.4	2.2	3.7	2.1	2.1	2.1
30–39	10.8	11.2	11.3	8.3	6.2	6.2	5.3
40–49	26.4	26.7	26.7	24.6	19.9	20.0	18.3
50–59	32.8	32.2	34.3	35.1	38.9	38.9	39.2
60–69	22.7	23.2	19.1	22.9	24.3	24.3	25.5
70 or older	5.5	5.4	6.4	5.4	8.6	8.6	9.5
Total	100.0	100.0	100.0	100.0	100.0	100.0	100.0

a   N equals the number of boards whose membership is described in the body of the tables.

b   Three or fewer boards governing 2 or 3 institutions.

c   More than 3 boards governing more than 3 institutions.

Source:
Association of Governing Boards, *Composition of Governing Boards 1985*, Table III.

Unduplicated Percentage of Undergraduates, by Sex, Source of Support, and Control and Level of Institution, Fall 1986

105

	Number of Undergraduates	Financial Aid Only	Parents Only	Student Only	Parents and Student Only	Financial Aid and Parents Only	Financial Aid and Student Only	Financial Aid, Parents and Student
Men								
Total	4,561,410	3.4	9.6	18.4	33.3	5.0	9.6	20.7
Public								
Total undergraduates	3,672,535	3.7	9.5	20.6	35.7	4.3	9.7	16.6
4-year doctoral	1,229,993	2.5	9.8	10.4	39.1	4.5	10.4	23.4
Other 4-year	750,649	2.7	9.5	13.4	35.4	5.7	9.7	23.6
2-year	1,691,893	5.0	9.2	31.2	33.4	3.6	9.1	8.5
Private								
Total undergraduates	888,875	2.4	10.3	9.2	23.2	7.7	9.4	37.7
4-year doctoral	382,374	1.8	11.1	7.7	25.7	7.9	8.2	37.6
Other 4-year	464,270	2.6	9.5	10.5	21.0	7.5	10.3	38.5
2-year	42,231	5.0	11.6	9.5	25.0	8.0	10.4	30.4
Women								
Total	5,487,871	5.0	10.5	24.9	25.0	6.1	9.8	18.7
Public								
Total undergraduate	4,420,158	5.2	10.4	28.1	26.7	5.3	9.5	14.8
4-year doctoral	1,308,794	3.1	13.0	13.0	31.5	6.9	8.8	23.7
Other 4-year	892,997	4.8	10.7	18.7	27.4	7.1	10.9	20.5
2-year	2,218,367	6.6	8.7	40.8	23.5	3.7	9.4	7.3
Private								
Total undergraduates	1,067,713	4.3	11.0	11.6	18.1	9.3	10.9	34.7
4-year doctoral	367,735	2.6	13.1	9.5	22.2	8.6	8.5	35.5
Other 4-year	620,196	4.5	9.7	12.8	15.9	9.6	12.0	35.5
2-year	79,782	10.8	11.4	12.0	16.8	10.3	13.5	24.8

Source:
ACE, special tabulations from the National Center for Education Statistics' 1987 National Postsecondary Student Aid Study database.

Category	Men			Women		
	Total	Public	Private	Total	Public	Private
Race						
White	36.2	30.5	60.0	35.8	30.3	57.9
Black	50.3	45.1	76.6	56.9	52.1	79.6
Other	37.2	34.5	53.6	35.9	31.5	60.9
Age						
23 and younger	42.6	35.8	66.4	46.1	39.2	68.5
24–29	31.4	29.3	42.2	31.4	29.5	42.3
30 and older	24.8	23.6	35.1	24.4	22.1	40.4

Source:
ACE, special tabulations from the National Center for Education Statistics' 1987 National Postsecondary Student Aid Study, database.

Undergraduates Enrolled in Fall 1986 Who Were Awarded Federal Financial Aid, by Type of Federal Aid, Sex, and Control and Level of Institution

	Number of Undergraduates	Any Federal Aid	Any Title IV Aid	Percentage Receiving					
				Pell Grants	Supplemental Educational Opportunity Grants	College Work-Study	National Direct Student Loans	Guaranteed Student Loans	Any Other Federal Aid
Men									
Total[a]	4,759,595	31.1	26.3	14.2	4.4	5.9	5.3	16.6	1.4
Public									
Total undergraduate	3,839,909	27.0	22.4	14.0	3.4	4.1	3.7	12.6	1.4
4-year doctoral	1,254,512	33.9	30.1	15.7	4.3	5.3	6.8	20.4	1.7
Other 4-year	767,915	37.1	32.2	19.7	5.2	6.8	6.0	19.0	1.3
2-year	1,817,482	18.0	13.0	10.4	2.0	2.2	0.5	4.6	1.3
Private									
Total undergraduate	919,686	48.2	42.6	15.1	8.5	13.3	12.1	33.3	1.5
4-year doctoral	391,057	46.2	40.6	12.4	8.2	15.0	13.9	33.2	1.9
Other 4-year	478,302	50.6	44.8	16.7	9.2	12.4	11.4	34.2	1.1
2-year	50,327	41.7	37.1	21.2	3.8	7.8	4.2	26.2	1.3
Women									
Total[a]	5,705,656	31.0	28.0	16.9	5.1	6.6	5.7	15.9	0.6
Public									
Total undergraduate	4,602,961	27.0	24.2	16.4	4.1	4.8	4.3	11.8	0.5
4-year doctoral	1,327,043	35.8	32.8	18.1	5.1	7.2	8.4	20.3	0.7
Other 4-year	913,138	36.8	34.1	22.4	5.8	8.2	7.6	17.8	0.5
2-year	2,362,780	18.2	15.5	13.2	2.9	2.1	0.7	4.8	0.4
Private									
Total undergraduate	1,102,695	47.9	43.8	18.9	9.2	14.3	11.7	33.0	1.1
4-year doctoral	377,884	43.5	39.0	13.7	7.8	15.6	13.2	29.8	1.2
Other 4-year	641,359	50.1	46.0	20.7	10.5	14.6	11.8	34.9	1.0
2-year	83,452	51.1	48.6	28.2	5.6	6.1	4.2	33.5	1.2

a Totals do not include students enrolled in less than 2-year institutions.

Source:
ACE, special tabulations from the National Center for Education Statistics' 1987 National Postsecondary Student Aid Study database.

	All Students	Men	Women
Total aid	$3,856	$3,996	$3,740
Total federal aid	3,010	3,112	2,925
Total nonfederal aid	2,087	2,207	1,994
Total grants	2,377	2,436	2,329
Federal grants	1,503	1,505	1,502
Nonfederal grants	1,935	2,046	1,848
Total loans	2,438	2,500	2,386
Federal loans	2,282	2,324	2,247
Total work-study	1,493	1,693	1,314
Federal work-study	1,408	1,621	1,211
Nonfederal work-study	1,093	1,102	1,087

Source:
ACE, special tabulations from the National Center for Education Statistics' 1987 National Postseconary Student Aid Study database.

Number of Doctorate Recipients, by Sources of Support in Graduate School, Fiscal Years 1974, 1978, 1982, 1984 and 1985

Source of Support	Fiscal Year 1974				Fiscal Year 1978			
	Men	Percent-age	Women	Percent-age	Men	Percent-age	Women	Percent-age
Federal Support								
NSF fellowship	1,305	5.3	206	3.5	586	2.7	139	1.8
NSF traineeship	1,241	5.0	191	3.2	354	1.7	68	0.9
NIH fellowship	663	2.7	270	4.6	369	1.7	193	2.5
NIH traineeship	1,233	5.0	441	7.5	1,068	5.0	473	6.1
NDEA fellowship	2,789	11.3	707	12.0	738	3.5	315	4.0
National Direct Student Loan					1,789	8.4	650	8.3
Other HEW/HHS [a]					575	2.7	423	5.4
Other Education Department [b]								
Graduate/Professional Opportunity Program								
NASA Traineeship	324	1.3	22	0.4	57	0.3	8	0.1
GI Bill	3,263	13.2	22	0.4	2,657	12.5	50	0.6
Other Federal Support [c]	2,631	10.7	702	11.9	1,159	5.4	341	4.4
National fellowships [d]								
Institutional Funds								
University fellowship	4,680	18.9	1,360	23.1	3,844	18.0	1,422	18.2
Teaching assistantship	12,326	49.8	2,786	47.3	9,833	46.1	3,360	43.1
Research assistantship	9,079	36.7	1,421	24.1	8,249	38.7	1,957	25.1
Education funds, industry	979	4.0	108	1.8	632	3.0	142	1.8
Other university related	2,163	8.7	701	11.9	1,453	6.8	678	8.7
College work-study								
Personal Funds								
Own earnings	9,678	39.1	2,529	42.9	10,310	48.4	4,489	57.6
Spouse's earnings	4,948	20.0	1,232	20.9	6,411	30.1	2,590	33.2
Family contributions	1,632	6.6	495	8.4	2,876	13.5	1,215	15.6
Borrowings [e]	3,308	13.4	703	11.9	1,995	9.4	799	10.2
Other	1,282	5.2	331	5.6	1,550	7.3	537	6.9
Unduplicated Total [f]	24,761		5,894		21,323		7,799	

Number of Doctorate Recipients, by Sources of Support in Graduate School, Fiscal Years 1974, 1978, 1982, 1984 and 1985

109 *Continued*

Source of Support	Fiscal Year 1982				Fiscal Year 1984				Fiscal Year 1985			
	Men	Percent-age	Women	Percent-age	Men	Percent-age	Women	Percent-age	Men	Percent-age	Women	Percent-age
Federal Support												
NSF fellowship	496	2.5	135	1.4	422	2.2	168	1.7	393	2.1	161	1.6
NSF traineeship	139	0.7	41	0.4								
NIH fellowship	313	1.6	199	2.1								
NIH traineeship	906	4.6	546	5.7	1,045	5.4	688	6.8	919	4.8	651	6.5
NDEA fellowship	181	0.9	110	1.2								
National Direct Student Loan	2,390	12.2	1,436	15.1	1,443	7.5	1,035	10.2				
Other HEW/HHS [a]	460	2.3	442	4.7	223	1.2	277	2.7	193	1.0	296	2.9
Other Education Department [b]					163	0.8	142	1.4	185	1.0	137	1.4
Graduate/Professional Opportunity Program	33	0.2	43	0.5	51	0.3	45	0.4	95	0.5	96	1.0
NASA Traineeship												
GI Bill	1,421	7.2	53	0.6	1,120	5.8	89	0.9	924	4.8	66	0.7
Other Federal Support [c]	1,101	5.6	443	4.6	891	4.6	489	4.8	728	3.8	366	3.0
National fellowships [d]	563	2.9	383	4.0	777	4.0	616	6.1	638	3.3	507	5.0
Institutional Funds												
University fellowship	3,651	18.6	1,853	19.5	3,878	20.1	2,086	20.6	3,956	20.7	2,154	21.3
Teaching assistantship	9,317	47.4	4,063	42.8	9,432	48.8	4,487	44.3	9,330	48.7	4,463	44.2
Research assistantship	8,329	42.4	2,683	28.3	8,865	45.9	3,115	30.7	9,014	47.1	3,193	31.6
Education funds, industry	735	3.7	219	2.3	907	4.7	414	4.1	1,031	5.4	488	4.8
Other university related	1,430	7.3	892	9.4	1,124	5.8	938	9.3	1,087	5.7	911	9.0
College work-study					586	3.0	421	4.2	770	4.0	441	4.4
Personal Funds												
Own earnings	9,698	49.3	5,724	60.3	10,953	56.7	6,861	67.7	10,925	57.1	6,840	67.8
Spouse's earnings	5,459	27.8	3,235	34.1	5,651	29.2	3,558	35.1	5,578	29.1	3,592	35.6
Family contributions	3,432	17.5	1,698	17.9	4,417	22.9	2,332	23.0	4,734	24.7	2,336	23.2
Borrowings [e]	2,247	11.4	1,297	13.7	4,199	21.7	2,732	26.9	6,059	31.6	3,825	37.9
Other	1,545	7.9	584	6.1	1,440	7.5	563	5.6	1,367	7.1	488	5.8
Unduplicated Total [f]	19,664		9,496		19,327		10,131		19,147		10,090	

a Includes ADAMHA traineeships and fellowships.

b Includes Title IV language area and area studies fellowships.

c Includes AEC/ERDA fellowships and NASA traineeships that were formerly shown separately.

d Includes Woodrow Wilson Fellowships that were formerly shown separately.

e Includes Guaranteed Student Loans and other loans.

f Ph.D.s who did not report sources of support are omitted from the table.

Sources:

1 National Research Council, "Summary Report, Doctorate Recipients from U.S. Universities, 1974 to 1985."

2 Vetter, B. M. & Babco, E. L., *Professional Women and Minorities: A Manpower Data Resource Service*, 1987, Table 2-8.

Sources of Support in Graduate School	Total Number and Percentage	
	Men	Women
NSF research assistant	1,183	238
	5.7	2.1
NIH research assistant	517	287
	2.5	2.5
Other federal research assistant	752	208
	3.6	1.8
NSF fellowship	312	144
	1.5	1.3
NIH traineeship	722	630
	3.5	5.5
Other Department of Health and Human Services	102	153
	0.5	1.3
Department of Education	251	280
	1.2	2.5
GI Bill	638	65
	3.1	0.6
Other federal support	615	305
	2.9	2.7
Foreign government	885	167
	4.2	1.5
National fellowship (nonfederal)	800	522
	3.8	4.6
University teaching assistant	9,550	4,765
	45.7	41.9
University research assistant	7,903	3,137
	37.8	27.6
University fellowship	3,702	2,070
	17.7	18.2
Other university-related	1,508	1,210
	7.2	10.6
Business/employer funds	996	558
	4.8	4.9
Own earnings	9,892	6,811
	47.3	59.9
Spouse's earnings	4,402	3,211
	21.1	28.2
Family support	4,356	2,361
	20.8	20.8
Guaranteed Student Loans	4,380	3,050
	20.9	26.8
National Direct Student Loans	927	680
	4.4	6.0
Other loans	532	379
	2.5	3.3
Other sources	662	381
	3.2	3.4
Unduplicated total[a]	18,871	10,469

a   The 2,938 Ph.D.'s who did not report sources of support are omitted from this table.

Source:
National Research Council, Office of Scientific and Engineering Personnel, Doctorate Records File; "Summary Report 1987: Doctorate Recipients from United States Universities," preliminary tables, App. A, Table 5.

	Men	Women	Total
White, non-Hispanic	157,278	198,065	355,343
Black, non-Hispanic	14,192	21,607	35,799
Hispanic	8,561	10,846	19,407
Asian/Pacific Islander	5,492	4,422	9,914
American Indian/Alaskan Native	1,198	1,755	2,953
Nonresident aliens	3,696	2,711	6,407

Source:
Center for Education Statistics, "Degrees and Other Formal Awards Conferred, 1984–85" survey; *Digest of Educational Statistics, 1988*, Table 181.

Program Categories	Number of Programs by Type of Degree			
	AA	BA	MA	Ph.D.
Free Standing (Degrees are awarded in "Women's Studies.")		54	6	
Concentration (Degrees are awarded in other disciplines, with a concentration in women's studies.)		58	24	
Individualized/Interdisciplinary (Degrees awarded are interdisciplinary, often called "liberal studies" or "general studies." Women's studies courses taken resemble a minor.)		180	43	14
Minor		257	22	
Certificate		66	8	
Type of Program Unspecified	19			

Note: In addition, more than 30,000 women's studies courses are now being taught and more than 100 curriculum transformation projects are now underway.

Source:
National Women's Studies Association, University of Maryland at College Park.

Selected Characteristics of 1983–84 College Graduates and Their Ability to Repay Debts Incurred During Their College Years

113

Characteristic	Men	Women
	Percentage	
1983–84 College graduates with debts		
Total 4-year institutions	45	41
Public	42	38
Independent	51	46
	Percentage	
Level of debts owed by 1983–84 graduates		
Less than $3,000	32	32
$3,000–$6,999	33	35
$7,000 and above	36	33
Total	100	100
Average Salaries of 1983–84 College graduates who were employed full-time in 1985	$20,000	$16,300
First-year repayment of debt as percentage of pretax earnings	**Percentage**	
Less than 3%	43	36
3%–5.9%	28	28
6%–9.9%	23	23
10%–12.9%	3	7
13% and above	3	6
Total	100	100

Notes: In 1985, the National Center for Education Statistics conducted a survey of 18,000 1983–84 graduates of 4-year colleges. Data were collected on the frequency and amount of loans incurred while the students were enrolled as undergraduates, and on the graduates' ability to repay these debts one year later (in Spring 1985). Debts were defined in the survey to include only expenses directly related to the students' educations, such as tuition, fees, room, board, books, supplies, and transportation to and from school. To calculate the size of the loan burden on pretax earnings, a 10-year repayment period at 7% interest was assumed.

Source:
Henderson, Cathy, "College Debts of Recent Graduates" (ACE), 1987.

Bibliography

American Council on Education. 1987. *1986–87 Fact Book on Higher Education*. New York: ACE/Macmillan.

———.1987. *Minorities in Higher Education: Sixth Annual Status Report, 1987*. Washington, D.C.

———.1987. "College Debts of Recent Graduates," Cathy Henderson.

———.1988. Special tabulations of data from the National Center for Education Statistics' HEGIS tapes of 1975–76, 1980–81, and 1985–86.

———.1989. *Minorities in Higher Education: Seventh Annual Status Report, 1988*. Washington, D.C.

———.1989. *1989–90 Fact Book on Higher Education*. New York: ACE/Macmillan.

American Council on Education, Office of Women in Higher Education. "Women Chief Executive Officers in U.S. Colleges and Universities, Table XII, December 1989." July 1990. Washington, D.C.

Association of Governing Boards of Universities and Colleges 1986. *Composition of Governing Boards 1985*. Washington, D.C.

Astin, A. W., Green, K. C., & Korn, W. S. 1987. *The American Freshman: Twenty Year Trends*. Los Angeles: Cooperative Institutional Research Program, University of California.

Astin, A. W., Green, K. C., Korn, W. S., & Schalit, M. 1987. *The American Freshman: National Norms for Fall 1987*. Los Angeles: Cooperative Institutional Research Program, University of California.

Bureau of Labor Statistics. Sept. 1987. *Monthly Labor Review,* 110, No. 9. Washington, D.C.: GPO.

———. 1988. "Geographic Profile of Employment and Unemployment 1987." Washington, D.C.: GPO.

———. Aug. 1988. *Employment and Earnings*, 35, No. 8. Washington, D.C.: GPO.

Bureau of the Census. February, 1978. *Current Population Reports,* Ser. P-20, No. 319, "School Enrollment—Social and Economic Characteristics of Students October: 1976." Washington, D.C.: GPO.

———. May, 1984. *Current Population Reports*, Ser. P-25, No. 952, "Projections of the Population of the U.S. by Age, Sex, and Race: 1983–2080." Washington, D.C.: GPO.

———. Nov. 1986. *Current Population Reports*, Ser. P-25, No. 995, "Projections of the Hispanic Population: 1983–2080." Washington, D.C.: GPO.

———. 1986. *Statistical Abstract of the United States, 1987*. Washington, D.C.: GPO.

———. Aug. 1987. *Current Population Reports*, Series P-60, No. 161, "Money, Income, and Poverty Status in the United States, 1987." Washington, D.C.: GPO.

———. Sept. 1987. *Current Population Reports*, Series P-70, No. 11, "What It's Worth: Educational Background and Economic Status, Spring, 1984." Washington, D.C.:GPO.

———. 1987. *Statistical Abstract of the United States, 1988*. Washington, D.C.: GPO.

———. Aug. 1988. *Current Population Reports*, Ser. P-20, No. 428, "Educational Attainment in the United States March, 1987 and 1986." Washington, D.C.: GPO.

———. Aug. 1988. *Current Population Reports*, Ser. P-20, No. 429, "School Enrollment—Social and Economic Characteristics of Students: October 1986." Washington, D.C.: GPO.

Chronicle of Higher Education 34, No. 7. (Oct. 14, 1987): A36.

Chronicle of Higher Education 35, No. 14. (Nov. 30, 1988): A34.

College and University Personnel Association. 1988. Special tabulations of data from *1987–88 Administrative Compensation Survey*. Washington D.C.: Richard C. Creal, Jan P. Miller, and John M. Toller. 1975.

Equal Employment Opportunity Commission. "EEO-6 Summary Report." Washington, D.C.

National Center for Education Statistics. July 1986. Unpublished tabulations from "The Timing of Abnormal Progression Among 1980 High School Seniors Entering Postsecondary Education in October, 1980." Washington, D.C.

———. Aug. 1987. "College Faculty Salaries 1976–1986." Washington, D.C.: GPO.

———. Aug. 1987. "Trends in Bachelor's and Higher Degrees: 1975–1985." Washington, D.C.: GPO.

———. Dec. 1987. "Bachelor's and Higher Degrees Conferred in 1985–86." Washington, D.C.: GPO.

———. 1987. *Digest of Education Statistics, 1988*. Washington, D.C.: GPO.

———. 1987. Unpublished tabulations from "Associate Degrees and Other Awards Below the Baccalaureate 1983 to 1985." Washington, D.C.

———. Jan. 1988. "Ed Tabs: Earned Degree Data 1984–85." Washington, D.C.: GPO.

———. April 1988. "Trends in Minority Enrollment in Higher Education, Fall 1976–Fall 1986." Washington, D.C.: GPO.

———. May 1988. Preliminary tables from the National Postsecondary Student Aid Study (NPSAS). Washington, D.C.

———. July 1988. Preliminary tables from the National Postsecondary Student Aid Study (NPSAS). Washington, D.C.

———. 1988. *Digest of Education Statistics*. Washington, D.C.: GPO.

National Research Council. August, 1988. Preliminary tables from "Summary Report 1987: Doctorate Recipients From United States Universities." Washington, D.C.

The College Board. 1985. *Profiles, College-Bound Seniors, 1985*. New York.

———. 1988. *College-Bound Seniors: 1988 Profile of SAT and Achievement Test Takers*. New York.

Vetter, B. M. & Babco, E. L. 1987. *Professional Women and Minorities: A Manpower Data Resource Service*. Washington, D.C.: Commission on Professionals in Science and Technology.

Index